Praise for *A New Song*

One of the strengths of this volume is the diversity of voices and approaches that Robin Leaver has brought to the conversation. *A New Song We Now Begin* celebrates not just Lutheran hymnody but Lutheran hymnals in all their materiality, with attention to the organization and printing (and politics) of the books themselves, as well as to the theology and music that bring them to life.
—Rev. Dr. Kathryn A. Kleinhans, dean, Trinity Lutheran Seminary at Capital University, Columbus, Ohio

A more fitting title for this collection of essays could not have been chosen than *A New Song We Now Begin*. Spanning the creation of the first Lutheran song books (*Liederbücher*) to the publication of the most recent North American Lutheran hymnals, the scholarship displayed in these essays addresses significant lacunae within the fields of liturgical studies and the history of Lutheranism. In no other single volume can one learn about the Lutheran tradition of *cantionals*, the controversial influence of Pietism in the production of Lutheran hymnals, alongside a pan-Lutheran history of North American Lutheran hymnary in the twenty-first century. Scholars and lovers of Lutheran hymnody alike will find this volume enlightening and enriching.
—Rev. Dr. James Ambrose Lee II, associate professor of theology, Concordia University, Chicago

A half-millennium glance back at the Lutheran hymnal is a tall order, but Robin Leaver has collected a series of essays that provide both a broad narrative of Lutheran hymnody (with plenty of twists, turns, and compelling stories) and deep dives into salient moments and movements along the way. The text includes all one would expect in a rich retelling, including attention to the music itself, people in varied roles, theology, tenets, poetry, social life, education, issues, and exemplars. This recognition of five hundred years of Lutheran hymnals is enlivened with plenty of texts and tunes, stories within stories, and excellently written scholarship—a collection most worthy of a half-millennium celebration!
—Dr. Jeff Meyer, professor of music, Concordia College, Moorhead, Minnesota

Robin Leaver's *A New Song We Now Begin* is an outstanding work: researched to a high academic standard, while written in a compelling way for the reader. This is an important resource for all church musicians,

clergy, students, professors in the academy, and anyone with a love for hymnody and its origins.
—Dr. Richard Nance, professor emeritus, School of Music, Theatre & Dance, Pacific Lutheran University

In *A New Song We Now Begin*, Robin Leaver and a stellar array of scholars take the reader on a fascinating five-hundred-year tour of Lutheran hymnals that is a must-read for lovers of Lutheran hymnody. The church's hymnals have always been a trustworthy theological repository. Therefore, this volume offers a wealth of musical, historical, and theological insight into the church's beliefs and practices over time that will inform and engage the reader.
—Rev. Richard C. Resch, professor and kantor emeritus, Concordia Theological Seminary, Fort Wayne, Indiana

A New Song We Now Begin is a thorough but accessible resource for conductors, pastors, and anyone who is interested in the history of hymnody in the Lutheran church. The text details what continues to be at the core of Lutheranism: corporate song in worship. This resource helps the reader put into historical context the events, musical traditions, and songs that influenced not only congregations but remarkable composers. This scholarly work should be on the shelves of every Lutheran church musician and pastor.
—Dr. Jennaya Robison, DMA, artistic director, National Lutheran Choir, Minneapolis

LUTHERAN QUARTERLY BOOKS

Editor
Paul Rorem, Professor Emeritus, *Princeton Theological Seminary*

Associate Editors
Timothy J. Wengert, Professor Emeritus, *United Lutheran Seminary (Philadelphia)*
Mary Jane Haemig, Professor Emerita, *Luther Seminary, St. Paul*
Mark C. Mattes, *Grand View University, Des Moines, Iowa*

Lutheran Quarterly Books will advance the same aims as *Lutheran Quarterly* itself, aims repeated by Theodore G. Tappert when he was editor fifty years ago and renewed by Oliver K. Olson when he revived the publication in 1987. The original four aims continue to grace the front matter and to guide the contents of every issue, and can now also indicate the goals of *Lutheran Quarterly Books*: "to provide a forum (1) for the discussion of Christian faith and life on the basis of the Lutheran confession; (2) for the application of the principles of the Lutheran church to the changing problems of religion and society; (3) for the fostering of world Lutheranism; and (4) for the promotion of understanding between Lutherans and other Christians."

For further information, see www.lutheranquarterly.org.

The symbol and motto of *Lutheran Quarterly*, VDMA for *Verbum Domini Manet in Aeternum* (1 Peter 1:25), was adopted as a motto by Luther's sovereign, Frederick the Wise, and his successors. The original "Protestant" princes walking out of the imperial Diet of Speyer in 1529, unruly peasants following Thomas Müntzer, and from 1531 to 1547 the coins, medals, flags, and guns of the Smalcaldic League all bore the most famous Reformation slogan, the first Evangelical confession: The Word of the Lord remains forever.

For the complete list of *Lutheran Quarterly Books*, please see the final pages of this work.

A New Song We Now Begin

A New Song We Now Begin

*Celebrating the Half Millennium
of Lutheran Hymnals 1524–2024*

ROBIN A. LEAVER, EDITOR

FORTRESS PRESS
MINNEAPOLIS

A NEW SONG WE NOW BEGIN
Celebrating the Half Millennium of Lutheran Hymnals 1524–2024

Copyright © 2024 Fortress Press, an imprint of 1517 Media. All rights reserved. Except for brief quotations in critical articles and reviews, no part of this book may be reproduced in any manner without prior written permission from the publisher. Email copyright@1517.media or write to Permissions, Fortress Press, PO Box 1209, Minneapolis, MN 55440-1209.

All Scripture quotations, unless otherwise indicated, are from the New Revised Standard Version Bible, copyright © 1989 National Council of the Churches of Christ in the United States of America. Used by permission. All rights reserved worldwide.

Library of Congress Cataloging-in-Publication Data

Names: Leaver, Robin A., editor.
Title: A new song we now begin : celebrating the half millennium of Lutheran hymnals, 1524-2024 / Robin A. Leaver, editor.
Description: Minneapolis : Fortress Press, 2024. | Includes bibliographical references and index.
Identifiers: LCCN 2023040699 (print) | LCCN 2023040700 (ebook) | ISBN 9781506487441 (paperback) | ISBN 9781506487458 (ebook)
Subjects: LCSH: Hymns--History and criticism. | Church music--Lutheran Church.
Classification: LCC ML3168 .N49 2024 (print) | LCC ML3168 (ebook) | DDC 781.71/41--dc23/eng/20230830
LC record available at https://lccn.loc.gov/2023040699
LC ebook record available at https://lccn.loc.gov/2023040700

Cover design: Kristin Miller

Cover art: excerpts of Ein neues Lied, Martin Luther, Walter Gesangbuchlein - 1525 and O Beauty Ever Ancient, from All Creation Sings, Augsburg Fortress, 2020

Print ISBN: 978-1-5064-8744-1
eBook ISBN: 978-1-5064-8745-8

Contents

Tables, Figures, and Musical Examples ... ix
Preface ... xi
Acknowledgments ... xv
Abbreviations ... xvii

1. Introduction
   Robin A. Leaver ... 1

Part 1. The German Background

2. Hymnals 1524
   Robin A. Leaver ... 33
3. Luther as Hymnal Editor
   Paul J. Grime ... 63
4. The Cantional Tradition
   Markus Rathey ... 85
5. A Most Popular Hymnal: *Praxis Pietatis Melica*
   Joseph Herl ... 109
6. The Most Controversial Hymnal: 1704–1771
   Dianne M. McMullen ... 133

Part 2. Influential American Hymnals

7. "Walther's Hymnal" for the Missouri Synod Saxons
   Jon D. Vieker ... 159

8. A Hymnal for Uniting Lutherans: *Common Service Book with Hymnal*, 1917/18
   Paul Westermeyer 181
9. The Scandinavian Hymnal Tradition
   Gracia Grindal 203
10. Chasing Mühlenberg's Dream: From SBH to LBW
    Mark A. Granquist 225
11. An Extraordinary Hymnal Supplement
    Daniel Zager 245
12. Hymnals 2024
    Daniel Zager and Robin A. Leaver 265

Select Bibliography 285

Contributors 293

Index 297

Lutheran Quarterly Books 303

Tables, Figures, and Musical Examples

Tables

1.1	Bach's Cantatas on Chorales that First Appeared in the Earliest Lutheran Hymnals.	18
2.1	Contents of the *Achtliederbuch*.	47
2.2	New Hymns That Made Their Appearance in the Earliest Lutheran Hymnals.	53
2.3	Relationships between Wittenberg Hymnals 1524–1526.	57
2.4	New Wittenberg Hymns 1524.	58
2.5	Church Year Hymns, Wittenberg 1524.	62
3.1	Summary of Relationships between Prayerbook, Catechism, and Hymnal.	70

Figures

4.1	Lucas Osiander *Fünfzig Geistliche Lieder und Psalmen* (1586), title page.	88
4.2	Johann Herman Schein, *Cantional* (1627), title page.	99
5.1	Seth Calvisius, *Harmonia Cantionum Ecclesiasticarum*, 1597, fol. B4^v.	119
5.2	Johann Hermann Schein, *Cantional, Oder Gesang Buch Augsburgischer Confession*, 1645, fol. B2^r.	121
5.3	Johann Crüger, *Praxis Pietatis Melica*, 1653, fol. H1^r.	122
8.1	Title page, *Common Service Book with Hymnal*, 1917/18.	182

Musical Examples

4.1 Lucas Osiander *Fünfzig Geistliche Lieder und Psalmen* (1586), No. XXI. *Unser Vater im Himmelreich.*   90

4.2 Seth Calvisius, *Kirchengesenge* (1597), No. XLVI. *Vater unser im Himmelreich.*   93

4.3 Johann Herman Schein, *Cantional* (1627), No. LXXVI. *Vater unser im Himmelreich.*   100

5.1 A possible realization of *Vom Himmel hoch* from PPM, 1653.   122

5.2 Crüger's tune for Paul Gerhardt's Advent hymn *Wie soll ich dich empfangen* (O Lord, how shall I meet you, CW^2 324, ELW 241, LSB 334), from PPM, 1653, no. 81.   123

5.3 Crüger's tune for Paul Gerhard's *Auf, auf, mein Herz, mit Freuden* (Awake, my heart, with gladness, CW^2 443, ELW 378, LSB 467), from PPM, 1653, no. 160.   124

5.4 Beginning of Giovanni Giacomo Gastoldi's *balletto, A lieta vita* with a German contrafactum, *In dir ist Freude* (In thee is gladness, CW^2 513, ELW 867, LSB 818).   124

6.1 Freylinghausen's tune for *Die lieblichen blicke/die Jesus mir giebt.* (1704/1708, No. 453; Zahn 6956b).   152

Preface

This collection of essays celebrates the distinctive and extensive succession of Lutheran hymnals that began five centuries ago in Wittenberg, Nuremberg, Erfurt, and Strassburg in the year 1524: the *Achtliederbuch, Chorgesangbuch, Enchiridia,* and *Teütsch Kirchen ampt*.[1] These collections of hymns marked the beginning of the remarkable sequence of Lutheran hymnals that expanded throughout the centuries and throughout the world—a vast and overflowing chronological procession of anthologies of corporate song that not only identify the essence of what it is to be a Lutheran,[2] but at the same time have contributed significantly to the content of the hymnals in use in other denominations. Indeed, what began as a specific Lutheran phenomenon quickly became the distinctive feature of Protestantism as whole.[3] By the middle of the sixteenth century hymnals of other Protestants were regularly including Lutheran hymns. The converse, the inclusion of non-Lutheran hymns in Lutheran hymnals, took a little longer, and it was not until the mid- to late nineteenth century that it could be regarded as commonplace, especially in Germany. On the other hand, even before the end of the sixteenth century what had been a strict separation between Protestant and Catholic hymnals began to blur, so that by the eighteenth century there were some striking examples

---

1. The reforming movement in Strassburg, while not exactly "Lutheran," was quick off the mark in singing the early Wittenberg hymns and publishing their own hymnals; see Daniel Trocmé-Latter, *The Singing of the Strasbourg Protestants, 1523–1541* (Farnham: Ashgate, 2015).
2. See Ernest E. Ryden, "Hymnbooks," in *The Encyclopedia of the Lutheran Church*, ed. Julius Bodensieck (Minneapolis: Augsburg, 1965), 2: 1072–1090; and Gracia Grindal, "Hymnody," in *Dictionary of Luther and the Lutheran Traditions*, ed. Timothy J. Wengert (Grand Rapids, MI: Baker, 2017), 350–352.
3. Robin A. Leaver, *"Goostly Psalmes and Spiritual Songes": English and Dutch Metrical Psalms from Coverdale to Utenhove 1535–1566* (Oxford: Clarendon, 1991), esp. 1–54; and Robin A. Leaver, "Hymns and Hymnals" EP 2: 908–20.

of hymnals that included hymns sung by both Catholic and Lutheran congregations.[4]

Of course, the hymnal was not a Lutheran invention. Manuscript *Hymnaria* dating from the eleventh century, and printed *Hymnaria* dating from the late fifteenth century, supplied hymns to be sung in the daily offices as well as on the festivals, Sundays, and celebrations of the church year. But these services and the hymns sung within them were in Latin rather than the vernacular. The singing was therefore confined to clergy and choirs, especially the monks and nuns of the various monastic orders, rather than the congregations of the people. Nor were Lutherans the first to issue vernacular hymnals from which the people could sing. That honor belongs to the followers of Jan Hus (*ca.* 1372–1415), known as the Bohemian Brethren, or Unitas Fratrum (United Brethren). In the final decades of the fifteenth century, they compiled manuscript hymnals of Czech translations of familiar Latin hymns which were widely sung among the brethren. In 1501 they published a Czech hymnal in Prague, and in 1519 a hymnal containing German versions of the Czech hymns was published in Leitomishl (Litomyšl).[5] Luther was, of course, familiar with the typical Latin *Hymnarium* from which he would have sung during his years as an Augustinian monk. He was also well aware of the Hussite movement and especially its vernacular hymnody, as is demonstrated in his adaptation of a melody and his revision of a text, both found in the Bohemian Brethren hymnal, *Ein New Gesangbuchlen* (Jungbuntzlau: Wylmschwerer, 1531): the former, to create the melody Vater unser im Himmelreich, and the latter, the revised hymn text *Nun laßt uns den Leib begraben*.[6]

We remember hymns one at a time and forget that the reason we can do so is because they have been made available to us in hymnals; their popularity and dissemination have occurred because of their presence in successive hymnals. Most hymnals are straight-forward and functional—almost mundane, one might say—practical songbooks from which the people sing. But throughout these five hundred years there have been significant and notable collections of hymns that introduced new styles

---

4. For example, see Robin A. Leaver, "A Catholic Hymnal for Use in Lutheran Leipzig: *Catholisches Gesang–Buch* (Leipzig, 1724)." *Bach and the Counterpoint of Religion*, ed. Robin A. Leaver [Bach Perspectives 12] (Urbana: University of Illinois Press, 2018), 36–62.
5. Regrettably neither hymnal has survived. The texts and tunes of the Bohemian Brethren are explored in the encyclopedic Zdenek Nejedly, *Dejiny husitskeho zpevu* (History of Hussite Singing), 6 vols. (Prague: Nakl. Československe akademie ved, 1954–56); see also Jan Kouba, "Die ältest Gesangbuchdruck von 1501 aus Böhmen." JbLH 13 (1968): 78–112.
6. See AWA 4, 114–116, 120–122; LW 53:295–96, 331 and 333 respectively.

of music or different kinds of poetry, for intensifying spirituality in the face of social and political unrest, for creating new approaches to the liturgical use of hymns in public worship, or for developing new avenues of hymnody within family worship or private devotion. Such hymnals not only influenced their own time but also had far-reaching ramifications for the hymnals that succeeded them. A variety of some of these seminal collections of hymns forms the focus of the discussions in the essays of this volume that celebrates the half-millennium of Lutheran hymnals, 1524–2024.

Robin A. Leaver

Acknowledgments

I wish to thank a number of people who have shared their expertise and knowledge in the making of this book, notably: Ruth Tatlow, for assistance in locating copies of rare sources; Matthew Carver, for unraveling difficult passages of Latin; Uwe Steinmetz, leader of the global celebration marking the five hundred years of Lutheran hymnals, 1524–2024, sponsored by the Lutheran World Federation and the Liturgical Institute of Leipzig University, for keeping me informed of its progress; Rebecca Wagner Oettinger for permission to use excellent literal translations from her *Music as Propaganda in the German Reformation* (Aldershot: Ashgate, 2001); and especially the contributors to this volume who accepted the challenge of creating significant snapshots of this five-hundred-year history and doing it so well. Particular thanks go to Paul Rorem, editor of *Lutheran Quarterly* and *Lutheran Quarterly Books*, the enthusiastic supporter and encourager of every stage of the project from the day I first suggested the possibility to him.

A slightly different version of chapter 2 was originally published as "The First Hymnals of 1524" in *Lutheran Quarterly* 37.4 (Winter, 2023), and appears here by permission of Lutheran Quarterly and Johns Hopkins University Press Journals.

Abbreviations

Literature

AWA 4 — *Archiv zu Weimarer Ausgabe der Werke Martin Luthers 4: Luther's Geistliche Lieder und Kirchen gesänge: Vollständige Neuedition in Ergänzung zu Band der Weimarer Ausgabe*, ed. Markus Jenny. Cologne: Böhlau, 1985.

BC — *The Book of Concord: The Confessions of the Evangelical Lutheran Church*, ed. Robert Kolb and Timothy J. Wengert. Minneapolis: Fortress Press, 2000.

CDH — *The Canterbury Dictionary of Hymnology*, edited by Richard Watson and Emma Hornby. <http://www.hymnology.co.uk>

CLM — *Celebrating Lutheran Music: Scholarly Perspectives at the Quincentenary*. Eds. Maria Schildt, Mattias Lundberg, and Jonas Lundblad. Uppsala: Uppsala University, 2019.

DKL — *Das deutsche Kirchenlied*. Dates with superior numbers (e.g., DKL 1524[13]) are references to the bibliography: *Das deutsche Kirchenlied I/1: Verzeichnis der Drucke*, ed. Konrad Ameln, Markus Jenny, and Walther Lipphardt. Kassel: Bärenreiter, 1975. Other references (e.g., DKL A327) are to specific melodies: *Das deutsche Kirchenlied: Kritische Gesamtausgabe der Melodien. Abteilung III: Die Melodien aus gedruckten Quellen bis 1680*, ed. Joachim Stalmann, et al. Kassel: Bärenreiter, 1993–. *Das deutsche Kirchenlied I/2: Verzeichnis der*

	Drucke, ed. Markus Jenny. Kassel: Bärenreiter, 1980 is a comprehensive index volume for the bibliography *Das deutsche Kirchenlied I/1*.
EP	*The Encyclopedia of Protestantism*, 4 vols., ed. Hans J. Hillerbrand. New York: Routledge, 2004.
JbLH	*Jahrbuch für Liturgik und Hymnologie* (1955–).
Koch	Eduard Emil Koch, *Geschichte des Kirchenlieds und Kirchengesangs der christlichen, insbesondere der deutschen evangelischen Kirche*, 3rd ed. Stuttgart: Belfer, 1866–1877; reprint, Hildesheim: Olms, 1973.
LQ	*Lutheran Quarterly. New Series* (1987–).
LSB–CH	*Lutheran Service Book. Companion to the Hymns*, ed. Joseph Herl, Peter C. Reske, and Jon Vieker. (St. Louis: Concordia, 2019).
LW	*Luther's Works: American Edition*, 82 vols. St. Louis and Philadelphia: Concordia and Fortress, 1955–.
WA	*Luthers Werke: Kritische Gesamtausgabe*, 65 vols. Weimar: Böhlau, 1883–1993.
WA BR	*Luthers Werke: Kritische Gesamtausgabe. Briefwechsel*, 18 vols. Weimar: Böhlau, 1930–1985.
WA TR	*Luthers Werke: Kritische Gesamtausgabe. Tischreden*, 6 vols. Weimar: Böhlau, 1912–1921.
WB	Philipp Wackernagel, *Bibliographie zur Geschichte des deutschen Kirchenliedes im XVI. Jahrhundert*. Frankfurt: Heyder & Zimmer, 1853; reprint, Hildesheim: Olms, 1961.
WDKL	Philipp Wackernagel, *Das deutsche Kirchenlied von der ältesten Zeit bis zu Anfang des XVII. Jahrhunderts*. Leipzig: Teubner, 1864–1877; reprint, Hildesheim: Olms, 1964.
Zahn	Johannes Zahn, *Die Melodien der deutschen evangelischen Kirchenlieder*, 6 vols. Gütersloh: Bertelsmann, 1889–1893; reprint Hildesheim: Olms, 1963.
Zedler	*Grosses vollständiges Universal Lexicon Aller Wissenschafften und Künste*. Leipzig: Zedler, 1731–1754.

ABBREVIATIONS · xix

Hymnals

ACH	*All Creation Sings: Evangelical Lutheran Worship Supplement.* Minneapolis: Augsburg Fortress, 2020.
Achtliederbuch	*Etlich Cristlich lider Lobgesang/ und Psalm/ dem rainen wort Gottes gemeß/ auß der heyligen Schrifft/ durch mancherley hochgelerter gemacht/ in der Kirchen zu singen/ wie es dann um tayl berayt zu Wittenberg in übung ist. Wittenberg. M.D.X[X]iiij* ([Nuremberg]: [Gutknecht], 1524). Facsimile: ed. Konrad Ameln. Kassel: Bärenreiter, 1957.
AH	*Hymnal and Order of Service, Evangelical Lutheran Augusta Synod.* Rock Island: Augustana Book Concern, 1925.
CH	*The Concordia Hymnal: A Hymnal for Church, School and Home.* Expanded edition. Minneapolis: Augsburg, 1932.
Chorgesangbuch	Johann Walter, *Geystlich gesangk Buchleyn. TENOR. Wittemberg. M. D. [xx]iiij.* (Wittenberg: [Cranach & Döring], 1524). 2nd ed: *Tenor. Geystliche Gsangbüchlin/ Erstlich zů Wittenberg/ und volgend durch Peter schöffern getruckt im jar. M, D. XXV. Mense Maio* ([Worms]: Schoeffer, 1525). Facsimile: ed. Walter Blankenburg. Kassel: Bärenreiter, 1979.
CSB	*Common Service Book.* Philadelphia: Board of Publication of the United Lutheran Church in America, 1918.
CW	*Christian Worship: A Lutheran Hymnal* [Wisconsin Evangelical Lutheran Synod]. Milwaukee: Northwestern, 1993.
CWS	*Christian Worship: Supplement* [Wisconsin Evangelical Lutheran Synod]. Milwaukee: Northwestern, 2008.
CW²	*Christian Worship: A Lutheran Hymnal* [Wisconsin Evangelical Lutheran Synod]. Milwaukee: Northwestern, 2021.
EG	*Evangelisches Gesangbuch* (1993) is the core repertory of 535 hymns for the fourteen different regional editions that also include additional hymns for each region.

ELH	*Evangelical Lutheran Hymnary* [Evangelical Lutheran Synod, Mankato, MN]. St. Louis: Morning Star, 1996.
ELW	*Evangelical Lutheran Worship* [Evangelical Lutheran Church in America] Minneapolis: Augsburg Fortress, 2006.
LBW	*Lutheran Book of Worship*. Minneapolis: Augsburg, 1978.
LSB	*Lutheran Service Book*. St. Louis: Concordia, 2006.
LW	*Lutheran Worship*. St. Louis: Concordia, 1982.
LH	*Lutheran Hymnary*. Minneapolis: Augsburg, 1913.
PPM	Johann Crüger, *Praxis Pietatis Melica*, various editions from 1647.
SBH	*Service Book and Hymnal*. Minneapolis: Augsburg, 1958.
SS	Vilhelm Koren, *Salmebog for Lutherske Kristne i Amerika* (Hymnal for Lutheran Christians in America). Decorah: Synodens Forlag, 1903; informally known as *Synodens Salmebog*.
TFBF	*This Far by Faith: An African American Resource for Worship*. Minneapolis: Augsburg Fortress, 1999.
TLH	*The Lutheran Hymnal*. St. Louis: Concordia, 1941.
WOF	*With One Voice: A Lutheran Resource for Worship*. Augsburg Fortress, 1995.
WS	*Worship Supplement*. St. Louis: Concordia, 1969.

1.

Introduction

Robin A. Leaver

It all began with a single song, Luther's *A new song we now begin* (*Ein neues lied wir heben an*),[1] written in 1523 to commemorate the martyrdom of two young friars in his Augustinian order who were executed for espousing what was regarded as Luther's heresy. Like contemporary news ballads, it was printed on a single sheet of paper, a broadside. Other poems/hymns by Luther and his Wittenberg colleagues soon followed, and they too were printed on one side of a single sheet. Now that there was a handful of vernacular hymns it was possible to emulate the small, printed collections of German folk songs that had begun to appear around this time. By folding a single folio sheet of paper one might create a small pamphlet of either four leaves (eight pages) or eight leaves (sixteen pages), depending on the dimensions of the pages. Each sheet was printed on both sides, then folded and cut to form a pamphlet. Further, it was possible to expand the number of pages by stitching together multiple gatherings (folios), each one comprising eight or sixteen pages. Over the winter of 1523/24 the hymns were first printed in Wittenberg as single broadsides and then reprinted in the single sheet format in other places where there were printing presses. But during 1524 the Wittenberg broadside hymns were gathered together and reprinted in the pamphlet format in such places as Nuremberg, Augsburg, and Erfurt.

Thus the long history of Lutheran hymnals began in the year 1524.

---

1. AWA 4: No. 18; LW 53:211. See also Robin A. Leaver, *Luther's Liturgical Music: Principles and Implications* (Minneapolis: Fortress Press, 2017), 13–14. The five hundredth anniversary of Luther's song was marked by the essay Robert J. Christman, "The Antwerp Martyrs and Luther's First Song," LQ 36 (2022): 373–389.

This collection of essays celebrates the five hundred years, the half-millennium 1524–2024, of the Lutheran hymnal, the popular format that made the texts of the hymns (and sometimes also their melodies) accessible for corporate worship and personal devotion in churches, schools, and homes—some small enough to be carried in pockets and handbags, others large enough for a group of choristers to sing from a single copy. What began as a trickle of publications in 1524 soon accelerated to become a veritable avalanche of hymnal production. By the end of the sixteenth century around two thousand different editions of German Lutheran hymnals had been issued. Although there is uncertainty concerning the extent of each print run of these editions, it has been estimated that, from the appearance of the first hymnals in 1524 to the end of the sixteenth century, between two and four million hymnals must have entered into circulation.[2] This was a pattern repeated in every century that followed. In the sixteenth and seventeenth centuries the Lutheran Reformation expanded northeastward through the Baltic States (Lithuania, Latvia, and Estonia), north through the Scandinavian countries (Denmark, Norway, and Sweden), and also to the Nordic countries in the east and west (Finland and Iceland), and this expansion was accompanied by millions of hymnals published and circulated in the different languages.[3] By the eighteenth and nineteenth centuries Lutheran churches were well established in many other European countries as well as in Germany, and the hymnals of the individual church bodies—some regional state churches, others free synods—established their particular Lutheran identity. During the eighteenth and nineteenth centuries European Lutheran churches—in parallel with other denominations—exported their faith and practice to countries in the continents of North America, Africa, India, and elsewhere, as part of the process of colonization. Later in the nineteenth and twentieth centuries, as part of the global missionary imperative, the former colonial churches gradually became more indigenous and independent. But, as always, it was the hymnal that in many respects defined the identity of the individual worshiper, that established that worshiper within a specific congregation, and that confirmed the status of that congregation within the particular Lutheran synod. Thus, as in every century, millions upon millions of Lutheran hymnals have been published and circulated

---

2. See Christopher Boyd Brown, "Devotional Life in Hymns, Liturgy, Music, and Prayer," in *Lutheran Ecclesiastical Culture, 1550–1675*, ed. Robert Kolb (Boston: Brill, 2008), 233–234. Others are of the opinion that the figure was even higher; for example, see Andew Pettegree, *Reformation and the Culture of Persuasion* (Cambridge: Cambridge University Press, 2005), 46.
3. See, for example, Otfried Czaika, "A Vast and Unfamiliar Field: Swedish Hymnals and Hymn-Printing in the Sixteenth Century," in CLM, 125–138.

because they literally enshrine what a Lutheran believes and practices, giving the Lutheran hymnal a status second only to the Bible and the Book of Concord.

COLLECTING AND EDITING HYMNALS

A hymnal is a very familiar object. There are many of them around. We hold them in our hands every Sunday. We perhaps also use them in our daily devotions. Like other familiar things the danger is to take hymnals for granted. Toward the end of the seventeenth century some Lutheran clergy in Germany set themselves the task of exploring the many-faceted contents of these practical songbooks of poetry and music in order to promote the theology they expressed, the liturgy they undergirded, the devotion they stimulated, and the identity they created. This was the period between 1690 and 1710 that saw the emergence of the first phase of hymnological research in Lutheran Germany.[4] It is noticeable that those who wrote on aspects of the contents of hymnals in the early eighteenth century tended to be the editors of significant hymnals. For example, Johann Friedrich Mayer (1650–1712), sometime superintendent in Hamburg, was the primary editor of the *Neu-vermehrtes Hamburgisches Gesang-Buch* ... (Hamburg: König, 1700; still in print in 1772), the hymnal used by Georg Telemann when he was Cantor in Hamburg (1721–1767). Georg Heinrich Götze (1667–1728), superintendent in Lübeck, edited the *Lübeckisches Gesang-Buch* ... (Lübeck: Wiedermeyer, 1703; still in print in 1775), the hymnal used by Dieterich Buxtehude during his final years as organist of the Marienkirche in Lübeck. Johann Christoph Olearius (1668–1747), deacon and librarian of the Arnstadt church library, later superintendent, edited the *Neu-verbessertes Arnstädtisches Gesangbuch* (Arnstadt: Bachmann, 1701; further editions in 1703 and 1705), the hymnal used by Johann Sebastian Bach when he was organist of the Neuen Kirche, Arnstadt (1703–1707).

A hymnal editor needs to have access to earlier hymnals in order to locate, verify, and incorporate hymns into the new hymnal being compiled. So, it is not surprising to discover that hymnal editors were also frequently collectors of hymnals. However, while it is known who these collectors were, the extent and content of most of their hymnal collections are either partially or totally unknown. These collectors were theologians

---

4. See Martin Rößler, "Die Frühzeit hymnologischer Forschung," JbLH 19 (1975): 123–86. The term "hymnology" (and cognates), however, did not come into general use until much later than the early eighteenth century.

and pastors who were not only intent on collecting hymnals but also in assembling substantial libraries of books on all aspects of theology. When these collectors died, their often vast libraries were generally sold by auction, with sale catalogues being prepared, printed, and circulated beforehand. These catalogues followed the accepted practice of book auctions in general of classifying the listing of the lot numbers according to book format—folio, 4to, 8vo, 12mo, 24mo—rather than by subject matter. Numerous lot numbers including the short titles of groups of books reflected, on the one hand, the economical practice of the time of including several books within a single binding, and on the other hand, the bundling of many books together under one lot number by the auctioneer in order to ensure the sale of as many books as possible. Thus, the number of books being offered for sale was frequently greatly in excess of the total lot numbers. Some theological catalogues did have their books arranged topically before being subdivided according to format, generally following a sequence of topics such as: exegetics, polemics, symbolics, catechetics, homiletics, etc. It would therefore seem probable that clues concerning the content of these hymnal collections in the first half of the eighteenth century would likely be found in these comprehensive libraries, even though not every personal library was auctioned, and not all auction catalogues have survived.

Georg Heinrich Götze must have owned a significant collection of hymnals, to judge from the published version of the sermon he preached in the Marienkirche introducing the *Lübeckisches Gesang-Buch* on the third Sunday in Advent, 1703,[5] his connections with other hymnologists such as Johann Christoph Olearius, and his various *Lieder Predigten* (hymn sermons).[6] A few years before his death in 1728 Götze auctioned his extensive library, catalogued as *Bibliotheca Theologica Selecta, Variis ex Historia Literaria Observationibus atqve accuratioribus Eruditorum Judiciis illustrata* (Greifswald: Fickweiler, 1722) (Select Theological Library, Illustrated with Various Observances from Literary Histories and with the more Accurate Judgments of the Learned).[7] The unusual feature of the catalogue is that unlike other auction catalogues, which simply give the title, place, and year of publication, here Götze offers annotations on many of the books, hence it was necessary for the statement on the reverse

---

5. Georg Heinrich Götze, *Christliche Lieder-Predigt . . . Alß das Lübeckische Gesang-Buch Der Christl. Gemeinde zu St. Marien bekandt gemacht wurde . . .* (Lübeck: Wiedemeyer, 1704).
6. Rößler, "Die Frühzeit hymnologischer Forschung," 138–9; Zedler 11 (1735): cols. 87–89.
7. It is difficult to estimate the total number of books offered in the catalogue because the lot numbers revert to "1" at the beginning of every subsection, but it must have been somewhere between five thousand and ten thousand.

of the title page that the auction catalogue was issued "with the censure and approval of the most reverend faculty of theology in the university of Rostock." Götze's comments either commend or criticize the content of a book. For example, on Augustus von Schönfeld [Johann Peter Grünenberg], *Erwegung, der Erläuterung der Fürstl. Mecklenburg. Kirchen-Ordnung, so Anno 1708, publiciret* (Hamburg: [Liebezeit], 1709) (Examination and Explanation of the Ducal Mecklenburg Church-Order, Published Anno 1708),[8] he remarks that the author "gives good advice regarding all sorts of errors in the church hymns."[9] Scattered among the books on offer are selected titles on hymnological matters by various authors, editions of the religious verse of poets like Paul Gerhardt and Johann Rist, as well as titles by Götze himself, such as a group of several books devoted to expositions of different individual hymns, published in Lübeck in 1715 and 1716.[10] But hymnals of the type that were regularly used in church, at home, or in private are almost non-existent. In the Götze catalogue I have only discovered reference to a copy of the Mühlhausen *Gesang-Buch*, 1712,[11] and the 1711 imprint of the *Neu-vermehrtes Hamburgisches Gesang-Buch*, edited by Johann Friedrich Mayer.[12] This was something of a surprise given the comprehensive nature of this "vast library of books, equipped in every kind of learning, antiquarian, exegetical, polemical, moral, homiletic, philological, and philosophical, furnished and illustrated by various observations from literary history."[13] The auction catalogue had no subsection for Götze's collection of hymnals, which therefore had to have been dispersed by some other means.

Johann Christoph Olearius, the most significant among the early German hymnologists,[14] was an avid collector who assembled an impressive collection of hymnals and hymnal-related literature.[15] His collection is known through his hand-written manuscript listing of his hymnological library that today is preserved in the Forschungsbibliothek (Research Library), Gotha: "Index scriptorum Hymnod[icorum]: quae possidet Joh.

---

8. *Bibliotheca Theologica Selecta*, 247–248, Lot 223.
9. *Bibliotheca Theologica Selecta*, 247–248, Lot 223: "so gibt er gute Erinnerung von allerhand Fehlern der Kirchen-Liedern."
10. *Bibliotheca Theologica Selecta*, 247–248, Lot 223; 314–315, Lot 11/1, 11/3, 11/5.
11. *Bibliotheca Theologica Selecta*, 290, Lot 77.
12. *Bibliotheca Theologica Selecta*, 290, Lot 77; 315, Lot 12.
13. *Bibliotheca Theologica Selecta*, [unpaginated dedication:] "Bibliothecam selectam amplissimo librorum, apparatu in omni eruditionis genere antiquario, exegetico, polemico, morali, homiletico, philologico, et philosphico, instructam variusque ex historia literaria observationibus illustratam prolixo mentis . . ."
14. Rößler, "Die Frühzeit hymnologischer Forschung," 134–137.
15. Martin Rößler, *Geistliches Lied und kirchliches Gesangbuch* (Berlin: Strube, 2006), 204

Chr[isto]ph: Olearius Consistor: Ass: et Insp: Arnstadii 1732" (Index of Hymnodical Writings: in the Possession of Johann Christoph Olearius, Consistory Assessor and Inspector, Arnstadt 1732).[16] Somewhat reminiscent of auction catalogues that include many titles under a single lot number, Olearius structured his "Index" according to numbered sections, which could contain just one title or a whole group—sometimes as many as thirty or forty titles—under an individual section number.[17] This makes the task of estimating the extent of the collection somewhat challenging, but it is clear that it must have comprised between eight hundred and one thousand volumes. A small, but significant, section of Olearius's manuscript "Index" appeared in print during his lifetime. Between 1737 and 1738 Johann Jacob Gottschaldt, pastor in Saxony, issued installments of what he called his *Hymn Remarks*. In the third installment he included "Alle Gesang-Bücher des sechzehenden Seculi . . . , Welche . . . J. C. Olearius Superintendens in Arnstadt, An. 1738. Besitzen" (Hymnals All from the Sixteenth Century, which in 1738 are in the possession of J. C. Olearius, Superintendent in Arnstadt).[18] Listed are thirty-six historically important early hymnals published before the end of the sixteenth century. They include rarities, such as the so-called *Chorgesangbuch* of 1524, no less than four different 1525 imprints, and the extremely rare, sole surviving copy of the earliest extant edition of the *Geistliche Lieder*, published by Klug in Wittenberg in 1533.[19] The source for Gottschaldt's list of thirty-six hymnals was the section of sixteenth century hymnals in Olearius's manuscript "Index."[20]

Like father like son, Johann Christian Olearius (1699–1776), followed in the footsteps of his father, Johann Christoph, becoming successively deacon, archdeacon, and church librarian in Arnstadt. The year before his father died Johann Christian published a report on the church library:

16. Forschungsbibliothek, Gotha, shelfmark Chart. B 1694; accessible in digital form. It comprises forty leaves, thirty-three leaves of crowded, hand-written entries, the last seven blank; see Paasch,"Mit Lust und Liebe singen," 73.
17. "Das Verzeichnis weist 180 Nummern mit mehreren hundert Titeln aus" (The index reveals one hundred and eighty numbers with many hundreds of titles); Paasch, *"Mit Lust und Liebe singen,"* 128, see also 73.
18. Johann Jacob Gottschaldt, *Sammlung von allerhand auserlesenen Lieder–Remarquen, In Sechs Theilen* (Leipzig: Martini, 1748), 334–336.
19. See the facsimile: *Das Klug'sche Gesangbuch 1533 nach dem einzigen erhaltenen Exemplar der Lutherhalle zu Wittenberg*, ed. Konrad Ameln (Kassel: Bäreneiter, 1983), "Geleitwort," 5. During the time Olearius owned the volume it was reprinted, without music or woodcuts, in *Die Hauskirche, oder erbauliche Schiften welche zu haüslicher übung der Gottseligkeit mit sonderbaren Nutzen gebraucht werden konnen* (Gotha: Reyher, 1739).
20. Olearius, "Index scriptorum Hymnodicorum," fol. 24^r–25^r. Olearius also owned other sixteenth century hymnals that are listed elsewhere in his "Index."

Kurtze doch hinlängliche Nachricht von der öffentlichen Kirchen-Bibliothek in Arnstadt (Brief but Sufficient Report from the Public Church Library in Arnstadt) (1746). The report included a catalogue of the books that his father had also overseen as the Arnstadt church librarian. The books were classified according to their places in the bookcases in the library, which were shelved according to format—folio, quarto, octavo, etc.—and thus the pages of the library catalogue look very similar to those of the usual auction catalogues. Only one hymnological book was apparently in the church library, Georg Serpilius, *Lieder-Concordance* (Dresden & Leipzig, 1696), with a preface by Johann Friedrich Mayer,[21] and the only listing of hymnals in the library was apparently in Georgius's *Allgemienes Bücher-Lexicon* (Leipzig, 1742)[22] (see further below). The presentation of the content of the public theological library was therefore similar to the way in which private theological libraries were organized, confirming the custom whereby hymnal collections were treated differently from the more extensive theological collections, and instead of a public auction were passed on privately. Thus, when he died in 1747 Johann Christoph Olearius's hymnological library was passed to his son.[23]

Johann Friedrich Mayer owned one of the largest libraries in private hands at that time. The auction catalogue of his books compiled after his death is a massive bibliography, running to more than one thousand pages.[24] The catalogue is structured in two main parts: the first presents books on theology (pages 1–420); the second is devoted to books on various other subjects, such as philosophy, geography, medicine, etc. (pages 421–837); and the catalogue is furnished with a detailed index (from page 837). It is the first part that commands attention since this is where one might expect to find hymnals listed. This first part is classified topically with subsections on theological topics and further classified according to format. Like the Götze catalogue the numbering is not consecutive throughout but reverts to "1" at the beginning of each subsection, making it difficult to estimate the total number of books being offered, which was probably something in excess of ten thousand.

21. *Kurtze doch hinlängliche Nachricht von der öffentlichen Kirchen-Bibliothek in Arnstadt Kirchen-Bibliothek in Arnstadt . . . Verziechniß der Bücher* ([Arnstadt]: Schill, 1746), 74, No. 46.
22. *Kurtze doch hinlängliche Nachricht von der öffentlichen*, 136, No. 35.
23. Some time after Johann Christian Olearius's death (1776), several hundred hymnals were obtained by the ducal library, Gotha, and the Gotha Research Library today has around three hundred volumes from the Olearius collection; see Paasch, *"Mit Lust und Liebe singen,"* 73.
24. *Bibliotheca Mayeriana seu apparatus librarus Io. Frid. Mayeri . . . II. partibus constans,quarum classes post praefationem exhibentur, Berolini. anno MDCCXVI. die IIdo Januar. et sequentib . . . distrahenda* (Berlin: Nicolai, 1715). The catalogue also includes his extensive art gallery.

8   A NEW SONG WE NOW BEGIN

In searching for hymnals in the Mayer catalogue it is possible to find sermons on specific hymns, such as: *Wer nur den lieben Gott* (If you but trust in God to guide you); *Erhalt uns, Herr, bei deinem Wort* (Lord, keep us steadfast in your Word); *Nun komm der Heiden Heiland* (Savior of the nations, come); and *Jesu meines Lebens Leben* (Christ, the Life of all the living).[25] Similarly there are a few groupings of hymnological books, like the five titles offered together in the one lot, one each by Johann Christoph Olearius and Götze, and three by Serpilius,[26] and it is possible to locate a small group of hymnals with distinctly Danish-Baltic connections:

Rigisch, Liffländisches Gesang–Buch (Hamburg, 1703)
Das Wißmarische Gesang–Buch (Wismar, 1700)
Das Kopenhagener Teutsch Gesang–Buch (Copenhagen, 1697)
Dänisches Gesang– und Gebet–Buch. (No place nor year)
Dänisches Gesang– und Gebet–Buch (Copenhagen, 1647)[27]

But these appear almost at the end of the first part of the catalogue and give the impression of being added as afterthoughts. However, Mayer had to have owned a significant collection of hymnals which included some of the earliest Lutheran hymnals, as will be discussed later in this chapter.

Peter Busch (1682–1744) was the superintendent and pastor of the Kreuzkirche, Hannover;[28] he was also a hymnologist,[29] hymnal editor,[30] and hymnal collector. On his death in 1744 an auction catalogue of his books was issued, 372 pages in 8vo format, with the books classified according to theological topics, and subdivided by format, in 2,962 numbered lots. Since many lot numbers included various titles, sometimes as many as twenty or thirty, the number of books in the catalogue was probably somewhat in excess of five thousand.[31]

A few of the books in Busch's library were hymnological in content. On the one hand, like the Götze and Mayer catalogues, there were published sermons on individual hymns, such as: *Ein*

---

25. *Bibliotheca Mayeriana*, 405, Lot. 5; 410, Lot. 74; 412, Lot. 116; 413, Lot. 125, respectively.
26. *Bibliotheca Mayeriana*, 413, Lot. 125.
27. *Bibliotheca Mayeriana*, 414, Lot. 132; 414, Lot. 133; 414, Lot. 134; 420, Lot. 55; 420, Lot. 56, respectively.
28. Rößler, "Die Frühzeit hymnologischer Forschung," 162, n121.
29. See page 9 below.
30. He edited: *Nieder-sächsischer Lieder-Kern, oder Vollständiges auf die nieder-sächsischen Lande gerichtetes Gesang-Buch* (Braunschweig: Schröder, 1719); and *Evangelische Lieder-Theologie, Oder vollkomneres Lehr- und Geistreiches Gesang-Buch...* (Hannover: Schultze, 1737).
31. *Bibliotheca Buschiana, Sue Index Librorum... Petrus Busch* (Hannover: Schrader, 1744).

INTRODUCTION 9

Kindelein so löbelich (A little child so praiseworthy); *O Jesu Christ, meins Lebens Licht* (O Jesu Christ, light of my life); *Merckt auf merckt Himmel* (Take note heaven); *O Welt ich muß dich lassen* (O world I must leave thee); *Es ist das Heil uns kommen her* (Salvation unto us has come).[32] On the other hand, there were a few historically orientated hymnological studies, notably those by Johann Christoph Olearius: *Lieder-Bibliotheck* (Jena, 1702); *Lieder-Freude* (Arnstadt, 1717); and *Lieder-Schatz* (Jena, 1707).[33] However, similar to the Götze and Mayer catalogues, what is again striking is the overwhelming absence of the many hymnals that Busch certainly owned. But in this case the explanation is to be found in the preface to the auction catalogue: "We have not added the Catalogue of the Hymnodic Library, comprising nearly a thousand books... because these things have already been given away."[34] The extent of Busch's hymnal collection is thus established. At the same time, it suggests that the collections of Götze, Mayer, and others were probably of a similar size. While the extent of Busch's hymnal collection is known, the identity of each of the hymnals in that collection remains almost totally unknown. A small sampling of the collection can be gleaned from Busch's study of Luther's hymn *Erhalt uns, Herr, bei dienem Wort* (Lord, keep us steadfast in Your Word). The textual variants found in the texts of Luther's original three stanzas of the hymn were identified by Busch by consulting the hymnals in his personal collection (here identified by place and year of publication):

Stanza 1. Giessen 1664; Halle 1714; Braunschweig 1708; Leipzig 1546 and 1586; Strassburg 1634; Nuremberg 1557; Frankfurt 1668; Magdeburg 1545; Wittenberg 1573.

Stanza 2. Frankfurt 1694; Dresden 1679; Weimar 1681; Rostock 1694; Görlitz [year not given]; Leipzig 1689; Stockholm 1675; Berlin 1684; Leipzig 1679; Riga 1675; Freiberg 1686; Copenhagen 1686; Halberstadt 1672.

Stanza 3. Halberstadt 1672; Nuremberg 1660; Frankfurt 1684; Minden 1689; Strassburg 1634; Nuremberg 1597, 1631, and 1660; Regensburg 1690 Schleusingen 1691; Darmstadt 1697; Dresden 1679.[35]

32. *Bibliotheca Buschiana*, Lot. 1397/2; Lot. 1523/6; Lot. 2854; [Appendix] Lot. 193; [Appendix] Lot. 194, respectively.
33. *Bibliotheca Buschiana*, Lot. 2905; [Appendix] Lot. 192; [Appendix] Lot. 2847), respectively.
34. *Bibliotheca Buschiana*, verso of title page: "*Bibliothecae Hymnodicae, chiliadem fere librorum complectentis, Catalogum, non adiecimus, quia haec iam ... cessit.*"
35. Peter Busch, *Ausführliche Historie und Vertheidigung des Allgemeinen Evangelischen Kirchen–Liedes: Erhalt uns Herr bey deinem Wort!* (Wolfenbüttel: Meißner, 1735), 18–20; see also note 32.

The references are to thirty-two hymnals published between 1545 and 1714, just a small fraction of the almost one thousand hymnals that were in Busch's collection.

That Busch's hymnal collection was given away in advance of the auction meant that no inventory of his hymnals was apparently preserved. The fact that inventories of the hymnal collections of other hymnologists appear to be extremely rare suggests that there was some reason why the hymnals were kept separate from the general theological libraries of the pastor-hymnologists. For example, if the library was classified according to theological topics, it would be difficult to decide which theological subdivision would be appropriate for the hymnals; virtually every aspect of theology—biblical, catechetical, homiletical, polemical, liturgical, etc.— could be found expounded in the hymns of the hymnals. An important contributing factor is found in the published theological auction catalogues, that is, their extensive use of Latin: the titles of the auction catalogues are in Latin; if there is a preface, it will be in Latin; and the majority of the books offered for auction were written in Latin. In contrast, the hymnals, while including some Latin hymns, were essentially in the vernacular. The auction catalogues of the pastors and theologians were thus professional libraries. Their collections of hymnals were regarded as a different kind of literature—too personal, too intimate, and too different in character to be incorporated into the professional theological libraries, or to be disposed of by public auction. Collections of hymnals were therefore either passed on privately following the deaths of the original collectors,[36] or independently sold to book dealers.[37]

---

36. When the composer Bach died an inventory of his estate was drawn up. The twelfth chapter listed the religious books ("geistlichen Bücher") that Bach owned. On a number of levels this listing parallels the book auction catalogues of theologians and pastors, only on a much smaller scale. The books are classified according to format: folio, 4to, 8vo, but there are no hymnals, apart from the "professional" eight volume anthology of hymns: *Andächtiger Seelen geistliches Brand- und Gantz-Opfer/ das ist vollständiges Gesangbüch* (Leipzig: Zeidler, 1697); see Robin A. Leaver, *Bach's Theologische Bibliothek* (Stuttgart: Hänssler, 1983), No. 52. It has often been explained that Bach's collection of hymnals must have been divided among the family before the inventory was drawn up, something that was thought to be against custom. But the information reviewed here suggests that, to the contrary, it was an established practice.
37. Over the years hymnal collections changed hands and were gradually absorbed into the holdings of major libraries, such as: the Herzog August Bibliothek, Wolfenbüttel; the Forschungs- und Landesbibliothek, Gotha; the Gesangbucharchiv, Johannes Gutenberg Universität, Mainz; and the Sammlung Wernigerode, Deutsche Staatsbibliothek, Berlin. Individual *Gesangbücher* can be located by accessing the comprehensive bibliography at the Johannes Gutenberg Universität, Mainz (approaching 30,000 records at the time of writing, and a high proportion are of Lutheran hymnals): https://gesangbuchbibliographie.uni-mainz.de/index.php

Most hymnals were identified by place, the village, town, or principality, as declared on their title pages, which also carried information regarding whether the hymnals were printed and published locally or in a nearby larger town. Copies of the hymnal in use in a particular church would be obtained locally. But there are signs that many individuals owned more than one hymnal and were in effect small-scale collectors of hymnals that were either passed on within the family or purchased from individual book dealers.

Leipzig had many book dealers—at least twenty in 1736. In 1742 one of them, Theophilus Georgius (*ca.* 1674–1762), published his four-part *Allgemeines Bücher-Lexicon* containing information on many thousands of books. It was based on Georgius's records of book sales over a period of fifty-four years (1688–1742).[38] Each book was identified by author or editor, title, year published, format, place of publication, name of publisher, and, most important for other book dealers, the price that had been paid for a copy of the book. In the second part of his *Lexicon* Georgius lists almost two hundred *Gesangbücher* published between 1657 and 1739.[39] Of course, what it does not reveal is how many copies of each edition Georgius had sold over the years, but what it does convey is very interesting. First, it shows that a wide variety of hymnals had been sold during this period and, given that the specific hymnals in use in individual parish churches would have been obtained locally, a good many of these hymnals purchased from this book dealer in Leipzig most likely were in addition to the hymnal used in services on Sundays and other days. Second, Georgius's listing, while extensive, is not exhaustive; there had been many more hymnals published during this period than is recorded in *Allgemeines Bücher-Lexicon*. It is not clear how much this was conditioned by supply and demand or whether there were other factors—and, of course, Georgius was not the only book dealer in Leipzig, and Leipzig was not the only place with many book dealers. Third, it is noticeable that Georgius's listing only includes very few hymnal editions in 4vo or large 8vo format (in similar dimensions, approximately 5" × 8"). Two examples of these formats not found in Georgius's listing—*Geistliches Neu-vermehrtes Altenburgisches Gesang- und Gebeth-Buch* (Altenburg: Richter, 1735), 1250 hymns; and *Theologia in Hymnis, Oder: Universal-Gesang-Buch* (Leipzig: Martini, 1737), 1301 hymns—are cumbersome books to handle. It is notable that

---

38. Theophilus Georgius, *Allgemeines Bücher-Lexicon, In welchem nach Ordnung des Dictionarii die allermeisten Autores oder Gattungen von Büchern zu finden . . .* (Leipzig: Georgius, 1742).
39. Georgius, *Allgemeines Bücher-Lexicon*, 2: 135–137. This total is somewhat modest compared with Busch's hymnal collection.

the hymnals in these larger formats that Georgius does include tend to be hymnals with music notation and thus could have been used with some form of music stand. Fourth, the most striking thing about Georgius's listing of the editions of hymnals he had sold over the years is that the vast majority were in the smaller formats, 8vo, 12mo, and 24mo. This suggests that portability was a prime factor on the part of those who purchased these hymnals.

The small-scale hymnal collections were of two types: those for the individual and those for the family. Individuals would own a copy of the hymnal of the parish in which they lived and worshiped, with perhaps another copy or two of similar hymnals from elsewhere that contained different hymns. They would also have owned various devotional books, such as those to be used in preparation for participation in confession and communion. These books customarily included a small hymnal of around fifty hymns. Families would have a primary hymnal for daily devotions at the meal table, morning and evening, perhaps one of the bulkier hymnals that could easily rest on the table, and a large family would need to have more than one copy of the communal hymnal. If they were a musical family, they could have copies of a cantional style hymnal for four-part singing at the table devotions (see chapter 4). If they owned a keyboard instrument, they would most likely have owned a hymnal that included the chorale melodies with figured bass. Thus, households with, say, three or four adults and four or five children (a small family for the time) together could have possessed between six to twelve hymnals of various types, and quite possibly even more.

A SENSE OF HISTORY

The hymnals of individuals and households were collected for the practicality of their use; the hymnals on the bookshelves of notable clergy were assembled for detailed information regarding the nature and content of Lutheran hymnody. When early in the year 1700 Johann Friedrich Mayer came to write the preface to the *Neu-vermehrtes Hamburgisches Gesang-Buch* he was able to make effective use of copies of two of the earliest Lutheran hymnals that he apparently owned, even though neither was listed in the auction catalogue of his extensive library in 1715: *Etliche Christliche Lieder* (DKL 1524[12–14]); and *Geistliche Gesänge so man itzt Gott Lob in der Kirchen singt* (DKL 1525[08]).[40] Mayer wanted those who would

---

40. Johann Bartholomäus Riederer, *Abhandlung von Einführung des teutschen Gesangs in der evangelischlutherische Kirche über in die nürnbergische besonders* (Nuremberg: Endter, 1759; facsimile, Leipzig: Zentralantiquariat, 1975), 139.

sing from the Hamburg hymnal to know how it all began in 1524–1525. After quoting St. Paul's familiar words concerning the singing of psalms, hymns, and spiritual songs (Col 3:16), Mayer wrote:

> You have a blessed supply of such spiritual hymns. In order that right from the very beginning there might be no lack, the blessed father Luther ... did not insist that only the hymns he had composed should be sung in the congregation, but upheld the gift of the Holy Spirit in the creation of psalms and hymns of praise by others, valuing them very highly, and thus collected their spiritual hymns for use in the churches of God, generously sharing them.[41]

Mayer then listed the first lines of the hymns in the two historic hymnals. Together, allowing for duplicates, there were thirty-six different hymns in the two hymnals. Mayer did not identify the different authors because he knew that his readers would recognize the familiar hymns by Luther and thus easily discern those that had been written by others. But he did single out three hymns by Paul Speratus that were in the *Achtliederbuch*: *Es ist das Heil uns kommen her* (Salvation unto us has come), *In Gott gelaub ich* (In God I believe), and *Hilf Gott, wie ist der Menschen Not* (God's help is what the people need). The text of the first was included in the Hamburg hymnal (No. 363), but the other two were not, so all the stanzas of these other two hymns were printed in full in Mayer's preface. One of the distinctive features of Speratus's hymns in the *Achtliederbuch* is the scriptural warrant for every line of the poetry that is included in an appendix to each of the hymns. From his personal copy of the *Achtliederbuch* Mayer reprinted all three of these lists in full.[42] Apparently this was the first time that the appendices of these hymns had been republished and made easily accessible since their original appearance in the foundational Lutheran hymnal of 1524.

---

41. *Neu-vermehrtes Hamburgisches Gesang-Buch* (Hamburg: König, 1739), sig.) (3ʳ. The preface is dated Hamburg, March 27, 1700. "Ihr habt dieser geistlichen Lieder einen seligen Vorrath. Damit gleich Anfngs kein Mangel sein möchte, drang der selige Vater Lutherus ... nicht etwas darauf, daß man bloß die von ihm aufgesetzten lieder in der Gemeine muste anstimmen, sondern er hielte die Gabe des Heiligen Geistes, die sich durch Verfertigung der Psalmen und Lob-Gesänge erweise, an andern sehr hoch, daß er auch ihre Geistliche Lieder in der Kirchen Gottes zu Nutze einsammlete, und reichlich mittheilete."

42. Of the twelve pages of the preface eight were reprinted from the *Achtliederbuch*. Mayer's personal copy of the first edition of the *Achtliederbuch*, later owned by Johann Christoph Olearius, is now in the Gotha Universitäts- und Forschungsbibliothek; see *"Mit Lust und Liebe singen": die Reformation und ihre Lieder. Begleitband zur Ausstellung der Universitäts–und Forschungsbibliothek Erfurt/Gotha in Zusammenarbeit mit der Stiftung Schloss Friedenstein Gotha, 5. May bis August 12, 2012*, ed. Kathrin Paasch (Gotha: [Universitäts– und Forschungsbibliothek], 2012), Abbildung 1.

In many respects the Reformation debate turned on the question of authority: Does it rest with the Church or with Scripture? For Luther it was unequivocally Scripture, and here in the earliest Lutheran hymnal the hymns of Speratus demonstrated the thoroughness of their biblical content. Mayer wanted the people who were singing from the new Hamburg hymnal at the beginning of the eighteenth century to understand that while other primary Lutheran hymnals did not include such scriptural warrants for the hymns they contained, they were nevertheless as thoroughly biblical in content as were the specific examples by Speratus. Thus, the early hymnals contained hymns that expressed the content and meaning of the protest that had begun in 1517.

As Lutherans moved closer to the celebration of the bicentenary of the Reformation in 1717, Johann Christoph Olearius, while in essential agreement with Mayer, nevertheless went much further than the Hamburg superintendent. In a sense Olearius argued that if the early Lutheran hymnals epitomized the protest of 1517, then they should be fully in focus for any celebration of an anniversary of the Reformation, and especially for the bicentenary of the Reformation in October/November 1717, a celebration that would be observed more extensively than had been the case either in 1617 or 1667.[43] For the 1717 celebrations Olearius arranged for the copies of three early hymnals that were in his personal library to be reprinted (texts only; no music). The small octavo book of around ninety pages was titled: *Jubilirende Lieder-Freude/ Bestehend in erster Aufflage derer allerersten A[nno].C[hristi]. 1524. und 1525. in Druck gegangenen Lutherischen Gesängen zur Vermehrung schuldigster Devotion und Danckbarkeit/bey dem Andern von Gott verliehenen Lutherischen Reformations-Jubilaeo . . .* (Arnstadt: Meurer, 1717) (Jubilant Hymn-Joy: Established in the First Editions of Lutheran Hymns in Print anno Christi 1524 and 1525 to Increase Dutiful Devotion and Gratitude for the Other God-granted, Reformation-Jubilee). These were the hymnals:

[1.] *Etlich Cristlich Lider, Lobgesang und Psalm, dem rainen Wort Gottes gemeß . . . in der Kirchen zu singen . . .* [Achtliederbuch]. (DKL 1524[12–14])
[2.] *Etliche christliche Gesenge und Psalmen . . . mit eyner vorrede des . . . Marti Luther M.D.XXv . . .* Erfurt, [Enchiridia supplement]. (DKL 1525[05])
[3.] *Geystliche Gesenge so man ytzt Got zu Lob ynn der Kyrchen singt. . ., gebessert und mit Fleyß corrigyrt durch Martini Lutther, Vuittemberg, anno 1525.* (DKL 1525[08])

---

43. For the background, see Robin A. Leaver, *The Whole Church Sings: Congregational Singing in Luther's Wittenberg* (Grand Rapids, MI: Eerdmans, 2017), 1–7.

As I have written elsewhere: "For Olearius it was obviously not enough to sing the early Lutheran hymns as part of the bicentenary celebrations; it was necessary to have an awareness of how they were first published and disseminated, being the vehicles by which the Reformation was to a large degree defined, expressed, promoted and taken to heart."[44]

The corollary was that if the content of these early hymnals was appropriate for celebrating an important Reformation anniversary, then when a significant hymnal anniversary was approaching—as it was in 1724—the occasion deserved to be celebrated, perhaps not quite on the same scale as the major Reformation festival of 1717, but in a way that focused on how Lutheran identity was established, preserved and furthered by the massive genealogical tree of Lutheran hymnals that grew from roots firmly planted in 1524.

This was effectively the argument that Busch presented in a small book: *Jubilaeum Cantionem Ecclesiasticarum Lutheranarum, oder Evangelisch-Lutherarische Jubel-Freude, über die öffentliche Reformation Der Kirchen-Gesänge, von D. Mart. Luthero Anno 1524. geschehen, Nebst denen Wohlgegründeten Uhrsachen solcher Freude* (Hannover: Förster, 1724). (Jubilaeum Cantionem Ecclesiasticarum Lutheranarum, or Evangelical Lutheran Jubilee-Joy, on the public Reformation of Church-Hymns, accomplished by Dr. Martin Luther in the year 1524, together with the well-founded causes of such joy). Busch begins by referring first to the celebrations of the bicentenary of the beginning of the Reformation that had taken place a few years earlier in 1717, and then to the forthcoming bicentenary of the presentation of the Augsburg Confession in 1730, plans for which were already being made at the time of Busch's writing. He then makes this observation:

> It is not inappropriate to call the year 1724 such a jubilee year for the whole Evangelical Lutheran Church because in it the Evangelical Lutheran Church will acknowledge the undeniable and great beneficence of God, which he brought about by the first public printing of the Evangelical-Lutheran hymns, and reformation of the church-song in the year 1524...[45]

---

44. Leaver, *The Whole Church Sings*, 7.
45. Busch, *Jubilaeum Cantionem Ecclesiasticarum Lutheranarum*, 7: "Ein solches Jubel-Jahr der gantzen Evangelisch-Lutherischen Kirche ist auch das 1724. Jahr nicht unfüglich zu nennen, weil darinnen die Evangelisch-Lutherischen Kirche die unläugbahre und hohe Wohlthat Gottes, welche Er durch ersten öffentliche Druck der Evangelisch-Lutherische Gesänge, und Reformation der Kirchen-Gesänge anno 1524..."

Busch then detailed the contents of some of the early hymnals of 1524–25: Johann Walter's *Chorgesangbuch*, the *Achtliederbuch*, and an Erfurt *Enchiridion*. Here two of Busch's primary sources were Mayer's preface to the Hamburg *Gesangbuch* of 1700 and Olearius's Arnstadt reprint of the 1524–1525 hymnals in *Jubilirende Lieder-Freude*.[46]

What Busch does not reveal is how the hymnal jubilee was to be observed in the Hannover churches in 1724. The Augsburg Confession bicentenary in June 1730 was centered on Luther's hymn *Ein feste Burg ist unser Gott* (A mighty fortress is our God).[47] The bicentenary of Hannover's acceptance of the Reformation in September 1733 was similarly epitomized in a hymn by Luther: *Erhalt uns, Herr, bei deinem Wort*. (Lord, keep us steadfast in your Word).[48] If the 1724 hymnal bicentenary celebrations in Hannover had followed a similar pattern to these later celebrations, one would have expected, first, that Busch would have given the date(s) of when the celebration was to take place, and second, that he would have revealed a Luther hymn that would be the focus of the celebration. But he does neither. Instead, he gives almost the same lists of first lines of hymns originating in 1524–1525 that Mayer had included in his preface to the Hamburg *Gesangbuch*, and that Olearius had reprinted in full in his *Jubilirende Lieder-Freude*. Thus, instead of celebrating just one of the early hymns on a single occasion, such as on the annual Reformation Day, October 31, 1724, the decision may well have been to spread the celebration over the whole year, perhaps beginning on Advent Sunday 1724. After all, Busch called the celebration a "jubilee year," not a "jubilee fest." So perhaps the celebration involved a weekly sermon on the *Graduallied* of the day, possibly together with a chorale cantata on the same hymn, composed by the Hannover cantor,

---

46. Busch, *Jubilaeum Cantionem Ecclesiasticarum Lutheranarum*, 7–12.
47. See Peter Busch, *Ausführliche Historie und Erklärung Des Helden–Liedes Lutheri Eine feste Burg ist unser Gott! Bey Gelegenheit des gefeyerten zweyeten Evangelischen Jubel–Festes. . . .* (Hannover: Förster, 1731). "Detailed history and explanation of the heroic song by Luther A strong castle is our God! On the occasion of the celebrated second Evangelical [Lutheran] Jubilee Festival..."
48. The full title of Busch's book cited at note 35 above, is: *Ausführliche Historie und Vertheidigung des Allgemeinen Evangelischen Kirchen-Liedes: Erhalt uns Herr bey deinem Wort! mit einer in der Vorrede gegebenen Nachricht von dem gefeyerten Jubel-Gedächtniß der Reformation der Stadt Hanover; auch angehängter Jubel- und Gedächtniß–Rede bei solcher Feyer.* (Wolfenbüttel: Meißner, 1735), 18–20. [Detailed History and Defense of the General Evangelical Church Hymn: Preserve us Lord by your Word! with a Report given in the Preface of the Celebrated Jubilee Commemoration of the Reformation of the city of Hannover; also attached is a celebratory and commemorative speech for such an occasion.] The report of the celebration is given in the preface, sig.)(6ʳ–)(7ᵛ.

Johann Ernst Georg Pott (1699–1762).[49] Something like this had already begun to happen in the two primary parish churches in Leipzig that year. In June 1724 when Johann Sebastian Bach, as the St. Thomas cantor, began composing his second *Jahrgang* (annual series) of cantatas for alternate weekly performance in the St. Thomas and St. Nicholas churches in Leipzig, he did so with a significant change in the type of libretto he used. Instead of the usual combination of biblical verses, free poetry and one or two stanzas of a hymn, the whole libretto was both a quotation and exposition of a complete hymn/chorale: the opening movement, with the text of the first stanza, was treated as a chorale fantasia, with its melody as the *cantus firmus*; the inner recitatives and arias were poetic reworkings of the inner stanzas of the hymn; and the cantata was brought to a conclusion with a four-part setting of the final stanza of the hymn. The first of these newly composed chorale cantatas was heard on June 11, 1724 (Trinity I), *O Ewigkeit, du Donnerwort* II (BWV 20), based on Johann Rist's popular eternity hymn (1642; melody 1652). Seven of the weekly sequence of cantatas between the two churches—a series that continued until Easter 1725—were of hymns from the earliest Lutheran hymnals of 1524 (see Table 1.1). The other chorale cantatas of the *Jahrgang* were based on familiar later classic Lutheran hymns, successors to the hymns that began the tradition in 1524.

Although there is no extant statement or written authorization that this Leipzig sequence of chorale cantatas was intended to commemorate the bicentenary of the Lutheran hymnal, 1524–1724, it seems too much of a coincidence to suppose that the connection was accidental, especially when certain factors are taken into account. First, Lutherans were fond of celebrating significant anniversaries and it was only a few years earlier that they had made a big deal about celebrating the bicentenary of the beginning of the Reformation in 1717. Second, there was precedent regarding sermons being linked with chorale cantatas in the Leipzig churches. During the year 1688–1689, for example, Johann Benedict Carpzov [II], superintendent and pastor of the St. Thomas Church collaborated with the St. Thomas cantor, Johann Schelle, in a *Jahrgang* of sermons and chorale cantatas.[50] Third, there must have been collaboration between Bach and

---

49. Pott composed a cantata for celebration of the bicentenary of the Hannover Reformation in September 1733, which most likely have included *Erhalt uns, Herr, bei deinem Wort*; see Busch, *Ausführliche Historie und Vertheidigung des... Erhalt uns Herr*, sig.)(6ᵛ.
50. Outlines of Carpzov's sermons were published in 1689; see Robin A. Leaver, *Bach Studies: Liturgy, Hymnology and Theology* (New York: Routledge, 2021), 127.

the clergy, notably the superintendent and pastor of the St. Nicholas Church, Salomon Deyling, and Christian Weiß, pastor of the St. Thomas Church, since their sermons would be on the same chorales as were in Bach's cantatas and thus would be for them as much a commitment as it was for Bach.

Table 1.1 Bach's Cantatas on Chorales that First Appeared in the Earliest Lutheran Hymnals 1524–1525.[51]

Chorale		Author	English	Cantata	Occasion	Date
Ach Gott, vom Himmel sieh darein	𝔄	Luther	LH 260	2	Trinity II	18 Jun 1724
Herr Christ, der einig Gottessohn	ℭ	E. Cruciger	LBW 96	96	Trinity XVIII	8 Oct 1724
Aus tiefer Not schrei ich zu dir	𝔄	Luther	LBW 295	38	Trinity XXI	29 Oct 1724
Nun komm, der Heiden Heiland	ℭ	Luther	LBW 28	62	Advent I	3 Dec 1724
Gelobet seist du, Jesu Christ	ℭ	Luther	LBW 48	91	Christmas	25 Dec 1724
Christum wir sollen loben schon	ℭ	Luther	LH 104	121	Christmas 2	26 Dec 1724
Mit Fried und Freud ich fahr dahin	ℭ	Luther	LSB 938	125	Purification	2 Feb 1725

Busch had been a student in Leipzig between 1701 and 1706 and he may have kept in contact with his *alma mater* over the years. If so, he may have heard about what was taking place in the Leipzig churches in 1724, to celebrate the bicentenary of the Lutheran hymnal, and decided to do something similar in Hannover. Alternatively, he may have been inspired by the growing reputation over the previous fifteen years or so of

---

51. The first four columns relate to the chorales/hymns, the remainder the chorale cantatas of Bach: col. 1, first lines; col. 2, 1524 hymnals, where 𝔄 = *Achtliederbuch*, ℭ = *Chorgesangbuch*, and ℭ = Erfurt *Enchiridion*; col. 3, author; col. 4, English hymn translations (not Bach's libretti); col. 5; Bach's cantatas according to the catalogue numbers; col. 6, occasion for which the cantata were composed; date of first performance.

a publication that was almost certainly in his library at this time: Johann Christoph Olearius, *Evangelischer Lieder–Schatz* (1707).[52] Olearius's study presents an exposition of every *Graduallied* (Gradual hymn), sung in between the epistle and gospel on Sundays and festivals throughout the church year in most Lutheran churches. Each exposition of a hymn was accompanied by an outline of a sermon that suggested how homily and hymn could complement each other. In many respects it was the obvious handbook for such a series of hymn-sermons commemorating the bicentenary of the Lutheran hymnal in 1724, and may well have been used as such by Busch in Hannover.

Much of this, of course, has to be conjectural because, in contrast to the widely celebrated and centrally organized Reformation festivals of 1717 and 1730, the bicentenary of the Lutheran hymnal in 1724 was organized and celebrated locally. Such observances were probably varied and small-scale, and what documentation there may have been was quickly forgotten. What happened in later times, such as 1824 and 1924, I have not been able to discover. If such commemorative services were held, we do not have the evidence, but is it because the evidence does not exist, or because we have not been looking in the right places?

OVERVIEW OF WHAT IS EXPLORED IN THIS BOOK

Whatever the past was, or was not, this collection of essays was planned and prepared to ensure that the half millennium of the Lutheran hymnal 1524–2024 would not pass by unnoticed. The contributions are divided into two parts. The first deals with primary hymnals that were not only fundamental for their contributions to German hymnody as a whole, but also for their specific influence on the hymnals of Lutherans (and a good many non-Lutherans!) no matter what language or whatever country they sang in. The second part charts the development of Lutheran hymnals in America from approximately the early nineteenth century.

In the earliest hymnals of 1524/25, the original hymns created by Luther and his Wittenberg colleagues over the winter of 1523/24 were simply gathered together in no particular order (see chapter 2). As the number of hymns increased it became necessary to devise some kind of topical structure. This was essentially achieved by Luther and his colleagues in the Wittenberg hymnals published by Klug from 1529 (see chapter 3).

---

52. *Bibliotheca Buschiana,* No. 2847. Bach was the organist of the Neuen Kirche, Arnstadt, between 1703–1707, the same period when Olearius was writing and publishing this important hymnological reference work; for the background, see Leaver, *Bach Studies,* 127–131, 158–159.

Here was established the basic structure that was followed throughout the centuries and marked out what a Lutheran hymnal should look like: church year hymns usually forming the initial group, with the Advent hymn, *Nun komm der Heiden Heiland* (Savior of the nations come), being the first hymn; then hymns on the various sections of the Catechism; then a group of metrical versions of individual Psalms; and so on. If a hymnal lost its title page, it still would proclaim its Lutheran identity by the way in which the individual hymns were presented.

There were three principal spheres of Lutheran hymn-singing: church, home, and school. In the worship of the church and the devotion of the home the hymns were generally sung in unison. In the latter part of the sixteenth century, in the schools that supplied choirs for the churches, a note-against-note, vertical four-part harmonization of the simple chorale melodies was developed, the so-called cantional style, particularly associated with the names of Lucas Osiander, Johann Hermann Schein, and Gottfried Vopelius. Although it was a vocal style it nevertheless proved to be a strong influence in establishing the basic form of organ accompaniments of congregational hymn singing (see chapter 4).

In the century between approximately 1640 and 1740 one hymnal was dominant in Lutheran Germany: Johann Crüger, *Praxis Pietatis Melica, das ist: Übung der Gottseligkeit in Christlichen und Trostlichen Gesängen* (The Practice of Piety in Christian and Comforting Hymns). During this period around sixty editions were issued. Unlike many hymnals, which simply recorded the first lines of the associated melodies in the headings of the hymns, with no music notation, Crüger's hymnal included both melodies and harmonizations. A good many of the melodies were composed by Crüger and are still being sung today. For some churches the *Praxis Pietatis Melica* effectively became its musical resource; for other churches Crüger's hymnal introduced them to the hymns of Paul Gerhardt (see chapter 5).

Although "piety" was in the title of Crüger's hymnal it was not a "Pietist" hymnal; that was the controversial "Halle Hymnal," edited by Johann Anastasius Freylinghausen and first published in 1704: *Geist-reiches Gesang-Buch* (Spiritually Rich Hymnal). It was heavily criticized for its theological errors, for undermining the sturdy chorale melodies by its use of what was regarded as trivial music, and for what was considered its tasteless poetic expressions. Nevertheless, the hymnal went through numerous editions and was responsible for changing the content of many subsequent Lutheran hymnals as well as influencing other Protestant hymnals in many different languages and countries (see chapter 6).

The essays of the second part deal with primary American hymnals, dating approximately from the early nineteenth century, that lie behind the hymnals of today. A useful bibliography of the hymnal collections in the libraries of Wittenberg University, Springfield, Ohio, was edited by Louis Voigt and published as *Hymnbooks at Wittenberg* (Springfield: Chantry, 1975): the American Lutheran hymnals are classified according to the *Ministeria* or synods that issued them (Nos. 203–484). Carl Schalk was an avid collector of Lutheran hymnals which supplied him with the documentation that enabled him to produce two important books that not only identify the various editions of the hymnals but also discuss in detail the character, content, and significance of each of these collections of hymns: *God's Song in a New Land: Lutheran Hymnals in America* (St. Louis, Concordia, 1995); and *Source Documents in American Lutheran Hymnody* (St. Louis, Concordia, 1996).[53]

To emigrate is to put oneself at risk, a risk that provides more hope than staying put in one's country of origin. America, the goal of a new life, beckoned, but there were many fears to overcome: the fear and isolation from one's family who may never be seen again; the fear of the dangers of the journey across the Atlantic; the fear of the necessity of years of hard work that may only barely lift you out of poverty.

I have in my possession a copy of the following hymnal: *Singender Mund eines glaubigen Christen, Das ist: Vollständiges Gesang–Buch der Alten und Neuen Lieder . . . in der Kirchen und zu Haus abzusingen, aus auf den Reisen . . .* (Nuremberg: Endter, 1728) (Singing Mouth of a Believing Christian, That is: Complete Hymn Book of Old and New Hymns . . . to Sing in Churches and at Home, and when Traveling . . .). On the flyleaf is an undated and unsigned inscription: "Für trostreicher begleiter zur Reiß auf Amerika" (A consolatory companion for the journey to America"). When Lutherans emigrated to America, whether they came in groups or as individuals, they brought with them a variety of vernacular hymnals. Some, like this one in my collection, were given as the gift of a concerned friend or member of the family; other emigrants simply brought with them a copy of the hymnal they had been using in the home parish church that they were then leaving. But the need was for comfort and consolation because there would be tough times ahead, and the necessary support and encouragement would be found in the hymnals they brought with them.

---

53. Schalk donated his collection of hymnals, comprising more than five hundred and thirty volumes, to the Center for Church Music at Concordia University Chicago in 2010. The Schalk American Lutheran Hymnal Collection continues to add to its holdings.

Among the earliest migrants to America were Swedish Lutherans who founded Fort Christina on the Delaware River (present-day Wilmington) in 1638, though the settlement struggled to survive for decades. Eventually Trinity Church was built and consecrated in 1699, and the hymnal they sang from was *Den svenska psalmboken* (Stockholm: Burchard, 1694).[54]

In October 1731 the Catholic Prince-Archbishop of Salzburg issued an edict that demanded Lutherans to recant their faith, and if they refused, they would be expelled from the diocese. They chose expulsion, and these Salzburger emigrants spent the next few years traveling across German territories trying to find a new home for hundreds of displaced people. Ultimately in the later 1730s, under royal patronage of the Hanovarian British King George II, a significant group was granted land in the colony in Georgia.[55] They brought with them an assortment of hymnals, but Freylinghausen's *Geist-reiches Gesang-Buch* was particularly well-known among the Salzburgers.[56]

In research into the hymnal holdings of American libraries and special collections one frequently comes across various editions of a hymnal identified as the *Marburger Gesang–Buch*. At face value one assumes that it was like other hymnals emanating from a particular location, such as the *Altenburgisches Gesang–Buch* or *Dresdnische Gesang–Buch*, *Leipziger Gesang–Buch*. But closer inspection reveals that editions of this hymnal were not intended only for use in and around Marburg. The *Marburger Gesang-Buch* of 1698, published in Nuremberg rather than Marburg, included the following on the title page: "Hymnal . . . as is usual and customary in Nuremberg, Frankfurt and also in surrounding places such as Darmstadt, Giessen, Alsfeld, and other Upper Hessian churches. . . ."[57] Between 1698 and 1811, in fact, around fifty editions of the *Marburger Gesang-Buch* were printed and published in Nuremberg, Frankfurt, and

---

54. Robin A. Leaver, "More than Simple Psalm-Singing in English: Sacred Music in Early Colonial America," *Yale Journal of Music and Religion*, 1/1 (2015): 75–80; see also Richard Hulan, "Four Songs from the Delaware," LQ 2 (1988): 35–45. On the 1694 hymnal, see chapter 9, note 13.
55. W. O. B. Allen and Edmund McClure, *Two Hundred Years: The History of The Society for Promoting Christian Knowledge 1698–1898* (1898) (New York: Franklin, 1970), 386–393.
56. "Hymns Sung by the Salzburgers in 1759 and 1760," in *Detailed Reports on the Salzburger Emigrants Who Settled in America . . . : Volume XVII: 1759–1760*, ed. Samuel Urlsperger (Athens, GA: University of Georgia Press, 1993), 287–91; see also the collection of hymnals belonging to the Salzburgers of Ebenezer, GA, in the James R. Crumley Jr. Archives, 4201 N. Main St., Columbia SC 29203: https://www.crumleyarchives.com/
57. "Gesang-Buch . . . Wie diese in Nürnberg, Franckfurt auch denen umligenden Orten Als Darmstädt- Giessischen/ Alsfeldischen und andern Ober-Hessischen Kirchen üblich und gebräuchlich."

Marburg.[58] Because it was accessible and widely used in central Germany, it was the hymnal that many immigrants brought with them, and that eventually found its way into American libraries and special collections. The popularity of this hymnal encouraged printer Christoph Sauer, working in Germantown, Pennsylvania, to reprint it as *Vollständiger Marburger Gesang-Buch* (Germantown: Sauer, 1757, 1759, 1762, 1770, 1777), the first Lutheran hymnal printed in what became the United States.

When the Elector of Hannover became King George I of England in 1714 a Lutheran royal chapel was created in St. James's Palace, London. The services were in German and the hymns were sung from *Das Hannoverische ordentliche Gesang-Buch... Mit Königl. Groß-Britannischen und Churfürstl. Braunschw. Lüneb. Privilegio* (Hannover: Förster, 1716, or similar year). English-speakers who overheard this hymn-singing were impressed by the melodies that were unknown to them. In response the "Royal Chapel Keeper," Johann Christian Jacobi (1670–1750), translated a sampling of fifteen hymns and published them in 1720 as *A Collection of Divine Hymns, Translated from the High Dutch*, which were then incorporated into the enlarged edition: *Psalmodia Germanica: Or, a Specimen of Divine Hymns, Translated from the High Dutch. Together with Their Proper Tunes and Thorough Bass* (London: Young & Smith, 1722). A second edition appeared in 1732, and, after Jacobi's death, the London printer John Haberkorn issued an expanded third edition in 1765. There was also a New York imprint by Hugh Gaine (*ca.* 1726–1807), ostensibly dated 1756: *Psalmodia Germanica: or, the German Psalmody, Translated from the High Dutch*. The title page includes the following information: "London, printed; New York, reprinted and sold by H. Gaine, 1756." This establishes that the original hymnal had been printed in London and was then reprinted in New York. The problem is that there is no known London edition of 1756. However, if this New York reprint is compared with the third edition that Haberkorn published in London in 1765 a complete match is discovered, thereby establishing that the New York edition was thus a reprint of the London edition of 1765. The year "1756" on the New York title page is a typographical error; the "5" and the "6" have been transposed and the year should have been "1765." What is important to note is the confirmation that a New York edition of the *German Psalmody* was published, but some nine years later than has been

---

58. Information based on data gathered from the *Gesangbuch Bibliographie*, Mainz; see note 37 above.

generally accepted.[59] Even though some of these translations left much to be desired, they did point the way ahead regarding producing hymnals of English translations of German hymns. For example, John Christopher Kunze (1744–1807), "Senior of the Lutheran Clergy in the State of New York," edited the first English Lutheran hymnal published in America: *Hymn and Prayer-Book: For the Use of such Lutheran Churches as Use the English Language* (New York: Hurtin & Commardinger, 1795). In the preface Kunze explained: "Most all of the hymns are translations from the German, and were used before in their churches [in Germany]. All except those in the appendix are taken from printed books, particularly the German Psalmody, printed in London and reprinted at New York, by H. Gaine, 1756 [*sic*], with which many serious English persons have been greatly delighted . . ."[60] According to Carl Schalk, 144 of the 239 hymns are translations from German, and around half of them were taken from the Jacobi/Haberkorn *German Psalmody* of 1765.[61]

English would eventually become the dominant language, but that was a long way off in the later eighteenth century, and most congregations in Pennsylvania and New York continued worshiping and singing in German. As Kunze acknowledges in his preface to the 1795 *Hymn and Prayer-Book*, the continuation of German was promoted by two strong influences. On the one hand there were the settled congregants who were comfortable with German, and on the other hand there were the new immigrants who were decidedly uncomfortable with English.[62] But there was a major problem: there was no unified German hymnal that they could all use. This meant that when these congregations sang a hymn, they were simultaneously singing from different hymnals which were not always textually in agreement: different words were used and stanzas might be omitted (or added) in the different editions. The matter was addressed at the thirty-fifth Convocation of the Evangelical Lutheran Ministerium, meeting in Lancaster, Pennsylvania, June 4, 1782:

Unanimously resolved to have a new Hymn Book printed for our United Congregations.
Resolved, that Revs. Mühlenberg, Sen., Kunze, Helmuth and Mühlenberg, Jun., be a committee to prepare this for print.

---

59. See *The Hymnal 1982 Companion*, ed. Raymond F. Glover (New York: Church Hymnal Corporation, 1994), 2: 487–8. Many library catalogues and bibliographies still give the year incorrectly as 1756.
60. Cited in Schalk, *Source Documents*, 31.
61. Schalk, *Source Documents*, 32, n. 5.
62. Schalk, *Source Documents*, 30.

Resolved, that the committee be strictly bound by the following rules: As far as possible to follow the arrangement of the Halle Hymn Book [Freylinghausen; see chapter 6] Not to omit any of the old standard hymns, especially Luther and Paul Gerhardt . . . Not to admit more than 750 hymns into the collection. *Resolved*, that Senior Mühlenberg prepare the Preface.[63]

The hymnal was published four years later:

> *Erbauliche Lieder-Sammlung zum gottesdienstlichen Gebrauch in den Vereinigten Evangelisch-Lutherischen Gemeinen in Pennsylvanien und den benachbarten Staaten. Gesammelt, eingerichtet und zum Druck befördert durch die gesamten Glieder des hiesigen Vereinigten Evangelisch-Lutherischen Ministerium 1786* (A Collection of Devotional Hymns For Use in the Worship of the United Evangelical Lutheran Congregations in Pennsylvania and Neighboring States. Collected, arranged, and prepared for publication by the local German Evangelical Lutheran Ministerium 1786).[64]

The principal editor was Henry Melchior Mühlenberg (1711–1787), often called the "Father of American Lutheranism." In his preface he expressed his hope that the problems connected with the use of different hymnals would be eradicated, though he seems to suggest that he thinks that there may be some resistance to the use of the new hymnal in some congregations:

> We should note what until now has hindered complete unity in connection with singing in our public worship, namely, the many kinds of hymnbooks, since in almost every one various little alterations have been made, and in some there are few hymns, in others many. If only there were one hymnbook for all American congregations that would contain the best of the old and new spiritual songs, how much more convenient and harmonious it would be.[65]

The *Erbauliche Lieder-Sammlung* was the first hymnal to be specifically edited and published for the use of Lutheran churches in the United States.

---

63. *Documentary History of the Evangelical Lutheran ministerium of Pennsylvania and Adjacent States. Proceedings of the Annual Conventions from 1748–1821... translated*, eds. Adolph Spaeth, Henry Eyster Jacobs, and G. F. Speiker (Philadelphia: Board of Publication of the General Council of the Evangelical Lutheran Church in North America, 1898), 183–4.
64. Schalk, *Source Documents*, 11; for the background, see Schalk, *God's Song*, 39–50.
65. Cited in Schalk, *Source Documents*, 13. See page 9 above for variants in the three stanzas of Luther's *Erhalt uns, Herr, bei deinem Wort* that Busch discovered in numerous hymnals.

It therefore marks the beginning of the histories of the different American hymnals that are explored here in chapters 7 through 12.

During the second half of the eighteenth century, hymnals published in Germany increasingly moved away from the confessional objectivity of the earlier hymnals in favor of the subjectivity of personal piety, with the hymns gathered together less dogmatically than had been customary hitherto. "The more pietistic a hymnbook was, the more its traditional stock of hymns was crushed, modernized, and rationalized, and the more traditional hymns were discarded."[66] One notable example was the Lutheran *Gesangbuch zum gottesdienstlichen Gebrauch in den Königlich-Preußischen Landen* (Hymnal to be Used for Worship in the Territories of Royal Prussia) (Berlin: Mylius, 1780). The primary editor was Johann Joachim Spalding (1714–1804), Prussian Oberkonsistorialrat (chief consistorial councilor), propst (provost) and primary preacher of the two parish churches in Berlin, and above all, the ardent proponent of the Rationalist "Neology" that sought to displace both Lutheran orthodoxy and pietism.[67] This "new theology" promoted a beneficent God and the need for humanity to live ethically, with the aim of edification (Erbauung) in all things, both personal and corporate. The hymnal reflected this "Neology" and its "newness" was severely criticized as soon as it was published, but Spalding countered the critics—as strongly as they had written against the hymnal—in his "Sermon on what is edifying" (Predigt von dem, was erbaulich ist).[68] Despite the criticism, the official hymnal remained in print between 1780 and 1844, being published in a variety of Prussian cities, to the discomfort of traditional Lutherans. Discomfort became dismay for many some decades later when in 1817—the three-hundredth anniversary of Luther's protest—Frederick William III (1770–1840) decreed that the individual Lutheran and Reformed churches were to be merged to become the Protestant Prussian Union Church. At the inaugural synod of 1817 the need for a new hymnal was expressed. It was eventually published some twelve years later as *Gesangbuch zum Gottesdienstlichen Gebrauch*

---

66. Friedrich Blume, *Protestant Church Music: A History* (New York: Norton, 1974), 360.
67. Martin Greschat, "Johann Joachim Spalding," EP 4: 1796–7.
68. See Peter Weber, "Der Berliner Gesangbuchstreit 1781: Aporien der Aufklärung 'von oben'," in *Berliner Aufklärung: Kulturwissenschaftliche Studien*, ed. Ursula Goldenbaum and Alexander Kosenina (Hannover: Wehrhahn, 1999), 101–119; Christina Rathgeber, "The Reception of Brandenburg–Prussia's New Lutheran Hymnal of 1781," *The Historical Journal* 36 (1993): 115–136; Malte van Spankeren, "Johann Joachim Spalding und der Berliner Gesangbuchstreit (1781)," *Journal of Modern Theology / Zeitschrift für Neuere Theologiegeschichte*, 18/2 (2011): 191–211.

für Evangelische Gemeinen (Berlin: Riemer, 1829).[69] Even though the title page declared it "Lutheran" (Evangelische) its primary editor was Friedrich Schleiermacher, the prominent liberal theologian, who was Reformed rather than Lutheran, and his theology permeated throughout the hymnal.[70] Such realities were the among the pressures that led confessional Lutherans in Saxony to consider emigrating to America, and why, soon after they had established the pioneer congregation of what would become the Missouri Synod (Trinity Congregation, St. Louis), their early concern was with creating an appropriate Lutheran hymnal (see chapter 7).

Of course the Saxons were not the only Lutheran immigrants to North America, and when they arrived the different groups were faced with similar problems. They had left a European country that had a long history to settle in America, a country that had a very short history. They came as individuals as well as in groups and a primary concern was to form congregations so that their spiritual needs could be met. Thus, church building was a high priority as they created their communities, villages, and towns, each with their places of worship. Often there was a congregation but no ordained pastor to lead, teach, and guide them. In the German state churches all ecclesiastical matters, especially the examination, licensing, and ordaining of candidates for the ministry, were overseen by the designated government state department. But in the United States no state had any role in the decision-making process of such church affairs. A solution was needed. Thus, an individual church would form an alliance with other churches in the same geographical area to create a *Ministerium*, that is, a council of representative clergy who were given the responsibility to oversee such issues of joint concern. As the number of churches in these *Ministeria* increased, and as the areas of oversight expanded, they were replaced by synods modeled on the Protestant church synods of Germany but which were autonomous and free from any political involvement. Over the course of the nineteenth century new synods were founded, smaller synods joined larger synods, and larger synods were subject to breakaway synods. Many of these synods produced their own hymnals that established their identity and concerns.[71] However, unlike the original *Achtliederbuch* (1524), which was simply

---

69. See "Vorrede," *Gesangbuch zum Gottesdienstlichen Gebrauch für Evangelische Gemeinen* (Berlin: Riemer, 1829), unpaginated.
70. James M. Brandt, "Friedrich Daniel Ernst Schleiermacher," EP 4: 1656–1661; Ilsabe Seibt, *Friedrich Schleiermacher und das Berliner Gesangbuch von 1829* (Göttingen: Vandenhoeck & Ruprecht, 1998), especially 139–194.
71. See Voigt, *Hymnbooks at Wittenberg*, Nos. 203–484.

a collection of hymns, such synodical hymnals contained, in addition to many hymns, a complexity of liturgical, confessional, catechetical, and other matters that were important for that particular synod, though often similar to other synodical hymnals. Thus, from time to time there were conversations between the different Lutheran synods on how they should or could be connected. The goal of American Lutheran unity remained elusive—Mühlenberg's vision of "one hymnbook for all American congregations"[72]—but continued to be held as a practical possibility. This was manifested to a significant extent in the *Common Service Book with Hymnal* (1917/18), the hymnal that was "Common" to Lutherans in different synods, the culmination of synodical hymnals of the second half of the nineteenth century, and model for hymnals in the first half of the twentieth century (see chapter 8).

The contents of chapters 2–8 progress in an approximate chronology. Now, however, before continuing into the twentieth century, we must, as it were, return to Europe and the beginnings of 1524. The reason is that the Scandinavian/Nordic hymnal tradition of today is firmly rooted in the early Wittenberg hymnals. Over the winter of 1523/24 there were quite a few people from Scandinavia in Wittenberg, mostly Danish students, but the deposed King of Denmark, Christian II (reigned 1513–1523), a Lutheran sympathizer, was also there at that time. They were certainly witnesses, and possibly also participants in, the new hymns that were then being introduced. In subsequent years more students studied in Wittenberg as the Lutheran Reformation became a powerful underground movement in these northern kingdoms. German hymns, especially those by Luther, were selected and translated into the varied Scandinavian/Nordic languages. To these translations were added original hymns in the various languages by talented poets, creating the need to compile hymnals for the translations and original hymns:

1526 Stockholm, Swedish, probably edited by Olaus Petri
1528 Copenhagen, Danish, edited by Mortensen and Olufson
1533 Malmø, Danish, probably edited by Tausen

When Christian III (1503–1559) acceded to the Danish throne in 1536 the kingdom was declared officially Lutheran, and then in 1537, when he also became King of Norway, his kingdoms established a church government. Eventually each kingdom followed a similar pattern. Church and

---

72. See note 65 above.

state were not separate. Thus, in their connected histories, the individual churches of the kingdoms of Denmark, Norway, and Sweden, came under royal patronage and control. Like other matters of church government, the creation of hymnals was the result of royal initiative, oversight, and authority. When hymnals were ready for publication, they were produced by a royal printing house, either the "Kongelig Wäysenhuuses" [Royal orphanage printing house] in Copenhagen, or the "Kungl. tryckeriet" [Royal printing house] in Stockholm.

Thus, Scandinavian/Nordic hymnal trajectory continued to flourish and develop throughout the generations, as each generation extended the repertory not only in the three kingdoms but also in North America.[73] Much has been made of the impact of the so-called "Hymn Explosion" of English-language hymnals published in the second half of the twentieth century.[74] What is not often realized is that during approximately the same period there was also a Scandinavian/Nordic hymn explosion that was just as creative and effective in its impact on hymnals produced on both sides of the Atlantic (see chapter 9).

That hymnals should be thought of in explosive terms is not as extravagant as might first appear, since the hymns they contain evoke powerful emotions. Hymns, specific texts borne by memorable tunes, are connected to very personal experiences: "This hymn was sung at my wedding." "That hymn was sung at my mother's funeral." Such hymns form a kind of personal core repertory to be preserved. We assume that the emotion we experience while singing a particular hymn is transferable: "If this is what I feel when I sing this hymn, then those with whom I sing must be sharing the same emotion." But each singer will have different emotions associated with different hymns. Similarly, different synods have different criteria when contemplating the compilation of a new hymnal. It is when a hymnal is to be created for several synods that the difficulties arise, as the editors from the main Lutheran synods discovered when they attempted to create a single hymnal for the majority of American Lutherans in the second half of the twentieth century. There was a clash of core repertories. For example, those whose heritage was German expected that the proposed hymnal would have many hymns from the early chorale tradition, theologically objective with melodies in their original rhythmic forms. Those

---

73. See the respective articles in the online *Canterbury Dictionary of Hymnology*, CDH: "Danish Hymnody," by Peter Balslev-Clausen; "Swedish Hymnody," by Sven-Åke Selander; "Finnish Hymns and Hymnals," by Hannu Vapaavuor; "Norwegian Hymnody," David Scott Hamnes and Åge Haavik; and "Icelandic Hymnody," by Einar Sigurbjörnsson.
74. See chapter 11, p. 11.

whose heritage was Scandinavian/Nordic expected that a united hymnal would contain more hymns from their linguistic backgrounds, theologically pietist with folk-song-like melodies, and with fewer German chorale tunes—which should be in their later equal-note isometric forms. In the event the single pan-Lutheran hymnal proved elusive, and instead of one hymnal two were produced, LBW (1978) and LW (1982) (see chapter 10). However, there was a kind of silver lining in the earlier production of a *Worship Supplement* WS (1969) that introduced some striking new texts and tunes, compiled before the Missouri Synod withdrew from the project (see chapter 11). The intent of producing a united hymnal may not have succeeded, but the need for practical hymnals is a continuing concern, as is witnessed in the many American Lutheran hymnals that continue to be published: hymnals that are linguistically diverse, international in content, and increasingly global in scope (see chapter 12).

PART 1
The German Background

2.

Hymnals 1524

Robin A. Leaver

The first sentence of the previous chapter states a truism: "It all began with a single song, Luther's *A new song we now begin* (*Ein neues lied wir heben an*)." But how are we to understand this song in the context of its time?[1] A common interpretation emphasizes the singularity of Luther's voice. Felix Mendelssohn illustrated this in aural terms in the final movement of his Reformation Symphony. Out of silence a single flute—representing Luther's voice—plays the EIN FESTE BURG melody (which has significant echoes of Luther's EIN NEUES LIED melody). Then little by little the other instruments join the flute in playing the melody and its harmonization until all the orchestra has entered for the final emphatic statement of the familiar tune. But this is an aural representation of the wisdom of hindsight. The situation at the time, the winter of 1523/24, would have been more like Charles Ives's Second Symphony than Mendelssohn's Fifth. In Ives's symphony different tunes struggle against each other, a mixture of sound fragments of both nonreligious tunes—such as "Turkey in the Straw" and "Camptown Races"—and hymn tunes—such as NETTLETON, BRINGING IN THE SHEAVES, HAMBURG, and BEULAH LAND—that contend with each other, sometimes somewhat stridently. The truth is that Luther was not the only one singing a vernacular song in 1523; there was plenty of competition. As Rebecca Oettinger observes:

---

1. For background, see Rebecca Wagner Oettinger, *Music as Propaganda in the German Reformation* (Aldershot: Ashgate, 2001), 61–69; T. H. M. Akerboom, "'A New Song We Raise': On the First Martyrs of the Reformation and the Origin of Martin Luther's First Hymn," *Perichoresis* 4/1 (2006): 53–77; Grantley McDonald, "'A New Song We Raise' ("Ein neues Lied wir heben an"), *Encyclopedia of Martin Luther and the Reformation*, ed. Mark Lamport (Lanham: Rowan & Littlefield, 2017), 553–555.

Song, or more accurately, singing, was an important part of the popular culture of sixteenth-century Germany. While many people in late-medieval Europe would have experienced music as passive listeners within the boundaries of religious services, outside of the church they would have taken a more active role in music creation . . . The resulting genre of music, long studied under the umbrella title of "folksong," provided entertainment, information, creative opportunities, and even a measure of education to the people of sixteenth-century Germany.

Folksongs came in a wide variety of structures, including lighthearted ditties for celebrating saints' days, lengthy narrative ballads, laments and farewell songs. Songs were the mass media of the oral culture; they provided news from distant places (often scandalous or miraculous), they told stories of true and false love, and they provided moral and spiritual guidance.[2]

In the later medieval period the news, trivial and serious, was communicated to the general populous by singers who, for a few coins, would sing the latest news ballads in places where people congregated: taverns, town squares, inns, and the like. As printing presses became more commonplace in the sixteenth century, with even small towns having at least one printer, and larger towns many more, the tradition was modified. The news was still being sung by the singers, but they carried with them single-sheet printed copies of the news ballads they were singing. After the songs had been sung, the printed copies were then sold to those who were literate and who could afford to buy them, such as owners of taverns who had them pasted onto walls where the literate could read them to the nonliterate, or sing individually or corporately for pleasure.[3]

Anything that was controversial, mysterious, macabre, gossipy, such things as earthquakes, fires, wars, famines, monstrous births, as well as current issues in politics and religion, were recounted in these many ballads. Thus the polarizations that came about because of the indulgence debate that Luther had stirred up in 1517 were promoted and demoted in ballads: a good many were pro-Luther; others were anti-Pope, anti-clergy,

---

2. Oettinger, *Music as Propaganda*, 21.
3. Oettinger's ground-breaking study, *Music as Propaganda,* includes a carefully assembled catalogue of two hundred and thirty "Songs of the Reformation," that are found in extant printed "Flugschriften" (broadsides, pamphlets, and small booklets) of the sixteenth century: Oettinger, *Music as Propaganda*, 210–402. It needs to be stated that such printed material is usually referred to as "ephemera" because of its transitory nature. The extant copies of such ephemera are but the tip of an iceberg and that hundreds if not thousands of broadside imprints have disappeared without trace. But what survives is significant. Oettinger's catalogue is alphabetical and covers the whole of the sixteenth century; however, in this chapter citations from this catalogue are restricted to editions printed within a few years of the publication of Luther's first song, that is, approximately between 1520–1525.

and anti-monasticism;[4] and there were those that were decidedly anti-Luther.[5] The particularly popular subgenre of the news ballad, familiar throughout Europe across many generations, was the execution ballad that narrated the crimes of the guilty and the details of their excruciating deaths.[6]

The ballad tradition was both a long history and a contemporary reality that enabled Luther to refashion elements of this vernacular singing into something that was new but at the same time was not entirely unfamiliar.

NEWS BALLADS

The news ballads generally followed a common sequential structure. First, there was the call for the people to hear, given in a variety of forms that in the preprinting era was expressed in the first line or two of the song, such as: *Ein lied will ich eüch singen*[7] (A song I will sing to you), or *Nun hört ich wil euch singen*[8] (Now hear what I will sing to you). The practice of such first-line, "listen–up" expressions continued at a later time when the ballads were also being circulated on single printed sheets called broadsides. However, these expressions were now more commonly, though not exclusively, transferred from the first line of the news ballad to the heading of the broadside on which the song was printed. Oettinger, for example, records that between 1519 and 1524 the title headings of nine extant broadside ballads included basically the same three words, *Ein neues lied* (A new song), variously spelled.[9]

Once the song was thus begun it then established the contexts of the news that was about to be divulged, such as where it happened and who was involved. For example:

[1.] Aber will ich singen But I want to sing
und singen ain news gedicht and sing a new poem
von Rumensattels dingen of Rumensattel's things
und was er hat außgricht . . . and what he did . . .

---

4. For example, Oettinger, *Music as Propaganda*, Nos. 8, 16, 30, 78, 90, 95, 112, 129, 135, 162, 178.
5. For example, Oettinger, *Music as Propaganda*, Nos. 37, 51, 136, 155.
6. See Una McIlvenna, *Singing the News of Death: Execution Ballads in Europe 1500–1900* (New York: Oxford University Press, 2022).
7. Oettinger, *Music as Propaganda*, No. 59.
8. Oettinger, *Music as Propaganda*, No. 158; see also 129 and 126.
9. Oettinger, *Music as Propaganda*, Nos.6, 8, 62, 76, 111, 137, 147, 200, 201.

[2.] Er saß bei güten gesellen   He went with good friends
      zü Weissenstain in der stat . . .   to the town of Weissenstein . . .[10]

After the contextual introduction the narrative of the news began, which could be fairly brief, comprising just a few stanzas, or quite lengthy, running to thirty, forty or more stanzas.

As already referred to, after a song had been sung single-sheet printed copies were made available for sale by the ballad singer. Local printers were among the purchasers because it offered them the possibility of making some money. By collecting together some of these sheets issued by other printers elsewhere and then reprinting these broadside songs in a small pamphlet, they could, without much outlay, produce a modest profit. The process had the important byproduct of preserving songs that might otherwise not have survived. Luther's *Ein neues lied wir heben an* is a case in point. The song must have been printed on a single sheet broadside although no such copy has survived.[11] Fortunately printers in Erfurt included the song in small pamphlets of reprinted broadsides in 1524, and thus it was preserved for posterity.

What is clear is that Luther's *Ein neues lied wir heben an* is not a hymn. It is a news ballad that shares many of the characteristics of the subgenre of the execution ballad. It is the narrative of the condemnation and execution of the two young men in the Augustinian order, who were accused of being too close to Luther in their thinking. Luther began:

[1.] A new song we now begin,
      may our Lord God help us
      to sing what he has done
      to his glory and honor
            in Brussels, in the Netherlands.
            Indeed, through two young men
      he has made his wonders known,
      with his gifts
      he has adorned them richly.[12]

---

10. Rochus von Liliencron, *Deutsches Leben im Volkslied um 1530* (Berlin: Spemann, 1885; reprint, Hildeseim: Olms, 1966), No. 16; Franz M. Böhme, *Altdeutsches Liederbuch: Volkslied der Deutschen nach Wort und Weise aus dem 12. bis zum 17. Jahrhundert*, 3rd ed. (Leipzig: Breitkopf & Härtel, 1925), 78.
11. Böhme claimed to have seen a broadside of Luther's *Ein neues Lied* dated with the year "1523"; see Böhme, *Altdeutsches Liederbuch*, 386.
12. Oettinger, *Music as Propaganda*, No. 61 (p. 261).

The execution took place in Brussels on July 1, 1523, but it took a month or more before Luther received the news in Wittenberg. The assumption is that he wrote the original ten stanzas of the news ballad around the end of August, or perhaps a little later. He then had second thoughts, and at some later date—sometime before the end of the year 1523—wrote two more stanzas which were inserted before the last two stanzas that were to remain in their place at the end of the ballad. This twelve-stanza version appeared in Johann Walter's so-called *Chorgesangbuch* printed and published in Wittenberg in 1524. Wilhelm Lucke, one of the editors of the volume of Luther's hymns and liturgies in the *Weimar Ausgabe* of Luther's writings, was of the opinion that Luther intended the two new stanzas to replace the original final two stanzas but that the Wittenberg printer misunderstood his instructions and included both of them.[13] I cannot believe that the twelve-stanza version was an accident that occurred in Wittenberg, the center of Luther's activity, especially as no one corrected the "error" at a later date. There is a simpler and more powerful explanation: Luther had more to say, and in particular was concerned that the martyrdom of the two Augustinian brothers should be seen in the light of the martyrdom of Abel. Consequently, he wrote the new stanzas (9–10):

[new 9.] Now they [their accusers] regretted the mockery,
and wished to make everything well.
They did not want word to spread,
and to bury the story.
Shame bites their hearts,
and they mourn their deeds to their friends,
but the Spirit cannot be silent.
Abel's blood was poured out,
and Cain must pay.[14]

Having written the new stanzas Luther intended that his expanded ballad should end with the same two stanzas as did his first version, especially what was now the twelfth stanza:

[10/12.] Let them [accusers in Brussels] go on lying for ever,
it is of no use.

---

13. WA 35: 10–11, 94; Akerboom, "A New Song We Raise," 67–8.
14. Oettinger, *Music as Propaganda*, No. 61 (p. 262).

> We shall thank God
> because his Word has come again.
> Summer is at the door,
> Winter is past,
> and the sweet flowers are in bloom,
> He who was at the beginning
> will be at the end.[15]

At face value the allusion to the coming of summer seems somewhat prosaic, especially since at the time it was written summer must have been on the way out. However, the imagery is more figurative than literal and echoes a passage in the Song of Songs:

> For now the winter is past, the rain is over and gone.
> The flowers appear on the earth;
> the time of spring has come,[16]
> and the voice of the turtledove is heard in our land. (Song 2: 11–12)

It is the same biblical allusion that Luther made near the beginning of his *Open Letter to the Christians in the Netherlands* (1523), in commiseration over the executions in Brussels: "But now is the time when we hear the voice of the turtledove and the flowers bloom in our land."[17] The figurative connection becomes much stronger when one realizes that Song of Solomon 2: 8–13 was the reading for the second nocturn at Matins, and again as the epistle for the mass, on the feast of the Visitation on July 2. The connection was not lost on Luther that the two Augustinians were executed on the eve of the Visitation, July 1.

News of the executions shook Luther deeply because it was he who was condemned as an outlaw and heretic at the Diet of Worms, not these two young men who, in a sense, died in his place. In particular, he was moved and impressed by his monastic brothers' faith, especially their singing as they were consigned to the flames: "Mit freuden sie sich gaben drein, | Mit Gottes lob und singen" (With joy they gave themselves up, with praises of God and singing), as Luther expressed it in stanza eight of *Ein neues lied*. But what

---

15. Oettinger, *Music as Propaganda*, No. 61 (p. 263).
16. English Bible versions translate this phrase somewhat freely as "the time of singing has come," whereas the literal version is "the time of pruning has come [i.e., Spring]."
17. WA 12:77: "Aber nun ist der zeit widder kommen, das wir der dordel tauben stym hören und die blumen auffgehen ynn unsern land."

were they singing? Since it was the eve of the Visitation, and as friars they were committed to monastic liturgical life, it could have been a Visitation antiphon. On the other hand, instead of a Latin liturgical chant it could have been a vernacular strophic song, such as the one intended for singing extra-liturgically on the feast of the Visitation: *Es flog ein kleins waldvögelein aus himelstrone* (A little forest bird flew out of the heavens).[18] We simply do not know, because it was not recorded. What we do know is that whatever it was, their singing made a very strong impression on Luther: first, in impelling him to write his news ballad, *Ein neues lied*; second, in awakening him to consider strophic song as the medium for congregational singing.

THE WINTER OF 1523–1524[19]

The approximate four-month period between when Luther completed writing his twelve-stanza news ballad, *Ein neues lied*, around September/October 1523, and the appearance of the first Lutheran hymnals in early 1524, was an astonishingly creative period. Although it is difficult to construct an accurate chronological sequence of events because there are so many gaps in our knowledge caused by the non-survival of sources, it is nevertheless possible to gather together the various elements that impinged upon each other during this period.

Luther had been working on his evangelical mass, the *Formula missae*, towards the end of 1523 and probably had to put it temporarily to one side while he wrote *Ein neues lied*. The Latin liturgy was still incomplete at the end of October,[20] not finished until a month later,[21] and not published until late in December 1523. Toward the end of the document, implying that it was written after almost everything else in the evangelical mass, possibly sometime in November, there is a significant section that deals with vernacular hymnody:

> I also wish that we had as many songs as possible in the vernacular for the people to sing during mass, immediately after the Gradual and also after the Sanctus and Agnus Dei. For who doubts that originally all the

---

18. Böhme, *Altdeutsches Liederbuch*, No. 599. The text is found in the hand-written copies of fifteenth- and sixteenth-century printed broadside ballads (with other poetry), made by Valentin Holl in Augsburg, between 1524 and 1526; Germanisches Nationalmuseum, Nuremberg, Ms. Merkel 2° 966, fol. 159ʳ.
19. For a different perspective on what is discussed in the remainder of this chapter will be found Robin A. Leaver, *The Whole Church Sings: Congregational Singing in Luther's Wittenberg* (Grand Rapids, MI: Eerdmans, 2017), 81–116.
20. Letter, Luther to Nicholas Hausmann, late October 1523; WA BR 3: 184; LW 49: 55–6.
21. Letter, Luther to Hausmann, 23 November 1523; WA BR 3: 198.

people sang these which now only the choir sings or responds to while the bishop [pastor] is consecrating? The bishops may have these hymns sung either after the Latin chants, or use the Latin on one day and the vernacular one on the next, until the time comes that the whole Mass is sung in the vernacular. But poets are wanting among us, or not yet known, who could compose pious and spiritual songs, as Paul calls them [Col 3:16], worthy to be used in the church of God. In the meantime, one may sing after communion *Gott sei gelobet und gebenedeiet* . . . omitting the line, "and the holy sacrament, At our last end, From the consecrated priest's hand." . . . Another good one is *Nun bitten wir den heiligen Geist*, and also *Ein Kindelein so löbelich*. For so few are found that are written in a dignified and prudent spirit. I mention this to encourage any German poets to compose pious hymns for us.[22]

Here Luther sets out his twofold goal. His primary concern is to get new vernacular songs or hymns written, though he acknowledges that authors who could do this are "wanting among us or not yet known." His second concern is that, as well as encouraging new hymns to be written, a few of the familiar older folk hymns—customarily sung extra-liturgically on specific days of the church year—could be sung liturgically, though it might be necessary to rewrite some of them to maintain a coherent and consistent theology.

For Luther the biblical Psalms were fundamental for devotional life, personal and corporate. For the university of Wittenberg he had given two lengthy series of lectures on the Psalms between 1513–1516, and again between 1518–1521, and for the parish of Wittenberg he had included a modest group of vernacular prose translations of a few Psalms in his 1522 *Betbüchlein* [Little Prayer Book].[23] Thus it makes sense that when Luther came to terms with the creation of strophic vernacular verse to be sung corporately in services of worship, naturally a significant portion of the new songs would be hymnic versions of the biblical Psalms. Toward the end of 1523 Luther apparently sent letters to various friends and colleagues to encourage them to create versifications of specific Psalms. Unfortunately, only Luther's letter to Georg Spalatin (1484–1545)—Frederick the Wise's court chaplain and secretary—is extant, though its content suggests that he must have sent similar letters to others.

[Our] plan is to follow the example of the prophets and the ancient fathers of the church, and to compose vernacular psalms for the people, that is,

---

22. LW 53: 36–7; WA 12: 218.
23. WA 10[II]: 410–425.

spiritual songs, so that the Word of God may be among the people in the form of music. Therefore we are looking everywhere for poets. Since you are endowed with richness and elegance in the German language, which you have polished through much use, I ask you to work with us, and turn a Psalm into a hymn, as you may see in this [enclosed] example.[24] But I would like you to avoid any new words or language used at court. In order to be understood by the people, only the simplest and the most common words should be used for singing; at the same time, however, they should be pure and apt, and further, the sense should be clear and as close as possible to the Psalm. You need a free hand here: maintain the sense, but don't cling to the words but rather translate them with other appropriate words. I myself do not have so great a gift that I can do what I would like to see done here. So I shall discover whether you are a Heman, or an Asaph, or a Jeduthun.[25] I would like to ask the same of Hans [von] Dolzig[26] [whose German] is rich and elegant. Nevertheless do this only as you have leisure, which I suspect is not the case currently. You have my *Seven Penitential Psalms* [Wittenberg, 1517[27]] and the commentaries on them [Psalms 6, 32, 38, 51, 102, 130, 143], from which you can catch the sense of the Psalm. If this is satisfactory to you, either the first one [of the Penitential Psalms, that is Psalm 6], *Domine, ne in furore*, can be assigned to you, or the seventh [Psalm 143], *Domine, exaudi orationem*. To Hans [von] Dolzig I would assign the second [Psalm 32], *Beati, quorum*. I have done *De profundis* [Psalm 130], and *Miserere mei* [Psalm 51] has been assigned to someone else [Erhart Hegenwalt]. If these [Psalms] are too difficult then take these two: *Benedicam Dominum in omni tempore* [Psalm 34], and *Exultate justi in Domino* [Psalm 33]. But let us know what we can expect from you.[28]

The letter is undated but must have been written towards the end of the year 1523, since early in January 1524 Luther reminded Spalatin of his request: "I have no news to write, my Spalatin, except that I am waiting for your German poems, about which I recently wrote to you."[29] Luther's initial plan was to have all seven penitential Psalms in hymnic form, the seven Psalms that had a long history of forming the basis of personal devotion. Only two of the seven were completed, Psalm 130 by Luther and Psalm 51 by Erhart Hegenwalt (fl. 1520).[30] Spalatin and von Dolzig

---

24. Unidentified, though it could have been Luther's *Aus tiefer Not* he mentions later in the letter.
25. Authors of some of the Psalms; see 1 Chronicles 25.
26. Saxon court Marschall for Elector Frederick the Wise.
27. WA 1: 158–220; see Timothy Wengert, "Luther's First Major Publication," *Lutheran Quarterly* 36 (2022): 166–180.
28. WA BR 3: 220; translation based on LW 49: 68–70; see also LW 53: 221.
29. WA BR 3: 324; LW 49: 70.
30. Koch, 1: 287–288.

were either too busy at the Saxon court, or unsure of their poetic abilities, to comply with Luther's request. Luther's letters to other possible authors were probably similar to his letter to Spalatin, but, instead of drawing attention to his German prose versions of the *Seven Penitential Psalms* as guides, he may have mentioned instead his other set of seven vernacular prose Psalms included in his 1522 *Betbüchlein*: Psalms 12, 67, 103, 20, 79, 25, and 10.[31] Of these Luther created hymn versions of Psalm 12 and Psalm 67, and Michael Stifel (1487–1567), close friend and sometime houseguest, Psalm 10.[32] Whether authors were sought for the remaining four *Betbüchlein* Psalms is unknown, but other Psalm versions were written during this initial creative period at the end of 1523 and the beginning of 1524: for example, Justus Jonas (1493–1555), dean of the Allerheiligenstift in Wittenberg, produced an alternative version of Psalm 124, and Johann Agricola (1494–1566), who had acted as Luther's secretary at the 1519 Leipzig debate, contributed his version of Psalm 117. During that winter a basic corpus of ten metrical Psalms was created that individually and collectively became the model for many other such Psalms written and sung in subsequent generations:

Psalm 10	*Dein armer Hauf, Herr, tut klagen*	Michael Stifel
Psalm 12	*Ach Gott, von Himmel sieh darein*	Luther
Psalm 13	*Es spricht der Unweisen Mund wohl*	Luther
Psalm 51	*Erbarm dich mein, o Herre Gott*	Erhart Hegenwalt
Psalm 67	*Es wollt uns Gott genädig sein*	Luther
Psalm 117	*Fröhlich wollen wir Alleluia singen*	Johann Agricola
Psalm 124	*Wo Gott der Herr nicht bei uns hält*	Justus Jonas
Psalm 124	*Wär Gott nicht mit uns diese Zeit*	Luther
Psalm 127	*Wohl dem, der in Gottes furcht steht*	Luther
Psalm 130	*Aus tiefer Not schrei ich zu dir*	Luther

In his concern to provide the people of Wittenberg with strophic hymn-versions of the biblical Psalms, Luther created a genre of hymnody that had an enormous impact on Protestant worship, especially in the Reformed/Calvinist tradition.[33]

---

31. WA 10[II]: 410–425.
32. Stifel had published a decidedly pro-Luther ballad in 1522 (Oettinger No. 135), as well as a number of polemic ballads in 1523 (Oettinger, *Music as Propaganda*, Nos. 5 and 112).
33. See Markus Jenny, "Das Psalmlied—eine Erfindung Martin Luthers," *IAH Bulletin* 5 (1977): 34–35.

While Luther promoted metrical versions of the Psalms, they were not to be the only hymnic genre for congregational singing; freely-written hymns on theological and devotional themes were also encouraged, so long as they were biblical in content. Notable examples of this early period of hymn-writing include the following: on the fall, *Durch Adams Fall ist ganz verderbt* (By Adam's fall is all forlorn) by Lazarus Spengler (1479–1534), city clerk of Nuremberg; on the Epiphany, *Herr Christ, der einig Gotts Sohn* (The only Son from heaven), by Elisabeth Cruciger (*ca.* 1500–1535), former nun, wife of Luther's colleague Caspar Cruciger;[34] on law and gospel, *Es ist das Heil uns kommen her* (Salvation unto us has come), by Paul Speratus (1484–1551), ardent follower of Luther who had arrived in Wittenberg late 1523; and on justification, *Nun freut euch, lieben Christen gmein* (Dear Christians, one and all rejoice), by Luther.

FROM BROADSIDES TO HYMNALS

Writing hymns was one thing; making them known was another. It is possible that hand-written copies of these early hymns were circulated among Luther's friends and colleagues in Wittenberg. But the likelihood is that as soon as a hymn was completed it was set up in type so that any number of single-sheet broadsides could printed off. The literate would be able to sing directly from the broadsides, which could also be used to teach the nonliterate to commit the hymns to memory. There is strong evidence that suggests that these early hymns were first circulated on broadsides printed and published in Wittenberg, but regrettably not one has survived. The closest we can get to Wittenberg imprints of the early hymns is Speratus's German version of Luther's *Formula missae*,[35] published by the newly-formed Wittenberg partnership of painter Lucas Cranach the Elder, goldsmith Christian Döring, and printer Joseph Klug, who would later become the independent printer-publisher of Wittenberg hymnals.[36] Speratus's German translation of Luther's Latin liturgy was published in January 1524, but the printing is likely to have been

---

34. See Mary Jane Haemig, "Elisabeth Cruciger (1500?–1535): The Case of the Disappearing Hymn Writer," *The Sixteenth Century Journal* 32/1 (2001): 21–44.
35. WA 12: 202; WA 35: 123; Josef Benzing and Helmut Claus, *Lutherbibliographie, Verseichnis der Gedruckten Schriften Martin Luthers bis dessen Tod* (Baden-Baden: Heitz and Loerner, 1966–94), 1: 199 (No. 1700: *Ein weyse Christlich Mess zu halten und zum tisch Gottes. Martinus Luther* (Wittenberg: [Cranach and Döring], 1524).
36. See Hans Volz, "Die Wittenberger Gesangbuchdrucker Joseph Klug und Hans Lufft," JbLH 4 (1958/59): 129–33; and chapter 3 in this volume.

completed before the end of 1523, that is, soon after the publication of the Latin *Formula missae*. At the end of the German volume, on a page that would otherwise have been blank, Agricola's Psalm 117, *Fröhlich wollen wir Halleluja singen* (without music), was printed. A second imprint of Speratus's translation *Ein weyse Christlich Mess* was also published later in January 1524, but this time Luther's Psalm 67, *Es wollt uns Gott genädig sein* (without music), appeared with Agricola's Psalm 117 at the end of the volume.[37] If these two hymns had already been issued as broadsides it would have been a relatively easy task to reset them to fill the blank pages at the end of Speratus's translation of the *Formula missae*. These two hymns were examples of what Luther was calling for in his *Formula missae* and also in his letter to Spalatin: vernacular hymns, and especially versions of the biblical Psalms.

Broadside copies of the early Wittenberg hymns were something of a hot commodity during the winter of 1523/24 when printers in other towns and cities obtained the Wittenberg imprints and then reprinted them. Fortunately, some of these have survived. In Augsburg, Heinrich Steiner reprinted several Wittenberg broadsides during this period, of which four are extant: all the texts are by Luther, all include the music of the melodies, and two are identified as specifically emanating from Wittenberg:

Christ lag in Todes Banden (Christ Jesus lay in death's strong bands)[38]
Gelobet seist du Jesu Christ (We praise you Jesus, at Your birth), "Wittenberg" imprint[39]
Jesus Christus unser Heiland, der von uns (Jesus Christ, our blessed Savior)[40]
Jesus Christus unser Heiland, der von uns, "Wittenberg" imprint[41]

---

37. WA 12: 2002; WA 35: 123.
38. DKL 1524[20]; *Der lobesang Christ ist erstanden/ g[ebessert]* ... [Augsburg: Steiner, 1524]; facsimile, JbLH 17 (1972), 215.
39. DKL 1525[01]; *Ain Deütsch hymnus oderlobsang auff Weyhenacht ... Gelobet seystu Jhesu Christ ...* Wittenberg. ([Augsburg: Steiner], 1524–25); facsimile, Hans–Otto Korth, *Lass uns leuchten des Lebens Wort: Die Lieder Martin Luthers, Im Auftrag der Franckeschen Stiftungen anlässlich des Reformationsjubiläums 2017* (Halle: Verlag der Franckeschen Stiftungen, 2017), 106.
40. DKL 1524[02]: *Das lied S. Johannes Hus gebessert...Jhesus Christus unser Heiland, der von uns zorn*... ([Augsburg: Steiner, 1524]), facsimile, Korth, *Lass uns leuchten des Lebens Wort*, 132.
41. DKL 1524[19]: *Ain lobgsang auf das Osterfest ... Wittenberg* [Augsburg: Steiner, 1524]; facsimile, JbLH 17 (1972): 214; and Korth, *Lass uns leuchten des Lebens Wort*, 46.

Two other Augsburg printers also republished Wittenberg hymn broadsides, both including music notation. In January 1524, Melchior Ramminger issued Hegenwalt's version of Psalm 51, *Erbarm dich mein, o Herre Gott* (Have mercy on me, O Lord God), with a "Wittenberg" imprint;[42] and Philipp Ulhart issued *Nun freut euch, lieben Christen gmein* (Dear Christians, one and all rejoice), signed "1524 | Martinus Luther," in two imprints, one with and the other without a heading.[43]

At least one broadside is known to have been produced in Magdeburg by Hans Knappe the Younger, in early 1524, after he had just moved from Wittenberg to Magdeburg.[44] The broadside is of Luther's Psalm 67, *Es wollt uns Gott genädig sein* (May God bestow on us his grace), the hymn appended to Speratus's German translation of the *Formula missae*.[45]

ACHTLIEDERBUCH 1523–1524

In Nuremberg, Jobst Gutknecht, who had been printing and publishing broadsides and other formats in the city since 1514,[46] created the first Lutheran hymnal by reprinting eight hymns originally published on Wittenberg broadsides:

Etlich Cristlich lider Lobgesang/ und Psalm/ dem rainen wort Gottes gemeß/ auß der heyligen schrifft durch mancherley hochgelerter gemacht/ in der Kirchen zu singen/ wie es dann um tayl berayt zu Wittenberg in übung ist. Wittenberg. M.D.Xiiij. (Some Christian Hymns, Songs of Praise, and Psalms, According to the Pure Word of God from the Holy Scriptures, by Several

---

42. DKL 1524[09]: *Psalmus Miserere mei deus. . . . Wittenberg freytag nach Epiphanie im 15 24 Jar: Erhart Hegenwalt* ([Augsburg: Ramminger], 1524). This was the hymn version of the Psalm mentioned by Luther in his letter to Spalatin towards the end of 1523; LW49:70.
43. DKL 1524[10]: *Darunter in zehn je vierzeiligen Strophen das Lied: Nun frewdt euch Christen gmayn . . .* [Augsburg: Ulhart], 1524; facsimile, Rolf Wilhelm Brednich, *Die Liedpublizistik im Flugblat des 15. bis 17. Jahrhunderts.* 2: *Katalog der Liedflugblätter des 15. und 16. Jahrhunderts* (Baden-Baden: Koerner, 1975), Abb. 25; facsimile (without the heading), Martin Brecht, *Martin Luther: Shaping and Defining the Reformation 1521–1532*, trans. James L. Schaaf (Minneapolis: Fortress Press, 1990), 132, and Korth, *Lass uns leuchten des Lebens Wort*, 46.
44. Knappe had left Magdeburg by 1525. See Josef Benzing, *Die Buchdrucker des 16. und 17. Jahrhunderts im deutschen Sprachgebiet*, 2nd ed. (Wiesbaden: Harrassovitz, 1982), 309, 500.
45. DKL 1524[11]; *Der Lxvi. Deus Misereatur . . . Es wolt unß Gott genedig sein . . .* Magdeburg: Knappe, 1524; facsimile, Henrik Glahn, *Melodistudier til den Lutherske Samesangs Historie* (Copenhagen: Rosenkilde and Bagger, 1954), 1: 156, and JbLH 3 (1957): between 104 and 105. Music staves were printed without notation which was later added by hand.
46. Benzing, *Die Buchdrucker des 16. und 17. Jahrhunderts*, 354.

Learned Authors, to be Sung in the Churches as Prepared and Practiced in Wittenberg. Wittenberg. M.D.X[X]iiij). (Nuremberg: Gutknecht, 1524)[47]

Like the Augsburg broadsides of Steiner and Ramminger, the title page gives the impression that the pamphlet was published in Wittenberg. However, typographical evidence reveals that it was in fact printed and published by Gutknecht in Nuremberg in at least three different imprints, as well as being reprinted in Augsburg.[48] As in the other cases, "Wittenberg" on the title page signified the origin of the hymns rather than the place of publication, information that also increased the commercial viability of the imprint since the new hymns were very much in demand.

The hymnal is usually referred to as the *Achtliederbuch* (the Eight Song Book) because of the number of its hymns: four by Luther, three by Speratus, and one anonymous. Four are dated, two from 1523 and two from 1524; three carry a Wittenberg identification, reflecting their origin on individual Wittenberg broadsides; and five are given with musical notation (marked † in Table 2.1). The pamphlet comprises three sheets of paper, each one folded twice, cut, and stitched together to make twelve leaves (24 pages), measuring approximately 19 × 14 cm—certainly more convenient than individual sheets, each with a single hymn (see Table 2.1).

The first hymn, *Nun freut euch, lieben Christen gmein* (Dear Christians, one and all), is given the following heading: "Ein Christenlichs lied Doctoris Martini Luthers/ die unaussprechliche gnaden Gottes und des rechten Glaubens begreyffendt" (A Christian Song by Martin Luther which Comprehends the Inexpressible Grace of God and True Faith). This is different from both broadsides of the hymn printed by Ulhart in Augsburg, one that has no heading and the other that has a different heading.[49] This suggests that several different broadsides of Luther's hymn were in circulation before it appeared in the *Achtliederbuch*.

The next three hymns by Speratus have a treasury of biblical verses appended to each one. For example, the first hymn, *Es ist das Heil uns*

---

47. DKL 1524[12–14]; see Konrad Ameln, "Das Achtliederbuch vom Jahre 1523/24," JbLH 2 (1956): 89–91; the *Jahrbuch* volume also includes a complete facsimile of the first imprint. The year on the title page, "Xiiij" is a misprint for "XXiiij"; it was subsequently corrected. See also Ada Kadelbach, "Das 'Achtliederbuch' vom Jahre '1523/1524'. Zu unserer Faksimile–Beilage," JbLH 50 (2011): 30–4, and the facsimile appended to the volume.
48. DKL 1524[07]; *Etlich Cristliche lyeder Lobgesang/ und Psalm/ dem rainen wort gotes gemeß/ auß der hailigen gschrifft/ durch mancherlay Hochgelerter gemacht/ in der Kirchen zůsingen/ wie es dann zům tail berayt zů Wittenberg in yebung ist. Wittenberg. M. D. XXiiij* ([Augsburg: Ramminger], 1524); facsimile, *Etlich Cristlich lyeder Lobgesang und Psalm* (Aylmer, ON: Amish Historical Library, 1984).
49. See note 43 above.

Table 2.1 Contents of the *Achtliederbuch*.

Signature A		
Ai[r]	[Title page:] *Etlich Cristlich lider...*	
Ai[v]–Aii[v]	*Nun freuet euch, lieben Christen gmein* †	"1523 Mart. Luth."
Aii[v]–Aiv[v]	*Es ist das Heil uns kommen her* †	"Wittenberg 1523 Pau. Speratus"
Signature B		
Bi[r]–Biii[r]	*In Gott gelaub ich, daß er hat* †	"Wittenberg 1524." Speratus
Biii[v]–Biv[v]	*Hilf Gott, wie ist der Menschen Not*	"Wittenberg 1524." Speratus
Signature C		
Ci[r]–Ci[v]	*Ach, Gott vom Himmel sieh darein* †	Luther
Ci[v]–Cii[r]	*Es spricht der Unweisen Mund wohl*	Luther
Cii[r]	*Aus tiefer Not schrei ich zu dir*	Luther
Cii[v]–Civ[r]	*In Jesus Namen heben wir an* †	Anon
Civ[v]	[Blank]	

kommen her (Salvation unto us has come), has fifteen stanzas that are alphabeticalized, A to O, rather than numbered 1 to 15. After stanza O there is a heading that applies to all three hymns: "Anzaygung auß der schrifft warauff diß gesang allenthalben ist gegrundet/ Darauff sich alle unser sach verlassen mag" (Declaration that this song is based everywhere on Scripture, on which we may rely for everything). The letters of the stanzas are then repeated in sequence in order to list the biblical references for every line of each of the stanzas of the hymns—for example, the biblical references for *Es ist das Heil* fill two complete pages in smaller type.[50] Few of the ordinary folk in Wittenberg would be able to afford the complete German New Testament that Luther had published toward the end of 1522, and it would be another ten years before the German Old

---

50. See the discussion in chapter 1 of Johann Friedrich Meyer's use of these Speratus hymns and their Scripture proofs at the end of the seventeenth century.

Testament would appear in print. But here was a way to make Scripture familiar to the people: singing to teach the substance of the faith.

The Speratus hymns are followed by Luther's versifications of Psalms 12, 13, and 130, that together form a connected unit; indeed, they appear to have originally been published together on the same imprint as a kind of *Dreiliederflugschrift* (Three Song Pamphlet) before being reprinted in the *Achtliederbuch*. Here they have the following heading: "Die drey nachfolgenden Psalm. singt man in disem thon. Der. xi. Psalm. Salvum me fac" (The Three Following Psalms One Sings to the Tune of the Twelfth Psalm. *Salvum me fac*). The "Twelfth Psalm" is Luther's *Ach Gott vom Himmel sieh darein* (O God, look down from heaven), the first of these three Psalms and the only one with music notation. So, what the headline is indicating is that all three Psalms are in the same meter so that they can be sung to a single tune, here the one associated with Luther's version of Psalm 12. This strongly suggests that the three Psalms had appeared together on an earlier broadside, and only the first one appeared with music notation. The Nuremberg printer apparently simply reprinted what was on the earlier Wittenberg broadside. But the *Achtliederbuch* had already included the same tune with Speratus's first hymn, *Es ist das Heil uns kommen her* (Salvation unto us has come). This means that of the eight hymns of the *Achtliederbuch* five could be sung to a single melody, because Luther's *Nun freut euch, lieben Christen gmein* (Dear Christians, one and all) is also written in the same meter (8.7. 8.7. 8.8.7.). The *Achtliederbuch* prints two melodies in this meter: one for *Nun freut euch, lieben Christen gmein*,[51] the other for two texts, *Ach Gott vom Himmel sieh darein* (O God, look down from heaven),[52] and Speratus's *Es ist das Heil uns kommen her*. New texts in the same meter could therefore be sung to a single tune. The implication is that during this early period, the people could learn the texts of the different new hymns, by singing them to a single tune. This appears to have been the pedagogical strategy devised by Luther and his colleagues, so that the texts of these new hymns could be sung more readily if the singers did not have to learn a different tune for each new text. But the practice was only meant as a temporary measure while the new hymns were being committed to memory. The long-term intention, when the hymns had become familiar, was for as many as possible to have their own distinctive melodies. Thus over the next few months texts in the *Achtliederbuch* that had appeared without music notation began to be published with individual melodies: *Hilf, Gott, wie ist der Menschen Not*

---

51. Zahn 4427; DKL B15.
52. Zahn 4430; DKL Ea2.

(God's help is what the people need),[53] *Es spricht der Unweisen Mund wohl* (So speaks the unwise mouth),[54] *Aus tiefer Not schrei ich zu dir* (Out of the depths I cry to you),[55] and *Ach Gott vom Himmel sieh darein* (O God, look down from heaven) were each assigned a different tune.[56]

The last item in the *Achtliederbuch* is the anonymous *In Jesu namen heben wir an* (In Jesus's name, we raise up) that appears under the heading: "Ein fast Christliche lied vom waren glauben/ und rechter lieb Gottes und des nechsten" (A Very Christian Song about True Faith and Right Love for God and Neighbor):

[1.] In Jesu namen heben wir an.	In Jesus name, we raise up
das best das wir gelernet han/	the best that we have learned,
vom gottes wort zü singen,	to sing the Word of God,
hört zu jr frawen und auch jr man,	that you women and also you men
wie man die seligkait,	hear how blessedness
sol gewinnen.	is won.

This song, which has close affinities with contemporary ballads, only circulated for a short time during these early years. Therefore, because it did not enter into later common use, as did the other hymns of the *Achtliederbuch*, it tends to receive only passing reference. What is notable is that there is another ballad, written around the same time, set to the same melody, published by a different Nuremberg printing house, and sharing almost verbatim the same first three lines, the only variant being "ein newes lied" in place of "vom gottes wort":

[1.] *In* Gottes *namen heben wir an*	In God's name, we raise up
dz best das wir gelernet han,	the best that we have learned,
ein newes lied *züsingen*	to sing a new song
Von Hörtzog Friederich hoch geboren,	about high-born Duke Friedrich.
Gott hat jn selber außerkoren,	God himself has selected him
soll jm sein wort verfechten.	to defend his Word.[57]

---

53. Zahn 8392; DKL Ec19.
54. Zahn 4436; DKL Ec15.
55. Zahn 4437; DKL Ea6.
56. Zahn 4431; DKL Ea5.
57. Oettinger, *Music as Propaganda*, No. 126 (p. 294). Oettinger gives the complete ballad in German with a literal English translation.

On its own the concurrence may only reflect the commonality of the way in which many ballads began, and Ameln identified a list of the most obvious.[58] But there are several factors that demand further investigation. The ballad celebrates the role of Frederick the Wise, Elector and Duke of Saxony, in the movement for reform, not only in the first stanza but also in the sixth:

[6.] Hörtzog Friderich aus Sachsen ist er gennant	Duke Friedrich of Saxony he is called,
Gott hat jhn in die welt gesandt,	whom God sent into the world
soll uns den baum thün pflantzen,	to plant a tree for us.
Der also lang verdorret was,	For a long time it was desiccated,
yetz tregt er wider laub unnd graß,	now bears leaves and grass again,
unnd ist unns fruchtbar worden.	and has become fruitful for us.[59]

The ballad is not dated but has to have been written before the Elector's death in May 1525 and sometime after the Diet of Worms in April 1521, especially as there appears to be an allusion to Charles V, the Holy Roman Emperor who presided over the Edict of Worms condemning Luther and his writings in stanza 11: "Sybilla red geht auch daher | bey aynem Karl vernymb die mär . . ." (The Sybil also tells us about a Charles—recognize the tale. . . ?).[60] Similarly, there appears to be a cryptic allusion to Luther's safety in the Wartburg after the Diet, which was made possible through Duke Frederick's intervention. Stanza 2 begins: "Er hat beschütz den glerten man, | der unns die warheyt sagen kan . . ." (He [Frederick the Wise] has protected the learned man [Luther], | who can tell us the truth). If this is correct then the ballad was probably written after Luther's return to Wittenberg from the Wartburg, sometime after March 1522, and

58. Ameln, "In Jesus Namen heben wir an," 160–161.
59. Oettinger, *Music as Propaganda*, No.126 (p.294).
60. Oettinger, *Music as Propaganda*, No.126 (p.294). The reference is to the Sibylline Oracles, apocalyptic sayings originally in Greek hexameters dating from the seventh century.

possibly midyear when Luther's presence back in Wittenberg had become common knowledge. Therefore, *In Gottes namen heben wir an* appears to have predated *In Jesu namen heben wir an* by a few months. The two ballads have similar contents: the stanzas of *In Gottes namen* have no less than seven references to "the Word of God," together with several statements relating to the substance of the "Scriptures." Many of the stanzas of *In Jesu namen* either begin or end with a biblical reference, such as the Gospels of Matthew and John and the letters of Peter and Paul. Both ballads, like the hymns of Speratus in the *Achtliederbuch*, have the aim of communicating biblical content in hymnic form, though with less detail.

The two ballads exist side by side in the earliest extant print of *In Gottes namen: Bergkreyen. Etliche Schöne gesenge/ newlich züsamen gebracht/ gemehret und gebessert* (Bergkreyen [lit. Miners' songs] Some Beautiful Songs Newly Brought Together, Extended, and Improved) ([Nuremberg: Wachter], 1536). Like Gutknecht's *Achtliederbuch* Wachter's collection was compiled from earlier-published broadsides. Both ballads are assigned to the same melody that can be traced back to south Germany around 1490,[61] and the two texts occur one after the other in the Wachter imprint: *In Gottes namen*, number 18; *In Jesus namen*, number 19. This suggests that the two ballad-hymns were connected in some way, although it is not exactly clear what that connection was. But at the very least it is another witness to how the earliest Lutheran hymnals evolved from the broadside tradition of vernacular song.

ERFURT, ENCHIRIDIA, 1524

The new Wittenberg hymns were causing quite a stir in the early months of 1524. In Erfurt there were two printer-publishers who were in competition with each other to be the first to bring out a collection of Wittenberg hymns, which, like the *Achtliederbuch*, were reprintings of Wittenberg broadsides. One was the established Erfurt printer Mathes Maler, whose press had been set up "at the Black Horn, near the grocer's bridge," in 1511. The other was Johannes Loersfeld, a newcomer who had set up his press "in Permenter lane, at the dyer's vat," in Erfurt, only a matter of a few months before in 1523. The two printers almost simultaneously published virtually identical collections of hymns with basically the same title and

---

61. See Böhme, *Altdeutsches Liederbuch*, Nos. 375, 376, 532, 533, 547, 636; Zahn 1704a; DKL Ea13.

almost identical contents: *Eyn Enchiridion oder Handbüchlein ... geystlicher gesenge und Psalmen/ Rechtschaffen und kunstlich verteutscht.* ... (An Enchiridion or Handbook ... Spiritual Songs and Psalms, Righteously and Artfully Translated) (Erfurt, 1524).[62] Both editions show signs of being hastily prepared, suggesting the printers were racing to publish first and therefore make a handsome profit. From his detailed examination of the two editions Konrad Ameln concluded that the most likely explanation of how the two parallel editions came about is that Loersfeld, working from a collection of broadsides, or from a manuscript copied from such broadsides, had progressed as far as the first proofs. Somehow, almost certainly nefariously, a set of these Loersfeld proofs found their way into Maler's print shop, who then began to set up his own edition from Loersfeld's proofs.[63] There was probably bad blood between the two printers, with Maler, the established printer, resenting the upstart Loersfeld.[64]

The Erfurt *Enchiridion* contained twenty-four Wittenberg hymns, that is, all eight of the *Achtliederbuch* with sixteen others that were apparently making their first appearance, fourteen by Luther, and two by his colleagues (see Table 2.2).[65]

When compared with the contents of the *Achtliederbuch*, a few differences become clear. The tune for Luther's *Nun freut euch, lieben Christen gmein* was omitted, as were Speratus's detailed Scripture proofs for his hymns, and the tune for *In Jesu Namen heben wir an*—which in the *Achtliederbuch* appears in a twopart setting—is given in a variant form. The last two items of the hymnal are the ten-stanza version of Luther's *Ein neues Lied*, which is followed by *In Jesu Namen heben wir an*—the two again underscoring the connection between the old ballad tradition and the newly emerging Lutheran hymn tradition.

62. DKL 1524[03–04] (Loersfeld); DKL 1524[05] (Maler). For the background, see, Benzing, *Die Buchdrucker des 16. und 17. Jahrhunderts*, 109–110; Martin von Hase, "Die Drucker der Erfurter Enchiridien, Mathes Maler und Johannes Loersfeld," JbLH 2 (1956): 91–93; *Das Erfurter Enchiridion Gedruckt in der Permentgassen zum Ferbefaß 1524*, facsimile, ed. Konrad Ameln (Kassel: Bärenreiter, 1983), "Geleitwort/Introduction, 3–12 (German), 13–22 (English); see also the enlarged facsimile, which also includes a complete transcription of the hymn texts with the tunes in modern notation: *Ein Enchiridion oder Handbüchlein geistlicher Gesänge und Psalmen (Erfurt 1524)*, ed. Christiane und Kai Brodersen; Leaver, *The Whole Church Sings*, 93–95.
63. See Ameln, *Das Erfurter Enchiridion*, "Introduction," 19.
64. Accepting Ameln's hypothesis the following is based on the Loersfeld imprint.
65. This list, along with similar lists later in this chapter, records the hymn texts that appear in the original sources. The first two columns identify the tunes they were sung to in the original sources. The remaining four columns locate where English translations can be found. However, these hymnals do not always assign the same tunes.

Table 2.2 New Hymns That Made Their Appearance in the Earliest Lutheran Hymnals.

Luther	Zahn	DKL	LBW	ELH	LSB	LW 53
Christ lag in Todesbanden	7012b	Ea8	134	243	458	256
Christum wir sollen loben schon	297b	Ec10	—	267	385	238
Dies sind die heilgen zehn Gebot	1951	Ea1	—	490	581	278
Ein neues Lied wir heben an	7245	Ea12	—	—	—	214
Es wollt uns Gott genädig sein	—	—	335	591	823	234
Gelobet seist du, Jesu Christ	—	—	48	136	382	240
Gott sei gelobet und gebenedeiet	—	—	215	327	617	253
Jesus Christus, unser Heiland, der den Tod	1977	Ea9	—	—	—	250
Jesus Christus, unser Heiland, der von uns	1576	Ec16	—	316/7	627	258
Komm, Gott Schöpfer, Heiliger Geist	294	D14A	284	10	—	261
Komm, Heiliger Geist, Herre Gott	7445a	Ea11	163	2	497	266
Mitten wir im Leben sind	—	—	350	52	755	275
Nun komm, der Heiden Heiland	1174	Ea10	28	90	332	236
Wohl dem, der in Gottes Furcht steht	—	—	—	—	—	230
Elisabeth Cruciger						
Herr Christ, der einig Gotts Sohn	4297	Ea4	86	224	402	—
Erhart Hegenwald						
Erbarm dich mein, o Herre Gott	5852	Ea7	—	—	—	—

CHORGESANGBUCH, 1524

There were two primary churches in Wittenberg: the parish church of St. Mary, and the church of All Saints which served the liturgical needs of both Wittenberg University and the Saxon ducal court. The unreformed mass and offices were still in Latin in both churches, and the Allerheiligenstift, with its numerous clergy and musicians, often presented the liturgical propers in polyphonic settings.[66]

Toward the end of 1524 a set of partbooks was printed in Wittenberg by Joseph Klug: *Geystlich gesangk Buchleyn. TENOR. Wittemberg. M. D. [xx] iiij*, a collection of polyphonic settings of the new vernacular hymns, with a preface by Luther, commonly referred to as the *Chorgesangbuch*.[67] They were the work of Johann Walter, court composer (Hofcompositor) and singer (bass) in the ducal Hofkapelle. This was a very different phenomenon from what we have encountered thus far. In place of the ballad-style unison singing of the new hymns from broadsides and pamphlets by the people, here were partbooks containing sophisticated polyphonic settings requiring a relatively small group of accomplished musicians. It was the *Tenorlied* style[68] popular in German courts of the time and characterized by the music of such composers as Hofhaimer, Isaac, and especially Senfl, whose music Luther particularly admired. Walter took the *Tenorlied* style, and where these other composers used different kinds of strophic poetry for their *cantus firmi*, Walter used the new Wittenberg hymns and their melodies.

The collection comprised thirty-eight motets in four or five parts with the chorale/hymn melody/*cantus firmus* usually in the tenor voice. Some melodies had more than one setting and some texts had more than one tune. In all there were settings of thirty-two of the new hymn texts, together with five Latin motets,[69] that were composed for the Duke's Hofkapelle rather than Wittenberg's parish church.

---

66. See Robin A. Leaver, *Luther's Liturgical Music: Principles and Implications* (Minneapolis: Fortress Press, 2017), 32–36; Marie Schlüter, *Musikgeschichte Wittenbergs im 16. Jahrhundert: Quellenkundliche und sozialgeschichtliche Untersuchungen* (Göttingen: V & R Unipress, 2010), 19–26. The musicians of the Allerheiligenstift were joined by those of the ducal court chapel (Hofkapelle) when the duke was in residence in Wittenberg.
67. DKL 1524[18].
68. Hence the later descriptive term "Tenorlied" (tenor song); see the opening paragraphs of chapter 4.
69. Some of the partbooks of the first edition of the 1524 partbooks are no longer extant. The second edition published in Worms in 1525 has been issued in facsimile, Johann Walter, *Das geistliche Gesangbüchlein "Chorgesangbuch,"* ed. Walter Blankenburg (Kassel: Bärenreiter, 1979),

The *Chorgesangbuch* came into use in the Duke's Hofkapelle late in 1524 or perhaps early in 1525. There is an entry in one of the Duke's ledgers, dated December 31, 1524, recording payment for one or more sets of Walter's partbooks.[70] As Jonas, one of the authors of the new hymns, was dean of the Allerheiligenstift, it is possible that sets of the partbooks were obtained for the musicians of the foundation in Wittenberg;[71] again this would have been late 1524 or early 1525, when significant liturgical changes were being made. It has been suggested that these settings were sung in the parish church in order to encourage the congregation, which was thought to be somewhat reluctant to sing the new hymns. The primary reason for this, so it is claimed, is that they had no hymnals, only broadsides.[72] But in this timeframe of 1523–1524, how can the members of the congregation have been reluctant when their reputation for singing was promoting the printing and reprinting of the Wittenberg hymns in such places as Augsburg, Erfurt, Magdeburg, Nuremberg?—and probably elsewhere, as the people in such places wanted to sing what the Wittenbergers were singing. And this reputation for singing the new hymns in the Wittenberg parish church was established months before the *Chorgesangbuch* was even published. Similarly, the claim that "they had no hymnals" is an unfortunate conclusion created by the scarcity of extant copies of the early hymnals. For example, the earliest extant edition of the extremely important Wittenberg *Geistliche Lieder* was published in 1533, yet it is known that two different editions were published in 1529 and neither is extant.[73]

WITTENBERG, ENCHYRIDION, 1524–1526

Late in the nineteenth century a previously unknown copy of a vernacular hymnal, published in Wittenberg, came to light: *Enchyridion geistlicher gesenge und psalmen fur die leyen/ mit viel andern/ denn suvor/ gebessert* (Enchyridion [Handbook] Spiritual Songs and Psalms for the People

---

and the motets have been issued in modern notation, Johann Walter, *Geistliches Gesangbüchlein, Worms 1525*, ed. Christian Schmitt-Engelstadt (Cologne: Dohr, 2017).
70. Christa Maria Richter, "Walter–Dokumente," in *Johann Walter, Torgau und die Evangelische Kirchenmusik*, ed. Mätthias Herrmann (Altenburg: Kamrad, 2013), 173 (No. 3).
71. For more details of what is discussed here, see Leaver, *The Whole Church Sings*, passim; and Robin A. Leaver, "Did the Choir Introduce German Hymns to the Wittenberg Congregation?" in *Lutheran Music Culture: Ideals and Practices*, ed. Mattias Lundberg, Maria Schmidt and Jonas Lundblad (Berlin: de Gruyter, 2022), 47–67.
72. See Leaver, *The Whole Church Sings*, 102–103.
73. See Leaver, *The Whole Church Sings*, 151–154.

with Many Others than Before, Improved) (Wittenberg: Lufft, 1526). Its content of hymns is very similar to that of the *Chorgesangbuch*. Since the 1524 partbooks predate the 1526 *Enchyridion*, the tendency has been to regard the 1524 imprint as primary and the 1526 imprint as secondary. The result has been to give the *Chorgesangbuch* a predominance that distorts the relationship between the two imprints, implying that the *Enchyridion* was derived from the *Chorgesangbuch*. Both had similar contents, but the *Enchyridion* was somewhat different; it was a hymnal "fur die leyen" (for the people), as it states on the title page, in contrast to the partbooks which were intended in the first place for the musicians of the Duke's Hofkapelle. The *Chorgesangbuch* is based on thirty-two hymn texts that appear in no particular sequence or structure. The *Enchyridion* comprises forty-two hymns: the same thirty-two hymns—and in the same sequence—as in the *Chorgesangbuch*, plus ten additional hymns. The title page of the *Enchyridion* reveals that it had to have been preceded by at least one earlier edition, since this 1526 collection declares on the title page that it includes "many others [that is, of songs and Psalms] than before, improved." Comparison of the contents of the *Chorgesangbuch* with that of the *Enchyridion* reveals that of the ten extra hymns in the *Enchyridion*, three were inserted individually into the thirty-two–hymn sequence, and seven were added as a kind of appendix after all the other hymns. This strongly suggests that the 1526 *Enchyridion* was preceded by not one, but two no-longer-extant earlier editions, making it effectively a third edition. If the proposed two earlier editions had been published a year apart, then, tracing backwards, one can conjecture that a second *Enchyridion* edition is likely to have appeared around 1525, and that the first edition would then have been published in 1524. If so, then the first edition of the *Enchyridion* may well have been published around the same time as the *Chorgesangbuch*, that is, late in 1524. The implication is that instead of being without hymnals, the congregation of Wittenberg parish church had access to at least three different editions of its hymnal between 1524 and 1526 (see Table 2.3).

When the music of the two sources is compared, a significant fact emerges, and that is that the *Chorgesangbuch* often assigns different alternative tunes for some of the texts. The same tunes that had been associated with the texts circulating on Wittenberg broadsides and their reprints in other cities were found in the *Chorgesangbuch* and in the different editions of the *Enchyridion*, as established in the edition of 1526. However, Johann Walter, the composer of the *cantus firmus* settings, also composed new melodies for some of the texts. What is revealing is that none of Walter's new tunes were included in the 1526 *Enchyridion*. This suggests that two different manifestations of the same basic corpus of the Wittenberg hymns

Table 2.3 Relationships between Wittenberg Hymnals 1524–1526.

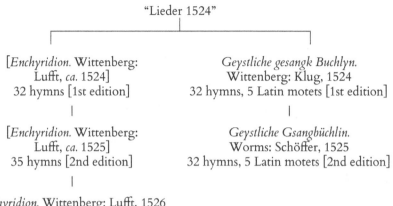

were published in 1524, the conjectural first edition of the *Enchyridion* and the *Chorgesangbuch*.[74] Since it was published some two years later than the partbooks, the *Enchyridion* would likely have included Walter's tunes if they were being regularly sung by the Wittenberg congregation. Instead, the 1526 *Enchyridion* throughout presents the melodies that were already known, rather than Walter's new tunes. The *Enchyridion* was thus the hymnal for the Wittenberg congregation, singing in unison, and Walter's *Chorgesangbuch* was the collection of polyphonic settings of the same hymns for the musicians of Frederick the Wise's Hofkapelle.

Once this is realized then a further probability comes into view, that in 1524, both the *Enchyridion* and the *Chorgesangbuch* would have been dependent on the same source for the thirty-two hymns they each contained. The conjectural common source, here designated "Lieder 1524" (see Table 2.3) would have included the thirty-two hymns found in the *Chorgesangbuch*, that is, the eight hymns of the *Achtliederbuch*, the sixteen hymns that had been reprinted in the Erfurt *Enchiridia*, together with a further eight hymns that were about to be published both in the *Chorgesangbuch* and in the conjectural first edition of the Wittenberg *Enchyridion* (see Table 2.4).[75]

---

74. For background and detail, see Leaver, *The Whole Church Sings*, 111–116.
75. In 1525 Loersfelt reprinted seven of these new hymns, the exception being Stifel's *Dein armer Hauf*, in: *Etliche Christliche Gesenge und psalmen/ wilche vor bey dem Enchiridion nicht gewest synd* . . . (Several Christian Songs and Psalms, Which Have Not Been Part of the *Enchiridion* Before . . .) (Erfurt: Loersfelt, 1525). Loersfelt was perhaps working from the tenor partbook of the *Chorgesangbuch* since he included Luther's preface.

Table 2.4 New Wittenberg Hymns 1524.

Luther	Zahn	DKL	LBW	ELH	LSB	LW 53
Gott der Vater wohn uns bei	8507	Ec17	308	18	505	270
Mensch, willst du leben seliglich	1956	Ec9	—	—	—	281
Mit Fried und Freud ich fahr dahin	3986	Ec13	350	52	938	248
Nun bitten wir den Heiligen Geist[76]	2029a	Eb8A	317	33	768	264
Wär Gott nicht mit uns diese Zeit	4434	Ec14	—	396	—	246
Wir glauben all an einen Gott	7971	Ec18	374	38	954	272
Michael Stifel						
Dein armer Hauf, Herr, tut klagen	3681	Ec2	—	—	—	—
Lazarus Spengler						
Durch Adams Fall ist ganz verderbt	7547	Ec7	—	430	—	—

In addition to these new hymns there were the significant revisions of two of Luther's texts. One was his version of *Aus tiefer Not schrei ich zu dir* that was revised and expanded from four to five stanzas.[77] The other was his narrative ballad, *Ein neues Lied wir heben an*, that was extended by two additional stanzas (see above, page 52). The earliest extant source for these rewritten texts is the tenor partbook of the *Chorgesangbuch*, but did Walter obtain them directly from Luther or from a common source where he found the other thirty texts, that is, the conjectural repertory here designated "Lieder 1524?" Although there is no documentation that would supply a categorical answer to this question, what was happening in Wittenberg at that time with regard to the worship of the two Wittenberg churches (see further below) would suggest that Walter took these revised versions from a common source, that is, the "Lieder 1524." Further, the reworking and expansion of *Aus tiefer Not schrei ich zu dir* and *Ein neues Lied wir heben an* and the addition of six new texts, together with the fact that most of the hymns in this basic repertory were his (75 percent), would suggest that Luther was its principal compiler.

---

76. Luther's expansion of the single stanza *Leise* dating from the thirteenth century.
77. See Leaver, *Luther's Liturgical Music*, 142–152.

LITURGICAL REFORM, 1524–1525

In 1523–1524 the three Wittenberg institutions—parish church, university, and Allerheiligenstift—were still struggling with the aftermath of "Die Wittenberger Bewegung" (The Wittenberg Movement) of 1521/22.[78] Differences of opinion remained regarding the need to reform patterns of worship to make them theologically consistent. Some agitated for radical reform; others resisted any proposal to make changes to the traditional Latin mass. For two years Luther had been writing and preaching against the daily celebration of endowed unreformed masses by the clergy (canons) and musicians of the Allerheiligenstift. Things came to a head in November 1524 when Luther gave the remaining recalcitrant priests of the foundation an ultimatum: either they accept the discontinuance of the daily masses, or they must resign.[79] On December 24, 1524 an important document was issued: *Ordinatio cultus Die in arce* (The Order of the Worship of God in the Castle [Church]).[80] It was drawn up by Johannes Bugenhagen, pastor of the parish church, also professor of theology,[81] and Justus Jonas, probst (provost) of the Allerheiligenstift, also professor and dean of the theological faculty.[82] These leaders of the two Wittenberg churches worked closely with Luther on the details of the document.[83] First, it declared that because the Castle Church did not serve a parish the mass in any form would no longer be celebrated in that church, not even on a Sunday.[84] Second, the document outlined in detail the revised form of the Latin daily offices that were then to be followed in the Castle Church, replacing the traditional daily offices and unreformed masses.[85] These revised offices would be led by the remaining musicians and clergy of the Allerheiligenstift who accepted the reform, and these daily services would be attended by the students and professors of the university.

---

78. See Leaver, *The Whole Church Sings*, 37–42.
79. For background, see Brecht, *Luther: Shaping and Defining the Reformation*, 127–129; Leaver, *The Whole Church Sings*, 119–121.
80. Karl Pallas, "Urkunden, das Allerheiligungsstift zu Wittenberg betreffend, 1522–1526," *Archiv für Reformationsgeschichte*," 12 (1915): 111–114.
81. *Professorenbuch der Theologischen Fakultät der Universität Wittenberg 1502–1815/17*, eds. Armin Kohnle and Beate Kusche (Leizig: Evangelische Verlagsanstalt, 2016), 34–36.
82. *Professorenbuch*, 95–98.
83. Pallas, "Urkunden," 114: "Disse ordenung ist durch Pomeranum [Bugenhagen] und D. Jonas gestellet mit rath D. Martini."
84. In a letter to Nikolaus von Amsdorf, December 2, 1524, Luther wrote: "At last we persuaded our canons to consent to the repeal of the mass." WA BR 3: 397.
85. See note 80 above.

Mass and communion were then confined to the parish church, where Luther's *Formula missae* was already the primary source of the liturgy. The information comes from a pamphlet made up of several disparate reformation documents reprinted by the Nuremberg printer, Hieronymus Höltzel, in 1524.[86] The fourth item is *Ordnung der Evangelischen Messz* (Wittenberg, 1524), a description by Bugenhagen of eucharistic worship in Wittenberg parish church.[87] In the *Formula missae* Luther had expressed his desire for vernacular hymns to be written so that the people could sing them in the mass, especially after the gradual.[88] Bugenhagen reveals that a year or so after Luther's words were published such hymns were available in the parish church and were being sung by the people. Bugenhagen writes: "The choir sings the gradual ... but the people sing a German psalm or hymn to Christ."[89] So what did the people sing from?

The worship of the Castle Church was then confined to the revised daily office and there was a similar provision for vernacular hymnody. After biblical readings at Vespers there is the directive: "A hymn should be sung, or, if they wish, they should sing a German hymn from those which Doctor Martin has carefully created, or some Latin hymn taken from the sacred scriptures."[90] When these daily offices came into use on New Year's Day, 1525, it was reported that at Matins "a German hymn was sung."[91] That the *Ordinatio cultus Die in arce*, dated Christmas Eve 1524, could request the corporate singing of a vernacular hymn by Luther, and that eight days later, on New Year's Day, 1525, a German hymn was indeed sung at Matins in the Castle Church, implies that the congregation must have had hymnals from which to sing. The statement in the *Ordinatio* regarding the hymns "carefully created" by "Doctor Martin" looks like a reference to the probable first edition of the *Enchyridion* (1524), since of the thirty-two hymns it would have had in common with the *Chorgesangbuch*, twenty-four were by Luther. The musicians of the Allerheiligenstift could have sung some

---

86. The composite volume is identified by the title of the first item: *Von der Evangelischen Messz*.
87. *Von der Evangelischen Messz*, sig. Biv^v-Dij^v.
88. LW 53: 36.
89. *Von der Evangelischen Messz*, sig. Biv^v: "Singt der Chor das Graduel ... Aber des volck singt dar für aynen verteütschten psalm/ oder lobgesang von Christo."
90. Pallas, "Urkunden," 111–112: "Hymnus emittatur aut, si volent, canant hymnum aliquem germanicum ex illis, quos curavit Doctor Martinus excudi, aut hymnum aliquem latinum ex scripturis sacris desumptum."
91. Pallas, "Urkunden," 114: "ein deutzsch liet gesongen."

of the settings in the *Chorgesangbuch* with the congregation—if indeed the partbooks had been published by this time[92]—but not all of them. This was because some of the melodies in the tenor partbook had been modified for compositional reasons, such as to enable a melody to be sung as a twopart canon within the polyphony, or for a melody to migrate from one voice to another. However, they could have adopted the familiar *alternatims praxis*, in which monodic chant alternated with polyphony, with the two groups singing alternate stanzas, the musicians of the Allerheiligenstift singing from the *Chorgesangbuch* partbooks and the congregation singing from the first edition of the *Enchyridion*: the two sources that made different usage of the same repertory, "Lieder 1524."

The conjectural first edition of the *Enchyridion* (1524) could be considered the work of the leaders of the two churches, Bugenhagen and Jonas, with the counsel of Luther—as they did with the preparation of the *Ordinatio* (1524). Both were concerned with liturgical reform that would actively involve the people through their singing. Until this point, the concern had largely been with individual hymns, and the *Enchyridion* was a practical means in which the hymns were conveniently gathered together; while they were in no particular order, the hymnal made them accessible for singing. However, now that significant progress had been made to the reform of worship in the two churches, we can detect a shift. Thus, the basic repertory, "Lieder 1524," begins with the hymn that blends the old with the new, Luther's expansion of *Nun bitten wir den Heiligen Geist*. Was it assigned the status of the first hymn simply because it was a favorite of Luther's?[93]—or because it could be sung as a vernacular alternative to the Latin *Veni sancti Spiritus* that the *Ordinatio* directs should begin Saturday Vespers?[94] Similarly, although the "Lieder 1524" had no categories of hymns of like content, it is noticeable that all the major seasons of the church year were specifically represented, suggesting that the question of how a hymnal should be structured was already being considered (see Table 2.5).

The "Lieder 1524" thus marks the beginning of the development of the Lutheran hymnal with the reminder that it grew out of the roots of the broadside ballad tradition: Luther's non-hymn, *Ein neues lied wir heben*

---

92. See note 70 above.
93. LW 53: 25, 37 (*Formula missae*).
94. Pallas, "Urkunden," 111.

an, appearing as number six in the basic repertory, as it does in the 1526 edition of the *Enchyridion* (and presumably the earlier editions as well) and the *Chorgesangbuch*.

Table 2.5 Church Year Hymns, Wittenberg 1524.

Major Seasons	LBW	ELH	LSB	LW 53
Advent				
Nun komm, der Heiden Heiland	28	90	332	236
Christmas				
Christum wir sollen loben schon	—	267	385	238
Gelobet seist du, Jesu Christ	48	136	382	240
Epiphany				
Wohl dem, der in Gottes furcht steht	—	—	—	243
Pre–Lent				
Es spricht der Unweisen Mund wohl	—	—	—	230
Lent				
Dies sind die heiligen zehn Gebot	—	490	581	278
Mensch, willst du leben seliglich	—	—	—	281
Aus tiefer Not schrei ich zu dir	295	452	607	223
Easter				
Christ lag in Todesbanden	134	243	458	256
Jesus Christus unser Heiland, der den Tod	—	—	—	258
Pentecost				
Nun bitten wir den Heiligen Geist	317	33	768	264
Komm, Heiliger Geist, Herre Gott	163	2	497	266
Komm, Gott Schöpfer, Heiliger Geist	284	10	498/9	261
Trinity				
Gott der Vater wohn uns bei	308	18	505	270
Wir glauben all an einen Gott	374	38	954	272

3.

Luther as Hymnal Editor

Paul J. Grime

Near the end of his life, Martin Luther (1483–1546) wrote the preface for a republication of his earlier church postils that was edited by his colleague Caspar Cruciger. This 1544 publication afforded Luther the opportunity to take note of the progress that had been made over the preceding quarter century. Whereas in the days before the Reformation the common people had to settle for fables and myths that corrupted the pure gospel, Luther noted how changed the landscape now looked. He began his preface by declaring that his fellow preachers of the gospel could, with a good conscience, join him in boasting before God. Why? Because—and here he quoted almost verbatim the words of St. Paul to the Corinthians—God's people had "become rich in all aspects of all teaching and in all knowledge," and how "the preaching of Christ" had become strong in them.[1]

After having spent decades addressing one issue after another, either simultaneously or in rapid succession, Luther's advancing years made it possible for him to step back and remind both himself and his readers of all that he and his colleagues had accomplished, all by God's grace. Thus, Luther makes note first of the catechism, referencing not only each of the chief parts but even the importance of the table of duties. He went on to point out the significance of the postils, giving thanks that the lay people were now able to read sermons on the epistles and gospels for themselves and thus have easy access to the essential Reformation insights. Similarly, faithful prayer books and Christian songs were now available for the

---

1. WA 21:200–1; my translation; cf. 1 Corinthians 1:4–9. For background on the production of the 1544 postil, see Martin Brecht, *Martin Luther: The Preservation of the Church, 1532–1546*, trans. James L. Schaaf (Minneapolis: Fortress Press, 1993), 251.

people's use. And, of course, there was Luther's translation of the Bible, which served as the foundation for every form of the gospel's delivery.

Luther's review, as it were, of this aspect of his life's work serves as a cautionary reminder that an examination of early Lutheran hymnals must not proceed outside the context of his broader effort to inculcate the gospel in the hearts of the people. Unlike the initial collections of hymns discussed in the previous chapter, the first fully developed hymnals of the Reformation in Wittenberg were intentionally integrated with other significant resources that served to shape the piety of the people, in particular Luther's prayer book and catechism.

TOWARD A SHAPING OF THE PEOPLE'S PIETY

A culmination of Luther's efforts to inculcate the gospel in the hearts and minds of the laity occurred in significant measure in the year 1529 with the publication of three crucial resources: a revision and expansion of his 1522 prayer book, the Small and Large Catechisms, and the first (more or less) complete hymnal in Wittenberg. Much like the three legs of a stool, all three publications, which bear clear evidence of Luther's direct involvement, served in a complementary way toward the shaping of the people's piety. What is seldom recognized, however, is how the appearance of all three publications was the product of more than a decade of development.

Consider, for example, the catechisms. Already in the year prior to the posting of the Ninety-Five Theses in late 1517, Luther had preached the first of what would be many series of sermons on the chief parts of the catechism. Most popular was his exposition of the Lord's Prayer, which appeared in numerous editions between 1519 and 1522.[2] Very quickly, however, Luther moved beyond these extended expositions to develop a more condensed form of instruction for the purpose of teaching the laity the chief doctrines of the faith. In 1520 he published his *Short Form of the Ten Commandments, the Creed, and the Lord's Prayer*.[3] Already here we find an early attempt at demonstrating how the first three parts of the catechism work together:

> The Commandments teach a man to know his sickness. . . . After that the Creed shows him and teaches him where he may find the

---

2. See Martin Bertram's historical introduction, LW 42:17, as well as Luther's exposition, LW 42:19–81. See also Martin Brecht, *Martin Luther: His Road to Reformation, 1483–1521*, trans. James L. Schaaf (Minneapolis: Fortress Press, 1985), 351–352.
3. WA 7: 204–29. For an English translation, see Martin Luther, *A Brief Explanation of the Ten Commandments, the Creed, and the Lord's Prayer* (1520), trans. C. M. Jacobs (Philadelphia: Holman, 1915), 2:351–386.

remedy . . . [showing] him God, and the mercy which He has revealed and offered in Christ. In the third place, the Lord's Prayer teaches him how to ask for this grace. . . . These three are the chief things in all the Scriptures.[4]

Here, for example, Luther expounded on the Ten Commandments by means of lists that invited the individual to probe what it meant to break each of the commandments as well as how to fulfill them. Likewise, we see Luther for the first time breaking from the medieval tradition of treating the creed in twelve separate articles, opting instead for a tripartite, trinitarian exposition.[5] He also handled the Lord's Prayer differently from his earlier expositions, which were extensive third person treatments, opting instead for a briefer treatment that was cast as an extended prayer addressed to God.

This *Short Form*, drawn up while the battle lines were forming with Rome, demonstrates the deep pastoral concern Luther had for his dear German people. Two years later, following his return from the Wartburg, Luther expanded the *Short Form* by adding it to the typical medieval prayer books to produce his own *Personal Prayer Book* of 1522.[6] In addition to his explanations of the commandments, creed, and Lord's Prayer, Luther provided an evangelical interpretation of the Hail Mary, the texts of eight psalms (10, 12, 20, 25, 51, 67, 79, and 103), and his freshly minted translation of the book of Titus, which would appear together with the entire New Testament in September of that year.

Luther's interrelated view of catechism and prayer book spilled over into the church's worship a few years later with the publication of his *Deutsche Messe*. In his introduction he forthrightly stated that "the German service needs a plain and simple, fair and square catechism" and identified as the constitutive elements of the catechism the three parts that he had previously treated in the *Short Form* and *Personal Prayer Book*.[7] With a nod to the ancient practice of focusing on the three chief parts he had treated in his prayer book, Luther was more explicit in directing how such a catechism was to be used, namely, in the home. Lengthy expositions would no longer do; thus, we find for the first time examples of the pithy explanations that would later characterize Luther's explanations in the

---

4. Ibid., 2:354–5; WA 7: 204–205. Essentially the same text appears in Luther's *Personal Prayer Book* (1522), LW 43:14; WA 10^{II}: 377. Luther later incorporated these thoughts into his Large Catechism, II 1, 67–69 and III 1–2.
5. The brilliance of Luther's treatment of the creed would later reach its zenith in his conclusion to the creed in the Large Catechism; see LC II 63–66.
6. Luther, *Personal Prayer Book*, LW 43:3–45. For background, see Brecht, *Martin Luther: Shaping and Defining the Reformation, 1521–1532*, 119–121.
7. LW 53: 64–65.

Small Catechism.[8] Luther, acknowledging the need to develop a way of teaching young children the rudimentary elements of the faith, even went so far as to suggest a simple game that would teach children how to distinguish the concepts of faith and love.[9] While a complete catechism along the lines of the examples Luther provided in the *Deutsche Messe* was still a few years off, the direction was clearly set.

For nearly a decade, Luther—and others, too—had been making various attempts at inculcating the evangelical faith in a way that would build up faithful Christians. One last factor that likely led to the pivotal publications of 1529 was the visitation of churches in Saxony that Luther, Melanchthon, and others carried out in the preceding year. While chief among Luther's concerns at that time was the poor working conditions of many of the pastors, often exemplified by the pitiful remuneration they received, others also believed that a visitation of the congregations would be helpful in working toward a unified confession.[10] The evidence for this is plain in the articles for visitation that Melanchthon drew up. Though not comprehensive in their coverage, they touched upon the main teachings of the evangelical faith, focusing in particular on the relationship between faith and repentance. It was in light of these articles that the visitors were to inquire as to the state of Christian knowledge and understanding in the churches of Electoral Saxony.

What were the results of those visits? Luther was most blunt when, in the following year, he recounted the findings in his preface to the Small Catechism:

> The deplorable, wretched deprivation that I recently encountered while I was a visitor has constrained and compelled me to prepare this catechism, or Christian instruction, in such a brief, plain, and simple version. Dear God, what misery I beheld! The ordinary person, especially in the villages, knows absolutely nothing about the Christian faith, and unfortunately many pastors are completely unskilled and incompetent teachers. Yet supposedly they all bear the name Christian, are baptized, and receive the holy sacrament, even though they do not know the Lord's Prayer, the Creed, or the Ten Commandments! . . .
>
> Therefore, my dear sirs and brothers, who are either pastors or preachers, I beg all of you for God's sake to take up your office boldly, to have pity on

---

8. Examples for the Lord's Prayer and the creed may be found at LW 53:65–66.
9. LW 53:66–67.
10. For a helpful overview of the visitations, see Brecht, *Martin Luther: The Preservation of the Church, 1532–1546*, 259–273.

your people who are entrusted to you, and to help us bring the catechism to the people, especially the young.[11]

Deplorable conditions. Wretched catechesis. Bishops shirking their duties. It was time for decisive action, and a good, German catechism was just the first step.

AN INFLUENTIAL GROUNDBREAKING TRILOGY

As noted earlier, 1529 became something of a culmination in Luther's work of providing faithful resources that could serve to implant the evangelical faith into the hearts of the people. Within the span of a few short months, three small octavo volumes appeared—the *Small Catechism*, the *Personal Prayer Book*, and the *Geistliche lieder*—all with clear indications that Luther was directly involved in their preparation.[12] While each book deserves attention in its own right—and the *Geistliche lieder* will indeed receive due consideration shortly—it is instructive first to consider the amazing interconnectedness that exists among all three.

Consider the following: Luther's catechism contained not only questions and answers on the chief parts of Christian doctrine, but also brief orders for morning and evening prayer, prayers at meals and for several other occasions, rites for baptism and marriage, a short form of confession, and Luther's German translation of the Litany. In addition, the book included twenty illustrations covering the Ten Commandments, the three articles of the Creed, and the seven petitions of the Lord's Prayer.[13]

Consider next the revised edition of Luther's *Personal Prayer Book*. Once again, Luther retained his earlier exposition of the first three parts of the catechism. While Luther's pithy explanations contained in the *Small Catechism* would eventually eclipse these earlier forms, the latter served as a contrasting vehicle for inculcating the faith into the hearts

---

11. Martin Luther, *Small Catechism*, Preface, 1–3, 6; BC, 347, 348.
12. Markus Jenny suggests a clear relationship between these three resources, noting Luther's desire to provide the necessary resources to shape the piety of the people. See Markus Jenny, AWA 4:37; see also his significant discussion in "Luthers Gesangbuch" in *Leben und Werken Martin Luthers von 1526 bis 1546: Festgabe zu seinem 500. Geburtstag*, ed. Helmar Junghans (Göttingen: Vanden hoeck & Ruprecht, 1983),1: 312; see also Christopher Boyd Brown, "Devotional Life in Hymns, Liturgy, Music, and Prayer," in *Lutheran Ecclesiastical Culture, 1550–1675* [Brill's Companions to the Christian Tradition, 11], ed. Robert Kolb (Leiden: Brill, 2008), 206.
13. For more on the contents of the catechism, see Michael Reu, *Dr. Martin Luthers Small Catechism: A History of Its Origin, Its Distribution and Its Use* (Chicago: Wartburg, 1929), 25–31.

and minds of the people. Concrete examples of how Christians both break and keep the commandments, for example, could assist the laity in self-examination.[14] The inclusion of eight psalms imparted something of a devotional character to the book. It was, however, the new additions to the 1529 edition that led the user more intentionally into the corporate worship life of the church. Sermons on the sufferings of Christ, holy baptism, confession and the Sacrament, and preparation for death—all previously published separately—were now included in the prayer book. Additionally, there was a calendar with a Latin verse for each month that paid homage to significant events in the church year. But most significantly, Luther included his Passional, which consisted of a collection of fifty full-page woodcuts together with biblical passages.[15] About one-fourth of the illustrations depict Old Testament events, beginning with the creation, with the remainder covering the life and ministry of Jesus, particularly focusing on his suffering, death, and resurrection. In an age when literacy could not be presumed, the Passional made possible the use of the prayer book by a wider audience.

Finally, there is the 1529 *Geistliche lieder*, which we will examine only briefly at this juncture. Its unique contribution to this *trifecta* of devotional resources was, of course, the inclusion of hymns. Yet, in so many ways it echoed and complemented the contents of the other two volumes. Consider these four examples. First, among the hymns were several that were based on the catechism, a practice that would reach fruition before the end of Luther's life with hymns devoted to each of the chief parts of the catechism. Second, several of the illustrations found in the Passional were also included in the hymnal, linked to particular hymns in the church year. Thus, viewing the image in the prayer book of Jesus's triumphal entry into Jerusalem might easily call to mind that same image in the hymnal, where it appears next to the very first hymn, *Nun komm, der Heiden Heiland*, the hymn for the first Sunday in Advent when the Gospel reading is the account of the triumphal entry. Third, it was not only the prayer book

---

14. LW 43:17–24. An attempt to carry forward this concrete unpacking of the commandments can be found in the development of *Lutheran Service Book* (LSB 2006), where a series of questions on each of the commandments, in the manner of a *Beichtspiegel* (confessional mirror), was intended in connection with the rite of Individual Confession and Absolution. Delays prevented its inclusion in the hymnal, though it was subsequently included in the *Lutheran Service Book: Pastoral Care Companion* (St. Louis: Concordia, 2007), 657–663.
15. Luther's introduction to the Passional, together with descriptions of each illustration and the related biblical passages, are found at LW 43:42–45; see also the facsimile ed. Frieder Schulz, *Martin Luther. Ein Betbüchlein mit Kalender und Passional Wittenberg 1529* (Kassel: Stauda, 1982). The *Geistliche lieder* of 1533 (and presumably the no longer extant first edition of 1529) is physically the same in size and format as the 1529 *Betbüchlein*.

that contained prayers—so did the hymnal, with a number of seasonal collects appearing with the corresponding hymns for those seasons.[16] In addition, several of the liturgical hymns, such as the Te Deum and the Litany, had multiple prayers attached.[17] Fourth, the prayer book contained a selection of psalms just as did the hymnal, where psalms account for 20 percent of the entries, appearing in both metrical paraphrase and, in two cases, as prose texts set to chant (see Table 3.1).

What all three resources demonstrate with amazing clarity is the pastoral concern that guided Luther's reforming efforts. While erudite treatises like *The Bondage of the Will* or the *Great Confession* of 1528 and other writings against the Sacramentarians were part and parcel of Luther's output as a "Doctor of the Church," he instinctively knew that such inquiries would accomplish little if the essentials of the faith were not imbedded in the hearts of the people. The ancient maxim *lex orandi lex credendi* was clearly operative in Luther's work as he provided a variety of resources that would positively shape the beliefs of the faithful, not only in the early days of the Reformation but to the present.[18]

GEISTLICHE LIEDER (1529)

The preceding background on the various publications prepared by Luther in 1529 provides the essential context for examining the early Lutheran hymnals. Turning our attention now to the *Geistliche lieder*, published by Wittenberg printer Joseph Klug in 1529, the uniqueness of this hymnal becomes evident not only from the perspective of the advancements it made when compared to previous collections of hymns but also in regard to the influence it exerted on the design of hymnals in the years and centuries that followed.

Because there is no extant copy of the 1529 edition, a reconstruction of its contents requires significant investigation, something well beyond the scope of this modest examination.[19] Our primary source is the 1533

---

16. Because an extant copy of the 1529 hymnal does not exist, there is not complete certainty that the seasonal collects were included in the 1529 edition; see Jenny, "Luthers Gesangbuch," 315–316.
17. One should note also the catechism's inclusion of daily prayers for morning and evening, as well as those both before and after meals.
18. See Jenny, "Luthers Gesangbuch," 320–321, where he points out the irony that Luther, though never a pastor, produced immensely pastoral resources, while reformers like Zwingli and Calvin, who actually were pastors, did not.
19. Markus Jenny provides the most extensive effort toward this goal; see "Luthers Gesangbuch," 303–307. For helpful summaries of the evidence, see Robin A. Leaver, *The Whole Church Sings:*

Table 3.1 Summary of Relationships between Prayerbook, Catechism, and Hymnal.

Category	Prayerbook	Catechism	Geistliche lieder
Catechism	Lists of how the commandments are broken and kept; phrase-by-phrase explanation of the Creed; sermons on the sacraments	Pithy explanations of the six chief parts that were in embryonic form in the *Deutsche Messe*	Hymns on several of the chief parts that presented the teachings in rhymed verse
Resources for the service	Eight prose psalms	Rites for confession, baptism, and marriage; brief order for morning and evening prayer; German Litany	German Sanctus; German Te Deum; German and Latin Litany; metrical and prose psalms; four-part settings of Biblical canticles
Prayers	Evangelical translation of the Hail Mary	Morning and evening, mealtime	Prayers covering the church year; prayers attached to the Litany and Te Deum
Church year	Calendar with Latin verses highlighting events in the church year	—	Ten hymns grouped together covering the church year
Illustrations	Passional (50 woodcuts) depicting salvation history	Illustrations interspersed with explanations of the first three parts	Woodcuts scattered throughout the hymns

edition, which is not only extant but also available in a facsimile edition published in 1954.[20] A letter late in 1529 from Georg Rörer, Luther's trusted assistant who oversaw his publications, suggests that a second, expanded edition appeared already in the same year. Further changes,

---

Congregational Singing in Luther's Wittenberg (Grand Rapids, MI: Eerdmans, 2017), 151–154, and also Robin A. Leaver, *Luther's Liturgical Music: Principles and Implications* (Minneapolis: Fortress Press, 2017), 247–249.

20. *Das Klug'sch Gesangbuch 1533 nach dem einzigen erhaltenen Exemplar der Lutherhall zu Wittenberg*, ed. Konrad Ameln (Kassel Bärenreiter, 1954).

minor in nature, likely crept into the 1533 edition. For purposes of this study, the 1533 edition will serve admirably to demonstrate Luther's goals, all of which were largely achieved in the 1529 edition.

There is abundant evidence of Luther's hand in the design of this hymnal. These include, in no particular order: (1) the publication of the hymnal just months apart from the prayer book and catechism as described above; (2) Luther's coat of arms included on the title page; (3) the first three sections of hymns all coming from Luther's pen; (4) a section devoted to hymns on, or pertaining to, the catechism; and (5) a new preface by Luther that is referenced internally within the hymnal.[21] An examination of the last three of these points will suffice to demonstrate Luther's own hand in the development of a vibrant piety among the faithful in Wittenberg.

Turning to the last point first, the 1529 hymnal contained two prefaces, both by Luther. The first initially appeared in Johann Walter's 1524 *Geystlicher gesangk Buchleyn*, the so-called *Chorgesangbuch*. In contrast to the general discussion in that earlier preface about the importance of hymnody, Luther's "New Preface," which appeared for the first time in 1529,[22] deals primarily with matters of hymnal publication and, in particular, editorial decisions. Especially revealing is the similarity of language that the preface shares with the heading that precedes the fifteen hymns written by other authors, grouped in their own section toward the end of the hymnal:

Luther's New Preface:

I have placed other hymns which we think are good and the most useful in the second section.[23]

Section Heading:

There are others who have made contemporary spiritual songs. . . . I have not included them all in our hymn booklet, but have selected the best; they follow here.[24]

---

21. Jenny, "Luthers Gesangbuch," 303–309; see also AWA 4, 37–38.
22. In the American Edition of *Luther's Works*, Ulrich Leupold carries forward an opposing opinion of Wilhelm Lucke that this New Preface first appeared in a 1528 hymnal published in Wittenberg by Hans Weiss; see Jenny, "Luthers Gesangbuch," 304, for his reasons rejecting this opinion.
23. LW 53:318; see also Jenny, AWA 4:31.
24. *Geistliche Lieder* (1529), fol. 94^{r-v}; translation from Robin A. Leaver, *"Goostly Psalmes and Spirituall Songes": English and Dutch Metrical Psalms from Coverdale to Utenhove 1535–1566* (Oxford: Clarendon, 1987), 284.

No one disputes Luther's authorship of the preface; that it corresponds so closely to the introduction to this group of hymns is strong evidence of Luther's direct hand in the entire production.

It is the intentional placement of the hymns into distinct groupings that provides unique insights into Luther's goals for this seminal hymnal. A comparison with earlier collections of hymns dating from 1524 reveals that they were just that: collections. This description is not meant to disparage these earlier collections in any way. Given the rapidly changing efforts at reform that characterized the 1520s, spurred on, no doubt, by the appearance of Luther's *Formula Missae* at the end of 1523 and Luther's call for "evangelical hymns,"[25] the need for a collection—any collection—of hymns was urgent.

Nearly all these earliest collections of hymns trace their organization back to Walter's *Gesangbuch*.[26] Published in 1524, this collection of thirty-two hymns, twenty-four of them from Luther's own pen, were arranged in no apparent order.[27] The initial publication appeared in five partbooks for choir. Already in 1525 and the years following, several editions for the laity appeared, with the hymns appearing in the same random order. Prior to the publication of the *Geistliche lieder*, and for a long time after in other places, hymnals seldom displayed any intentional organization of the hymns.[28]

In contrast, the 1529 *Geistliche Lieder* displays a remarkable degree of intentional organization. According to Luther's New Preface, the impetus for this reorganization appears in part to be motivated by the "wild west" state of printing in the early years of the Reformation, where printers were naturally on the lookout for anything that might sell. The use of Luther's name to sell all sorts of texts forced him to risk the appearance of "vainglory" (*umb rhumes willen vermidden*) so that authorship might be properly attributed.[29] That explains the initial organization of the hymns,

---

25. LW 53:36–7.
26. The following discussion is based on a summary by Leaver, *"Goostly Psalmes and Spirituall Songes,"* 6–9. See also Chapter 2 where Leaver explores the possibility that Walter relied on a Wittenberg source for his repertory of the hymns.
27. For example, hymns for the church year appear randomly at numbers 1, 2, 9/10/11, 20, 21, 22, 29, 31, 32, 33. Similarly, Luther's paraphrases of psalms are scattered at numbers 4, 8, 12, 26, 28, and 30.
28. See, for example, the Leipzig *Enchiridion* of 1530 and the Madgeburg *Enchiridion* of 1536, both of which are available in facsimile editions: *Das erste Leipziger Gesangbuch*, ed. Hans Hofmann (Leipzig: Spamerschen Druckerei, 1914) and *Enchridion Geistliker Leder unde Psalmen, Magdeburg 1536: Introductory Study and Facsimile Edition by Stephen A. Crist* (Scholars Press for Emory University, 1994).
29. LW 53:318.

with three groups of hymns attributed solely to Luther. A closer examination, however, reveals that within these groupings there are pastoral, liturgical, and even theological motives at play.

The first grouping immediately makes plain that Luther has a bigger picture in mind than simply protecting the integrity of his hymns. Ten hymns covering the church year appear in order, beginning with Advent and ending with Trinity Sunday.[30] Woodcuts highlighting five of those seasons are likewise placed in the proper order. With the 1533 edition, eight translations of historic collects for the major seasons of the year appear with the corresponding seasonal hymns and woodcuts.[31] This section, though quite small, left no doubt that this new publication was more than a collection; it was for use by the Church in the church.

The second section, a gathering of hymns on the catechism, stands out as another unique contribution of Luther, perhaps even more so than the intentional grouping of hymns for the church year. Just as the prayerbook and the catechism present the essential teachings of the faith from different perspectives, so do the hymns in this section, though in yet another way, namely, through rhymed verse. There are several striking features in this section. First, Luther makes no attempt to include hymns for every part of the catechism. Just as in the first part, where there are gaps in coverage of the church year, such as no hymn for the passion or ascension, so here Luther resists the attempt to systematize his efforts.[32] It would be over a decade before Luther would get around to writing hymns for the Lord's Prayer and baptism, hymns that would appear in later editions to complete the cycle of catechism hymns.

Second, there are hymns in this section that would appear at first glance not to belong. Unlike the Bapst *Gesangbuch*, where the catechism section essentially includes only hymns on the chief parts of the catechism, the collection of catechism hymns in 1529 must be considered more broadly. For example, following Luther's two hymns on the Ten Commandments, we find the hymn *Mitten wir im Leben sind* (In the very midst of life, LSB 755), Luther's versification of the medieval antiphon *Media vita in morte sumus*. The hymn, which is a confession of the sinner's utter helplessness, perfectly complements the same truth found in the hymns on the commandments. Just as in the final stanza of *Dies sind die heilgen zehn*

---

30. Note that in Walter's *Chorgesangbuch*, these same ten hymns appeared out of order as numbers 20, 21, 22, 27, 9/10/11, 31/32, 33, 2, 1, and 34.
31. One curious feature of the corresponding collects is that there are two that address the Passion of Christ, even though there is no hymn for Lent or Holy Week.
32. Jenny, "Luthers Gesangbuch," 311.

Gebot (These are the Holy Ten Commands, LSB 581), where we make our plea to Christ as our only mediator, so do we make the same plea in *Mitten wir*, appealing in each stanza to the thrice-holy God to have mercy on us sinners.

Other additions to this catechism section are equally intriguing. Consider, for example, the inclusion of *Nun freut euch Christen lieben gmein* (Dear Christians, One and All, Rejoice, LSB 556), which Luther placed immediately after his hymn on the Creed, *Wir glauben all in einen Gott* (We All Believe in One True God, LSB 954). While *Nun freut euch* does not present a tidy creedal summary in the way that *Wir glauben all* does, it explores the inner-trinitarian relationships in a way that *Wir glauben all* does not. There is, for example, an amazing correspondence in the way that the hymn *Nun freut euch* echoes what Luther says in the conclusion to the section on the Creed in the Large Catechism:

> For in all three articles God himself has revealed and opened to us the most profound depths of his fatherly heart and his pure, unutterable love.... For, as explained above, we could never come to recognize the Father's favor and grace were it not for the Lord Christ, who is a mirror of the Father's heart. Part from him we see nothing but an angry and terrible judge. But neither could we know anything of Christ, had it not been revealed by the Holy Spirit.[33]

Note specifically the language of turning a "father's heart" (*vatter hertz*) in stanza four of the hymn and the description of the Son as a "mirror of the father's heart" (Spiegel des väterlichen Herzens) in the Large Catechism.[34]

The last hymn in the catechism section—*Ein neues Lied wir heben an* (A new song we now begin[35])—is an equally intriguing insertion. More of a ballad than a hymn, this entry was Luther's first known attempt at hymn writing, spurred on by the occasion of the martyrdom of two monks in Brussels who remained steadfast in their confession of the teaching of Luther.[36] Its placement at the end of the collection of catechism hymns may have simply been due to the fact that there was no other obvious place

---

33. LC II 64, 65; BC 439–440.
34. Luther's description of the inner-trinitarian relationships, which is found in neither the prayerbook nor the Small Catechism, represents a major advancement in trinitarian teaching precisely because of his easy-to-understand language. It even goes beyond his brief exposition on the Trinity in his 1528 *Confession Concerning Christ's Supper*; see LW 37:365–366; cf. LC II 24.
35. LW 53:211–216,
36. For more on the use of song as a vehicle for disseminating significant news events and on Luther's ballad in particular, see Leaver, *The Whole Church Sings*, 18–20, and 55–64; and chapter 2 in this volume.

within the three groupings of Luther's hymns. Markus Jenny, however, has surmised that its placement here is likely quite intentional as a demonstration that instruction in the Christian faith is not only for the sake of knowledge but, ultimately, for one's personal confession as one's faith is lived out in a hostile world that can sometimes even bring suffering and death to the faithful confessor.[37]

Thus far we have examined two of the three sections of Luther's hymns, neither of which is preceded by a heading.[38] The final section, however, does have a heading:

> Now follow several psalms which have been made into spiritual songs by Dr. Martin Luther.[39]

Included in this section are two somewhat distinct groups of hymns: first, those based on specific psalms and, second, several liturgical pieces. That Luther has brought these together in the same section is not surprising, given that his psalm paraphrases were understandably used liturgically within the service.

It is not an exaggeration to say that the paraphrase of a psalm in hymn form—a metrical paraphrase—originated with Luther.[40] His earliest attempts at hymn writing, very shortly after the composition of his ballad *Ein neues Lied*, were such paraphrases. In his letter toward the end of 1523 to Georg Spalatin, Luther urged the court chaplain to take up the pen and write hymns based on psalms, mentioning that he was sending along an example—which of the six psalm hymns that Luther composed at the end of 1523 and beginning of 1524 is not clear.[41] All six can be found in Johann Walter's 1524 *Chorgesangbuch*. By 1529 there was a seventh hymn to add to the group, *Ein feste Burg ist unser Gott* (A mighty fortress is our God, LSB 656). In contrast to the earlier examples, however, the latter

---

37. Jenny, "Luthers Gesangbuch," 309.
38. While the 1529 hymnal did not have a heading that preceded the catechism hymns, the 1545 Bapst *Gesangbuch* did:

> Now follow spiritual songs in which the Catechism is covered, since we certainly must commend Christian doctrine in every way, by preaching, reading, singing, etc., so that young and unlearned people may be formed by it, and thus in this way it will always remain pure and passed on to our descendants. So may God grant us his grace and his blessing through Jesus Christ. Amen. *Geystliche Lieder mit einer newen vorrhede D. Mart. Luth.* (Leipzig, 1545), preceding hymn XIIII; translation from Leaver, "*Goostly Psalmes and Spirituall Songes*," 283.

39. *Geistliche Lieder*, fol. 38ʳ; translation from Leaver, "*Goostly Psalmes and Spirituall Songes*," 283.
40. Jenny, "Luthers Gesangbuch," 310–311.
41. LW 49:68–70.

was not so much a paraphrase as a hymn based more loosely upon the primary themes of Psalm 46.

It is perhaps noteworthy that Luther never attempted to produce a more systematic corpus of psalm hymns. As the letter to Spalatin suggests, Luther was interested in encouraging others to take up the task, which they did in fact do. Already in the *Geistliche lieder* (1529) Luther could include several other psalm hymns;[42] in subsequent years more translators and authors would step forward.[43] By the beginning of the seventeenth century, a complete metrical paraphrase of the psalter was published by Cornelius Becker, a Lutheran pastor in Leipzig, and subsequently set to music by various musicians, Heinrich Schütz chief among them.[44]

The remaining five items in this section that bring Luther's contributions to a close are liturgical pieces. These include (1) his version of the Sanctus that he prepared for the *Deutsche Messe*, *Jesaia dem Propheten* (Isaiah, mighty seer, LSB 960); (2) *Verleih uns Frieden* (Grant peace, we pray, LSB 778), an adaptation of a medieval prayer for peace; (3) Luther's translation of the Te Deum, *Herr Gott, dich loben wir* (Lord God, thy praise we sing, WS 745); 4) Luther's translation of the Litany, newly prepared in 1529; and (5) the Latin version of the same, likely added in the second printing in 1529 for use by the school boys.[45]

With Luther's hymns and the Latin Litany accounted for, the *Geistliche lieder* continues with hymns written by other hymn writers. The first grouping contains just two metrical psalms with a simple heading that reads, "Now follow other songs of ours."[46] The hymns, *Wo Gott der Herr* (Psalm 124)[47] and *Fröhlich wollen wir* (Psalm 117), were written by Justus Jonas and Johann Agricola, respectively.[48] The phrase "of ours" is a reference to the Wittenberg circle of hymn writers—Jonas, Agricola, and

---

42. In the *Geistliche Lieder* there are paraphrases of Psalm 124 by Justus Jonas (fol. 82^r, erroneously labeled as Psalm 134), Psalm 117 by Johann Agricola (fol. 85^r), Psalm 51 by Erhardt Hegenwalt (fol. 99^v), and Psalm 127 by Johann Kohlrose (fol. 128^r).
43. For example, the 1541 Strasburg hymnal contained fifty-seven hymns, twenty-four of which were metrical psalm hymn paraphrases. A collection from 1537 had included even more psalm hymns. Such a large number of psalm hymns is not surprising, given how Strasburg straddled the Lutheran and Swiss Reformations. John Calvin, a strong proponent of metrical psalmody, resided in Strasburg from 1538 to 1541 and set his own hand to the development of this genre; see Leaver, "*Goostly Psalmes and Spirituall Songes*", 30–31, 40–46.
44. Walter Blankenburg, "Becker, Cornelius," in *The New Grove Dictionary of Music and Musicians*, 20 vols., ed. Stanley Sadie (London: Macmillan, 1980), 2: 337–338.
45. See Luther's comments in the *Deutsche Messe* concerning the retention of Latin at LW 53: 63.
46. *Geistliche Lieder*, fol. 81^v.
47. For an English translation see *Walther's Hymnal: Church Hymnbook* (St. Louis: Concordia, 2012), 351
48. *Geistliche Lieder*, fols. 82^r and 85^r.

Paul Speratus, whose hymns appear later in the collection—who were all present in Wittenberg in the mid-1520s when the burst of hymn-writing activity had first begun.[49]

Two groupings of hymns now follow with substantial explanations concerning their inclusion. The first contains the heading: "Now follow several hymns written by the fathers," followed by Luther's rationale:

> We have included the old hymns, which follow here, to clearly show how certain pious Christians, who have lived before us in the great darkness of false doctrine, nevertheless still witness to all times and peoples how to know Christ aright, and through God's grace remain immovably constant to this decision.[50]

The phrase "by the fathers" (*von den Alten*) must be understood to encompass hymns written from a wide span of time. For example, the Office hymn *Christus qui lux es et dies*, translated by Urbanus Rhegius (1489–1541) as *Christe, der du bist Tag und Licht* (O Christ, who art the Light and Day, LSB 882), is attested as early as the beginning of the sixth century. In contrast, the hymn *Dies ist letieiae*, which appears here in both Latin and German, *Der Tag, der ist so freudenreich* (Hail the day so rich in cheer, TLH 102), was of more recent origin—the thirteenth century. The two other entries included the macaronic hymn *In dulci jubilo* (Now sing we, now rejoice, LSB 386), and *Christ ist erstanden* (Christ is arisen, LSB 459). The latter was, in a sense, already represented in the 1524 *Chorgesangbuch* as the inspiration for Luther's Easter hymn *Christ lag in Todes Banden* (Christ Jesus lay in death's strong bands, LSB 458). Here it now appears in its own right.

In reality, this small grouping of hymns reflects the sources of many of Luther's own hymns that appear earlier in the hymnal. His recognition that "certain pious Christians" in the past were able to "witness ... how to know Christ aright" led him to draw upon the rich storehouse of earlier hymns. Thus, in the *Geistliche lieder* we find Luther's translations and "improvements" of hymns from the Latin tradition (e.g., *Nun komm, der Heiden Heiland*; *Christum wir sollen*; *Komm, Gott Schöpfer*) as well as numerous hymns from medieval sources that he frequently improved and enlarged (e.g., *Nun bitten wir*; *Gelobet seist du*; *Gott, der Vater, wohn uns bei*).

---

49. Leaver, *The Whole Church Sings*, 137–138. In later editions of the *Geistliche Lieder*, certainly by 1543, Agricola's hymns were removed, likely an acknowledgement of his falling out of favor with Luther as a result of the Antinomian controversy.
50. *Geistliche Lieder*, fol. 86ʳᵛ; translation from Leaver, *"Goostly Psalmes and Spirituall Songes,"* 284.

Unquestionably, Luther held a fond appreciation for those in previous centuries who had written hymns that faithfully expressed the truths of the Scriptures. As Markus Jenny so diplomatically puts it, Luther proceeded "more prudently" than other reformers who were all too eager to reject hymns and chants that had been handed down from earlier times.[51] When one takes into account the various sources that lay behind many of the hymns in the *Geistliche lieder*—psalms and other biblical texts, early and medieval Latin hymns, German *Leisen*—well over half of the contents of this first hymnal draw in one way or another directly from the Scriptures and the tradition.

The next grouping of hymns comprises more recently written hymns by various authors who were sympathetic to the Reformation. The introduction to this section reads:

> There are others who have made contemporary spiritual songs. However, since they are very numerous and in the greater part not especially good, I have not included them all in our hymn booklet, but have selected the best; they follow here. But in order to inform you of my motives in this, there is the New Preface above.[52]

This section makes plain what Luther had voiced in the opening words in his New Preface, namely, that some hymn writers had actually surpassed him. One notes here a certain level of discernment that Luther also voiced in the preface, even though he provides no particulars, saying only that he has selected "the best." One can, however, begin to intuit that discernment process by noting what was not included—namely, seven of the hymns that had appeared in the 1526 Wittenberg *Enchyridion* that Luther did not carry over into the *Geistliche lieder*. These include two hymns each by Hans Sachs, Johann Agricola, and Michael Stifel, as well as an anonymous paraphrase of the Lord's Prayer. Given that both Sachs and Agricola are represented by one hymn each that were included, the reason for the other omissions cannot necessarily be a personal one. Other criteria were at play, though Luther does not explicitly provide them.[53]

The fifteen hymns in this section represent a wide range of early Lutheran hymn writers. The first hymn, which stands out because of its heading: "A fine Christian hymn," is none other than Paul Speratus's

---

51. Jenny, "Luthers Gesangbuch," 309–310.
52. *Geistliche Lieder*, fol. 94ʳ; translation from Leaver, *"Goostly Psalmes and Spirituall Songes,"* 284.
53. Leaver, *The Whole Church Sings*, 155–157, where Leaver carefully traces these omissions and explores some possible reasons for their exclusions.

tour de force summary of the Reformation teaching, *Es ist das Heil uns kommen her* (Salvation unto us has come, LSB 555). The two other hymns of Speratus that had also appeared in the very first hymn collection, the 1524 *Achtliederbuch*, also appear here: *Hilf Gott, wie ist der Menschen Not* and *In Gott gelaub ich, daß er hat*. Other familiar names represented in this grouping of contemporary hymn writers include Hans Sachs, the famed Meistersinger of Nuremberg; Lazarus Spengler, also of Nuremberg, who as town clerk played a significant role in promoting the Reformation in that imperial city; Elizabeth Cruciger, the wife of Luther's colleague Caspar Cruciger; and another hymn by Johann Agricola, *Ich ruf zu dir, Herr Jesu Christ*. One important hymn, its origin unknown, is *O Herre Gott, dein Göttlich Wort* (O Lord, our God, thy holy Word, TLH 266), a hymn that would become associated with celebrations of the Reformation long before "A Mighty Fortress."[54] Lastly, several hymns present in this section originated from a small group of German nobility who supported the Reformation.[55] All in all, this section represented a nascent Lutheran hymn-writing tradition that would blossom in the coming generations.

The final section in the *Geistliche lieder* consisted not of hymns but liturgical chants drawn from both the Old and New Testaments. Luther's most extensive explanation is reserved for this section, which represented a considerable advancement beyond the collections of hymns published prior to 1529:

> In this booklet we have also taken—as good examples—the sacred songs of Holy Scripture, which the dear patriarchs and prophets made and sang. Thus we are not now as new masters contemplating this work but are following the example of all the saints before us. So each Christian will affirm, without great pains, how they—as we do likewise—praise only the grace of God and not the works of men. One may despise these hymns and us, but cannot condemn them along with us.
>
> But above all, we have desired to sing these songs or psalms with sobriety and devotion, with heart and mind, and not as in religious foundations and monasteries, where still today, with great abuse and idolatry, one bleats and roars without knowledge, understanding and trouble, instead of singing with devotion and profit, and thus God is angered rather than pleased.[56]

---

54. Leaver, *The Whole Church Sings*, 111n37.
55. Leaver, *The Whole Church Sings*, 158
56. *Geistliche Lieder*, fols. 132ᵛ, 133ʳ; translation from Leaver, "*Goostly Psalmes and Spirituall Songes*," 284.

The 1526 *Enchyridion* had included, along with several psalms, the traditional canticles for Vespers, Compline, and Matins—namely, the Magnificat, Nunc Dimittis, Te Deum, and Benedictus. These canticles are retained in the *Geistliche lieder*, though the Te Deum is placed earlier in the book together with other compositions of Luther.

Luther's more significant addition to the *Geistliche lieder*, however, was the group of eleven canticles from the Old Testament, many of which were assigned in the monastic tradition to the weekdays at Matins. As Luther intimates in the explanation that heads this section, his strong condemnation of monastic abuses since the early days of the Reformation did not apply to these magnificent canticles, hence his desire that they be sung "with sobriety and devotion." To facilitate such a salutary use of these canticles, brief explanations appear before each canticle. All indications are that it was Luther's amanuensis, Georg Rörer, who authored them, though some show the clear influence of Luther, such as the introduction to the Magnificat where significant themes from Luther's 1522 commentary on the same are evident.[57]

LATER EDITIONS DURING LUTHER'S LIFETIME

Editions of the 1529 *Geistliche lieder* occurred at various intervals during Luther's lifetime, culminating in the exquisitely produced 1545 *Geystliche lieder*, the so-called Bapst *Gesangbuch*. The ordering of materials shifted somewhat in these later editions. Not surprisingly, new hymns also appeared. Luther, for example, completed his catechism series with two additions: *Vater unser im Himmelreich* (Our Father, who from heaven above, LSB 766) and *Christ, unser Herr, zum Jordan kam* (To Jordan came the Christ, our Lord, LSB 406).[58]

The 1545 Bapst *Gesangbuch* was the last hymnal to which Luther made a contribution, authoring yet another preface that was, in effect, his last word on the role of congregational singing. Turning to Psalm 96, Luther ponders the "new song" that Christians are so eager to sing about:

> For God has cheered our hearts and minds through his dear Son, whom he gave for us to redeem us from sin, death, and the devil. He who believes

---

57. Leaver, *Luther's Liturgical Music*, 264–74, where Leaver provides translations of each summary. See also Leaver's description of the musical settings of these canticles, which consisted of plain Gregorian tones in the first printing and then four-part faburden settings in the second printing at the end of 1529; Leaver, *Luther's Liturgical Music*, 261–264.
58. See Leaver, *The Whole Church Sings*, 161, for a complete list of the hymns Luther wrote after 1529 that would eventually appear in the 1545 Bapst *Gesangbuch*.

this earnestly cannot be quiet about it. But he must gladly and willingly sing and speak about it so that others also may come and hear it.[59]

Luther expressed great pleasure in the finished product, one that went far beyond earlier hymnals. Printed in a larger size, the volume boasted a new and much larger collection of exquisite woodcuts. In addition, every page contained decorative borders that could not help but capture the attention of anyone who opened the book. Just as Luther had commended the use of the arts in his 1524 preface to the *Chorgesangbuch*, so could he in his last preface write, "printers do well if they publish a lot of good hymns and make them attractive to the people with all sorts of ornamentations, so that they may move them to joy in faith and to gladly sing."[60]

The Bapst *Gesangbuch* still exhibits the general structure of the 1529 *Geistliche lieder*, though with some notable adaptations. Several hymns are added to the first section, which covers the church year. As noted earlier, the catechism hymns are now prefaced with an explanation but reduced in number just to those that are based on the chief parts of the catechism. The section of hymns from preceding centuries includes several additions that appear only in Latin, such as *Resonet in laudibus* (No. 53) and *Nunc angelorum gloria* (No. 54), as well as *Puer natus in Bethlehem*, which interleafs the German text (*Ein Kind geboren zu Bethlehem*) with the Latin.

A few additional liturgical hymns and chants appear in 1545, namely, a chant version of the Kyrie (No. 60) and a metrical paraphrase of the Gloria in Excelsis (No. 61). They are separated considerably from the German Sanctus (No. 29). No setting of the Agnus Dei is provided, though options were certainly available by this point.[61]

The most notable addition in 1545 was a section of hymns and chants for funerals, drawn nearly verbatim from a 1542 publication of the same.[62] An extended preface by Luther lays out the reformer's understanding of the purpose of the church's burial rites:

> For it is meet and right that we should conduct these funerals with proper decorum in order to honor and praise that joyous article of our faith, namely, the resurrection of the dead, and in order to defy Death, that terrible foe who so shamefully and in so many horrible ways goes on to devour us.[63]

---

59. LW 53:333.
60. LW 53:316, 333.
61. Indeed, options would have already been available for inclusion in 1529; see Jenny, "Luthers Gesangbuch," 311.
62. LW 53:325–331.
63. LW 53:326.

A magnificent woodcut depicting the Last Day closes out both this section and the entire first part of the hymnal.

A second part follows with an additional forty hymns. The purpose of this second part is not entirely clear. Given that the printer, Valentin Bapst, was based in Leipzig, it is possible that he included this separate collection of hymns by contemporary writers for the churches in that city, though this does not fully explain the choice of hymns. Whether Luther even saw this second part is doubtful.[64]

* * *

The uncertainty concerning the origin and purpose of that second part of the Bapst *Gesangbuch*—an *Anhang*, so to speak—serves as a fitting entrée into remaining chapters in this book. The evidence is clear that during Luther's lifetime he took a very active role in shaping the Wittenberg hymnal tradition. While the extravagantly produced Bapst *Gesangbuch* often catches one's eye, as well it should, by all accounts Luther was not actively involved in its formation, despite its inclusion of his newest and last hymnal preface. His groundbreaking contribution in shaping the 1529 *Geistliche Lieder* and its subsequent editions (1533, 1535, 1543), however, set the stage for all subsequent Lutheran hymnals, including the Bapst *Gesangbuch*.

Luther's call for others to take up the pen and write good hymns was answered already in his lifetime, with more hymns and hymnal editions appearing than he would have thought possible when he wrote his first hymns in 1523. The outpouring of hymns in the coming generations—even down to the present day—would have been beyond his wildest imagination.[65] Never could he have anticipated, for example, a complete metrical psalter in both French and English just four decades later that emulated his own initial attempt at casting psalms in hymn form. And neither could he have foreseen the voluminous translations of hymns into English in the nineteenth century, even his own hymns—a practice of respecting the tradition that he pioneered when he made translations of ancient Latin hymns and medieval religious folk songs.

64. Konrad Ameln, the editor of the facsimile edition, notes that six of the hymns included in the second part had been removed from the last edition of Klug's *Geistliche lieder* in 1543, presumably at Luther's direction. In addition, several of the other hymn writers had connections with those in the Schwenkfeld and Anabaptist traditions. Konrad Ameln, *Das Babstsche Gesangbuch von 1545* (Kassel: Bärenreiter, 1966), 13–14.
65. See Brown, *Devotional Life in Hymns, Liturgy, Music, and Prayer*, 233–234, where he provides data concerning the nearly two thousand hymnals—the vast majority of them Lutheran—that were published by the year 1600.

With that plethora of religious song came the necessity of judging the suitability and value of each hymn. Like Luther, every hymnal editor or committee has experienced the challenge of discerning which hymns to include and which to reject. While the criteria have varied somewhat over the centuries, the starting point for Luther and his theological heirs is the one that he voiced already in his 1524 preface of the first significant collection of hymns, namely, that "we should know nothing to sing or say, save Jesus Christ our Savior."[66]

---

66. LW 53:316.

4.

The Cantional Tradition

Markus Rathey

Ever since the beginning of Lutheran hymnody in the 1520s, hymns were not only transmitted as simple melodies but also in settings for four or more voices. In addition to complex chorale motets, the melodies often appeared in simple, homophonic settings. As was common in settings of songs in the decades around 1500, the melodies were mostly sung by the tenor, while the other voices provided a simple counterpoint. The texture followed the same stylistic form as the *Tenorlied* (tenor song) in secular music.[1]

TENORLIED

The aesthetic beauty of the hymn setting with tenor cantus firmus was bought at a price: the hymn tune was surrounded by the other voices, and unless the tenor voice was reinforced by additional singers or instruments, it could be difficult to hear. Cantors in the sixteenth century noticed soon that the *Tenorlied* was not ideal for the accompaniment of congregational singing.

In the middle of the sixteenth century, a shift took place in the realm of song settings. The *Tenorlied* was replaced by secular song forms that featured the main voice in the discant (or soprano), such as the Italian

---

1. For a comprehensive discussion of the German *Tenorlied*, see N. Böker-Heil, H. Heckmann, and I. Kindermann, eds., *Das Tenorlied. Mehrstimmige Lieder in deutschen Quellen 1450–1580*, 3 vols. (Kassel: Bärenreiter, 1979–1986); see also Franzpeter Messmer, *Altdeutsche Liedkomposition. Der Kantionalsatz und die Tradition der Einheit von Singen und Dichten* (Tutzing: Schneider, 1984).

frottola, the early madrigal, and the French *chanson*. While this transition first took place within secular song repertoires, it soon influenced sacred music as well.[2] The first traces of this shift can be seen in the Reformed tradition, especially in the settings of the *Genevan Psalter*. While Calvin had originally prohibited the use of polyphonic settings within the Reformed liturgy, the Genevan melodies were soon set as motets and simple homophonic settings to be used at home and outside of the liturgy. The French composer Loys Bourgeois (1510–1559) not only contributed many melodies to the psalter, but he also set the melodies in *contrapunctus simplex* with the melody in the upper voice. His first publication of hymns appeared in Lyons in 1547 and an expanded edition followed in 1554.[3] The settings by Bourgeois served as a model for other composers in France, Switzerland, and Germany, such as Johannes Heugel and Siegmund Hemmel.[4]

The homophonic setting with the melody in the upper voice became common in metrical psalters, even before this texture was adapted for settings of other hymns. It remained the norm into the seventeenth century, as can be seen in the *Becker Psalter* by Heinrich Schütz, which closely follows the model of Bourgeois.[5]

OSIANDER AND THE EARLY YEARS OF THE CANTIONAL

What had become a convention in metrical psalters was soon adopted in settings of hymns. The first composer to do so on a larger scale was Lucas Osiander (1534–1604), a theologian and composer, and son of the Lutheran theologian and Reformer Andreas Osiander. Lucas Osiander's *Fünfzig Geistliche Lieder und Psalmen* (1586) (see Figure 4.1) stands at the beginning of the *cantionalsatz* tradition and influenced the setting of Lutheran hymns for the next centuries. Osiander's goal was the creation of a hymn collection that allowed the congregation to sing together with the choir. While he appreciates (and even defends) polyphonic singing and Latin

---

2. See Édith Weber, "'Nota contra Notam' et ses incidences sur le Choral Luthérien et sur le Psautier Huguenot," JbLH 32 (1989): 73–93.
3. *Pseaulmes de David... à voix de contrepoinct égal consonante au verbe* (Lyon 1547) and *Pseaulmes LXXXIII de David* (Lyon 1554).
4. Cf. Michael Zywietz, "Osiander, Lucas," in: *MGG Online*, ed. by Laurenz Lütteken (New York, Kassel, Stuttgart, 2016ff.), https://www-mgg-online-com.yale.idm.oclc.org/mgg/stable/51326
5. Heinrich Schütz, *Psalmen Davids Hiebevorn in Teutzsche Reimen gebracht durch D. Cornelium Beckern Vnd an jetzo Mit Einhundert vnd Drey eigenen Melodeyen darunter Zwey vnd Neuntzig Newe vnd Eylff Alte Nach gemeiner Contrapuncts art in 4. Stimmen gestellet...* [op. 5] (Freiberg 1628).

motets, his preface for the *Fünfzig Gesänge* advocates for hymns in the vernacular that allow the congregation to participate and to understand the words of the text:

> Jedoch / ob man gleich die Melodi vnnd den Text versteht / so kan doch ein Ley / so der Figural Music nicht berichtet / nicht mit singen / sondern muß allein zuhören. (sig. A iij^r) (However, even if one understands the melody and the text, a lay person, who has not been instructed in figural music, will not be able to sing [with the choir] and can only listen.)[6]

Osiander's pastoral concerns to allow the congregants full participation (both musically and intellectually) led him to the composition of hymn settings that made it easier for the congregation to sing together with the choir. Osiander explains in his preface:

> Derwegen ich vor diser zeit nachgedenckens gehabt/ wie bey einer Christlichen Gemein ein solche Music anzurichten were / da gleichwohl vier stimmen zusammen giengen / vnd dannoch ein jeder Christ wol mit singen köndte. Hab deswegen / als zur prob (in denen stunden / da ich sonsten von andern wichtigern geschefften müd gewesen) diese fünffzig geistliche Lieder vnnd Psalmen mit vier Stimmen also gesetzt / das eine gantze Christliche Gemein / auch junge Kinder mit singen können / vnnd dennoch dise Music daneben (zur zierde des Gesangs) iren fortgang hat: Wie auch mit der zeit andere dergleichen mehr Compositiones (welche ich allbereit vnterhanden) erfolgen mögen. Vnd bin der tröstlichen zuuersicht / das durch solche mein ringfüge arbeit / das Christlich allgemein gesang in der Kirchen nicht allein nicht gehindert / sondern auch die guthertzige Christen / durch solche liebliche Melodeien noch mehr zum Psalmen singen angereitzt werden sollen. (sig. A iij^r) (Therefore, I have been thinking for a while, how a [form of] music for the Christian congregation could be devised in which four voices sing together but that would still allow every Christian to join in. I have, therefore, as an experiment (during those hours during which I was too tired for my other obligations), set these fifty sacred hymns and psalms for four voices. [I have set them] in a way that the whole congregation, and even young children, can join in. At the same time, I have made sure that the [correct harmonic] progression of the music was observed (as well as the beauty of the singing). In the future, I will publish more compositions of this kind (which I have already written). And I am confident that my small contribution will not only not be an obstacle to the Christian singing of the church but that Christians with a good heart will be inspired by these pleasant melodies to sing the psalms even more.)

---

6. All translations, unless stated otherwise, are my own.

Figure 4.1 Lucas Osiander *Fünfzig Geistliche Lieder und Psalmen* (1586), title page.

It was not the first time that Osiander had emphasized accessibility as an important criterion for sacred music. Already two decades earlier he had contributed a preface for Sigmund Hemmel's metrical psalter, *Der gantze Psalter Davids, wie derselbig in teutsche Gesang verfasset* (1569).[7] Hemmel's settings are simple and homophonic, and the German texts aligned with Osiander's wish to have sacred music that was accessible to the congregation. Osiander's involvement in the publication of Hemmel's psalter also highlights the direct connection between the homophonic psalter in the Reformed tradition and Osiander's newly created *cantionalsatz*.

In the preface for his *Fünfzig Geistliche Lieder und Psalmen*, Osiander concedes that he had to take some contrapuntal liberties in order to make the settings work as intended. The focus for Osiander is on the discant (with the melody) and the bass (as the harmonic foundation). The intervallic progression in the other voices is handled more freely.

---

7. Already Walter Blankenburg had suggested that Hemmel's psalter might have been a model for Osiander; see Blankenburg, "Osiander, Lucas," in *Grove Music Online*, https://doiorg.yale.idm.oclc.org/10.1093/gmo/9781561592630.article.20527.

THE CANTIONAL TRADITION   89

Osiander explains: "Daher vnterweilens die Interualla im Alt vnnd Tenor etwas vngewönlicher werden." (sig. A iiij^r) (Therefore, the intervals in the alto and tenor can be somewhat uncommon.) Practicality is the primary goal: "Wiewol ich mich beflissen / dieselbige also zu machen / daß sie die Knaben leichtlich lernen mögen." (sig. A iiij^r) (However, I have written the settings in a way that the boys [of the choir] can easily learn them.). Example 4.1 shows an example from Osiander's *Cantional*. The voice leading of the middle voices of Luther's setting of the Lord's Prayer, "Unser Vater im Himmelreich" lacks organic flow. Noteworthy is also the beginning in unison, which gives the setting a particularly archaic character.

Osiander's settings reflect the general shift within sixteenth-century composition from a horizontally oriented counterpoint to a vertical concept of harmony that relies on the bass as the foundation. It is doubtful that Osiander was aware of this major change in compositional theory and practice, but his *Cantional* has, nevertheless, contributed to the establishment of the new understanding of harmony in a significant way. Harmonically, the settings are rather simple, and Walter Blankenburg has commented that they were of "slight musical value."[8] And yet, their historical significance rests in their model character, which influenced the following decades and even centuries.

Osiander compiled the *Cantional* in his capacity as court preacher in Stuttgart and it was intended for the schools and churches in the territory of Württemberg. The book was printed outside the country in the Frankonian city of Nuremberg, one of the centers of music publishing at the time. Osiander's collection is not a complete hymnal, but rather it compiles fifty songs of the Lutheran core repertoire, which were either by Luther himself or the early Lutheran tradition.

Osiander's *Cantional* was followed by several other composers who used the same texture. For some, Osiander served as a direct model; in other cases, the composers might have come to a similar conclusion without Osiander's direct inspiration. Among the earliest examples are the settings by Andreas Raselius (1562–1602). In 1586, the year of Osiander's publication, the city of Regensburg commissioned Raselius to furnish settings of the hymns that were commonly used in the city.[9] The commission explicitly asked for settings that would allow the congregation to sing together with the choir. Raselius completed his

---

8. See previous note.
9. For Raselius's activity in Regensburg, see Fabian Weber, *Protestantische Kirchenmusik in Regensburg 1542–1631: Aspekte des Repertoires vor dem Hintergrund von Stadtgeschichte, Kantorat und Gottesdienst im ersten Reformationsjahrhundert* (Regensburg: ConBrio, 2020), 104–114.

Example 4.1 Lucas Osiander *Fünfzig Geistliche Lieder und Psalmen* (1586), No. XXI. *Unser Vater im Himmelreich.*

first *Cantionale* in 1588. Other than Osiander's work, Raselius'*Cantionale* remained unpublished, and it was only used in a manuscript copy, which is today incomplete.[10] As Weber points out, the twenty-two settings of

---

10. Weber, *Protestantische Kirchenmusik in Regensburg*, 194.

German hymns that have survived represent the traditional repertoire of Lutheran hymnody.[11]

Like Osiander before him, Raselius's settings are strictly homophonic and almost exclusively for four voices.[12] However, only a part of the settings features the hymn melody in the discant; in some of the compositions, the hymn melody is still sung by the tenor (including core hymns such as *Erhalt uns, Herr, bei deinem Wort* or *Verleih uns Frieden*).

A second manuscript by Raselius, *Psalmen und geistliche Lieder*, was written in 1591 and instead of using score notation, the hymns are now noted in five separate partbooks. While the settings are still simple and homophonic, the number of voices is expanded to five. This gave the composer a greater spectrum of harmonic possibilities. By composing for five voices, Raselius followed the model of other contemporary composers such as Johann Eccard and Bartholomäus Gesius, who also favored five-part harmony in their hymn settings. Raselius also (partly) abandons Osiander's model by assigning the cantus firmus again to the tenor.

While the earlier hymn settings by Raselius had remained in manuscripts, the *Regensburger Kirchen Contrapunct* from 1599 did finally appear in print. The publication relied heavily on the repertoire transmitted in the earlier manuscripts.[13] The chorale melody now appears in the upper voice[14] while the total number of voices fluctuates between four (eleven settings) and five (forty settings). Most of the settings are homophonic but, in some cases, the lower voices show small embellishments.[15] The size of the print (12.8 × 7.2 cm) makes it hardly usable for the choir, so it clearly is a book that was intended for use by the congregation while the choir either continued using the earlier manuscripts or new manuscript copies based on the print.

While the hymn collection had been compiled for Regensburg, it can also be found in music inventories of other cities and churches in the Upper Palatinate in the early seventeenth century.[16] The example of

---

11. Weber, *Protestantische Kirchenmusik in Regensburg*, 196; however, Weber adds that some variants of the melodies might represent local traditions in Regensburg. See also the list of hymns in Weber, 198–200.
12. See the example in Weber, *Protestantische Kirchenmusik in Regensburg*: "Nun freut euch lieben Christen gmein," 197–198.
13. For an overview of the repertoire and its relationship to the earlier manuscripts see Weber, *Protestantische Kirchenmusik in Regensburg*, 212–215.
14. Only the settings of *In dich hab ich gehoffet, Herr* and *Gelobet seitst du, Jesu Christ* have the melody in the tenor.
15. But even in those cases, the interdependence of the lower voices develops within the framework of a homophonic setting, and it does not amount to truly independent voice leading in a polyphonic sense.
16. See Weber, *Protestantische Kirchenmusik in Regensburg*, 209.

Raselius shows the complexity of the *cantionalsatz* genre in the early years of its inception. Some of the settings by Raselius increase the number of voices, present melody in the tenor, and occasionally afford the voices a greater degree of independence than Osiander had envisioned. On the other hand, the first printed collection of cantional settings by Raselus again conforms to Osiander's focus on the congregation and on the ability for follow the singing of the choir.

Contemporaneously with Raselius's efforts to create cantional settings for Regensburg, other Lutheran composers likewise wrote simple hymn settings in the tradition of Osiander. In 1593, Rogier Michael (1554–1619) edited the Dresden hymnal, *Der Gebreuchlichsten vnd vornembsten Gesenge D. Martin Lutheri,* which presented the hymn tune in the upper voice of a homophonic texture. As the title suggests, the print was not a complete hymnal but again a selection of core hymns that focused on hymns by Luther and from the early Lutheran tradition. Michael's print is not only important as an early example for the cantional tradition, but it also influenced two *Cantionals* that were published in Leipzig. Michael and Osiander served as models for Seth Calvisius's *Kirchengesenge* from 1597. And, even more importantly, Michael was the teacher of composer and cantor Johann Hermann Schein, who would publish one of the most important *Cantionals* of the seventeenth century.

Calvisius was cantor at St. Thomas in Leipzig and his print with one hundred and fifteen four-part settings is one of the most substantive collections of cantional settings from the late sixteenth century. The hymn settings appear in choir-book notation, with each of the four voices printed separately (and not lined up like in a score). Calvisius's settings, while simple, show the hand of a more experienced composer than Osiander and his settings are usually more skillful and harmonically interesting than Osiander's. The setting of Luther's *"Vater unser im Himmelreich"* features middle voices that are more organic and thus easier to sing; also, the harmonic progression shows a clearer direction (see Example 4.2).

Calvisius's preface explains that the use of four-part settings for the school choir had been favored by Martin Luther. What he does not mention, however, is that Luther would have been familiar with tenor *cantus firmi* while Calvisius places the tune in the upper voice. Despite this historical difference, Luther proudly serves as a justification for the texture Calvisius is using in his *Cantional*:

> Es hat aber der H. Lutherus auch dieses für rahtsam vnd notwendig geacht / das solche Kirchengesenge / auch in vier Stimmen gebracht würden / Damit der Jugend / die von Natur zur Musica heneiget / das gute mit lust beygebracht / vnnd durch das Euangelium / wie ander

THE CANTIONAL TRADITION 93

Example 4.2 Seth Calvisius, *Kirchengesenge* (1597), No. XLVI. *Vater unser im Himmelreich.*

gute Künste / also auch die Musica zum dienst dessen der sie gegeben [...] angewendet würde. (preface, 10) (Mr. Luther thought this advisable and necessary that such hymns should be set for four voices, so that the youth, which is inclined to music by nature, can be taught the good with pleasure; and that the gospel can utilize music (just like other good arts) to serve the one who has given it [to us]).

Calvisius's preface highlights another performance convention for the singing of cantional settings. In addition to singing the hymns in four-part harmony, they can also be performed by instruments:

> ... weil eine liebliche schöne Melodey / oder auch die Harmoney / wann die Lieder mit menschlicher stim[m] gesungen oder auff Instrumenten gespielt werden / die gemüter der Menschen vielmehr und krefftiger bewegen vnd zur andacht erwecken: Als wenn die Wort nur blos geredet vnd gehöret werden. (preface, 5) (... since a pleasurable, beautiful melody, or harmony (when a song is sung by human voice or played on instruments) can move the spirit of humans more and more strongly; and it can inspire devotion. [Much more effectively,] than when the word is only spoken or heard.)

We are still decades away from the time when organ accompaniment for congregational singing became a common practice; however, we can see here that an instrumental execution was within the scope of the collection (in this, it was similar to other compositions of the time, such as motets or madrigals, which also often suggested that the pieces could be performed by voices or instruments).[17] Erasmus Widmann (1572–1634) also mentions that the hymn settings in his *Cantional* were not only intended for voices but that an instrumental performance was possible as well.[18]

The genre of the *Cantional* became increasingly popular and other composers followed these early models. Around the turn of the century, we have *Cantionals* by Erasmus Widmann, Melchior Vulpius, and one of the leading Lutheran composers of his generation, Hans Leo Hassler:

> Erasmus Widmann, *Geistliche Psalmen und Lieder, wie sie deß Jars uber auff alle Fest, Sonn unnd Feyertag zu Weickersheim in der Gravenschafft Hohenloe etc. gebraucht werden : Mit vier Stimmen componirt* (Nürnberg 1604).
> Melchior Vulpius, *Kirchen Geseng vnd Geistliche Lieder D. Martini Lutheri vnd anderer frommen Christen, [. . .] im Discant der Choral richtig und eigentlich behalten* (Erfurt 1604).
> Hans Leo Hassler, *Kirchengesäng: Psalmen und geistliche Lieder auff die gemeinen Melodeyen mit vier Stimmen simpliciter gesetzt* (Nürnberg 1608).

---

17. See Stephen Keyl, "Tenorlied, Discantlied, Polyphonic Lied: Voices and Instruments in German Secular Polyphony of the Renaissance," *Early Music* 20 (1992): 434–442.
18. Erasmus Widmann, *Geistliche Psalmen*: "Vocaliter vnd Instrumentaliter zu singen vnnd zu gebrauchen" (3ᵛ).

The *Cantional* by Vulpius can serve as an example for how these composers amalgamated the simple form of the cantional setting with their individual musical styles.

While Vulpius mentions that the settings feature the melody in the discant voice, he does not feel compelled to provide a longer explanation for this practice. The discant texture, which still had been new in hymn settings when Osiander had introduced it two decades earlier, was by now an accepted convention and an explanation (or even justification) was not necessary anymore. As the prefaces by Weimar superintendent Antonius Probus and by Vulpius himself point out, the settings were intended to be used in churches and schools. In other words, they were composed to provide material both for the singing of the boys in school but also for their duties as members of the cantorei in the local church. The didactic purpose is also reflected in Vulpius's decision to include not only four-part settings for soprano, alto, tenor, and bass (SATB) for several hymns; he also added alternate versions, often for equal voices. This allowed school choirs that lacked deeper voices to perform the settings and it also made it possible to alternate between different settings during a performance. In addition to being simply a collection of settings of the most important hymns, the *Cantional* now becomes a repository of material that caters to the needs of the choir—a feature that will become even more important as we come to the second generation of *Cantionals* in the 1620s.

A second feature that distinguishes Vulpius's *Cantional* from his predecessors is the inclusion of not only core hymns from the Lutheran tradition but also more than thirty hymns by Vulpius himself.[19] Noteworthy is Vulpius's interest in contemporary vernacular forms, such as dances. Several of his hymn melodies are influenced by the Italia *balletto*, with which his hymns shared not only the rhythm but also the emphasis on the top voice.[20] Vulpius's *Cantional* was widely received and numerous of his hymns were adopted by other hymn collections. As Vulpius was cantor

---

19. The first edition of his cantional (1604) only included two of his own melodies; that number increased to thirty-one in the second and expanded edition from 1609: Melchior Vulpius, *Ein schön geistlich Gesangbuch Darinnen Kirchen Gesänge vnd geistliche Lieder [. . .] nicht allein auff eine, sondern des mehrentheils auff zwey oder dreyerley Art, mit sonderm Fleiß Contrapuncts Weise gesetzt, im Discant oder Choral richtig behalten, vnd zum Andernmal sehr vermehrt* (Jena 1609).
20. Vulpius was not the first German Lutheran composer to use the Italian *Balletto* as a model for sacred music; Johannes Lindemann's *Amorum filii Dei decades duae* (1594–1598) preceded Vulpius's publication by a decade; however, Lindemann's settings were mostly *contrafacta* of Italian compositions; see Stephen Rose, "Patriotic Purification: Cleansing Italian Secular Vocal Music in Thuringia, 1675–1600," *Early Music History* 35 (2016): 203–260.

in Weimar, he might have influenced Johann Hermann Schein, who was court capellmeister here in 1615/16.

The end of the first generation of Cantionals is marked by the extensive publications of Michael Praetorius. Praetorius, music director at the court in Wolfenbüttel, was one of the most prolific composers in the early decades of the seventeenth century. His theoretical treatises and compositions introduced German musicians to the most recent developments in Italian music, such as the small-scale concerto and the Venetian polychoral style. Praetorius was particularly important for combining these recent styles with settings of German hymns. In several of his printed collections, he also included older settings by Johann Walter and more recent ones by Raselius, reflecting the developments in hymn settings from the Reformation to the later years of the sixteenth century.

In his multi-volume collection *Musae Sioniae* (1605–1610), Praetorius explores the multitude of ways in which hymns can be set effectively. The volumes VI–VIII (published 1609–10) together form a *Cantional* in the classical sense with hymn settings in *contrapunctus simplex* and the melody in the upper voice. But already *Musae Sioniae* V provided performers with simpler hymn settings, ranging from small *bicinia* for two voices to larger (yet still manageable) settings for seven voices. In his preface, Praetorius explains the practical implications. His use of the term *"Cantional"* in this context shows that it was not limited to hymn collections in Osiander's style but rather referred to collections of hymn settings for practical use:

> Dabeneben aber auch betrachtet und angesehen / daß an allen Orten und bey allen Städten / Flecken und Märckten der Christlichen *Religion* verwandten Kirchen vnd Gemeinden / wie gerna manns offtmals auch gewolt / mit so viel Stimmen nicht fort kommen mögen: Habe derowegen Ich mir die Mühe nicht wollen verdriessen lassen / Auch ein *Cantional,* so gut es der liebe Gott verliehen / auff 2.3.4.5.6.7. Stimmen / für deroselben Chor und Kirchen zu vorfertigen. (preface, unpaginated) ([I have] also taken into account that the Christian churches and congregations in all places and cities, in hamlets and villages do not have enough voices [to execute the larger-scale compositions] even if this is desired: Therefore, I have made an effort, as good as God allowed me to do so, to compose a *Cantional* as well, for 2, 3, 4, 5, 6, 7, voices, for the choirs and churches.)

Noteworthy in this context is also Praetorius's later collection *Urania* (1613). The composer takes hymn settings in *contrapunctus simplex* and divides the lines among several choruses, so that a polychoral dialogue ensues. Praetorius shows how the simple cantional setting can be expanded onto a Venetian-style concerto. This spatial and sonic expansion, however, remains within the original scope of Osiander's *Cantional*; the resulting compositions are still intended to be sung together with the congregation, as Praetorius's title page for *Urania* announces:

> Auff 2. 3. vnd 4. Choren zu gebrauchen / ganz schlecht vnd einfeltig gesetzet / Also daß auch das Gemeine Volck in der Kirchen den *Choral* zugleich mit drein singen kan. Benebenst gnugsamen Bericht vnd Anleitung / wie man alle andere Teudsche Psalmen vnd Kirchen Gesänge (welche sonstn allein mit 4. Stim[m]en *simpliciter componirt* seyn) ohn sonderbahre Mühe vnd mit wenig Knaben / in 2. 3. vnd mehr Chroren in der Kirchen an vnterschiedlichen Orten anordnen vnd gebrauchen könne. (Title page) (To be performed by 2, 3, and 4 choirs, set simply and plainly, so that the common people in the church can sing the chorale melody as well [with the choir]. Also including a report and guide for how to arrange and use all other German Psalms and church hymns (which are usually set in four-part contrapunctus simplex) for 2, 3 and more choirs for churches in different places, without particular effort and with only a small number of choirboys.)

In his performance instructions, Praetorius makes suggestions for how to perform the settings, including using a soloist with organ accompaniment, contrasting instrumental choruses, and spatially separated vocal choruses—all while the congregation keeps singing the hymn tune. To facilitate the participation of the congregants, Praetorius points out that the discant melody should always be sung in a way that it can be heard clearly by the congregation.[21] In addition to his own compositions, Praetorius suggests that other cantional settings could easily be expanded in a similar way and he suggests the collections by Rogier Michael, Seth Calvisius, Melchior Vulpius, and Andreas Raselius.[22]

SCHEIN AND THE SECOND PHASE OF THE CANTIONAL STYLE

Johann Hermann Schein was born in 1586, the year in which Osiander published his *Cantional* and established the cantional setting as one of the main forms of Lutheran church music. Consequently, when Schein began his professional career as a composer, the cantional setting had already been firmly established in the repertoire of Lutheran church music. Throughout his short life, he crossed paths with numerous composers of

---

21. Michael Praetorus, *Urania*, "Praeoccupatio Autoris."
22. Praetorius, *Urania*, preface, X.

Cantionals: Rogier Michael had been his teacher in Dresden, during a short stint in Weimar he worked with Melchior Vulpius, and he had frequently interacted with Michael Praetorius. When Schein became cantor at St. Thomas in Leipzig in 1616, the students of the choir used the *Cantional* by Schein's predecessor Seth Calvisius.

When Schein published his *Cantional* in 1627,[23] he did not have to establish a new genre. Rather, his *Cantional* is characterized by reform and innovation. As Schein laments in the preface for his *Cantional*, a lot of hymnals included many unknown and unused hymns while hymns by Luther and his circle had been omitted, or they had accumulated many mistakes both in text and melody.[24] The expressed goal of Schein's hymnal was to provide corrected versions of these hymns and to restore the body of Reformation-time hymnody while also including newer melodies.[25]

The first edition of Schein's *Cantional* includes 286 individual hymns in 228 settings (see Figure 4.2). Most of these settings were by Schein himself; only thirteen were borrowed from other composers (including three by his predecessor Calvisius).[26] Most of the hymn settings appear in *contrapunctus simplex* for four voices, following the model of Osiander. Schein, an experienced composer, is able to modernize the harmonic language of the settings without sacrificing their simplicity and their function as choral accompaniment for congregational singing.

Schein's setting of "Vater unser im Himmelreich" breaks up the strict homorhythm by introducing a syncopation in mm. 3/4 (see Example 4.3). We can also see more modern understanding of harmony as Schein interprets the melody strictly as being in D minor. While both Osiander and Calvisius had harmonized the beginning of the melody with an A-chord, Schein begins and ends in D.

Another part of this modernization is the inclusion of a figured bass line, which allowed organists (and other instrumentalists) to accompany the singing of the choir without having to resort to transcribing the settings into German organ tablature.[27] As the preface highlights, the figured bass

---

23. *Cantional oder Gesangbuch Augspurgischer Confession* . . . (Leipzig, 1627, enlarged 1645).
24. Schein, *Cantional*, sig. a iij^v.
25. Schein, *Cantional*, sig. a iij^r.
26. See the discussion of borrowings and Schein's revision of older settings in Walter Reckziegel, *Das Cantional von Johan Herman Schein* (Berlin: Merseburger, 1963), 136–138.
27. See the discussion of this practice in Henrik Glahn, "J.H. Scheins 'Kantional' in die Tabulatur transponiert von J. Vockerodt, Mühlhausen 1649," in *Festskrift Jens Peter Larsen, Studier udgivet af musikvedenskabeligt institut vid Københavns Universitetet* (Copenhagen,1972), 47–71; see also Markus Rathey, "Traditions of organ music and organ playing in Mühlhausen in the seventeenth century and in the times of Johann Sebastian Bach," *Organ Yearbook* 45 (2016): 111–131.

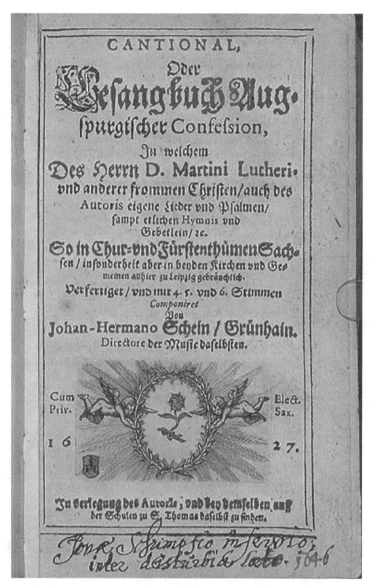

Figure 4.2 Johann Herman Schein, *Cantional* (1627), title page.

was added "für die Organisten/ Instrumentalisten vnd Lautenisten."[28] As in earlier *cantionals*, the settings appeared in a form of choir book notation in which the each of the voices was printed separately on the

---

28. Schein, *Cantional*, preface, sig. aiij[r–v].

Example 4.3 Johann Herman Schein, *Cantional* (1627), No. LXXVI. *Vater unser im Himmelreich.*

page. The bass figures (which were added to the vocal bass) allowed the accompanist to play with the singers without having a score in front of him. The figured bass line also made it possible to perform the hymns at home with only the discant melody and an instrumental accompaniment.

In addition to the simpler cantional-type settings for four voices, Schein included seven settings in *contrapuncto composito* for five voices (nos. 1, 5, 31, 44, 59, 64, 196). These more demanding settings appeared as alternate versions of hymns that were also available in *contrapunctus simplex*. These expanded settings are based on the major hymns of the seasons of the church year and usually appear at the beginning of a rubric of the Cantional: Advent, Christmas, Lent, Easter, Pentecost, and Trinity as well as for days of repentance.[29] Despite their more polyphonic, motet-like texture, these settings also feature the hymn melody in the upper voice, making them suitable for congregational accompaniment as well.

While Schein highlights his revision and corrections of Reformation-era hymns, he also included a significant number of his own hymns in the collection. Forty-one of the texts and melodies were by Schein, most of which were psalm paraphrases or funeral hymns.[30] The inclusion of these hymns straddled the gulf between the simple *Cantional* tradition (to which most of the settings belong) and the more expressive and personal compositions Schein had published outside of his *Cantional*.

The *Cantional* remained in use after Schein's untimely death in 1630, and in 1645, his successor, Tobias Michael, son of Schein's teacher Rogier Michael, published an expanded edition of the *Cantional*. Michael kept most of the book unchanged, but he added an appendix with twenty-two additional funeral pieces by Schein and four of his own. Michael did not revise the music of his predecessor, and the preface remained the same.

More than its predecessors, Schein's *Cantional* is a book for both congregational use and for use in the context of domestic devotion. The inclusion of the figured bass made it easier to sing the hymns at home with simple accompaniment by a keyboard instrument or a lute. Additionally, the inclusion of numerous funeral compositions catered to a revival of a Lutheran *ars moriendi* during the seventeenth century,[31] a shift in devotion that was significantly influenced by the devastation of the Thirty Years' War (1618–1648).

Another *Cantional* that belongs to the second generation of *Cantionals* is the *Psalmodia Sacra* by Melchor Franck (*ca.* 1579–1639), composer and music director in the Upper Frankonian city of Coburg. Already in his

---

29. Reckziegel suggests that the setting of the hymn *Wenn dich Unglück tut greifen an* was intended for funerals; however Schein's funeral compositions appear in a different rubric and the text of the hymn fits well the sentiment of days of Prayer and Repentance, which were frequently celebrated in the seventeenth century.
30. Five of these funeral settings had been composed for members of Schein's own family.
31. For an overview of the Lutheran *ars moriendi*, see Austra Reinis, *Reforming the Art of Dying. The ars moriendi in the German Reformation (1519–1528)* (Aldershot: Ashgate, 2007).

early motet collection *Contrapuncti Compositi deutscher Psalmen* (1602) Franck had acknowledged the popularity of simple cantional settings and highlighted that they allowed the congregation to join in with the choir so that their hearts might be moved. Realizing the strong emotional power of hymnody, Franck explains that he had taken these melodies and turned them into polyphonic motets. The musical style in this early collection is influenced by Hans Leo Hassler (with whom he might have studied) and by Orlando di Lasso. The settings were not intended (or suitable) to accompany the congregation. Almost a quarter of a century later, Franck did publish a *Cantional* that provided choirs with hymn settings in *contrapunctus simplex*. The print encompasses 102 settings (including a complete cycle of hymns for the church year). Only thirty-four of the settings, however, are for four voices; sixty-eight settings feature five voices instead.

While Schein's *Cantional* had targeted both choirs and the domestic sphere, Franck's print is explicitly intended for choirs. In his preface, Franck laments that previous *Cantionals* had usually printed all four voices together on one page, either in score notation or, as blocks, in choir book fashion. This was inconvenient for choirs and cantors often had to put effort and time into copying the voices into the individual partbooks which were much more common for choral music. By publishing his *Cantional* in partbooks, this was not necessary anymore and choirs were able to perform the hymns right away. While Franck's decision might have been convenient for choirs, it made the books impractical as hymnals for congregational or domestic use.[32] This transition of the *Cantional* into a book exclusively for the choir will continue in the second half of the seventeenth century.

STYLISTIC TRANSFORMATIONS:
FROM GOTHA TO LEIPZIG

Published in 1646, the *Gotha Cantional* is the first volume in our overview that is not connected to one specific composer. Up to the middle of the century, it was usually the creative effort of one composer who shaped the style and the content of the *Cantionals*. This was already the case with Osiander's *Cantional* and it was particularly apparent in the publications by

---

32. Franck was not the first to publish his settings in individual partbooks; already Hans Leo Hassler had done so in his *Kirchengesäng* from 1608; what is different about Franck, however, is that he explicitly rejects the common tradition of publishing the four voices together in one book.

Vopelius and Schein, who had included numerous of their own compositions as well.

The *Gotha Cantional*, on the other hand, was compiled by Gotha cantor Veit Dietrich Marold, who mostly borrowed settings from other composers. The largest body of settings stem from a previously unpublished collection of hymn settings by Bartholomäus Helder (*ca.* 1585–1635), a pastor and hymn writer who had lived near Gotha.[33] Thirty-four settings were by Melchior Vulpius and had originally appeared in his *KirchenGeseng und Geistliche Lieder* from 1604. Another group of thirty settings were from Johann Hermann Schein's *Cantional* and another thirty from Melchor Franck's *Psalmodia Sacra* (1631). A smaller number of settings (fifteen and nine respectively) originated in a *Cantional* by Erfurt composer Michael Altenburg, *Christlicher lieblicher und andechtiger newer Kirchen und Haus Gesänge* (Erfurt 1620–1622), and Heinrich Schütz's settings of the *Becker Psalter* (Freiberg, 1628).[34]

Of the 324 settings in the *Cantional*, 213 are in *contrapunctus simplex* while forty-five are more contrapuntal in texture. Although the emphasis is still on traditional cantional settings, Osiander's original goal of providing choral accompaniment for the congregation has faded into the background. Among the more elaborate pieces are, for instance, an *Allelluja, in resurrectione tua* for double chorus (No. 69), or the intimate vocal concerto *O Jesu mi dulcissime* (No. 590) for alto, tenor, and bass, which reflects the increasing shift toward an intimate and personal relationship with Christ during the seventeenth century.[35]

The *Gotha Cantional* returns to the traditional score notation. However, in form and texture, the settings are clearly intended as a repository of (simpler) choral music and not only as a collection of hymn settings. The historical significance of the *Gotha Cantional* lies in its relationship to a larger educational reform in the duchy of Gotha, which was spearheaded by Ernst der Fromme of Saxe-Gotha (1601–1675) and executed by the rector of the Gotha Gymnasium, Andreas Reyher. Based on the educational reforms of Jan Comenius (1593–1656), Reyher published an extensive reform program that combined modern pedagogical concepts with religious education. Reyher's *Spezial- und Sonderbarer Bericht* from 1642 is a curriculum that included not only the traditional disciplines

---

33. See Robin A. Leaver, "Chorales," Robin A. Leaver, ed., *The Routledge Research Companion to Johann Sebastian Bach* (New York: Routledge, 2017), 364.
34. Michael Praetorius is also represented with a small number of settings, see Leaver, "Chorales," 365.
35. See the overview of musical textures in the cantional in Walter Blankenburg "Das Gothaer Cantionale Sacrum," JbLH 15 (1970): 152.

of the medieval educational canon but also scientific and practical disciplines. Students were instructed in geography, physics, botanic, and other applied sciences. In addition, Reyher saw a great value in music and his curriculum fostered the theory and practice of choral singing as well. The *Gotha Cantional* grew out of this reform movement and Reyher was heavily involved in the compilation of the *Cantional* (in collaboration with Marold).[36] The title already highlights that the book is anchored in the educational efforts in Gotha:

> *Cantionale Sacrum, Das ist/ Geistliche Lieder/ von Christlichen und Trostreichen Texten/ Mit 3. 4. 5. oder mehr Stimmen unterschiedlicher Autorum, Für die Fürstl. Land- und andere Schulen im Fürstenthum Gotha Auff gnädige Fürstl. Verordnung in dieses bequeme Format zusammen gebracht.* (Cantionale Sacrum, that is, spiritual songs of Christian and consolatory texts, in 3, 4, 5, or more voices by various authors, for the Ducal land- and other schools in the duchy of Gotha, brought into a convenient format on ducal command.)

The three sections of the hymnal reflect the main occasions during which the boys of the school choir had to perform: during the liturgy, at school, and at funerals. The preface explains:

> First comprises the festival-songs according to the special feasts throughout the whole year . . . The second part contains other Christian songs for church and school arranged according to the structure of the holy catechism. . . . In the third part are assembled such sings that may conveniently be sued for Christian burials, and are appropriate for such use . . .[37]

As the preface adds, the settings were intended for the middle classes of the schools in Gotha and in the vicinity.[38] In other words, it was geared toward students who already had musical training but who did not yet sing the more demanding compositions that were expected from students in the upper classes.

The selection of hymns reflects the current trends in the middle of the seventeenth century. Contrary to some scholars, it is not a traditional *Cantional* that compiles settings of the hymns for the liturgical year. Those hymns were printed, as Blankenburg has shown, in the Gotha *Gesang-Büchlein*. The *Cantional*, on the other hand, was a collection of choral pieces and contained primarily hymns and sacred songs from

---

36. For the authorship, see Blankenburg, "Das Gothaer Cantionale Sacrum," 149–150.
37. English translation, Leaver, "Chorales," 362.
38. Blankenburg, "Das Gothaer Cantionale Sacrum," 149.

THE CANTIONAL TRADITION 105

the late sixteenth and early seventeenth century[39] But while it does not include the core repertoire of Lutheran hymnody (and thus differs from traditional *cantionals*), it fits into the historical development of the genre as it continues the shift away from purely congregational hymns toward a stronger emphasis on choral music—a feature we have already seen in both Schein and Vulpius, two composers who are represented among the settings of the *Gotha Cantional*.

The *Cantional* by Schein and its revision by Tobias Michael had been widely used in Leipzig when Cantor at St. Nicholas, Gottfried Vopelius, edited the *Neu Leipziger Gesangbuch* in 1682.[40] The name *Gesangbuch* is somewhat misleading as it is not a congregational hymnal but a *Cantional* for the use of the choir. The title page directly references Johann Hermann Schein's *Cantional,* and Vopelius borrows ninety-eight settings from his successful predecessor (sometimes in revised versions).

In the preface, Leipzig book binder Christoph Klinger gives an overview of previous cantionals and explains the rationale for publishing a new one for Leipzig:

Ob nun zwar bey so vielen Schaaren Evangelisten absonderlich bey denen hin und wieder albereit herausgegebenen Gesangbüchern man wol könnte beruhen/ massen hierinnen der sonderbare Fleiß und ungespahrte Mühe derer theils noch lebenden/ theils aber auch im HErrn entschlafenen geistreichen Männer billich zu rühmen; So hat doch darinnen bisher ein absonderlicher Mangel sich wollen spüren lassen/ daß/ wie *Vulpii* und *Decimatoris Cantional*-Bücher wegen der alten und unbekanten Melodeyen nicht allenthalben beliebet/ Herrn *Bartholomæi Gesii,* Herrn *Sethi Calvisii,* und Herrn Johan[n] Herman Scheins allseits berühmter *Musicorum,* bereits vor vielen Jahren herausgegebene Gesangbücher aber dermassen abgegangen/ daß keine *Exemplaria* mehr zubekommen/ als hingegen die neulich herausgegegangene entweder wegen der allzuvielen neuen Gesänge/ oder des unbequemen Format und Drucks in Kirchen und Schulen nicht wohl können gebrauchet werden.[41] (As there is already a large number of published hymnals among Protestants, one could have left it at that, especially since a lot of effort and diligence has been put into them and some of the authors are still alive (while others have passed away in the Lord). However, there was still a need for it since the Cantional books by Vulpius and Decimator are not very popular because of their old and unknown melodies; the hymnals by the widely famous musicians

---

39. Blankenburg, "Das Gothaer Cantionale Sacrum," 152.
40. *Neu Leipziger Gesangbuch, Von den schönsten und besten Liedern verfasset [. . .] Mit 4. 5. bis 6. Stimmen, deren Melodeyen Theils aus Johann Herman Scheins Cantional, und andern guten Autoribus zusammen getragen, theils aber selbsten componiret* (Leipzig 1682).
41. Vopelius, *Neu Leipziger Gesangbuch*, preface by Christoph Klinger, sig. a2[r-v].

Bartholomaeus Gesius, Seth Calvisius, and Johann Herman Schein have been published many years ago and the copies have been sold so that it is impossible to acquire them; hymnals that have been published more recently either have too many new songs or an inconvenient format or print and are thus unusable in churches and schools.)

Georg Moebius, dean of the theological faculty at Leipzig University, adds in his preface that the texts and melodies were revised and, if necessary, corrected. Especially the hymns by Martin Luther were revised based on the authoritative Jena Edition of Luther's works.[42]

As in the Schein *Cantional* before, the settings appear with a figured bass line that allowed organists and other instrumentalists to easily accompany the singers of the choir. While a *Cantional* in the traditional sense, it also includes settings that were not intended to accompany the singing of the congregation. Among the works included in the book are motet-style pieces (such as the anonymous *Virga Jesse floruit*, p. 77–83) and even pieces in a more modern concerto styles, like Andreas Hammerschmidt's *Alleluja, Fürchtet euch nicht* (p. 62f.) for three voices. Overall, however, the settings are more homophonic than the pieces in the *Gotha Cantional*.

Especially for the core hymns of the church year, Vopelius used the settings from Schein's *Cantional* as a resource.[43] In cases in which he modifies his models, Vopelius usually tends to simplify the older settings.[44] It is often not clear whether Vopelius made these changes himself or whether he used sources that already contained the revised compositions.[45] Other composers are only marginally represented in the *Gesangbuch*: Leipzig musicians Sebastian Knüpfer, Tobias Michael, and Johann Schelle are only each named once as composers, and so are Heinrich Schütz and Bartholomäus Gesius. With three settings by Melchior Franck and nine settings by Johann Crüger, Vopelius taps into the chorale and cantional tradition of the previous generation, whereas the seven works by Andreas Hammerschmidt represent the tradition of easy and accessible choral music that was popular in central Germany in the second half of the seventeenth century.

The Vopelius *Gesangbuch*, while musically not very innovative and mostly derivative, remained in use in Leipzig for the following decades.

---

42. Vopelius, *Neu Leipziger Gesangbuch*, preface by Moebius, preface, sig.)(3ᵛ.
43. See Jürgen Grimm, *Das Neu Leipziger Gesangbuch des Gottfried Vopelius (Leipzig 1682): Untersuchungen zur Klärung seiner geschichtlichen Stellung* (Berlin: Merseburger, 1969), 202–203.
44. Grimm, *Das Neu Leipziger Gesangbuch*, 203.
45. As Grimm suggests, Vopelius also knew the hymnals and settings by Johann Crüger and Christoph Peters, see Grimm, *Das Neu Leipziger Gesangbuch*, 205.

Expanded and revised editions appeared in 1693 and 1707 (both without music). The hymnal represents an important resource for the hymns used by Johann Sebastian Bach in his Leipzig cantatas and Bach was very familiar with the *Cantional* and its content.

Within the development of the genre of the *Cantional*, the Vopelius print represents the seventeenth century model which complements the core hymns of the reformation with newer songs that appeal to a more contemporary taste. With the inclusion of numerous polyphonic settings, the Vopelius *Gesangbuch* continues a tradition that had begun with Johann Hermann Schein, who had added more polyphonic hymn settings to the versions in strict *contrapunctus simplex*.

LEGACIES AND TRADITIONS

While the *Cantional* as a genre underwent a transformation during its one-hundred-year development from Osiander to Vopelius from a collection of core hymns of the Lutheran tradition to a repository of simpler compositions for the choir (with short moments in the 1620s during which the *Cantional* could also be used in domestic devotion), the texture of the cantional setting remained the norm: after Osiander, the hymn melody rarely appeared in the tenor anymore, and hymn settings in *contrapunctus simplex* appeared in choir books, *Cantionals*, and other books for choirs. Even in newer settings of religious songs, as in Johann Crüger's publications or in the popular sacred song-arias of the second half of the seventeenth century, the melody usually appears in the top voice and is supported by a more or less homophonic texture in the lower voices. With the establishment of the modern church cantata in the early eighteenth century, chorale settings in simple counterpoint also became part of larger scale works. And even if Bach's hymn settings in his cantatas and oratorios are harmonically and rhythmically more complex than Osiander's simple compositions, they continued the tradition shaped by Osiander.

Over the eighteenth century, hymns and settings in *contrapunctus simplex* could become synonymous. When Johann Kirnberger drafted his *Kunst des reinen Satzes in der Musik* (1771–1779), he elevated the simple setting in *contrapunctus simplex* as the basis for any kind of music and required any budding composer to master settings in this style before moving on to other genres.[46] Mozart learned from this tradition, and

---

46. See Markus Rathey, "Mozart, Kirnberger and the Idea of Musical Purity: Revisiting Two Sketches from 1782," *Eighteenth Century Music* 13 (2016): 235–252.

when the young Felix Mendelssohn Bartholdy studied with his teacher, Carl Friedrich Zelter, he had to study how to compose hymn settings in *contrapunctus simplex* before moving on to more complex forms. Listeners of his organ sonatas and other works still get a sense of his continuing interest in this genre.

While the four-part chorale setting in *contrapunctus simplex* remained a staple of church choirs throughout the seventeenth and eighteenth centuries in Germany, singing in harmony for the congregation never really caught on in the land of Luther and Osiander. Lutheran hymnals usually only contained the melody, while the choir (and later the organ) provided the accompaniment. Singing in harmony was a practice that remained more common in Reformed congregations and in some Lutheran traditions outside of Germany.

5.

A Most Popular Hymnal: *Praxis Pietatis Melica*

Joseph Herl

Praxis Pietatis Melica is the most important German hymnal that hardly anyone knows. By the time its first edition appeared in 1640 under the title *Newes vollkömliches Gesangbuch*, its compiler, Johann Crüger (1598–1662), was already an accomplished church musician, composer, author, and teacher. He was also well on his way to fathering nineteen children, five by his first wife and fourteen by his second. Since 1622 he had been cantor of the Nikolaikirche in Berlin, director of music for the city, and teacher at the Greyfriars Cloister Academy (Gymnasium zum Grauen Kloster). He held these posts until his death forty years later.

Ten editions of the hymnal would appear in Berlin under Crüger's editorship, and after his death another thirty-five editions would be published there through 1736, with at least sixteen further editions appearing in Frankfurt am Main, at least two editions in Stettin, and at least one in Hamburg, plus single editions in Lübeck and Gotha.[1] Johann

---

1. For a list of known editions, see *Praxis Pietatis Melica: Edition und Dokumentation der Werkgeschichte*, 2 vols. in 5, ed. Hans–Otto Korth and Wolfgang Miersemann (Halle: Franckesche Stiftungen, 2014–), vol. 2, part 1. This final volume in the set is scheduled for publication in 2024. The Berlin publications have edition numbers on the title page, so they are easy to count. The editions published in Frankfurt do not, so some edition may be unknown to us. The number sixteen is from Christian Bunners, *Johann Crüger (1598–1662): Berliner Musiker und Kantor, lutherischer Lied– und Gesangbuchschöpfer* (Berlin: Frank & Timme, 2012), 43, 51; Bunners lists the Frankfurt editions on pages 112–113. The list includes two editions in a large, bold typeface "for old and infirm eyes." These Berlin editions are available online (as of early 2023) at www.zvdd.de: 1st (1640), 5th (1653), 12th (1666), 15th (1671), 20th (1679).

Anastasius Freylinghausen, the compiler of the most important German hymnal of the eighteenth century, the *Geist-reiches Gesang-Buch* (Halle, 1704), named Crüger's book as one of his chief sources.[2]

What can account for this extraordinary record? Six features of the book seem especially important: two textual, two musical, and two dealing with the book itself: (1) the texts are a mixture of solid old hymns with new ones of high quality; (2) the new texts display a deeply personal piety that pervaded the seventeenth century; (3) harmonizations of tunes were provided in the form of figured bass; (4) new tunes by Crüger were both artistic and readily singable; (5) it was useful for both church services and private devotions; and (6) it was widely accepted by Lutheran Pietists and also by many in the Orthodox party.

OLD AND NEW

Lutheran hymnbooks of the late sixteenth century relied heavily on *Geystliche Lieder*, published in Leipzig by Valentin Babst in 1545. It was the last hymn collection with a new preface by Martin Luther, who died the next year; and its contents, mostly hymns by Luther, formed a sort of core that was carried into later books. To this core were added more recent hymns by authors such as Joachimsthal cantor Nicolaus Herman (*ca.* 1500–1561), the most popular author of the mid-sixteenth century, whose two hymn collections were themselves reprinted well into the 1600s.[3]

Hymnals intended for church use were conservative, and the bar was high for newer hymns to be admitted. The Frankfurt an der Oder collection *Geistliche Lieder* had nearly the same contents in 1604 as in

---

22nd (1684), 24th (1690), 25th (1690), 27th (1693), 29th (1702), 30th (1703), 31st (1708), 35th (1712), 38th (1718), 42nd (1732), 43rd (1733), and 44th (1736). Some Frankfurt editions are also available: 1662, 1668, 1670, 1674, 1676, 1693; also editions from Stettin (1688) and Hamburg (1703). A partial edition for choir and instruments, the *Geistliche Kirchen Melodien* (1649), is available online from the University of Pennsylvania.

2. Johann Anastasius Freylinghausen, *Geist–reiches Gesang Buch, Den Kern Alter und Neuer Lieder* (Halle, 1704; DKL 170404), fol.)(9a. See chapter 6 in this volume.
3. Herman's hymns were intended for private use, but they were so popular that they were included in church hymnals. His first collection, *Die Sontags Euangelia vber das gantze Jar, Jn Gesenge verfasset*, appeared in 1560, a year before Herman's death (DKL 1560⁰⁸). Its hymns were both paraphrases of the Sunday Gospels and devotional commentaries on them. His second book, the posthumous *Historien von der Sindfludt* (1562; DKL 1562⁰³) contained stories from the Old and New Testaments in rhyme along with other hymns and songs (such as the opening song, an acrostic paean to Joachimsthal and its mining industry). For a list of editions of these books, see DKL I/1 (under the sigla HermN–S and HermN–H).

the previous edition of 1579, and this was hardly unusual.[4] Virtually all the core hymns from the Dresden *Gesangbuch* of 1597 were retained in the edition of 1625, (though there were exceptions such as the Dresden hymnal of 1632 that contained hardly any of the old Lutheran hymns).[5] Even large publishing centers such as Nuremberg, where competition among hymnal publishers had been fierce since the 1550s, were quite conservative in this regard.[6]

When the *Newes vollkömliches Gesangbuch* appeared in 1640, it was one of just a few hymnbooks containing a well-balanced selection of old and new hymns. Of the 248 hymns, eleven appear in the book in Latin (these were dropped in later editions), six are German translations of Latin hymns, and nine are paraphrases of Latin devotional works. Martin Luther is represented by thirty-two hymns, Nicolaus Herman by seven, and Bartholomäus Ringwaldt (1530–99) by twelve. The only other sixteenth-century writers with more than one are Michael Weisse (*ca*. 1488–1534), Erasmus Alber (*ca*. 1500–1553), and Paul Eber (1511–1569) with four each; and Johann Kohlross (*ca*. 1487–1560), Nicolaus Selnecker (1530–1592), and the mystic Martin Moller (1547–1606), with two each. Post–1600 authors include Johann Hermann Schein (1586–1630), cantor of the Thomasschule in Leipzig, with four; poet laureate Martin Opitz (1597–1639), with two; Michael Schirmer (1606–73), Crüger's colleague at Greyfriars, with four; and another poet laureate, Silesian pastor Johann Heermann (1585–1647), with a whopping thirty-four. Around 40 percent of the hymns in the book are unattributed; they are not included in the above counts.

Heermann's two principal books of hymns had only recently appeared: *Devoti musica cordis: Hauß- und Hertz-Musica* in 1630 and *Sontags- und Fest- Euangelia* in 1636. Here is stanza 1 of the first hymn from Heermann's earlier book, headed "A faithful admonition from St. Augustine that one should not postpone the day of repentance":

---

4. The 1561 edition (DKL 1561[07]) had about the same number of pages as the 1579 edition (200 versus 212), so the contents may have been similar; but no copy of the 1561 edition has survived, so a comparison could be made only through a tedious analysis of the contents list in WDKL 1: 453–454; see also WB, 321–322 for an edition from 1562).
5. The book was first published in 1594 (DKL 1594[04]), but that edition was unavailable for inspection.
6. See, for example, the large collections printed by Abraham Wagenmann: *588. Geistliche Psalmen Vnd Lieder* (1609; DKL 1609[08]) and *834. Geistliche Psalmen Hymnen Lieder vnd Gebett* (1625; DKL 1625[11]), which were intended for singing "before and after the hearing of the holy divine Word and also at the distribution of the holy supper."

So war ich lebe, spricht dein Gott,	As I live, says your God,
Mir ist nicht lieb des Sünders Todt.	I do not desire the sinner's death.
Vielmehr ist diß mein Wuntsch vnd Will,	Much more is this my desire and will:
Daß er von Sünden halte still.	that he keep himself from sin,
Von seiner Boßheit kehre sich,	turn back from his evil,
Vnd lebe mit mir ewiglich.[7]	and live with me eternally.

Three things are notable about this brief excerpt. First, it flows easily when compared to the rougher poetry of Luther or Nicolaus Herman, which frequently contains stress accents in odd places and lacks endings on nouns and adjectives that display gender or number, such as Luther's *Ein feste Burg ist unser Gott* (A mighty fortress is our God, CW[2] 863, ELW 503, LSB 656)—which should grammatically be "*Eine* feste Burg ist unser Gott." In this respect, Heermann heeded a call by Martin Opitz in 1624 to regularize German poetry by applying the standards of Latin poetic writing.[8] Second, the language is simple and direct, with short phrases and words of one or two syllables (except for the final three-syllable word "ewiglich"); this is in contrast to Opitz's own poetry, whose phrases tend to be more convoluted and artificial.[9] Third, the stanza is strongly biblical, being a paraphrase of Ezekiel 33:11: "As I live, declares the Lord God, I have no pleasure in the death of the wicked, but that the wicked turn from his way and live; turn back, turn back from your evil ways." Crüger knew that Heermann's hymns would help to sell the book, so he highlighted them on the title page, saying that "not only the hymns of Luther and other learned individuals" were included, but also those of the "distinguished theologian and poet Johann Heermann."

PERSONAL PIETY

Heermann's hymns possessed another quality that distinguished them from earlier hymns: they were strongly personal in tone. As an example of an earlier hymn, here is the most intimate stanza from the more personal of Bartholomäus Ringwaldt's two hymns on the Sacrament of the Altar, published in 1582:

---

7. Johann Heermann, *Devoti musica cordis. Hauß und Hertz Musica* (Leipzig: Mintzeln, 1630; DKL 1630[05]), 1.
8. See Martin Opitz, *Buch von der Deutschen Poeterey* (Brieg: Gründer, 1624).
9. Nineteenth-century hymn translator Catherine Winkworth wrote concerning Opitz's hymns: "They are easy, correct, and elegant, but have scarcely a spark of originality or force" (*Christian Singers of Germany* [London: Macmillan, 1869], 172). For the texts themselves, see Albert F. W. Fischer, *Das deutsche evangelische Kirchenlied des 17. Jahrhunderts*, ed. Wilhelm Tümpel, 6 vols. (Gütersloh: Bertelsmann, 1904–16), 4: 236–249.

O HERR sterck vnsern glauben schwach,	O Lord, strengthen our weak faith
durch dis hoch Sacramente,	through this high sacrament,
Vnd vnser hertz gewisse mach,	and convince our hearts
auff dein war Testamente,	from your true testament
Das wir im todt	in death
vnd aller not,	and in all need
in deine wunden schawen,	to gaze into your wounds
gar künlich darauff bawen,	and boldly build on them,
Auch jeder zeit,	and also at any time
bald sein bereit,	to be prepared
Ehr, hab vnd gut,	for your sake to give up
Ja leib vnd blut,	honor, possessions,
deinthalben zuuerlassen,	even body and blood,
Vnd also recht,	and therefore rightly,
als dein geschlecht,	as your offspring,
ghen auff der schmalen strassen.[10]	to walk on the narrow pathways.

To be sure, this is a moving prayer for persistence in the faith; but it is corporate, coming from the whole body of believers, and there is a certain distance and formality between the petitioner and God. By contrast, here are the first two stanzas of a hymn on the sacrament by Heermann that was included in the *Newes vollkömliches Gesangbuch*:

O Jesu du mein Bräutigam,	O Jesus, my bridegroom,
Der du aus Lieb am Creutzes Stamm	who in love on the tree of the cross
Für mich den Todt gelidten hast,	suffered death for me
Genommen weg der Sünden Last.	[and] taken away the burden of sins.
Jch kom zu deinem Abendmal,	I come to your supper
Verderbt durch manchen Sünden Fall.	corrupted through many falls into sin.
Jch bin kranck, vnrein, nackt vnd blos,	I am sick, impure, naked and bare,
Blind vnd arm. Ach mich nicht verstoß![11]	blind and poor. Oh, cast me not away!

10. Stanza 3 of *Herr Christ, der du die deinen liebst*, in Bartholomäus Ringwaldt, *Die EVangelia Auff alle Sontag vnd Fest* (Frankfurt an der Oder: Eichorn, 1582), fol. O1r–v.
11. Heermann, *Devoti musica cordis*, 78; p. 261 in *Newes vollkömliches Gesangbuch*.

The prayer in this hymn is not to a powerful Lord, but to a personal Jesus, who is addressed intimately as bridegroom. Revelation 19:7 referred to the entire church as the bride of the Lamb (Christ); later, St. Bernard of Clairvaux (1090–1153) applied the term to individual believers in his sermons on the Song of Songs. It was not an uncommon image in seventeenth-century devotional literature and one that would have been familiar to Heermann from (among other places) Philipp Nicolai's 1599 tour de force *Wie schön leuchtet der Morgenstern* (How lovely shines the Morning Star, CW² 370; O Morning Star, how fair and bright, ELW 308, LSB 395), which Crüger also reprinted. In the second stanza, as many as six adjectives describe the singer, each one adding to the pathos of the moment, until finally the poet gives up trying to describe his sorry state and throws himself, and the singer, onto the mercy of God. This is much more personal than what we find in Ringwaldt.

In the *Newes vollkömliches Gesangbuch*, we see, along with historic Lutheran hymns, a move toward a more mystical and contemplative Christianity: seven hymns are paraphrases from St. Augustine, two from St. Bernard, two from the mystic Johann Tauler (*ca.* 1300–1361), and one from the *Paradiesgärtlein* of Johann Arndt (1555–1621), who more than any other single author inspired the Pietist movement of the late seventeenth century.[12] The *Paradiesgärtlein* (Little Garden of Paradise, 1612) was a prayer book divided into five sections: virtues from the Ten Commandments, thanksgivings for God's works, prayers of cross and comfort, prayers for various occasions, and praises to God. It was extremely popular during the seventeenth century and would have been a great comfort during the dark days of the Thirty Years' War (1618–1648).

Arndt's writings, especially his oft-reprinted and translated *Four Books on True Christianity* (1605–1610), show the influence of various contemplatives, especially Tauler. This trend toward an introspective faith gained momentum during the seventeenth century, and Crüger was well placed to capitalize on it. In 1647, he reissued his hymnbook with a new title: *Praxis Pietatis Melica* (The Practice of Piety in Song; hereafter PPM). Crüger himself reportedly called it the second edition of his book, demonstrating the continuity with the 1640 publication.[13]

---

12. This is close to the count in Heermann's complete output: ten paraphrases from Augustine, three each from Bernard and Tauler, and one from Arndt. See the hymn texts in Fischer/Tümpel, *Kirchenlied des 17. Jahrhunderts*, 1: 254–338. For more about Arndt's influence on hymns, see Elke Axmacher, *Johann Arndt und Paul Gerhardt* (Tübingen: Francke, 2001).
13. Philipp Spener, in his preface to the 1702 edition of PPM [fol.)(7ᵛ], stated clearly that the 1640 book was the first edition ("Praxis pietatis melica . . . erstmals 1640. verlegt war werden"), and that opinion is supported by Crüger's own words in the preface to the 1647 edition of PPM. He

The title is an apparent reference to *The Practice of Pietie* (2nd ed., 1612) by the Welsh Puritan Lewis Bayly (*ca.* 1575–1631). Bayly's book had been available since 1629 in a German translation called *Praxis Pietatis* and was reprinted many times in various cities.[14] The devotional appeal of Crüger's hymnal was increased when many editions were bound with a reprint of a popular prayer book by the sixteenth-century Lutheran theologian Johann Habermann.[15]

Between 1647 and 1653, PPM added two more authors of contemplative hymns to its roster whose hymns are still sung today: Johann Franck (1618–1677) and Paul Gerhardt (1607–1676).[16] Franck was a lawyer who had studied poetry with Simon Dach at the University of Königsberg; Gerhardt was a tutor or private secretary in Berlin. He was ordained in 1651 at the Nikolaikirche, where he would become first deacon (assistant pastor) and Crüger's colleague six years later. Most of their hymns were

---

reported that the first edition of six years earlier was no longer available, and so he has revised the same book ("selbiges nicht allein zu revidiren"). . . . The reference to the "same book" shows that Crüger considered PPM to be a new edition of the 1640 publication, not a new book altogether, and the edition numbers in subsequent publications bear this out. The second edition (1647) is no longer extant, but Wilhelm Tümpel reprints the quotation from 1647, together with surrounding context, in "Die Ausgabe der Crügerschen Praxis Pietatis Melica vom Jahre 1647," *Siona: Monatsschrift für Liturgie und Kirchenmusik* 30/11 (1905): 201–203, especially 202 (the author is grateful to Wolfgang Miersemann for this citation). The conclusion reported here is his. Six years before 1647 is of course 1641, not 1640; in 1641 a choral edition of the 1640 book was published (see below under "Church and Home"). For more on the relationship between the 1640 and 1647 editions, see Wolfgang Miersemann, "Vom neuem vollkömlichen Gesangbuch, Augspurgischer Confession (1640) zur PRAXIS PIETATIS MELICA (1647ff.): ein Gesangbuch auf Erfolgskurs," in *Crüger 1622: Ein Berliner Kantor schreibt Musikgeschichte*, ed. Albrecht Henkys, Hans–Otto Korth, and Wolfgang Miersemann (Beeskow and Berlin: Ortus, 2022), 175–198.

14. *Praxis Pietatis, das ist Übung der Gottseligkeit* (Basel: König, 1629). By 1647 it had been reprinted in Basel, Lüneburg, Nürnberg, and Wolfenbüttel. Philipp Spener, in his 1702 preface to PPM [fol.)(7ᵛ], stated that the title was a reference to Bayly's book; but Bunners is not convinced by the association with Bayly, saying that the question should remain open; see his *Johann Crüger*, 137.

15. *Christliche Gebet für alle Not vnd Stende der gantzen Christenheit* (Hof: Pfeilschmidt, 1567).

16. The dates when the hymns entered PPM are somewhat uncertain because the second edition (1647), third edition (1648), and fourth edition (date unknown) are no longer extant. Nineteenth-century hymnologists Philipp Wackernagel and Johannes Zahn both saw the 1647 edition, although the copy Zahn saw had no title page, and he thought it was the 1648 edition (see the notation at DKL 1647⁰⁸). We therefore have a good idea of the contents from 1647. We also have partial contents from 1648, because in 1649 Crüger published a book of hymns, *Geistliche Kirchen Melodien* (DKL 1649¹⁵), for (mostly) four-part choir with two instrumental parts. In its preface he explained that the hymns were all taken from the third edition of PPM, published in 1648. For more information, see the critical edition by Burkard Rosenberger, *Johann Crügers Geistliche Kirchen-Melodien (1649)*, Wissenschaftliche Schriften der WWU Münster, series XVIII, vol. 3 (Münster: Westfälische Wilhelms-Universität, 2014), 1, 5.

first published in PPM. Franck, best known today for his sacramental hymn *Schmücke dich, o liebe Seele* (Soul, adorn yourself with gladness, CW² 663, ELW 488, LSB 636), had twenty-seven in the 1653 edition; Gerhardt had eighteen in 1647 and eighty-two in 1653 (one-sixth of the total number of hymns in the book).[17]

Nineteenth-century translators of Gerhardt often toned down the more sensual parts of his hymns, but lest there be any doubt that they were representative of the new affective trend, here are the first seven stanzas of his fifteen-stanza Christmas hymn *Ich steh an deiner Krippen hier* (Beside Thy manger here I stand, LH 27). The hymn is beloved in Germany, but is all but unknown in America.

JCh steh an deiner krippen hier,	I stand here beside your cradle,
O Jesulein mein leben,	O Jesus, my life;
Jch komme, bring und schencke dir,	I come, I bring and give to you
Was du mir hast gegeben.	what you have given me.
Nim hin es ist mein geist und sinn,	Take it: it is my spirit and being,
Hertz, seel und muth, nimm alles hin	heart, soul and courage; take everything
Vnd laß dirs wol gefallen.	and let it be pleasing to you.
2. Du hast mit deiner lieb erfüllt	You have filled my veins and blood
Mein adern und geblüte,	with your love;
Dein schöner glantz, dein süsses bild	your lovely brilliance, your sweet portrait
Ligt mir gantz im gemüthe,	are ingrained in my heart.
Vnd wie mag es auch anders seyn,	And how could it be otherwise?
Wie könt ich dich, mein Hertzelein,	How could I leave you, my little heart,
Aus meinem hertzen lassen?	out of my own heart?

---

17. The hymn count for Franck is from Fischer/Tümpel, *Kirchenlied des 17. Jahrhunderts*, 4: 71–97; the counts for Gerhardt are from Christian Bunners, *Paul Gerhardt: Weg, Werk, Wirkung*, rev. ed. (Berlin: Buchverlag Union, 1993), 44–45. Many of the new hymns in the 1653 edition were also published in another book the same year from the same printer, Christoff Runge, who also took over as editor of PPM after Crüger's death in 1662: *D. M. Luthers Vnd anderer vornehmen geistreichen und gelehrten Männer Geistliche Lieder und Psalmen* (DKL 1653⁰¹). This book was commissioned by the 26-year-old Luise Henriette, consort of the "Great Elector," Friedrich Wilhelm of Brandenburg. It contained a selection of 338 Lutheran hymns for use by the electress, a member of the Reformed Church. The only known copies, in Hamburg and Berlin, were lost in the Second World War. A reprint of the hymn texts only (without music) was edited by G. Irenäus as *Andachtsbuch Luise Henriettens von Brandenburg* (Berlin: Schleiermacher, 1880). In 1657, an enlarged edition was issued, edited by Crüger, for use in the electoral court chapel. The following year a companion volume of Reformed psalms in four parts with three instrumental voices and basso continuo appeared, also edited by Crüger, with the title *Psalmodia Sacra* (DKL 1658⁰⁴).

3. Da ich noch nicht geboren war,
Da bist du mir geboren,
Vnd hast mich dir zu eigen gar,
Eh ich dich kant erkohren,
Eh ich durch deine hand gemacht,
Da hast du schon bey dir bedacht,
Wie du mein wolltest werden.

4. Jch lag in tieffter todesnacht,
Du warest meine Sonne,
Die Sonne, die mir zugebracht
Liecht, leben, freud und wonne.
O Sonne, die das werhte liecht,
Des glaubens in mir zugerichtt,
Wie schön sind deine strahlen!

5. Jch sehe dich mit freuden an,
Vnd kan mich nicht satt sehen,
Vnd weil ich nun nicht weiter kann,
So thu ich, was geschehen:
O daß mein sinn ein abgrund wär,
Vnd meine seel ein weites meer,
Daß ich dich möchte fassen!

6. Vergönne mir, o Jesulein,
Daß ich dein mündlein küsse,
Das mündlein, das den süssen wein,
Auch milch und honigflüsse
Weit übertrifft in seiner krafft,
Es ist voll labsal, stärck und safft,
Der march und bein erquicket.

7. Wann offt mein hertz im leibe weint,
Vnd keinen trost kann finden,
Da rufft mirs zu, ich bin dein freund,
Ein tilger deiner sünden:
Was traurest du mein brüderlein?
Du solt ja guter dinge seyn,
Jch zahle deine schulden.[18]

Before I was even born
you were born to me,
and you made me your own
before I ever knew you.
Before I met you,
you had already determined
how you would become mine.

I lay in deepest night of death:
you were my sun,
the Sun that brought me
light, life, joy, and bliss.
O Sun, who has placed in me
the true light of faith,
how lovely are your beams!

I look upon you with joy
and cannot have enough of the sight;
but because I cannot now go further,
I do what has happened.
If only my being were an abyss
and my soul a broad sea,
so that I might hold you!

Allow me, O little Jesus,
to kiss your tiny mouth,
the little mouth that in its power
surpasses sweet wine, milk, and honey.
It is full of refreshment,
strength, and nectar
that enliven marrow and bone.

When my heart often cries with grief,
unable to find comfort,
you call to me: "I am your friend,
exterminator of your sin.
Why are you sad, my brother?
You should be in a good mood,
for I atone for your guilt."

---

18. *Praxis Pietatis Melica*, Editio V (Berlin: Runge, 1653; DKL 1653[04]), 197–199.

This is unquestionably sensual, with phrases such as "How could I leave you, my little heart, out of my own heart?" and "Allow me, O little Jesus, to kiss your tiny mouth." But it is also profoundly theological, with Gerhardt decoding the doctrine of election for individual believers, a doctrine rarely addressed in Lutheran hymns. It is the ability of Gerhardt to combine fervent emotion with deep theology in image-filled poetry that caught the attention of his contemporaries and still delights us today, and it is all because Johann Crüger recognized his genius and published his hymns.

TUNE SETTINGS

In early Lutheran churches, organs were not used to accompany hymn singing; this practice developed gradually during the seventeenth and early eighteenth centuries. Since the 1580s, a popular way to sing hymns in churches with good choirs was for the congregation to sing the melody while the choir sang a homophonic or lightly contrapuntal setting with the tune in the top voice. Books containing tunes in this style are known today as *cantionales*.[19] Figure 5.1 is an example from a popular cantionale, *Harmonia Cantionum Ecclesiasticarum* by Leipzig Thomaskantor Seth Calvisius.[20]

It shows cantus, altus, and tenor parts for the last three lines of Martin Luther's hymn *Vom Himmel hoch da komm ich her* (From heaven above to earth I come, CW^2 331, ELW 268, LSB 358). The bassus part is on the next page (the right-hand page) so that when the book is open on a stand, all voices can read from the same copy.

If organists perchance wanted to play a hymn on the organ, they would have had to laboriously transcribe the vocal parts into organ tablature. During the seventeenth century, though, more and more organists learned to read a new notation that had worked its way up from Italy: *figured bass*. The bass part was accompanied by numbers and other symbols (the "figures") above or below that staff that informed the organist (or harpsichordist, or player of a stringed instrument such as a lute or theorbo) what harmonies to play. Johann Hermann Schein incorporated the system into

---

19. DKL lists fifty-six cantionales intended for Lutheran use printed between 1586 and 1640, including new and reprinted editions. There are also some cantionales in DKL that are not identified as such; for example, Rogier Michael's 1593 collection for the Dresden court (DKL 1593^{03}).
20. After its initial publication in 1597 (DKL 1597^{04}), this book was reprinted in 1598, 1605, 1612, and 1622.

A MOST POPULAR HYMNAL 119

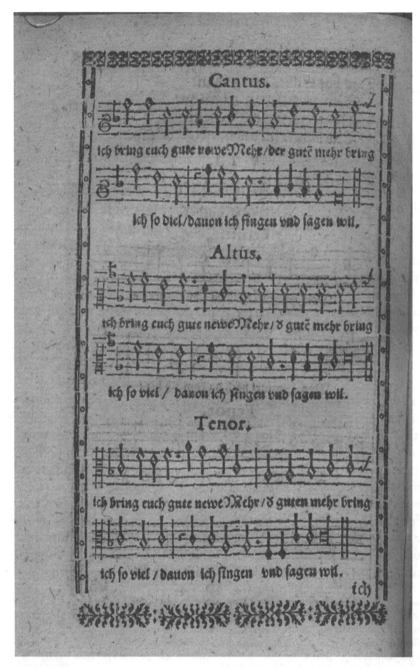

Figure 5.1 Seth Calvisius, *Harmonia Cantionum Ecclesiasticarum*, 1597, fol. B4ᵛ.

his cantionale of 1627, as shown in Figure 5.2 from the slightly expanded edition of 1645.[21]

The page shows the tenor and bassus parts of the same hymn, with the figures above the bass staff. The notes without figures are harmonized by root-position triads.

Johann Crüger followed Schein's example and included figured bass, but removed the altus and tenor parts, leaving only the melody and bass (Figure 5.3).[22]

This is much more compact than the previous examples: the entire tune takes up only a third of the page. In the 1640 edition, the first stanza of text was interlined with the music, but the 1653 edition shown here has only the text incipit, allowing more room for the figures. In both editions, the entire text was placed below the music. A musician who had learned to read figured bass could easily transform the music in Figure 5.3 at sight into something like Example 5.1 (the placement of the inner voices will vary according to each player's preference).

The convenience of this system was beyond dispute, and it became standard in later seventeenth- and eighteenth-century hymnals. It was first used here, in PPM.

NEW TUNES

In an era when little polyphonic music appeared in print, Johann Crüger had published two compositions by the time he was twenty-two years old, both eight-voice works written for weddings. Although a few collections of his music would be printed during his lifetime, his more important contribution to music history, aside from his hymnal production, was in music theory pedagogy. Crüger was thoroughly at home with the latest theoretical developments, and in his several books on the topic he was able to synthesize this knowledge and explain it in a comprehensible way. He was the first, for example, to present in a school textbook the idea that music was based on triadic harmony (that is, chords), still the foundation of traditional theory today.[23] He could, in other words, take complex ideas

---

21. Schein was not the first to attach figured bass to choral settings of Lutheran hymns. Michael Praetorius had done this in Part 9 of his *Musae Sioniae* (1610; DKL 1610¹³), but it was Schein's cantionale that caught the attention of seventeenth-century church musicians.
22. Crüger also copied several other features of Schein's publication; see the discussion in Elisabeth Fischer-Krückeberg, "Johann Crüger's Praxis pietatis melica," *Jahrbuch für Brandenburgische Kirchengeschichte* 26 (1931): 27–52, especially 32.
23. See his *Praecepta musicae practicae figuralis* (Berlin: Kall, 1625) and an extract in German published the same year, *Kurtzer und verstendtlicher Unterricht, recht und leichtlich singen zu lernen* (Berlin: Kall, 1625).

Figure 5.2 Johann Hermann Schein, *Cantional, Oder Gesang Buch Augsburgischer Confession*, 1645, fol. B2^r.

Figure 5.3 Johann Crüger, *Praxis Pietatis Melica*, 1653, fol. H1[r]. The last two bass notes are printed a step too high.

Example 5.1 A possible realization of *Vom Himmel hoch* from PPM, 1653.

and present them in a way that common people could understand. In the same way, he was able to take the complex harmonies employed in the art music of his day and adapt them to simple melodies easy for untutored congregations to learn and sing. Yet he was also able to produce memorable tunes in an older style. See Example 5.2 from the 1653 edition of PPM.

A MOST POPULAR HYMNAL 123

Example 5.2. Crüger's tune for Paul Gerhardt's Advent hymn *Wie soll ich dich empfangen* (O Lord, how shall I meet you, CW² 324, ELW 241, LSB 334), from PPM, 1653, no. 81.

Except for the last note, only two rhythmic values are used. There is a recurring half-note beat, but the rhythm is not simplistic, with syncopations at the words "setze" and "mir kund." The melody is mostly stepwise, and leaps are part of a triad, rendering the tune easy to navigate and to remember. Two notes strike us as being outside the key, both B naturals. But in Crüger's day, the concept of key had not yet fully developed, and this would have been seen as an instance of the principle that a B-natural rather than a B-flat should be used when the next note is C. This tune is therefore in an older style: there is nothing in it from a purely musical standpoint that was not in Luther's tune *Ein feste Burg ist unser Gott*, written more than a hundred years earlier. The one newer feature deals with how the music sets the text; namely, the highlighting of the word "Jesu," the most important word in the text, on the highest note of the melody. That is a nice touch.

Crüger's tune for Gerhardt's Easter text *Auf, auf, mein Herz, mit Freuden* (Awake, my heart, with gladness, CW² 443, ELW 378, LSB 467) is more innovative (see Example 5.3).

Immediately apparent is the triple meter, which is quite unusual for hymn tunes in this period, although it became popular decades later with the Pietist movement. In any case, the poetic meter does not require it here, and a more natural choice would have been some sort of iambic meter. But here Crüger writes in the style of a popular Italian dance tune, a *balletto*, as Christian Bunners has pointed out.[24] By comparison, Example 5.4 shows the beginning of an authentic *balletto* used as a hymn tune.

24. Bunners, *Johann Crüger*, 102.

Example 5.3 Crüger's tune for Paul Gerhard's *Auf, auf, mein Herz, mit Freuden*, (Awake, my heart, with gladness, CW² 443, ELW 378, LSB 467), from PPM, 1653, no. 160.

Example 5.4 Beginning of Giovanni Giacomo Gastoldi's *balletto A lieta vita* with a German contrafactum, *In dir ist Freude* (In thee is gladness, CW² 513, ELW 867, LSB 818).[25]

Both have the same triple meter and dotted rhythms, and their lively energy makes them superb vehicles for a joyful text. Crüger's tune bounces around like a small child: it is so excited at Jesus's resurrection that it cannot be confined to a single key, but escapes four times, cadencing (to use modern terminology) successively on D twice at "geschicht" and "grosses licht," on G at "hinträgt," and on C at "unser geist," which is remarkable for such a short tune. Despite this, the tune is easy to learn and sing, with only stepwise and triadic motion throughout. The opening descending minor third is mirrored as an ascending minor third at "Mein Heyland." The phrase "Mein Heyland war gelegt" is immediately repeated a step higher, which not only depicts growing excitement but also serves as a built-in musical mnemonic. There is a similar, but shorter, musical sequence on the words "von uns unser." In so constructing the tune, Crüger makes a complex musical task look easy.

With few exceptions, Crüger did not have the same success in gathering tunes by other contemporary composers as he had in collecting new texts.

---

25. The tune and Italian text are from Giovanni Giacomo Gastoldi, *Balletti a cinqve voci* (Venice, 1591), no. 1, transcribed here from the 1593 edition. The German text is from Johann Lindeman, *Amorvm filii dei decades dvae* (Erfurt, 1598; DKL 1598¹⁹), no. VII.

The following table reports the number of tunes by living or recently deceased composers in the editions of 1640 and 1653:

Composers	1640	1653
Johann Crüger (1598–1662)	22	71
Johann Hermann Schein (1586–1630)	1	6
Johann Schop (ca. 1590–1647)	—	4
Heinrich Schütz (1585–1672)	—	2
Johann Stobäus (1580–1646)	—	1
Unattributed and not by others named here	113	133
TOTAL	136	217

In both 1640 and 1653, most of the unattributed tunes were old tunes long established. In 1640, two tunes by Crüger and the one by Schein were unattributed, but attributions appear in some other editions of PPM. One tune attributed to Crüger in 1640 is anonymous; this was corrected in the tenth edition (1661). The count of twenty-two represents tunes actually by Crüger.

In 1653, Crüger's count of seventy-one includes twenty-one not attributed to him in this edition and excludes two erroneously attributed to him (one is by Schein and one anonymous). Schop's four tunes were all unattributed; three of those were revised by Crüger. Five of Schein's six tunes were not attributed to a composer, nor was the one tune by Stobäus, nor one of Schütz's two tunes. Two tunes whose assignment to Crüger is uncertain are included in the "unattributed" count.[26]

It is entirely possible that Crüger did not even try to find new tunes by other composers, since it was easy enough for him to write any that were required. Some of Crüger's tunes were really reworkings of preexisting tunes; Elisabeth Fischer-Krückeberg estimates that nearly a quarter of his tunes fall into this category.[27] Crüger also borrowed without alteration some older tunes that had rarely been used by Lutherans: the Genevan

---

26. The correct attributions are from *Praxis Pietatis Melica: Edition und Dokumentation der Werkgeschichte*, vol. 1, part 1, *passim*; see also Robin A. Leaver, "Genevan Psalm Tunes in the Lutheran Chorale Tradition," in *Der Genfer Psalter und seine Rezeption in Deutschland, der Schweiz und den Niederlanden 16–18 Jahrhundert*, eds. Eckhard Grunewald, Henning P. Jürgens and Jan R. Luth (Tübingen: Niemeyer, 2004), 145–166.
27. Elisabeth Fischer-Krückeberg, "Johann Crüger und das Kirchenlied des 17. Jahrhunderts," *Monatschrift für Gottesdienst und kirchliche Kunst* 34/11 (1929): 310–315, especially 312.

tunes of the Reformed psalter.[28] The psalm texts, in a German translation by Ambrosius Lobwasser, were anathema to most Lutherans because of their association with Reformed churches and their theology; but in the tenth edition of PPM (1661) Crüger printed some thirteen to seventeen Genevan tunes, depending on how they are counted, at times setting several texts to the same tune, so that around 8 percent of the hymns in the book used tunes from the Genevan Psalter.[29] Some scholars have detected characteristics of the Genevan tunes in Crüger's original tunes as well.[30]

A practical feature of PPM that would have appealed to users is the fact that nearly all the tunes are to be found somewhere in the book.[31] To be sure, if a tune was intended for use with more than one text, the tune itself was printed only once, with a cross-reference from the other texts; but users did not have to hunt for tunes in other books.

CHURCH AND HOME

Lutheran hymnbooks of the early seventeenth century often have a clear purpose that can be ascertained from the title page, such as with the books published in Dresden and Nuremberg mentioned in the section "Old and New" above. These books typically have few, if any, newer hymns, and the hymns they contain tend to be arranged according to the church year. Hymnbooks intended for private use, by contrast, usually contain new hymns by a single author, such as the *Devoti Musica Cordis* of Johann Heermann (Leipzig, 1630) and *Johann Risten... Himlischer Lieder* (series beginning in 1641). Their titles are often evocative: "Music of the dedicated heart" (Heermann) or "Heavenly songs" (Rist). Their contents do not attempt to cover the church year, but rather are arranged in other ways: the source of the text (a Bible passage or writings of early church fathers) or in categories pertaining to one's devotional life.

---

28. The complete psalter was issued in Geneva in 1562 with the title *Les Pseaumes mis en rime francoise.*
29. Hans-Otto Korth, "Inhalt als Bestimmung: Johann Crügers *Praxis Pietatis Melica*," in *Weil die Seelen fröhlich macht: Protestantische Musikkultur seit Martin Luther*, ed. Cordula Timm-Hartmann (Halle: Franckesche Stiftungen, 2012), 27–41, especially 27.
30. See, for example, Fischer-Krückeberg, "Johann Crüger und das Kirchenlied," 313–314, 315; also Korth, "Inhalt als Bestimmung," 38–39.
31. The first edition of 1640 contains 137 tunes for 248 texts, so 55 percent of hymns have tunes appearing with the texts. All the others have references to other tunes in the book, except that six have no cross-references at all: *Dancksagen wir alle Gott* (36), *Da Jesus an dem Creutze stund* (50), *Christ ist erstanden von der Marter alle* (63), *Also heilig ist der Tag* (65), *Christe qui lux es et dies* (127), and *Erhalt uns, Herr, bey deinem Wort* (208). In later editions even fewer tunes are lacking.

The intended use of Crüger's *Newes vollkömliches Gesangbuch* of 1640, though, is ambiguous. In the past, it was generally accepted that it was intended for private devotion.[32] But the hymns are arranged according to the church year, and although there are many newer hymns, the traditional hymns sung in church are also present. The title page states only that the book contains "not only the spiritual and consoling songs of Luther and other learned individuals, but also many lovely new songs of comfort . . . omitting those hymns that are unnecessary and unused." The preface is similarly unhelpful in determining the book's intended use. Christian Bunners points out, though, that the lengthy title also refers to hymn settings that have been composed in four voices, something that would have been useful only to a church choir.[33] The four-voice settings were published in 1641; we know this because hymn historian J. F. Bachmann saw a copy of the altus and tenor parts with that imprint, although they no longer survive.[34]

The 1647 edition bears the evocative title *Praxis Pietatis Melica: Das ist Vbung der Gottseligkeit in Christlichen und Trostreichen Gesängen* (*Praxis Pietatis Melica*; that is, Practice of Piety in Christian Songs Rich in Consolation). The book now begins with hymns for morning and evening, followed by penitential hymns, before continuing with hymns for the church year. These innovations suggest a hymnal intended primarily for devotion. But Crüger stated in the preface that he had written settings of hymns contained in the book for four voices and two instrumental parts (mainly violin or cornett); these would be published in 1649 as *Geistliche Kirchen-Melodien*.[35] This would have been unnecessary had the hymnal not been intended for use in church, and so Bunners concludes that Crüger's plan all along was to introduce the new hymns in church.[36] By 1653 this goal was explicit in the book's title, which contains the words "for the advancement of church as well as private services" ("zu Beforderung des so wol Kirchen- als Privat-Gottesdienstes"). The ambiguity concerning the book's intended use probably helped to sell it. The title, arrangement of contents, and presence of new hymns would have suggested to potential buyers that the hymns were meant for private devotion; but we now know that Crüger also made every effort to use them in public services.

32. See the citations to various scholars in Bunners, *Johann Crüger*, 69.
33. Bunners, *Johann Crüger*, 71.
34. Johann Friedrich Bachmann, *Zur Geschichte der Berliner Gesangbücher* (Berlin: Schultze, 1856), 20; cited by Bunners, 71.
35. Tümpel, "Die Ausgabe," 202.
36. Bunners, *Johann Crüger*, 69.

This is something that previous Lutheran hymnals had not accomplished, at least not since Luther's lifetime.

RECEPTION OF PRAXIS PIETATIS MELICA

Neither Johann Crüger nor Paul Gerhardt lived to see the full flower of the Pietist movement, which would divide German Lutheranism from the 1690s to the 1730s and beyond. Freylinghausen's *Geist-reiches Gesang-Buch* (Halle, 1704), mentioned at the start of this chapter, was the chief Pietist hymnbook, and it made ample use of Crüger's book. In the hymnal's preface, Freylinghausen referred to "the blessed Paul Gerhardt's splendid spiritual songs."[37] The book contained fifty-two hymns by Gerhardt, and the follow-up volume from 1714, the *Neues Geist-reiches Gesang-Buch*, included another thirty-one.[38] It is hardly surprising that the Pietists would have been attracted to the emotional intensity and personal devotion to Jesus expressed in the newer hymns by Gerhardt and others, which fit well with the goal for hymn singing that Freylinghausen expressed in his 1704 preface: for "the edification and awakening of Christian devotion."[39]

Freylinghausen's hymnal was not the only connection of PPM to Pietism. Philipp Spener (1635–1705), sometimes called the "father of Pietism," supplied the preface to the Berlin edition of 1702. Bunners makes a strong case that Spener was responsible for the 1668 Frankfurt preface as well.[40] In 1700, as provost of the Nikolaikirche, the chief church in Berlin and Crüger's place of employment for forty years, Spener delivered the funeral sermon for Crüger's widow Elisabeth. There is thus ample evidence of the connections between PPM and the Pietist movement, although all of this happened after Crüger's death.

What is interesting is that PPM, or at least Paul Gerhardt's hymns, did not fare so well among the Orthodox Lutherans as with the Pietists, at least at first. To be sure, one searches in vain for any direct criticism of

---

37. Freylinghausen, *Geist reiches Gesang Buch, fol.*)(11ᵇ. For more on the relationship between PPM and Freylinghausen's book, see Hans–Otto Korth and Wolfgang Miersemann, "*Das 'Berlinische Gesangbuch' Johann Crügers und Johann Anastasius Freylinghausens 'Hallisches Gesangbuch*,'" in *Doch der ist am besten dran, der mit Andacht singen kann": Festschrift der Paul-Gerhardt-Gesellschaft für Christian Bunners* (Berlin: Frank & Timme, 2016), 129–141.
38. The count is from Christian Bunners, "Paul Gerhardt und der Pietismus: Eine Skizze," in *Überliefern—Erforschen—Weitergeben: Festschrift für Hans Otte zum 65. Geburtstag*, ed. Inge Mager, *Jahrbuch der Gesellschaft für niedersächsische Kirchengeschichte* 113 (2015): 143–155, especially 149.
39. Freylinghausen, *Geist–reiches Gesang Buch,* fol.)(11ᵃ.
40. Bunners, *Johann Crüger,* 122–127.

Gerhardt or Crüger by Orthodox writers; and Conrad Tiburtius Rango, pastor of the Nikolaikirche in Greifswald and General Superintendent for Pomerania, a solidly Orthodox opponent of Pietism who generally disapproved of new hymns in church, nevertheless favored Gerhardt's hymns "because they do not spring from a poetic flight of fantasy, but are based in a theological spirit."[41] But Inge Mager found, in a study of hymnals from Lower Saxony, that hymnals from cities where Lutheran Orthodoxy prevailed included few hymns by Gerhardt (for example, five in the Hannover hymnal of 1657 and six in the new edition of 1698). Conversely, a 1686 hymnal from Lüneburg, where the city superintendent was an adherent of Spener, contained ninety Gerhardt hymns.[42] Gerhardt's hymns did not become broadly popular until the nineteenth century; but even early on, the Orthodox party accepted some of them. It seems that in supporting the new piety of the seventeenth century Crüger came close to the line that would have caused Orthodox Lutherans to reject his book, but he did not step over it.[43]

LEGACY

It was by no means inevitable that Crüger's hymnal would become so influential. About the same time as it appeared, Justus Gesenius and David Denicke edited the *New Ordentlich Gesang-Buch* (Hannover, 1646). Like PPM, it introduced many new hymns and also brought some traditional hymns into conformity with Opitz's rules for poetry.[44] But it had little influence, either in its own day or subsequently, even though it was named the official hymnal of Hannover in 1652 and remained so until 1740.[45] By

---

41. "weil sie nicht aus einer phantastischen Dicht-Art, sondern aus einem Theologischen Geist gesetzet sind." Conrad Tiburtius Rango, *I.N.R.J. Von der Musica, Alten und neuen Liedern* (Greifswald: Starcke, 1694), 29.
42. Inge Mager, "Die Rezeption der Lieder Paul Gerhardts in niedersächsischen Gesangbüchern," *Jahrbuch der Gesellschaft für niedersächsische Kirchengeschichte* 80 (1982): 121–146, especially 122–124, 127.
43. Although pious devotional writings in the seventeenth century are associated especially with writers who would later influence the Pietist movement, such as Johann Arndt and Heinrich Müller, there were plenty of devotional writers who were solidly Orthodox, including the most important Lutheran theologian of the century, Johann Gerhard (1582–1637), with his *Meditationes sacrae* (1606) and *Schola pietatis* (1622/23). When Gerhard was a youth, his pastor was none other than Johann Arndt.
44. The revised hymns were relatively few. See Hans-Christian Drömann, "Das Hannoversche Gesangbuch 1646," JbLH 27 (1983): 164–192.
45. Ingeborg Röbbelen, *Theologie und Frömmigkeit im deutschen evangelisch-lutherischen Gesangbuch des 17. und frühen 18. Jahrhunderts* (Göttingen: Vandenhoeck & Ruprecht, 1957), 22, note 20.

contrast, in the preface to the 1702 Berlin edition, Philipp Spener called PPM a hymnal that has "become known and used all over Germany."[46] In 1732, Christian Gerber, a moderate Pietist, wrote that "the newer hymns are great in number, and among them, like diamonds and rubies, shine the hymns of the blessed Paul Gerhardt, which nowadays are much used in the public service."[47]

PPM is still influential today, nearly four hundred years after its first edition was published. The following table counts in two present-day hymnals the hymns that first appeared in PPM. The core section (*Stammteil*) of the German Protestant hymnal, *Evangelisches Gesangbuch* (EG), was published in 1993; the American hymnal *Lutheran Service Book* (LSB) appeared in 2006.[48]

Editions	Texts in EG	Texts in LSB	Tunes in EG	Tunes in LSB
1640 Berlin	1	0	3	0
1647 Berlin	7	4	2	2
1648 Berlin	1	2	1	2
1653 Berlin	17	11	7	5
1656 Frankfurt	1	1	0	0
1668 Frankfurt	0	0	1	1
1690 Berlin	0	0	1	0
TOTAL	27	18	15	10

46. "in gantz Teutschland bekant gewordenen und gebräuchlichen Gesangbuch." Quoted in Bunners, *Johann Crüger*, 136.
47. "Der neuern Lieder aber sind noch eine grössere Zahl, und darunter leuchten des sel. Paul Gerhards Lieder wie Diamanten und Rubinen herfür, die auch numehr sehr beym öffentlichen Gottesdienste gebraucht werden." Christian Gerber, *Historie Der Kirchen Ceremonien in Sachsen* (Dresden and Leipzig: Sauereßig, 1732), 246. More evidence of PPM's influence is given in Walter Blankenburg, "Der Einfluß des Kirchenliedes des 17. Jahrhunderts auf die Geschichte des evangelischen Gesangbuches und der Kirchenmusik," in *Das protestantische Kirchenlied im 16. und 17. Jahrhundert: Text-, musik- und theologiegeschichtliche Probleme*, ed. Alfred Dürr and Walther Killy (Wiesbaden: Harrassowitz, 1986), 73–85.
48. The total for PPM Berlin 1647 in EG excludes Martin Rinckart's hymn *Nun danket alle Gott* (Now thank we all our God, CW² 597, ELW 839, LSB 895). Although EG assigns it to the 1647 book, it had previously appeared in *IESV Hertz Büchleyn* (Leipzig, 1636).

Here is a breakdown by author and composer.

Authors & Composers	EG	LSB
Authors		
Johann Franck	2	3
Paul Gerhardt	22	14
Michael Schirmer	1	0
Otto von Schwerin	2	1
Composers		
Anonymous	1	0
Johann Crüger	13	9
Peter Sohren	1	1

PPM is the most important hymnal of the seventeenth century not only because of its widespread use over a long period and its influence on its contemporaries, which was considerable, but also because its contents still appear in significant numbers in hymnals today.

6.

The Most Controversial Hymnal: 1704–1771

Dianne M. McMullen

The most controversial hymnal of the eighteenth century, Freylinghausen's *Geist-reiches Gesang-Buch*, was also the most popular of its time.¹ It has the largest number of editions in the history of German Lutheran hymnody other than *Praxis Pietatis Melica*, the work of Johann Crüger (1598–1662).² Hymnal compilers and music editors have borrowed much from the pages of Freylinghausen, including Johann Sebastian Bach (1685–1750) for the 1736 Schemelli *Gesangbuch*. Hymns first appearing in Freylinghausen traveled to distant parts of Europe as well as to North America, Asia, and Australia.

This chapter describes Freylinghausen's life, the environment in which he worked and ministered, the content of *Geist-reiches Gesang-Buch*, the controversy that ensued over this publication, and the hymnal's reception. The chapter also summarizes the renewal of interest, since the 1980s, in Freylinghausen's contribution to sacred music.

BIOGRAPHICAL SKETCH OF JOHANN ANASTASIUS FREYLINGHAUSEN (1670–1739)³

On December 2, 1670 Johann Anastasius Freylinghausen was born in Gandersheim, Germany, a small town near the Harz Mountains and

---

1. I thank Dr. Wolfgang Miersemann (Berlin) for making suggestions and corrections on a draft of this essay.
2. See chapter 5.
3. Freylinghausen wrote an autobiography in 1731; see Freylinghausen, *Wohlverdientes Ehren-Gedächtniß* (*Well-Earned Commemoration of Honors*) (Halle: Waisenhaus, 1740), 26–41. For

eighty-five kilometers south of Hannover. His father was a merchant and town mayor. Freylinghausen grew up in an Orthodox Lutheran family. From age twelve until eighteen he lived with his maternal grandfather, senior pastor at Einbeck, twenty-five kilometers from Gandersheim. At age eighteen Freylinghausen enrolled at the University of Jena to begin theological studies. During his second year he became involved with the Pietist movement at Jena, which led him to Erfurt two years later. There he met Joachim Justus Breithaupt (1658–1732), who later contributed hymns to Freylinghausen's hymnals. At Erfurt Freylinghausen also met August Hermann Francke (1663–1727), who became his mentor and more. Philipp Jakob Spener (1635–1705), the "father of Pietism," influenced both Breithaupt and Francke.

Breithaupt suggested that Freylinghausen continue his studies at Erfurt. Freylinghausen's parents, objecting at first, eventually gave their permission. After six months, Freylinghausen returned to Gandersheim on account of opposition in Erfurt to the Pietists. Francke and Breithaupt moved to Halle, taking professorships at the newly founded university. Simultaneously, Francke became pastor at Georgkirche in Glaucha, a town outside of Halle's city wall. In May 1692 Freylinghausen enrolled at the University of Halle, and after completing his studies, he returned in summer 1693 to Gandersheim, where he preached, taught children, and continued theological studies on his own. A few years later, Francke needed an assistant pastor, and he asked Freylinghausen to take the position. In January 1695 Freylinghausen moved to Halle, and thus began a long, productive relationship between the two men.

For twenty years Freylinghausen assisted Francke at Glaucha's Georgkirche. He received no salary, but Francke provided room and board. Freylinghausen preached, taught catechism lessons, and led devotional services. In 1715 Francke and Freylinghausen became, respectively, pastor and assistant pastor at Halle's Ulrichskirche. In the same year Freylinghausen married Francke's daughter, Johanne Sophie Anastasie, who was twenty-seven years younger than Freylinghausen. The similarity between

---

studies about Freylinghausen's life, see Matthias Paul, *Johann Anastasius Freylinghausen als Theologe des hallischen Pietismus* (Halle: Verlag der Franckesche Stiftungen, 2014); Wolfgang Miersemann, ed., *Johann Anastastius Freylinghausen (1670 Gandersheim–1739 Halle). Lebens-Lauf eines pietistischen Theologen und Gesangbuchherausgebers* [Katalog zur Ausstellung der Franckeschen Stiftungen aus Anlass des Jubiläums "300 Jahre Freylinghausensches Gesangbuch"] (Halle: Verlag der Franckeschen Stiftungen, 2004); and August Walter, *Leben Johann Anastasius Freylinghausen's* (Berlin: Schultze, 1865).

the groom's and bride's given names is no coincidence; Freylinghausen was her godfather.

Pastoral work took only a part of the day for Francke and Freylinghausen. Soon after Francke arrived in Glaucha, near Halle, in late 1691, he became concerned about the needs of children who asked for bread at his door. He offered them more, as well, namely, an education. Freylinghausen became Francke's assistant there also. Francke opened a school for poor children in 1695 and the Halle Waisenhaus in 1698, and he gradually added other schools, including a Paedagogium for children of nobility. By the late 1720s, the enrollment at the so-called Glauchasche Anstalten grew to about two thousand. It became a model for similar institutions across Europe. Francke and Freylinghausen lived and worked together, building up the Glauchasche Anstalten, while also ministering to a congregation.

Twice weekly, children at the Glauchasche Anstalten gathered in the Singesaal[4] (today named Freylinghausen-Saal) in the main building of the Glauchasche Anstalten to sing from *Geist-reiches Gesang-Buch*. People stood outside to listen through huge windows. Freylinghausen was among those who led these Singstunden. He and music teachers also taught children new melodies from *Geist-reiches Gesang-Buch* in their music lessons. In addition, Freylinghausen instructed older students in theology and religion.

In 1722 Freylinghausen became the assistant director of the Paedagogium and assistant director of the Waisenhaus. When Francke died in 1727, he bequeathed Freylinghausen the ministry at Ulrichskirche (along with supervision of the city's gymnasium) and codirectorship, with Francke's son, of the Waisenhaus (orphanage). In 1728 Freylinghausen became paralyzed. He recovered but was weakened. Suffering another attack in 1737, he died two years later, on February 12, 1739, at the age of sixty-eight. He and Johanne Sophie Anastasie had three children: Auguste Sophie (1717–1763), Gottlieb Anastasius (1719–1785), and Agnes Henriette (1726–1799). Gottlieb Anastasius eventually became a University of Halle theology professor and codirector of the Waisenhaus.

In addition to compiling the two Gesangbücher, Freylinghausen wrote hymns, forty-four of which are extant. Modern scholars use

---

4. The Singesaal, where two thousand children sat in a semicircle around a pulpit, was built in 1710 and dedicated in August 1711. It was renovated between 1992 and 1995. The first event in the nearly renovated Singesaal was a 1994 concert organized by Wolfgang Miersemann. It was part of a conference about Pietist hymnody.

words such as warmth and fire of expression to characterize them. The texts lean toward the conservative side compared with texts by other Pietist poets. Koch writes that Freylinghausen's hymns carry the stamp of a healthy devoutness and sincere inner godliness.[5] In addition to compiling the Gesangbücher, Freylinghausen published catechisms, theological tracts, and a series of sermons for Sundays and feast days, as well as other works.

CONTENT OF FREYLINGHAUSEN'S GESANGBÜCHER

Freylinghausen published two hymnals, understood by the 1730s as two parts of a whole. The first was *Geist-reiches Gesang-Buch*. It has twenty editions, published between 1704 and 17[71?]. Its first edition has 683 hymns, 174 with printed music. The second edition (1705) has an additional seventy-five hymns, twenty with printed music. Ten years after the first edition of *Geist-reiches Gesang-Buch*, Freylinghausen published *Neues Geist-reiches Gesang-Buch*, which has no duplication of texts or printed melodies with the first hymnal. *Neues Geist-reiches Gesang-Buch* has four editions, published between 1714 and 1733. Each edition of *Neues Geist-reiches Gesang-Buch* has 815 hymns, 158 with printed music. All editions of *Geist–reiches Gesang-Buch* and *Neues Geist-reiches Gesang-Buch* are in small duodecimo format and tightly bound. While they fit well into a singer's hand, organists must have someone hold the hymnal open for them or they must copy the music. In 1708 Freylinghausen published *Einige/Theils neue/theils nicht überall bekante Melodeyen* (Some Melodies, Partly New and Some Not Known Everywhere), also called *Melodien-Büchlein* (Booklet of Melodies). It has an additional one hundred hymns (one stanza only), all with printed music.

Freylinghausen's brother-in-law, Gotthilf August Francke (1696–1769), published a compilation of *Geist-reiches Gesang-Buch* and *Neues Geist-reiches Gesang-Buch* in 1741, two years after Freylinghausen's death, giving the compilation the title *Johann Anastasius Freylinghausen [. .] Geistreiches Gesang-Buch*. A second edition appeared in 1771. The 1741 and 1771 compilations, in octavo format, have, respectively, 1,581 and 1,582 hymns, 597 with printed music. In addition, there is a collection of hymns selected from *Geist-reiches Gesang-Buch* and *Neues Geist-reiches Gesang-Buch*

---

5. Koch, 4:332.

published without music, the so-called "Auszug." It has twenty editions that appeared between 1728 and 1775. The publisher of the Freylinghausen Gesangbücher was the Waisenhaus printing house, founded shortly after the establishment of the Waisenhaus. Noteworthy is the fact that the repertoire of hymn titles remains constant across Freylinghausen editions, unlike Crüger's *Praxis Pietatis Melica*.

Most seventeenth- and eighteenth-century German Lutheran hymnals have no printed music. That makes Freylinghausen's hymnals unusual. Even more unusual is the fact that Freylinghausen also printed basso continuo lines. He gave priority to melodies that had never appeared in print. Almost half of the melodies in *Geist-reiches Gesang-Buch* and most in *Neues Geist-reiches Gesang-Buch* are new. The oldest printed melodies in each originate in fourteenth-century chant. Well-known composers are Heinrich Schütz (1585–1672), Johann Crüger (1598–1662), and Joachim Neander (1650–1680). Freylinghausen also printed many melodies that first appeared in the 1698 Darmstadt hymnal. The 1741 and 1771 compilations have more older melodies than *Geist-reiches Gesang-Buch* and *Neues Geist-reiches Gesang-Buch*, including melodies from pre-Reformation and Reformation times.

The hymn texts change little across the twenty editions of *Geist-reiches Gesang-Buch* and the four editions of *Neues Geist-reiches Gesang-Buch*, but alterations to the music in *Geist-reiches Gesang-Buch* are many and sometimes significant. The first edition (1704) has a lot of errors in music notation, sometimes even omitting notes. Maybe the music editors are to blame, or maybe it is the fault of a printing press that had little or no experience with music notation. The basso continuo figuration, crude and often missing in the first edition, was improved in the second (1705) and third (1706) editions. With the fourth edition (1708), one has a reliable text. Freylinghausen himself writes in the preface to the fourth edition that it is to be preferred over the preceding three editions because "two Christian and experienced musicians from here," [6] whose names remain anonymous to this day, worked on it. For these reasons, Wolfgang Miersemann and I based the modern critical edition of *Geist-reiches Gesang-Buch* on the fourth edition (1708).[7] The alterations across editions are not limited

---

6. Freylinghausen, *Geist-reiches Gesangbuch*, 4th ed. (Halle: Waisenhaus, 1708), sig.):()2ʳ.
7. *Johann Anastasius Freylinghausen. Geistreiches Gesangbuch. Edition und Kommentar.* Im Auftrag der Franckeschen Stiftungen zu Halle, ed. Dianne Marie McMullen and Wolfgang Miersemann. Bd I/1: *Geist-reiches Gesang-Buch (Halle, vierte Ausgabe 1708). Text [Lied 1–395]* (Tübingen: Niemeyer, 2004). Bd. I/2: *Geist-reiches Gesang-Buch (Halle, vierte Ausgabe 1708). Text [Lied*

to pitches, rhythms, and basso continuo figures. For instance, the music editors of some editions of *Geist-reiches Gesang-Buch* replaced melodies printed in earlier Freylinghausen editions with other melodies.[8]

For more than a century and a half, scholars have sought to discover the identity of those who composed the melodies, edited the music, or wrote the basso continuo lines in the hymnal, but without a great deal of success. Through archival work, Miersemann hypothesized that Johann Gotthilf Ziegler (1688–1747), an accomplished musician who matriculated at the Paedagogium in March 1708, might have worked on the fourth edition (1708) of *Geist-reiches Gesang-Buch*.[9] Of significance is the fact that Ziegler, age twenty when he matriculated, received a personal invitation from the Paedagogium's Inspector. Unrelated to Miersemann's work and before his uncovering of the possibility of Ziegler, I was studying basso continuo figuration in the fourth edition. I discovered a distinct change about one-quarter of the way into the hymnal. The figuration is more accurate and more complete in the last three-quarters of the hymnal than in the first quarter.[10] Maybe Ziegler was the second of the two "Christian and experienced musicians from here" to whom Freylinghausen referred in the preface of the fourth edition. Miersemann's hypothesis is the most plausible to date.

Poets from across the spectrum of German congregational and devotional song wrote the hymns in Freylinghausen's Gesangbücher. The oldest texts are German translations of Gregorian chant. Freylinghausen includes many Reformation-Era hymns. From later times are texts by Johann Rist (1607–1667) and Paul Gerhardt (1607–1676) on the one hand,

---

396–758; Melodien-Büchlein] (Tübingen: Niemeyer, 2007). Bd. I/3: *Geist-reiches Gesang-Buch (Halle, vierte Ausgabe 1708). Apparat* (with Rainer Heyink) (Berlin: De Gruyter, 2013). Bd. II/1: *Neues Geist-reiches Gesang-Buch (Halle 1714). Text [Lied 1–434]* (Tübingen: Niemeyer, 2009). Bd. II/2: *Neues Geist-reiches Gesang-Buch (Halle 1714). Text [Lied 435–815]* (Berlin: De Gruyter, 2010). Bd. II/3: *Neues Geist-reiches Gesang-Buch (Halle 1714). Apparat* (with Rainer Heyink) (Berlin: De Gruyter, 2020).

8. These are documented in *Johann Anastasius Freylinghausen. Geistreiches Gesangbuch. Edition und Kommentar*; see Bd. I/3, IV. Notenanhang.

9. See Wolfgang Miersemann and Rainer Heyink, ed. *Die güldne Sonne. Lieder von Paul Gerhardt in Fassungen des Freylinghausenschen Gesangbuches. Musikalische eingerichtet von Axel Gebhardt auf Grundlage der kritischen Edition des Freylinghausenschen Gesangbuches von Dianne Marie McMullen und Wolfgang Miersemann* (Halle: Verlag der Franckeschen Stiftungen Halle/ortus musikverlag, 2007), 56–57.

10. See Dianne Marie McMullen, "'. . . von Christlichen und erfahrnen Musicis aufs neue fleißig untersuchet/und...verbessert. . .'. Unterschiede in der Generalbaßhandlung als Spuren zu den anonymen Musikredatoren des *Geist-reichen Gesang-Buches* (Halle 1704 u.ö.)," in *"Singt dem Herrn nah und fern." 300 Jahre Freylinghausensches Gesangbuch*, ed. Wolfgang Miersemann and Gudrun Busch (Tübingen: Verlag der Franckeschen Stiftungen Halle im Max Niemeyer Verlag, 2008), 55–76. This essay was based on a 2004 Halle conference paper.

and by Gottfried Arnold (1666–1714) and Johann Wilhelm Petersen (1649–1727) on the other. Also included are hymns by poets such as Johann Daniel Herrnschmidt (1675–1723) and Christian Friedrich Richter (1676–1711), Freylinghausen's colleagues at Halle.

GENERAL OBSERVATIONS RELATED TO THE CONTROVERSY

The typical German Lutheran congregational hymnal of the seventeenth and early eighteenth centuries has many hymns that paraphrase Scripture or that embed elements of church doctrine. Martin Luther's hymns represented the ideal. Alongside the congregational hymnal was a stream of devotional hymnals, often penned by a single author. In these, poets sometimes express topics such as their love for Jesus or their reflection on Christ's passion in tones more personal than one might expect in texts for congregational singing. A few poets also write about mystical visions. Orthodox theologians found some of the more personal texts inappropriate for church use and even for individual use.

Freylinghausen cast the net broadly. He drew from both traditional and devotional repertoires. Several of the devotional hymns caught the critics' attention. Commenting on some hymns in the *Geist-reiches Gesang-Buch*, Wittenberg theologians and professors wrote that through God's mercy, the Protestant church had never allowed such texts into its hymnals.[11] They wrote that it would have been better and more straightforward if Freylinghausen had issued a separate hymnal for the new "fanatic" hymns, since not everyone could tell the difference between them and older hymns.[12]

Freylinghausen was not the first to mix these genres. Other hymnal editors had paved the way,[13] but none had gained a following so quickly. The growing popularity of Freylinghausen's Gesangbuch was undoubtedly one of the critics' concerns. *Geist-reiches Gesang-Buch* appeared in 1704, and one new edition after another followed. The Waisenhaus's

---

11. *Der Löblichen Theologischen Facultaet zu Wittenberg Bedencken über das zu Glauche an Halle im Waisen-Hause daselbst edirte Gesang-Buch eingeholt und zum Druck befördert durch Hoch-Gräfliche Waldeckische zur Regierung Verordnete Land-Drost und Räthe* (Frankfurt and Leipzig: Zimmermann 1716), 25. For a transcription and an English translation of the Wittenberg pamphlet see Dianne Marie McMullen, "The *Geistreiches Gesangbuch* of Johann Anastasius Freylinghausen (1670–1739): A German Pietist Hymnal." Volumes I and II. Ph.D. dissertation, The University of Michigan-Ann Arbor, 1987, Vol. II, 567–631.
12. *Bedencken*, 8.
13. The Darmstadt 1698 hymnal, from which Freylinghausen drew, is an example.

burgeoning enrollment accounted for this in part, but copies were also going well beyond the city. Halle missionaries transported barrels of the Gesangbücher to distant lands, and hymnal editors from several continents took new hymns from its pages. Orthodox critics were cognizant of the influence that hymn singing can have on the development of a person's faith and were eager to stem the infiltration of hymns of which they disapproved into the church and into the homes of the faithful.

SOME PRIMARY PARTICIPANTS IN THE CONTROVERSY

Who praised Freylinghausen's *Geist-reiches Gesang-Buch* soon after it appeared? Who censured the work? It comes as no surprise that theologians and professors at Wittenberg, a stronghold of the Protestant Reformation, were among the first critics. Most other critics had studied or taught there also. Supporters usually had connections with Halle.

1. The Wittenberg Theologians

Theologians at the University of Wittenberg wrote a twenty-six-page pamphlet, *Der Löblichen Theologischen Facultaet zu Wittenberg Bedencken über das zu Glauche an Halle im Waisen-Hause daselbst edirte Gesang-Buch* (Frankfurt and Leipzig: Gottfried Zimmermann, 1716) (The Laudable Wittenberg Theology Faculty's Deliberations about the Hymnal Edited at the Waisenhaus in Glaucha/Halle), about *Geist-reiches Gesang-Buch* in 1714 and published it in 1716. The senior deacon and "the rest of the doctors and professors of the theology faculty at Wittenberg" signed it. They did not write the pamphlet on their own initiative. The nobility of Waldeck, fifty kilometers southwest of Kassel, had requested their opinion, asking if they should introduce Freylinghausen's hymnal to the public. The Wittenberg theologians answered in the negative. They feared that Freylinghausen's Gesangbuch would bring "Pietist ferment" to the people.[14]

2. Dassov vs. "Cordatus Evangelici"[15]

The Orthodox theologian Theodor Dassov (1669–1721) and a Pietist writer who called himself "Cordatus Evangelici" sparred over Freylinghausen's

---

14. *Bedencken*, 8.
15. Literally, "one whose heart is fervently beating for the evangelical cause."

hymnal. Dassov, born in Hamburg, taught at Wittenberg for some years and in 1714 became the General Superintendent in Schleswig-Holstein. The identity of Cordatus Evangelici is unknown. Dassov commented on Freylinghausen's work in *De Pura Doctrina* (Frankfurt and Leipzig, 1713) (Concerning Pure Doctrine). Cordatus Evangelici countered in the same year in *Fraternum Alloquium de Puritate Doctrinae* (Frankfurt and Leipzig, 1713) (Brotherly Encouragement about the Purity of Doctrine). Dassov also criticized Freylinghausen's work in *Justa Animadversio* (Hamburg: Christian Liebezeit, 1716) (Just Observation) and *Treuherzige Warnung vor die Quakerish und Enthusiastische Lieder Welche im Hallischen Gesang-Buch . . . Häuffig enthalten sind* (Flensburg: Balthasar Otto Bosseck, 1720) (Sincere Warning concerning the Hymns by Quakers and Enthusiasts [the spiritual radicals among the Pietists] often found in the Halle Hymnal), a thirty-one-page tract addressed to Holstein clergy and devoted to a discussion about the Halle Gesangbuch.

3. Löscher vs. Lange

The Orthodox Valentin Ernst Löscher (1673–1749) and the Pietist Johann Joachim Lange (1690–1744) also clashed over Freylinghausen's Gesangbuch. Recognized as the last important representative of Lutheran Orthodoxy, Löscher was born in Wittenberg to a theology professor there and eventually attended its university. After stints in Jüterbog and Delitzsch, Löscher was professor at Wittenberg from 1707 until 1709 and then pastor and superintendent in Dresden from 1709 until his death forty years later. Löscher founded a theological journal in 1701 that was published in Leipzig and continued until late in the eighteenth century under different titles.[16] One name was *Unschuldige Nachrichten* (Innocent News)[17]. He mentions Freylinghausen's Gesangbuch occasionally in this publication as well as in his six-volume *Evangelische Zehenden* (Magdeburg and Leipzig: Seidel, 1704–1707) (Protestant Tithes) and in *Timotheus Verinus* (Faithful Timothy),[18] which are reprinted columns from the 1711 and 1712 issues of *Unschuldige Nachrichten*.

Lange, Löscher's opponent, was a close associate of Francke and Freylinghausen. Lange lived with Francke in 1689 when they studied

---

16. For information about title changes, see Zedler, 49: cols. 1979–81.
17. "Innocent" in the sense of "frank."
18. Löscher also used the title for a two-part publication called *Vollständiger Timotheus Verinus* (Wittenberg, 1718–1722); Valentin Ernst Loescher, *The Complete Timotheus Verinus*, trans. James L. Langenbartels and Robert J. Koester (Milwaukee: Northwestern, 1998).

at the University of Leipzig. When Francke moved to Erfurt in 1690 and to Halle soon after, Lange followed. After a few years in the Berlin area, Lange became a professor of theology at the University of Halle in 1709. In response to Löscher's *Unschuldige Nachrichten,* Lange published *Aufrichte Nachrichten von der Unrichtigkeit der sogenannten* Unschuldigen Nachrichten (Leipzig: Heinichen, 1707–1714) (Sincere News about the Insincerity of the So-Called Innocent News). Countering Löscher's *Timotheus Verinus,* Lange issued *Die Gestalt Des kreutzreichs Christi In Seiner Unschuld/Mitten unter den falschen Beschuldigungen und Lästerungen sonderlich unbekehrter und fleischlichgesinnter Lehrer: Erstlich insgemein vorgestellet Und hernach mit dem Exempel Herrn D. Valentin Ernst Löschers In seinem so genannten* Timotheo Verino (Halle: Waisenhaus, 1713) (The Essence of the Kingdom of the Cross of Christ in its Innocence in the midst of False Accusations and Defamations especially made by Unconverted and Flesh-Minded Instructors, put forth first in general terms and then with the example of Herr D. Valentin Ernst Löscher in his So-Called Timotheus Verinus).

4. Freylinghausen vs. Löscher

In *Abgenöthigte Vertheidigung der Gründlichen Beantwortung/Wider eine unter dem Titel einer geziemenden Gegen-REMONSTRATION in denen so genannten* Unschuldigen Nachrichten *von A. 1709. Ordn. 2. und 3. hervorgetretene abermalige höchst-unbillige CENSUR gegen das hiesige Wäysen-Haus* (Halle: Waisenhaus, 1710) (A Defense, Given by Force, of the Thorough Reply against a Highly Unjust Censure against this Waisenhaus, a Censure appearing again under the Title of a "Fitting Counter-Remonstration" in the So-Called Innocent News A. 1709. Ordn. 2 and 3), an "admirer of innocence and truth" ("Liebhaber der Unschuld und Wahrheit") writes a response to Löscher's criticisms in 1709 issues of *Unschuldige Nachrichten* and in *Evangelische Zehenden* about many aspects of the Waisenhaus. Freylinghausen was the "admirer" who wrote *Abgenöthigte Vertheidigung,* a volume with more than 260 pages, ten devoted to the Gesangbuch. In addition, Freylinghausen counters Löscher in his preface to *Neues Geistreiches Gesang-Buch* (Halle, 1714).

DISCUSSION ABOUT THE HYMN TEXTS

The controversy about *Geist-reiches Gesang-Buch* focuses mostly on texts, not music, although music also was important in the debate. Driving many of the disputes were the beliefs held by both sides that a hymnal is as important as the Bible in spreading Scripture and church doctrine and that it serves as a Bible for the layperson.

The Wittenberg theologians, following Martin Luther and others, point to Satan's tricks in transmitting false teaching.[19] They were on the lookout for hymns that incorrectly portrayed church doctrine and for hymns with ambiguous phrases. They cite fifty-seven hymns in Freylinghausen's *Geist-reiches Gesang-Buch* as examples with offensive lines.[20] Accounting for more than half are hymns by Gottfried Arnold (1666–1714), Johann Wilhelm Petersen (1649–1727), and Christian Friedrich Richter (1676–1711). Arnold, who wrote nine of them, and Petersen, who wrote eleven, were church separatists. Richter, Waisenhaus physician and pharmacist, wrote ten. Richter's hymns first appeared in Freylinghausen's hymnal.

Orthodox and Pietist theologians tended to have differing views about the means of salvation. The typical Orthodox view was that a Christian is assured of eternal life on the merits of baptism and faith (the doctrine of justification). Many Pietist theologians wrote that one must also deny the old, sinful self and strive for a new being through a conscious conversion (rebirth or *Wiedergeburt*). Löscher writes that among the suspicious expressions of the time nothing is more vulgar than the phrase "the process of Christ in us" ("Der Process Christi in uns"). He interprets it to mean that one must go through a process and allow it to work within if one wants to be saved.[21] He argues that the phrase appears nowhere in the Bible and thus one should avoid it. This excerpt from Arnold's *Wenn vernunfft von Christi leiden und von dessen nutzen spricht* (When Reason Talks about Christ's Suffering and its Usefulness) captures the viewpoint of some Pietists:

... I should concern myself mostly
with this wonder:
only Christ's death in me
– while I continually die –
bears new life,
leads to the victory in judgment.[22]

---

19. *Bedencken*, 4.
20. While the titlepage of the Wittenberg treatise refers to the first edition of Freylinghausen's hymnal, it is clear that they also had the second edition because they refer to hymns in that edition's "Zugabe."
21. Löscher, *Unschuldige Nachrichten ... Eilffte Ordnung/A. 1704, Andere Auflage* (Leipzig, 1708), 683.
22. I thank Prof. Dr. Barbara Mahlmann (Bern) for corrections of and suggestions about some of my English translations.

> ... meine gröste sorgen
> sollen auf diß wunder gehn/
> das nur Christi tod in mir
> durch ersterben für und für
> zu dem leben ausgebieret/
> im gericht den sieg ausführet.[23]

The Wittenberg theologians complain that *DU sagst: ich bin ein Christ*[24] (You say: I am a Christian), a hymn by Johann Adam Haßlocher (1645–1726) that first appeared in the 1698 Darmstadt hymnal, encompasses ideas that smack of the "new theology." Haßlocher, like Arnold and Petersen, belonged to Spener's circle. The Wittenberg theologians write that the following stanza is contrary to the Lutheran doctrine that a Christian is so called based solely on belief in Christ.[25] The text demonstrates the Pietist emphasis on conversion.

> You say: I am a Christian.
> He is the one who knows Jesus.
> He not only names Him
> his God and Lord,
> but also diligently does
> what His Law requires.
> If you do not do this also,
> whatever you say is a mockery.

> Du sagst: ich bin ein Christ.
> Der ists/der JEsum kennet/
> und seinen GOTT und HErrn
> ihn nicht alleine nennet/
> sondern thut auch mit fleiß/
> was fordert sein gebot:
> thust du nicht auch also/
> ist/was du sagst/ein spott.[26]

---

23. *Geist-reiches Gesang-Buch*, no. 104, stanza 3.
24. *Geist-reiches Gesang-Buch*, no. 244.
25. *Bedencken*, 11–12.
26. *Bedencken*, no. 244, stanza 2.

Eschatology was another topic that prompted conflict. Especially contentious was the interpretation of the thousand-year reign of Christ (Revelation 20). Chiliasts take the account literally. They believe that there will be a time before the end of the world during which believers will reign with Christ. A small faction of Pietists were chiliasts. Most Orthodox, on the other hand, believed that Revelation 20 refers to the Christian afterlife in heaven where Christ will reign, not to an earthly kingdom. The Wittenberg theologians found chiliastic references in stanza 5 from Arnold's *DEin Erbe/HErr/liegt vor dir hier*[27] (Your heir, Lord, rests here before You):

O! Lord of life, manifest Yourself
with total power in Your people,
who fearfully cry day and night
until You appear as the Savior.
We stop until Your word of consent comes [and]
determines the whole victory and breakthrough for us.

Ach! HErr des Lebens/äussre dich
mit voller stärcke in den deinen/
die tag und nacht schrey'n ängstiglich/
bis du/als Retter/wirst erscheinen;
wir halten an/bis daß dein Ja–Wort kömmt/
den gantzen sieg und durchbruch uns bestimmt.[28]

Some devotional hymnals have texts that describe visions or mystical experiences, or even a mystical union with God. The Wittenberg theologians complain that selected texts in Freylinghausen's hymnal have "enthusiastic" expressions, such as "transport, divine flesh, a little spark in the soul, fire of divinity, and tangible unity with the Lord."[29] They write that a Lutheran hymnal should have no hymns with "ambiguous, insidious, or suspicious phrases," even if they appear devout.[30] In their search for questionable phrases, the Wittenberg theologians point to the following lines from Arnold's *SO führst du doch recht selig/HErr/die*

---

27. *Bedencken*, no. 306.
28. *Bedencken*, no. 306, stanza 5.
29. *Bedencken*, 15.
30. *Bedencken*, 6.

deinen[31] (How well, o Lord! art thou Thy people leading), lines which, they say, imply that one may enter into the Lord's being. They write that such expressions do not conform to the articles of faith.[32]

Draw me, then, into Your Will,
and carry and protect and lead Your poor child!
Your inner testimony is to alleviate the doubt:
Your Spirit conquers the fear and cravings.

So zieh mich dann hinein in deinen willen/
und trag und heg und führ dein armes kind!
Dein inners Zeugniß soll den zweiffel stillen:
dein Geist die furcht und lüste überwind'.[33]

Johann Scheffler (1624–1677), also known as Angelus Silesius, was a mystic. Born Lutheran, he converted to Roman Catholicism, eventually becoming a priest. The Wittenberg theologians call the following stanza from *JEsu! wie süß ist deine liebe*[34] (Jesus! How sweet is Your love), which originally appeared in Scheffler's *Heilige Seelen-Lust* (Holy pleasure of the soul) (Breslau, 1657), pseudo-mystical.

How sweet it is to be lit
and fully aglow with your flames
and to be flown together with You
in complete, eternal peace.
How sweet it is to be fused into a single unity
with You, My Treasure!

Wie süß ist es mit deinen flammen
entzündet werden und durchglü't/
und gantz und gar im ew'gen fried'
mit dir geflossen seyn zusammen:

---

31. *Geist-reiches Gesang-Buch,* no. 210. Translation of hymn title, *Moravian Hymn Book,* Part 1 (1751), no. 601.
32. *Bedencken,* 10.
33. *Geist-reiches Gesang-Buch,* no. 210, stanza 12, lines 1–4.
34. *Geist-reiches Gesang-Buch,* no. 455.

wie süß ists in ein ein'ges Ein
mit dir/mein Schatz! geschmoltzen seyn.[35]

The Wittenberg theologians write that Richter's *Wo ist meine Sonne blieben?*[36] (Where has my sun gone?) incorrectly describes the Holy Spirit's action and that Petersen's *Das Wort ist Fleisch worden*[37] (The Word has become Flesh) inaccurately depicts Christ's Incarnation. Concerning *Hilff Jesu, hilff siegen*[38] (Help, Jesus, help conquer) by Johann Christian Nehring (1671–1736), a hymn that features a dialogue between Soul and Jesus, they write that the phrase recovering "in the essence of the divinity" means nothing. The stanza reads:

Save my soul
and give me oils.
Let me recover only
in the essence of the divinity.
O Jesus, help me!
I cry to You.

Errette die seele/
und gib mir doch öle;
laß mich nur im wesen
der Gottheit genesen;
O Jesu/hilff mir!
ich schreye zu dir.[39]

Pietists responded quickly to criticism about Freylinghausen's hymnal, as one sees from the dates on the publications discussed earlier. Their defense is as fervent as the Orthodox objections. At times the two factions speak past one another, coming at topics from different angles and experiences. Part of the problem was that some Pietists used vocabulary stemming from Pietist devotional literature, as demonstrated

---

35. *Geist-reiches Gesang-Buch*, no. 455, stanza 3.
36. *Geist-reiches Gesang-Buch*, no. 624.
37. *Geist-reiches Gesang-Buch*, no. 642.
38. *Geist-reiches Gesang-Buch*, no. 310.
39. *Geist-reiches Gesang-Buch*, no. 310, stanza 2 ("Seele").

already.[40] In the preface to his 1711 hymnal and prayerbook, Christoph Heinrich Zeibich (1677–1748), pastor and superintendent at Baruth, publishes a list of Pietist expressions.[41]

Pietists argue that the Orthodox misinterpreted hymn texts. The debate over Arnold's *HErrlichste Majestät/himmlisches wesen!*[42] (Most magnificent Majesty! Heavenly Essence!) offers an example. The last lines of the first stanza read:

The shadow has covered us long enough.
Now the light will reveal the [Spiritual] Being.

Lang' genug hat uns der schatten bedecket/
nun wird das wesen vom Lichte entdecket.[43]

Lange writes that nothing in this text supports Löscher's claim in *Timotheus Verinus* that these words refer to the coming of a new light and to a newly erected church.[44] Pietists also argue that the Orthodox distorted texts and took lines out of context.

Johann Martin Schamelius (1668–1742), a well-known hymnologist of the time, writes complimentary words about Freylinghausen's work. Schamelius studied at Leipzig and Halle and served at Naumburg from 1703 as deacon and from 1708 as pastor. He edited a two-part, annotated hymnal (Naumburg, 1712–1714) and wrote *Evangelische Liedercommentarius* (Leipzig: Lanckisch, 1737) (Commentary on Protestant Hymns), among other works. In *Andrer Theil oder Fortsetzung der Theologischen Vindiciarum* (Leipzig: Lanckisch, 1715) (Second Part or Continuation of the Theological Vindicia), he writes that he likes the ordering of the rubrics called the "Order of Salvation," ("Ordnung des Heils"[45]) in Freylinghausen's Gesangbuch, but he thinks that "ordinary folk" might not

---

40. Wolfgang Miersemann analyzes Pietist expressions in "'anstößige und höchst verdächtige Redens–Arten.' Orthodoxe Kritik an sprachlicher 'Neurung' in Liedern des Pietismus" in Irmtraut Sahmland, Hans-Jürgen Schrader, ed., *Medizin- und kulturgeschichtliche Konnexe des Pietismus. Heilkunst und Ethik, arkane Tradition, Musik, Literatur und Sprache* (Göttingen: Vandenhoeck & Ruprecht, 2016), 279–301.
41. Miersemann, 289f.
42. *Geist–reiches Gesang-Buch*, no. 540.
43. *Geist–reiches Gesang-Buch*, no. 540, stanza 1, lines 5 and 6.
44. Lange, *Die Gestalt*, 325.
45. Rubrics in congregational hymnals of the time typically feature the calendar of the church year, as well as hymns for specific occasions (morning, Communion, etc.).

understand it thoroughly.⁴⁶ In *Kurzgefasste Historia der Hymnopoeorum* (Leipzig, 1737) (Brief History about Hymn-Writing), Schamelius calls several of Freylinghausen's hymns "scriptural."⁴⁷

Freylinghausen himself defends *Geist-reiches Gesang-Buch* in the preface (dated September 28, 1713) to *Neues Geist-reiches Gesang-Buch* (Halle, 1714). First, he notes the success of *Geist-reiches Gesang-Buch*, which reached its eighth edition in only ten years, the same year in which he published *Neues Geist-reiches Gesang-Buch*. He considers this fact evidence of its role in bringing people to salvation. Because of this, he sees no reason to respond formally or at length to "several unkind and unfounded criticisms" ("einige lieblose und ungegründete Censuren"). Instead, Freylinghausen points the reader to Lange's *Die Gestalt*.⁴⁸

Freylinghausen also directs attention to his 1710 *Abgenöthigte Vertheidigung*. In that volume Freylinghausen complains that Löscher uses the word chiliastic to describe Scheffler's *KOmm/Liebster/komm in deinen garten*⁴⁹ (Come, beloved, come into your garden), as well as *LIebster Jesu/du wirst kommen*⁵⁰ (Dear Jesus, You will come), possibly by Julius Franz Pfeiffer (?-1703?); the anonymous *NUr mein JEsus ist mein leben*⁵¹ (Only my Jesus is my Life); and the anonymous *O JEsu! komm zu mir*⁵² (O Jesus, come to me). These hymns follow one another in the same rubric, "Von der Begierde zu GOtt und Christo" (On the Desire for God and Christ). He writes that Löscher gives no evidence of chiliastic lines. Freylinghausen furthermore points out that *KOmm/Liebster/komm in deinen garten* had long been in use—citing the 1686 Lüneburg Gesangbuch, a hymnal approved by Superintendent Caspar Hermann Sandhagen (1639-1697)— and that people sang the hymn in Wolfenbüttel churches.⁵³ These are not strong arguments since Sandhagen was a Pietist and some Pietists lived in Wolfenbüttel.

Returning to the preface of *Neues Geist-reiches Gesang-Buch*, one notes that Freylinghausen makes the same argument that others do, namely, that critics misinterpreted poetic expressions. Concerning complaints about hymns by controversial poets, Freylinghausen writes that these poets

---

46. Schamelius, *Andrer Theil*, 8-9.
47. Schamelius, *Kurzgefasste Historia der Hymnopoeorum* (=second part of *Evangelische Liedercommentarius*), 13.
48. *Neues Geist-reiches Gesang-Buch*, Vorrede, sig.):(3ᵛ–):(4ʳ).
49. *Geist-reiches Gesang-Buch*, no. 351.
50. *Geist-reiches Gesang-Buch*, no. 352.
51. *Geist-reiches Gesang-Buch*, no. 353.
52. *Geist-reiches Gesang-Buch*, no. 354.
53. *Abgenötigte Vertheidigung*, 131-32.

understood the same simple mystical union that the Orthodox church teaches. He argues that critics would recognize this if they judged the hymns according to true hermeneutic principles and without bias. Since this is obvious, he writes, he sees no need for a lengthy defense.[54]

The division between the Orthodox and Pietists was already longstanding by the early eighteenth century. Freylinghausen's hymnal marks an important intersection for the debate between the two sides. While there are already studies, the theological debate surrounding the hymnal deserves additional analysis.

DISCUSSION ABOUT THE MELODIES

The Wittenberg theologians give less space to discussing melodies than to texts, but they had important concerns here also, aware that music has the power to introduce into the church a text contrary to Scripture or accepted doctrine. The reason that they gave great attention to texts is probably because they were theologians. Well-versed in the Bible and Lutheran doctrine, they easily spotted objectionable phrases. While some may have studied music, their terminology suggests that none had expertise.

The Wittenberg theologians address melodies twice in the twenty-six-page *Bedencken*, for less than a page near the start and for about a page and a half near the end.[55] They write that melodies in a Lutheran hymnal should be serious, devotional, and pious in terms of meter and composition. The melodies should not resemble the "elaborate, light, and almost sloppy manners found in secular tunes."[56]

One type of melody drew considerable criticism. The Wittenberg theologians write that with "a certain springing and dancing type of melody," the heart can be moved to a delicate transformation and to "the beginning of a frenzy."[57] To them the offending melodies were "unsacred" and "almost luxuriant." The words "springing" and "dancing" could describe many melodic types. Musicologists might have been left with speculation if the Wittenberg theologians had not given examples. They name eight hymns, seven of which have two things in common: the poetic meter is either dactylic (long-short-short) or amphibrachic (short-long-short), and the musical meter is triple. This combination hops and leaps. Already in 1645, Martin Rinckart (1586–1649), author of *Nun danket alle Gott* (Now

---

54. *Neues Geist-reiches Gesang-Buch*, Vorrede, sig.):4ʳ.
55. *Bedencken*, 6–7 and 25–26.
56. *Bedencken*, 6–7.
57. *Bedencken*, 7.

thank we all our God), notes that triple meter is the natural choice for dactylic verse.[58]

The Wittenberg theologians argue against the use of dactylic poetic meter on the basis that Martin Luther, whose hymns were the standard by which they measured congregational song, did not write in dactyls.[59] Maybe they were not aware that dactylic meter was not introduced into German poetry until the 1630s and 1640s, almost a century after Luther died. Scholars give the credit to August Buchner (1591–1661). It took a while before dactylic meter became common in German poetry. Early seventeenth-century German poets and composers such as Matthaeus Apelles von Löwenstern (1594–1648) and Philipp Harsdörffer (1607–1658) wrote sacred pieces with dactylic texts in triple meter, but these appear primarily in collections of devotional hymns.[60] Slightly later, Johann Scheffler (1624–1677) and Joachim Neander (1650–1680) added to this repertoire. Early eighteenth-century Orthodox theologians were anxious about the infiltration of this hymn type into church hymnals. Eventually, dactyls entered congregational hymnals, as one sees, for instance, in Gesangbücher published at Nuremberg in 1676 and at Darmstadt in 1698, the latter of which was an important source for Freylinghausen.

Some evidence supports the Wittenberg theologians' claim that a springing and dancing type of melody can transform the heart and even bring a person to a state of frenzy.[61] Quoting a Pietist theologian from Wolfenbüttel named B. Meyer, C.T. Rango writes in 1694 about the emotional reaction that some women had upon hearing Lange's *MEin JEsu/der du mich zum lust–spiel ewiglich dir hast erwählet*[62] (My Jesus, who has eternally chosen me for a joyful play). Meyer had told Rango that two young women became rapturous when they heard it.[63] Orthodox Lutherans opposed religious enthusiasm and thus also hymns that provoked it. Many towns and provinces even issued edicts against so-called fanatic sects. Some of the other hymns that caught the Wittenberg theologians' attention for the same reasons are *DIe lieblichen blicke/die JEsus mir giebt*

---

58. Martin Rinckart, *Summarischer Discurs und Durch-Gang von Teutschen Versen, Fuß-Tritten und vornehmsten Reim-Arten* (Leipzig, 1645) (Summary Discussion and Careful Deliberation about German Verses, Meters, and the Most Important Rhyme Types], 13–15.
59. *Bedencken*, 7.
60. One example is Joachim Neander's *Glaub- und Liebes-übung* (Bremen: Herman Brauer, 1680) (Practice of Faith and Love).
61. *Bedencken*, 7.
62. *Geist-reiches Gesang-Buch* no. 546.
63. C.T. Rango. *Von der Musica* (Greiffswald, 1694) [*About Music*], 41. Francke wrote a 1692 report about a similar incident. See *Eigentliche Nachricht von Dreyen Begeisterten Mägden* ([Halle], 1692) (True Report about Three Enthusiastic [Possessed] Girls).

152 A NEW SONG WE NOW BEGIN

Example 6.1 Freylinghausen's tune for *Die lieblichen blicke/die Jesus mir giebt* (1704/1708, No. 453; Zahn 6956b).

(The lovely glances that Jesus gives me) by Johann Quisfeld (1642–1686) (see Example 6.1),[64] *O Jesu/ mein Bräut'gam! wie ist mir so wohl*[65] (O Jesus, my bridegroom, how well I feel) by Heinrich Müller (1631–1675), Richter's *ES gläntzet der Christen inwendiges Leben*[66] (The Christian's inner life shows its splendor), and *JHr kinder des Höchsten! wie stehts um die Liebe?*[67] (Children of the Most High, how do you deal with love?) by Christian Andreas Bernstein (1677–1699). Given the nature of some of the sources from which Freylinghausen drew, one might have predicted his inclusion of dactylic, triple-meter hymns.

As noted in the earlier discussion about hymn texts, the Wittenberg theologians had written that it would have been better if Freylinghausen had printed a separate hymnal for the "new fanatic hymns." Their opinion about leaping melodies is at least as strong, if not stronger. They write that they find such hymns inappropriate for both church and home devotions.[68] Later in the treatise they write that poets may express their divine thoughts in any type of meter, but that it is inappropriate to offer the type of melody that they found offensive to a Christian congregation.[69]

Why did some seventeenth-century poets choose dactylic meter for sacred poetry? The doctrine of affections may offer an explanation. Baroque poets had differing opinions about the affects of iambic and trochaic meters, but they were unanimous about the affect of dactylic meter. They used words such as laughter, love, and joy to describe it. Both

64. *Geist-reiches Gesang-Buch*, no. 453.
65. *Geist-reiches Gesang-Buch*, no. 459.
66. *Geist-reiches Gesang-Buch*, no. 515.
67. *Geist-reiches Gesang-Buch*, no. 386.
68. *Bedencken*, 7.
69. *Bedencken*, 25.

Orthodox and Pietist poets wrote cheerful texts, but for some reason, Pietist poets were more drawn to the dactyl than Orthodox poets. Timing also might have had something to do with it, for the introduction of dactylic meter into German poetry happened around the time of the rise of the Pietist movement.

Of the eight melodies about which the Wittenberg theologians lodged complaints, five fall under the rubric of "Joy in the Holy Spirit" in Freylinghausen's hymnal. This rubric has a Pietist theological bent and would have caught the eye of an Orthodox theologian. The Wittenberg theologians note that "the matter is not improved with such [rubric] titles," citing this one and others such as "Longing for Christ," "Love for Jesus," "Spiritual Marriage with Christ," and "Zion's Hope."[70] The affect of dactylic meter apparently suited the tone of some Pietist texts.

Some scholars forget the fact that Freylinghausen included most of the standard congregational hymns. Pietists valued knowledge of Scripture and doctrine. At the same time, they were interested in spiritual rejuvenation. In the preface to *Geist-reiches Gesang-Buch*, Freylinghausen writes that he believes that God uses Christian hymns and songs as a means to touch people's hearts, to persuade them, and to introduce them to a better way.[71] He writes that his hymnal offers more than enough material to strengthen, nourish, and refresh one's soul.[72] Hymns with new modes of expression, including hymns with dactylic texts written in triple meter, were a part of that repertoire.

The Orthodox and Pietists worshiped in congregational settings. Many Pietists also often gathered at one another's homes to read and discuss Scripture and to sing hymns. In these "conventicles" Pietists sang from publications and manuscripts that the Orthodox, who were less likely to have such gatherings (some even opposing them), would probably not have used. These cultural differences offer some explanation for the divergent styles of artistic expression.

RECEPTION OF FREYLINGHAUSEN'S *GEIST-REICHES GESANG-BUCH*

The popularity of Freylinghausen's *Geist-reiches Gesang-Buch* was apparent right from the start, with the production of a new edition of the first hymnal every one, two, or three years for thirty years. One might attribute

---

70. *Bedencken*, 25–26.
71. *Geist-reiches Gesang-Buch*, Vorrede, sig.):():1ʳ.
72. *Geist-reiches Gesang-Buch*, Vorrede, sig.):():1ᵛ.

this in part to the growing enrollment at the Glauchasche Anstalten, but it was much more than that. Contemporary references in hymnal prefaces across Europe and in America, in letters, and in journals, demonstrate the *Geist-reiches Gesang-Buch*'s appeal.

The new content of *Geist-reiches Gesang-Buch* influenced hymnody far and wide, despite the initial controversy. Texts and melodies from it appear in hymnals on several continents in many languages. Already in the early eighteenth century, European congregations from southern parts of Switzerland to Scandinavia, Latvia, Transylvania, Lithuania, and Silesia were singing texts and melodies that originated with the Freylinghausen Gesangbücher. John Wesley (1703–1791) introduced texts to English speakers. Halle pastors and missionaries brought large quantities of Freylinghausen's work to North America, Siberia, India, and Australia. When German immigrants in America sought to produce a unified hymnal,[73] Freylinghausen's Gesangbuch was their primary source, although one might have predicted it since the editor, Henry Melchior Mühlenberg (1711–1787), the "father of American Lutheranism," had close connections with Halle. Count Nicolaus Zinzendorf (1700–1760), who had been a student at the Glauchasche Anstalten for five years, printed in his Moravian (Brüdergemeine) hymnals hymns from Freylinghausen's hymnals, altering some to suit his theological taste. Zinzendorf once wrote to Freylinghausen that he had memorized two hundred and fifty hymns from the Freylinghausen hymnal, calling it a treasure.[74] Modern hymnals of many denominations include hymns that originate in Freylinghausen.

RECENT SCHOLARSHIP ABOUT THE FREYLINGHAUSEN GESANGBÜCHER

Starting in the 1980s the Freylinghausen Gesangbücher received a burst of scholarly attention. Working separately and never having met one another before, an American, a Dane, and a Finn wrote doctoral dissertations on different aspects of Freylinghausen. In 1987 I completed *The Geistreiches Gesangbuch of Johann Anastasius Freylinghausen (1670–1739): A German Pietist Hymnal* (The University of Michigan-Ann Arbor), having spent a year and a half researching in Germany. Also in the 1980s,

---

73. *Erbauliche Lieder-Samlung* (Germantown: Leibert and Billmeyer, 1786) (Devotional Hymn Collection).
74. See Dietrich Meyer, "Johann Anastasius Freylinghausen und Nikolaus Ludwig Graf von Zinzendorf" in *Pietismus und Liedkultur* (Tübingen: Niemeyer, 2002): 298.

Steffen Arndal studied the work of Hans Adolph Brorson (1694–1764), who translated hymns from Freylinghausen from German into Danish. Arndal's dissertation, *"Gen store hvide Flok vi see . . .". H.A. Brorson og tysk pietistisk vaekkelsessang,* appeared in 1989 at Odense Universitet. Tracing predecessors to Freylinghausen's work for more than a decade, Suvi–Päivi Koski completed *Geist-reiches Gesang-Buch vuodelta 1704 pietistisenä virsikirjana. Tutkimus kirjan toimittajasta, taustasta, teologiasta, virsistä ja virsirunoilijoista. Zusammenfassung: Das Geist-reiche Gesang-Buch aus dem Jahre 1704 als ein pietistisches Gesangbuch-eine Untersuchung zu dem Herausgeber, zu dem Hintergrund, zu der Theologie, zu den Liedern und Liederdichtern des Buches* in 1996 at the University of Helsinki. Together these dissertations, completed at universities outside of Germany, cover a lot of literary, theological, historical, and musicological territory.

This was only the start. Soon research picked up in Freylinghausen's homeland with great momentum! Igniting it was the work of Germanist Wolfgang Miersemann (Berlin) and musicologist Gudrun Busch (Bonn), who discovered their common interests in Pietist hymnody at Wolfenbüttel. Starting in 1994 they coordinated several conferences held at the very place where Freylinghausen had produced his hymnals, today called the Franckesche Stiftungen. Miersemann and Busch invited scholars from around the world to take part.

Supported by the Deutsche Forschungsgemeinschaft (DFG) and the Franckesche Stiftungen, in 2000 Miersemann established the Forschungsstelle Freylinghausen-Edition (Freylinghausen Edition Research Center) at Halle's Franckesche Stiftungen. There Miersemann worked with other scholars on the Freylinghausen modern critical edition. Simultaneously, I worked on it in the United States, equipped with hard copies of all twenty-six Freylinghausen editions with printed music and making frequent research trips to Halle. At the Franckesche Stiftungen Miersemann, our colleagues, and I collaborated, probably only steps from where Freylinghausen and his associates worked three centuries earlier.

The Freylinghausen Project began in 2000 with the collection of copies of all editions of Freylinghausen's hymnals, a difficult task since it was hard to gain permission to copy some of the rare editions. We reached our initial goal of publishing the first volume of the modern critical edition in 2004, the three hundredth anniversary of the publication of the first edition (1704) of *Geist-reiches Gesang-Buch*. At the same time, we celebrated with an international conference at the Franckesche Stiftungen, organized by Miersemann and Busch. This followed other conferences on Freylinghausen and Pietist hymnody that they coordinated in 1994 and 1999. Conference proceedings accompanied each one.[75] In 2020 we completed the six-volume modern critical edition: for *Geist-reiches Gesang-Buch*, two volumes for the content of the Gesangbuch and one volume for the critical apparatus, and the same for *Neues Geist-reiches Gesang-Buch*.[76] A large commentary volume, with essays about Freylinghausen and his work written by scholars from many disciplines, is in the works.

Freylinghausen scholarship during the last four decades has been international, vast, in depth, interdisciplinary, and exciting. While scholars have pursued dozens of angles, fascinating questions and topics are open. Those interested in researching at the Franckesche Stiftungen will find welcoming staffs at the library and archive, as well as first-rate collections. Scholars will discover stimulating subjects that will expand upon the current understanding of sacred music at the time of Bach and particularly of the work of Freylinghausen—Francke's respected colleague and son-in-law, pastor, educator, hymn writer, theologian, and compiler of Gesangbücher of great importance.

---

75. Gudrun Busch and Wolfgang Miersemann, ed., *"Geist-reicher-Gesang." Halle und das pietistische Lied*. Hallesche Forschungen 3 (Tübingen: Niemeyer, 1997); Wolfgang Miersemann and Gudrung Busch, ed., *Pietismus und Liedkultur* (Tübingen: Niemeyer, 2000); and Wolfgang Miersemann and Gudrun Busch, *"Singt dem Herrn nah und fern." 300 Jahre Freylinghausens Gesangbuch* (Tübingen: Niemeyer, 2008).
76. Important to the production of the volumes have been ortus verlag, Verlag der Franckeschen Stiftungen, Max Niemeyer Verlag, and Walter deGruyter GmbH. Prof. Dr. Paul Raabe, Prof. Dr. Thomas Müller-Bahlke, and Dr. Britta Klosterberg of the Franckesche Stiftungen also gave tremendous support to the Freylinghausen Project from the start.

PART 2

Influential American Hymnals

7.

"Walther's Hymnal" for the Missouri Synod Saxons

Jon D. Vieker

In April 1847, a small cadre of German Lutheran pastors and congregational representatives from Illinois, Indiana, Missouri, Michigan, New York, and Ohio, met in Chicago at First Saint Paul Lutheran Church. There they approved the first constitution of *Die Deutsche Evangelisch Lutherische Synode von Missouri, Ohio, und andern Staaten,* "The German Evangelical Lutheran Synod of Missouri, Ohio, and Other States."[1]

This modest gathering represented the culmination of several earlier meetings that had been held over the previous three years in Cleveland, St. Louis, and Fort Wayne, as the men from Franconia, who were affiliated with J. K. W. Löhe, (1808–1872), separated themselves from the Ohio Synod and drew C. F. W. Walther (1811–1887) and the Saxons of Missouri into their conversations about forming a confessional, Lutheran synod on the American frontier. At this first convention, these Saxons and Franconians, along with a third group of German immigrants fleeing the effects of the Prussian Union, elected the Saxon, C. F. W. Walther, to be their first president.[2]

Just three months later, in June 1847, Walther the Saxon announced in his biweekly publication, *Der Lutheraner,* that a "new *Church Hymnal for Ev. Lutheran Congregations of the Unaltered Augsburg Confession* . . . has now

---

1. Carl S. Meyer, ed., *Moving Frontiers: Readings in the History of The Lutheran Church—Missouri Synod* (St. Louis: Concordia Publishing House, 1964), 142–143.
2. W. F. Hussmann, "Erster Synodalbericht der deutschen Evangelisch-Lutherischen Synode von Missouri, Ohio und andern Staaten, vom Jahre 1847," *Der Lutheraner* 3 (July 27, 1847): 132–133.

159

left the press."[3] This hymnal, which was born as a kind of fraternal twin to the Missouri Synod, became the first and only German hymnal that this strand of American Lutheranism would ever have. Edited by Missouri's founding president and foremost theologian, "Walther's Hymnal" became for the Missouri Synod a kind of hymnological and theological plumb line against which all subsequent hymnals would be measured.[4] In this chapter, we will examine the formation and reception histories of Walther's Hymnal and then consider the impact of Walther's Hymnal on the congregational song of the Missouri Synod and beyond.

PIETISM AND THE ENLIGHTENMENT

The Lutheran Church at the dawn of the nineteenth century presented a theologically bleak state of affairs—both in Saxony as well as throughout most German lands. From the accounts of the Saxons and others who emigrated to the United States and elsewhere during the 1830s onward, the twin influences of Pietism and Rationalism had severely affected both the theology and practice of the Lutheran churches in Germany.[5]

The movement known as Pietism is often reckoned from the publication of Philipp Jacob Spener's *Pia Desideria* ("Pious Wishes") of 1675, which sought primarily to address the social injustices and wild living of many Lutherans of his day, as well as the perceived spiritual lifelessness of Lutheran orthodoxy.[6] During the course of the eighteenth century,

---

3. [C. F. W. Walther], "Lutherisches Kirchen-Gesangbuch," *Der Lutheraner* 3 (June 1, 1847), 112; as translated in Joel R. Baseley, trans., *C. F. W. Walther's Original Der Lutheraner, Volumes One through Three (1844–47): The LCMS in Formation* (Dearborn: Mark V Publications, 2012), 3:112.
4. *Kirchengesangbuch für Evangelisch-lutherische Gemeinden ungeänderter Augsburgischer Confession* (New York: Ludwig, 1847). For an English translation of the 1892 edition of this hymnal, see: Matthew Carver, trans. and ed., *Walther's Hymnal: Church Hymnbook for Evangelical Lutheran Congregations of the Unaltered Augsburg Confession* (St. Louis: Concordia, 2012).
5. For source readings on the effects of Rationalism and Pietism on German Lutheranism, see Robert C. Schultz, "The European Background," in Meyer, *Moving Frontiers*, 47–89. For further reading see August R. Suelflow and E. Clifford Nelson, "Following the Frontier," in *The Lutherans in North America*, rev. edition (Philadelphia: Fortress, 1980), 147–159; and for a primary source in nineteenth-century European historiography, see C. F. A. Kahnis, *Internal History of German Protestantism Since the Middle of the Last Century*, tr. Theodore Meyer (Edinburgh: Clark, 1856; Philadelphia: Smith & English).
6. Douglas H. Schanz, *An Introduction to German Pietism: Protestant Renewal at the Dawn of Modern Europe* (Baltimore: The Johns Hopkins University Press, 2013), 86–91. See also pages 1–11 for a helpful introduction and overview of the most important studies of Pietism over the last sixty years.

Pietism flowered into a variety of shades and aromas, but by the time its long-range effects had reached young Walther and his university compatriots in the late 1820s, it presented as a kind of radical internalization of the Christian faith, where one took a reading off of one's self in order to determine whether or not one was truly a Christian.

Walther poignantly recounts his struggle with Pietism as a young university student at Leipzig:

> ... I had an older brother who had entered the university ahead of me. Just before I got to university, he joined a society of converted students. When I arrived, he introduced me to this circle of Christians.... This went on for nearly a half year. Then a theology student who was a good deal older—a genuine Pietist—joined our group.... This theology student came to us and said, "You think you are all converted Christians, do you? But you are not. You have not yet passed through any real penitential agony."... He kept repeating his claim until I finally began to ask myself whether I was really a Christian ... I went to the student and asked him, "What must I do to be saved?" He prescribed a number of things I had to do and gave me several books to read, among them Fresenius's *Book on Confession and Communion*. The more I read in that book, the more uncertain I became as to whether I really was a Christian.[7]

Walther and his university friends became convinced that they could not find salvation until they had struggled so much with their sin that they felt the terrors of hell itself. Then they would need to fully repent of their sin and completely dedicate their lives to God. The counsel from Fresenius's volume was like kerosene on the open flame of a troubled conscience,[8] as Walther described:

> His advice to cry to God "until you obtain grace" means, as the words that follow show, "until you have a *feeling* of grace." The sweet sensation that satisfies the heart—that is what these people call grace. But grace is [actually] not something for which you must look in your heart. It is in the heart of God. Grace cannot be found *in* me. It is *outside* of me.[9]

Pietism downplayed the external means of grace in favor of an internal renewal and holiness. Likewise, the observance of the church year, formal

---

7. Carl Ferdinand Wilhelm Walther, *Law and Gospel: How to Read and Apply the Bible*, trans. Christian C. Tiews (St. Louis: Concordia, 2010), 157–158.
8. Johann Philip Fresenius, *Beicht- und Comunion-Buch*, 3rd ed. (Franckfurt: Brönner, 1753).
9. Walther, *Law and Gospel*, 161.

liturgy, and Christian ceremony gave way to more subjective and emotional approaches toward corporate worship. Frank Senn notes:

> Pietism did not have a liturgical program of its own with which to replace that of [Lutheran] orthodoxy, but its emphases did have a profound impact on public worship . . . Pietist influences were evident at points in the liturgy where extempore prayer could be offered, as in the pulpit office, and where hymns could be selected. The old objective church hymns, which celebrated the saving acts of God in Christ, were set aside in favor of hymns that concentrated on the conditions of the soul. As new hymnals were published, they were arranged according to the theological order of salvation rather than the liturgical calendar and church year. New melodies, better suited to the emotional character of Pietist hymn texts, replaced the old chorales.[10]

In addition to Pietism, the other major *Zeitgeist* at play for Walther and the Saxons was the enduring effects of the Enlightenment, otherwise known as Rationalism. Although the influences of the Enlightenment on Western thinking are usually dated from the late seventeenth century, they did not become especially pronounced in much of German Lutheranism until the second half of the eighteenth century, when Rationalist principles began to impact the revision of hymnals and agendas, and especially the preaching in congregations.[11] What this meant for weekly worship was that the orders of service, the hymns, and baptismal rites all had to be revised and "updated" to fit the rationalistic notions of the day. In particular, Rationalist thinkers in the church did not have much use for the deity of Christ, for superstitious talk of the devil, or for miracles in the Bible—to one degree or another. Quite often all that was left was ethics, with a moralizing imperative for parish preaching. And so one sees sermon topics during this period ranging from such spiritually weighty

---

10. Frank C. Senn, *Christian Liturgy: Catholic and Evangelical* (Minneapolis: Augsburg Fortress, 1997): 498.
11. Paul Graff, *Geschichte der Auflösung der alten gottesdienstlichen Formen in der Evangelischen Kirche Deutschlands*, 2 vols. (Göttingen: Vandenhoeck & Ruprecht, 1937–39), 2:35. "The old liturgical orders had already been greatly depreciated, undermined, and gutted by prior occurrences, prevailing trends, and especially by Pietism. As an example showing to what degree Pietism paved the way . . . the Schwerin hymnal of 1764 left out many hymns by Luther and Paul Gerhardt while taking up Pietistic ones instead, independently of the Freylinghausen hymnal. The Rationalist view of worship coincides with that of Pietism in measuring the value of the divine service according to its effect on the individual . . . In Pietism, the divine service has in mind a consideration for personal feeling; Rationalism, for the individual man and his particular situation . . . What was properly ecclesial was dissolved at the cost of individualism and subjectivism . . ." Translation by Matthew Carver (unpublished manuscript).

matters as "On the Hardiness of Shepherds and a Warning against the Use of Fur-Caps"; or, "On Going for Walks: A Sermon for Hypochondriacs."[12] Likewise, the hymnals and agendas at the end of the eighteenth century and beginning of the nineteenth century were almost inevitably revised away from orthodox, Lutheran doctrine toward the free-thinking and moralizing notions of rationalistic idealism.[13]

The twin influences of Pietism and Rationalism had altered indelibly the worship life of German Lutheranism by the dawn of the nineteenth century. Pietism emphasized small groups that gathered for prayer and discipline toward living a holy life and personal religion. Rationalism demanded moralizing and didactic preaching. And yet, change was around the corner. Theodore Tappert notes regarding the years 1800–1830:

> The excesses of the French Revolution, culminating in a radical repudiation of Christianity were interpreted by many as the bitter harvest of the infidelity stemming from the Enlightenment. The subsequent conquests of Napoleon imposed on occupied countries hardships such as merely human powers seemed incapable of overcoming. In time resistance to Napoleon grew, and the wars of liberation were accompanied by a great surge of patriotic feeling . . . At times, the spirit of nationalism seemed to contribute to religious awakenings; at others, religious sentiment appeared to support military or political resistance.[14]

The Napoleonic Wars raged from 1803 to 1815, and by the end, Germany and the rest of Western Europe was in a shambles. The idealism of eighteenth-century Rationalism had lost much of its luster after a dozen years of destruction and the bloodshed of some six million casualties. Germans began to look to the past and to their own history for unity, and the Reformation consequently became a kind of national myth, with Luther as its hero. Scattered calls began to arise for a renewal of Lutheranism according to its first principles.[15]

---

12. Senn, *Christian Liturgy*, 540.
13. Graff, *Geschichte der Auflösung*, 2:12 notes regarding Saxony in particular: "Already in 1787, the state parliament expressed a desire to change the divine service. The opportunity was ripe when in 1799 a new edition of the *Kirchenbuch* was needed. An opinion report by Reinhard stressed the fact that, since the 16th century, there had been changes in the use of language and method of presentation concerning the essence of religion, and hence the prayers, collects, etc., had to be changed." Translation by Matthew Carver (unpublished manuscript).
14. Theodore G. Tappert, ed., *Lutheran Confessional Theology in America, 1840–1880*. A Library of Protestant Thought. (New York: Oxford University Press, 1972), 5.
15. Joseph Herl, "Germany from 1620 to the Present," in *Lutheran Service Book: Companion to the Hymns*, edited by Joseph Herl, Peter C. Reske, and Jon D. Vieker (St. Louis: Concordia, 2019), 2:46.

The most influential of these calls happened in 1817, on the three hundredth anniversary of Luther's posting of the Ninety-Five Theses. In that year, Claus Harms (1778–1855), a German pastor in Kiel, republished Luther's Ninety-Five Theses along with another ninety-five theses of his own, in which he attacked reason as "the pope of our time" who "dismisses Christ from the altar and throws God's Word from the pulpit."[16] Harms's Ninety-Five Theses pamphlet was so popular that some two hundred responses to it appeared in newspapers and various periodicals of the day, arguing the pros and cons of his proposals.[17]

Harms's incisive and forceful criticism of Rationalism was directed not only against its ideology, but especially against its deleterious effect on the hymnody and preaching of the Lutheran Church. In Thesis 84, Harms noted:

> [There is] confusion with the authorized and accepted church agendas, hymnals and catechisms, just as already the public preaching in many instances stands as a glaring, horrid contradiction in holy places.[18]

Harms goes on to cite an older hymn by Johann Arnschwanger (1625–1696):

> "Two places, O man, you have before you," said the old hymnal. In modern times, the devil has been killed and hell has been dammed up.[19]

For Harms, the old hymnals proclaimed the doctrines of heaven and hell; in recent times, talk of the supernatural and eternal realities had been discarded on the ash heap of history.

Harms's clarion cry of 1817 advocated for a return to a Lutheranism grounded in the orthodox teachings of Luther and the Lutheran Confessions of the sixteenth century—a return to first principles among Lutherans. As a result, churchmen and scholars began to dig out the original forms of those confessional documents and of Luther's writings. Others began to recover the original forms of hymn texts and melodies, as well as the

---

16. Claus Harms, *Das sind die 95 theses oder Streitsätze Dr. Luthers, theuren Andenkens: zum besondern Abdruck besorgt und mit andern 95 Sätzen als mit einer Uebersetzung aus Ao. 1517 in 1817 begleitet* (Kiel: im Verlage der academischen Buchhandlung, 1817), 30 (Thesis 71).
17. Tappert, *Lutheran Confessional Theology in America*, 7.
18. Harms, *Das sind die 95 theses*, 33.
19. Harms, *Das sind die 95 theses*, 23 (Thesis 24): "'Zwei Ort', o Mensch, hast du vor dir,' hieß es im alten Gesangbuch. In neuern Zeiten hat man den Teufel totgeschlagen und die Hölle zugedämmt."

liturgies of the sixteenth century, which had been corrupted by Rationalist churchmen. Even Harms himself worked to restore the hymnody of the Reformation. His own research led him to discover several original texts by Luther, Gerhardt, and others. He was less successful in restoring the original "rhythmic" form of hymn melodies of the sixteenth century; a preference for the isometric versions was still firmly entrenched.[20]

As awareness of primary sources grew, scholars in the nineteenth century began to assemble them into critical editions, which they then published and which hymnal editors began to draw from when new hymnals were produced.[21] This was all part of the larger, nineteenth-century renaissance of Luther studies and Lutheranism, with a return *ad fontes* through the study of hymns and liturgies, the collected writings of Martin Luther, and the texts of the Lutheran Confessions and what they meant theologically.[22] Walther's Hymnal and the formation of the Missouri Synod arose out of this fertile renaissance of confessional Lutheranism and its liturgy and hymnody during the nineteenth century, and this is reflected in how Walther approached his editorship of this hymnal.

PREDECESSOR HYMNALS

When considering which hymnals might have served as a model for Walther's Hymnal, we can begin by looking at the hymnals that Walther and his Saxon compatriots would have brought with them from their German homeland. There is evidence that in some of the congregations that eventually joined the Missouri Synod, there was more than one hymnal in use prior to 1847. This was because members of those congregations had come from different parts of Germany and so brought different hymnals with them. Such an arrangement could become confusing, of course, when it came time to put hymn numbers on hymn boards, with two or three different hymnals being used all in the same

---

20. Günther Gassmann, Mark W. Oldenburg, and Duane H. Larson, *Historical Dictionary of Lutheranism* (Lanham: Scarecrow, 2011), 174.
21. Herl, "Germany from 1620 to the Present," 2:48, notes that first large-scale effort to recover Reformation era hymn texts was August Jakob Rambach, *Anthologie christlicher Gesänge aus allen Jahrhunderten der Kirche*, 6 vols. (Altoona, 1817–33). Rambach's collection foreshadowed the critical editions of Philipp Wackernagel, *Das deutsche Kirchenlied von der ältesten Zeit bis zu Anfang des 17. Jahrhunderts*, 5 vols. (Leipzig, 1864–1877); and Albert. F. W. Fischer, *Das deutsche evangelische Kirchenlied des 17. Jahrhunderts*, completed and edited by Wilhelm Tümpel, 6 vols. (Gütersloh, 1904–1916).
22. For an overview of the recovery of Luther's writings and the birth of modern Luther studies during the nineteenth century, see: Bernhard Lohse, *Martin Luther: An Introduction to His Life and Work* (Philadelphia: Fortress, 1986), 217–226.

service.[23] Then there was the problem of variations of hymn texts among the different hymnals being used. Many hymn texts during this period had been corrupted by Rationalist churchmen, and others had been slightly emended for various reasons along the way. There were even different numbers of stanzas included for a particular hymn, or different orderings of those stanzas, or both. These kinds of problems were somewhat evident in Walther's Trinity Congregation as well, at least for a time.[24]

However, when all is said and done, it is evident that, at least for Walther's Trinity Congregation in St. Louis, the predominant hymnal in use prior to 1847 was the *Dresdnisches Gesangbuch*, the "Dresden Hymnal."[25] Of course, the publication of hymnals in Dresden went back to the sixteenth century, but this particular hymnal was a new edition that had first been published in 1796 under the editorship and oversight of Church Superintendent Karl Christian Tittmann (1744–1820).[26] Tittmann was a churchman and university professor, who is regarded as having stood philosophically "between the eudaemonism of the Enlightenment and Kantian moralism." Tittmann's most famous work was titled *Christliche Moral* ("Christian Morality") which was written with the intention of "maintaining a middle ground between the lax compliance of a frivolous philosophy and the overly severe rigor of an exaggerated and rational philosophy."[27] Tittmann was clearly a product of his philosophical age, and this showed in his editorship of the 1796 Dresden Hymnal.[28]

23. Meyer, *Moving Frontiers*, 181–182; see also Mühlenberg's observation cited in Chapter 1, note 61.
24. See "Von dem amerikanisch-luth. und reformirten Gesangbuch," *Der Lutheraner* 5 (August, 7, 1849): 197–204; and "Die Kirchen-Gesangbücher," *Der Lutheraner* 7 (October 1, 1850): 20; as well as additional documentation regarding the various problems the Missourians encountered with the existing German hymnals of this period, as noted in James L. Brauer, "The Hymnals of The Lutheran Church–Missouri Synod" (STM Thesis, Concordia Seminary, 1967), 16–20.
25. In a sermon dated Advent 1842, Walther makes the following reference to the Dresden Hymnal as being in common use at Trinity Congregation: "Lasset uns zuvor Gott im stillen Gebete um seinen Gnadenbeistand anrufen, wenn wir mit einander werden gesungen haben (Dresdner Gesangb.) 225, 9." ["Let us before God in silent prayer call upon his gracious assistance, as soon as we have sung with one another (Dresden Hymnal) 225:9."]. C. F. W. Walther, *Gnadenjahr: Predigten über die Evangelien des Kirchenjahrs von Dr. C. F. W. Walther. Aus seinem schriftlichen Nachlaß gesammelt* (St. Louis: Concordia, 1891), 31. Walther would not have so specifically referenced a hymn number and stanza had not that hymnal been readily available to the worshiper. The parenthetical reference appears to be an editorial insertion made decades later so as to not be confused with Walther's Hymnal of 1847.
26. The second edition was printed in 1798: *Dresdnisches Gesangbuch auf höchesten Befehl herausgegeben* (Dresden: Churfürstl. Hofbuchdruckerey, 1798).
27. Paul Tschackert, "Tittmann, Karl Christian," in *Allgemeine Deutsche Biographie* (1894), https://de.wikisource.org/wiki/ADB:Tittmann,_Karl_Christian. Accessed March 31, 2023.
28. Tschackert observes: "In the practical field, [Tittmann] then tried to redesign the hymnals and agendas that had been in use up to that point, an undertaking that cannot be judged to be

When it was first published, there was an article in the local newspaper that demonstrates the kind of over-confidence typical of the times. It noted:

> We should have no need of a new hymnal for centuries because Dr. Tittmann has provided the Dresden Hymnal with the greatest possible perfection, and the proper teaching, as is here submitted in the selected songs, is exalted above all other improvements.[29]

Tittmann's hymnal, produced under the influence of German Rationalism, continued to be reprinted as late as 1837, just a year before Walther and the Saxons came to Missouri.[30] This Dresden hymnal, therefore, was the hymnal that Walther and his young, Saxon colleagues grew up with, that they and their compatriots brought with them to America, and which was, in fact, used at Trinity Congregation, St. Louis, when Walther began serving there as pastor in May 1841.

THE BIRTH OF WALTHER'S HYMNAL

The minutes of Trinity Congregation indicate that, for most of 1842, Walther's congregation was consumed with the details of constructing a new sanctuary. The total cost for the sanctuary project was about $5,000.[31] However, shortly after the dedication of the sanctuary,[32] the congregation resolved in February 1843 that in the public divine services "only pure

---

fruitful according to our present-day ... It was a time of the "watering down" of evangelical hymnody..." Additionally, Graff, *Geschichte der Auflösung,* 2:49, notes: "There is a great deal, says Tittmann, ... which has been 'pointlessly altered' in the divine services, but 'far from the amount' that needed to be done, 'and much of it not with the considerations' that were needed. He notes that the right means were not always chosen and argues that it would be better through 'a prudent flexibility to make up for what was neglected before, and through expedient improvements to the liturgy to prevent everything from ultimately being destroyed.'"

29. As quoted in Christoph Albrecht, *Einführung in die Hymnologie* (Göttingen: Vandenhoeck und Ruprecht, 1973), 95.
30. *Dresdner Gesangbuch auf höchsten Befehl herausgegeben* (Dresden and Leipzig: Teubner, 1837).
31. Walter A. Baepler, *A Century of Grace* (St. Louis: Concordia, 1947), 48, as noted in Brauer, "The Hymnals," 29.
32. Brauer, "The Hymnals," 25, n. 48, notes that a service folder from the church dedication on December 4, 1842 survived and is described in William G. Polack, "Two Rare Antiquities of Unique Interest," *Concordia Historical Institute Quarterly* 1 (July 1928): 26–27. The service folder provides a window into the kinds of hymns were being used at Trinity Congregation already at this early date. These included: *Allein Gott in der Höh sei Ehr, Wir glauben all an einen Gott, Nun bitten wir den heiligen Geist, Schmücke dich, o liebe Seele, Nun danket alle Gott.* For the afternoon service: *Herr Gott, erhalt uns für und für* (sung by the children alone), *Wie schön ists doch, Herr Jesu Christ,* and *Unsern Ausgang segne Gott.*

Lutheran hymns should be used."[33] Not surprisingly, they had encountered issues with a number of the hymns in Tittmann's hymnal. This went on for a while, and so in November 1845, the congregation resolved to publish a new hymnal.[34] Pastor Walther was appointed as general editor, and several laymen in the congregation were appointed to keep the finances straight.[35] The price of a bound copy was to be seventy-five cents, unbound fifty cents.

It is also important to note that "several area pastors" served as part of the editorial team with Walther.[36] The names of these pastors have never been clearly identified, but it seems very likely that Friedrich Lochner was among them. Lochner was one of the *Sendlinge* of J. K. W. Löhe and was serving as pastor at St. John, Pleasant Ridge (Maryville), Ilinois at the time, just across the Mississippi River from St. Louis.[37] He had also just married Walther's sister-in-law in 1846. Lochner's special interest and expertise was Lutheran hymnody and liturgy, so it seems very likely that Walther would have enlisted his gifted brother-in-law to be among the "several area pastors" working on this project.[38]

33. Minutes of Trinity Congregation, St. Louis, Missouri, February 3, 1843, typed transcript, Concordia Historical Institute, St. Louis, Missouri.
34. Minutes of Trinity Congregation, St. Louis, Missouri, November 17, 1845.
35. Carl S. Mundinger, *Government in the Missouri Synod* (St. Louis: Concordia, 1947), 162, n. 73, reports, on the basis of a document described as "MS. history" and which had been inserted in the cornerstone of Immanuel Congregation on July 30, 1847, the following record regarding the printing of Walther's Hymnal: "Der Druck mit Stereotypen, welches in New York besorgt worden ist, kostete inclus. des Einbandes circa $10,000." Considering the number of copies in the first printing (500 bound, 100 unbound) and the price being charged to members (seventy-five cents), the report of $10,000 seems extremely high, even considering the possibility that the congregation may have subsidized the cost to purchasers in some fashion. The manuscript from Immanuel's cornerstone could not be located to verify.
36. [C. F. W. Walther], "Lutherisches Kirchen-Gesangbuch," *Der Lutheraner* 3 (June 1, 1847): 112, as translated in Meyer, *Moving Frontiers,* 182.
37. See Meyer, *Moving Frontiers,* 97. These "missionaries" were men who received partial theological training from Löhe in Franconia and were then sent to the United States to complete their training at a Lutheran seminary and receive ordination. Carl Schalk, *The Roots of Hymnody in The Lutheran Church—Missouri Synod,* Church Music Pamphlet Series 2 (St. Louis: Concordia, 1965), 14, n. 19, notes: "Loehe had arranged for Friedrich Hommel, a renowned liturgiologist to instruct his *Sendlinge* ('emissaries') in the musical sections of the Lutheran liturgy." See also Baepler, *A Century of Grace,* 69.
38. Friedrich Lochner went on to teach liturgics at the Missouri Synod seminary in Springfield, Illinois, and became the Missouri Synod's first liturgiologist of note, publishing his *opus magnum* at the end of his career: Friedrich Lochner, *Der Hauptgottesdienst der evangelisch-lutherischen Kirche: Zur Erhaltung des liturgischen Erbtheils und zur Beförderung des liturgischen Studiums in der americanisch-lutherischen Kirche erläutert und mit altkirchlichen Singweisen* (St. Louis: Concordia, 1895). See also the recent English translation: *The Chief Divine Service of the Evangelical-Lutheran Church: Explained, and Furnished with Historic Church Melodies for the Preservation of the Liturgical Heritage and for the Advancement of Liturgical Study in the

In June 1847, nineteen months after resolving to publish a new hymnal, Trinity Congregation's new, German-language hymnal was printed in New York City and shipped to St. Louis for distribution. It did not arrive until August of that year.[39] The hymnal was titled *Kirchengesangbuch für evangelisch-lutherische Gemeinden ungeänderter Augsburgischer Confession* (Church Hymnal for Evangelical Lutheran Congregations of the Unaltered Augsburg Confession). The title page of Walther's Hymnal is instructive:

> Church Hymnal
> for
> the Evangelical Lutheran
> Congregations
> of the Unaltered Augsburg Confession
> in which
> the
> Blessed Dr. Martin Luther's
> and Other Gifted Teachers'
> Commonly-used Hymns
> Are Contained.
>
> New York:
> Printed for the Editors by G. Ludwig
> Published by the German Ev. Luth. Congregations UAC
> in
> St. Louis, Mo
> 1847.

The most intriguing aspect from the title page of Walther's Hymnal is the use of the word "congregations" in the plural. It shows up in the fourth line from the top, and then again in the fourth line from the bottom. In the bottom instance, "congregations" may be a reference to the *Gesamtgemeinde*, or "joint congregation" that Walther pastored in St. Louis. By 1847, Walther was pastor of Trinity, St. Louis, but he was also

---

American-Lutheran Church, trans. Matthew Carver; ed. Jon D. Vieker, Kevin J. Hildebrand, and Nathaniel S. Jensen (St. Louis: Concordia, 2020).

39. Minutes of Trinity Congregation, August 12, 1847. The first printing was for five hundred bound copies and one hundred unbound copies.

pastor of Immanuel, St. Louis. This was a "joint congregation" arrangement. In the years following, Holy Cross and Zion, St. Louis were also added to this *Gesamtgemeinde* arrangement. There were assistant pastors at each of these locations, but Walther was the chief pastor of all four. That said, however, this instance of "congregations" (plural) may also be referencing the other Lutheran congregations in the St. Louis area—like Friedrich Lochner's congregation on the Illinois side of the Mississippi, or perhaps the congregations of the other local pastors who had assisted Walther in editing this hymnal.

When considering the reference to "congregations" (plural) in the fourth line from the top, however, we cannot ignore the "fraternal twin" aspect of Walther's Hymnal—that it was born right alongside the birth of the Missouri Synod. During that same, three-year period, when preliminary meetings were being held to hammer out the first constitution of this new synod, Walther and his editorial team were also hard at work preparing a hymnal for "congregations [plural] of the Unaltered Augsburg Confession." *Walther war klug.* He knew that the prospective congregations for this new synod were having many of the same hymnal problems that Walther and his congregation were having—multiple hymnals, confusing numbers on the hymn boards, corrupted hymn texts, and so forth. A new hymnal for a new synod would solve those problems, and so Walther, his congregation, and an editorial team of pastors were ready to offer a solution. Their "Church Hymnal for Evangelical-Lutheran Congregations [plural] of the Unaltered Augsburg Confession" was born for such a time as this.

The sales of the first printing of Walther's Hymnal speak volumes. The first copies of the hymnal arrived in St. Louis in August, and it was nearly sold out by the middle of September. A second printing was ordered in early October.[40] With a subsequent printing early the next year, Walther's Hymnal was officially registered with the US Library of Congress. By the fourth printing in 1849, several additional items were added at the request of the local St. Louis pastoral conference: the epistles and gospels, the passion harmony account, and Josephus's Description of the Destruction of Jerusalem.[41] Overall, sales of Walther's Hymnal were brisk.

40. Minutes of Trinity Congregation, October 7, 1847, note that one thousand bound copies and one hundred unbound copies were to be ordered for the second printing.
41. Minutes of Trinity Congregation, November 13, 1848; an announcement of these additions was also carried in *Der Lutheraner* 5 (April 17, 1849): 136.

What was included in the first printing of Walther's Hymnal?

- 437 hymns
- Table of Contents outlining the organization of the hymns
- Alphabetical hymn index organized by page number
- Melodic index consisting of 167 melodies in 103 different meters
- Appendix of various prayers with an index to their content
- A Formula for Emergency Baptism
- The Antiphons and Proper Prefaces
- Luther's Small Catechism, including Luther's Preface and the "Christian Questions with Their Answers"
- The Augsburg Confession
- The Three Ecumenical Creeds

In addition to the items added in the fourth printing of 1849, in 1857, six hymns were added in an appendix; and in 1917, a second appendix was included with an additional 41 hymns.[42] In 1863, Trinity Congregation gave the rights and the printing of Walther's Hymnal over to the Missouri Synod, and eventually Concordia Publishing House as the Synod's publisher. Walther's Hymnal continued to be printed into the 1960s.[43]

For the entire life of this hymnal, it was published in text-only editions. The music was made available for organists in a variety of publications over the decades, as well as to families and schoolteachers through various smaller volumes for use at home and in the classroom.[44] Likewise, the hymnal originally contained no orders of service. The order for the Divine Service in the Missouri Synod was not clearly established until the arrival

---

42. Brauer, "The Hymnals," 45–46.
43. Brauer, "The Hymnals," 42, noted in 1967 that "the *Kirchengesangbuch für Evangelisch-Lutherische Gemeinden* may still be purchased from Concordia Publishing House...."
44. See Schalk, *The Roots*, 31–38 for a discussion of the music editions published during this period, both in melody-only editions to instill the use of the "rhythmic chorale" among congregants, and in editions with fully harmonized settings for the organist to lead congregational singing. These musical volumes included various editions and expanded printings of Friedrich Layritz, *CXVII Geistliche Melodien meist aus dem 16. Und 17. Jahr, in ihren ursprünglichen Rhythmen zweistimmig gesetzt* (Erlangen: Bläsing, 1839); H. F. Hölter, ed., *Choralbuch: Eine Sammlung der gangbarsten Choräle der evang.-lutherischen Kirche, meist nach Dr. Fr. Layritz, nebst den wichtigsten Sätzen* (St. Louis: Concordia, 1886); and Karl Brauer, ed., *Mehrstimmiges Choralbuch: zu dem Kirchengesangbuch für evangelisch-lutherische Gemeinden Ungeänderter Augsburgischer Confession* (St. Louis: Concordia, 1888).

of the *Kirchen-Agende* of 1856,[45] also edited by Walther, and an outline for that service did not start appearing in printings of Walther's Hymnal until the 1870s. This absence of liturgical orders in the hymnals was actually a continuation of the tradition found in the Dresden hymnals of the eighteenth century, which also had no printed orders of service.

It was noted earlier that the Dresden Hymnal of 1796 was the hymnal that Walther and his compatriots brought with them, that Walther and his congregation used as their primary hymnal prior to 1847, but which could not be relied on because of the influences of Rationalism. This returns us to the question of which predecessor hymnal Walther did use as a model for his hymnal.

The table of contents and organization of the hymns in the Dresden Hymnal of 1796 bears very little resemblance to the outline found in Walther's Hymnal. The hymns in Tittmann's hymnal are organized into two large sections: Part I: *Glaubenslehre* (Doctrine); and Part II: *Sittenlehre* (Ethics.) All of the hymns are organized under these two large categories, within a tightly constructed and logical system of doctrine and ethics.[46] It is clear that Tittmann's hymnal was certainly not a model for Walther's Hymnal.

However, when one reviews the line of Dresden Hymnals that came *before* Tittmann's hymnal of 1796, a whole new world opens up. In these older Dresden hymnals, from 1795 and earlier,[47] one sees an outline of hymns that begins with Advent and Christmas, and then follows through the church year. Next come hymns on the catechism, justification, baptism, and the Lord's Supper. The outline of this older stream of Dresden hymnals is almost *exactly* the same outline found in Walther's Hymnal of 1847.[48] In other words, Walther reached back beyond the Rationalist hymnals of his childhood and shaped his hymnal according to the outline of the older, orthodox Lutheran hymnals from Dresden.[49]

---

45. *Kirchen-Agende für evangelischlutherische Gemeinden ungeänderter Augsburgischer Confession* (St. Louis: Druckerei der Deutschen Ev-Luth. Synode v. Missouri, O. u. à. St., 1856).
46. In the Lutheran tradition, the separation of ethics from doctrine has been attributed to Georg Calixtus (1586–1656). Kurt Galling, ed., s.v. "Calixtus, Georg," *Die Religion in Geschichte und Gegenwart*, 6 vols., 3rd ed. (Tübingen: Mohr Siebeck, 1957–65), 1:1586.
47. For example, *Das Privilegirte Ordentliche und vermehrte Dresdnische Gesang-Buch* (Dresden and Leipzig: Richter, 1791).
48. For a translation and comparison of the respective Tables of Contents for these two hymnals, see: Jon D. Vieker, "The Doctrine of Baptism as Confessed by C. F. W. Walther's *Gesangbuch* of 1847" (STM Thesis, Concordia Seminary, St. Louis, 1990), 29–31; Jon D. Vieker, "C. F. W. Walther: Editor of Missouri's First and Only German Hymnal," *Concordia Historical Institut Quarterly* 65/2 (1992): 62–64.
49. Walther's pattern of "reaching back" beyond the Rationalist worship materials of his day to older, orthodox resources has also been observed in his editing of the baptismal order for his

Walther's preference for the outline and shape of the older Dresden hymnals is reflected in an 1850 article in *Der Lutheraner,* where the writer (undoubtedly Walther) notes:

> Only the *old* hymn books—which are also now and then in this land found among immigrant German Lutherans, such as the *old* Dresden, the *old* Marburg, the *old* Silesian, the Pomeranian, Prussian, Hamburger, Bayreuther, etc.—exhibit a sufficiently large stock of the *old* pure Lord's Supper hymns containing the teachings of the Lutheran Church. And whoever has no such *old* hymnal in his possession, this alone should be enough to convince him to get the "St. Louis Lutheran Hymnal" [i.e., Walther's Hymnal].[50]

Walther's promotion of his new hymnal with the old Lutheran hymns in it was more than salesmanship. The publication of Walther's Hymnal represented a repudiation of the Rationalist hymnals that he and his compatriots had grown up with, and a restoration of the "old," pre-1796, Dresden line of hymnals, fine-tuned to engage German Lutherans in America as the first hymnal of the new Missouri Synod.

WALTHER'S STATED PURPOSE FOR HIS HYMNAL

Returning to June 1847, just three months after the birth of the Missouri Synod, Walther published his article in *Der Lutheraner,* which we noted earlier, and announced the birth of a new hymnal. But in this article, he goes on to describe the intended purposes of this publication and how the editors went about their task. He writes:

> In the selection of the adopted hymns the chief consideration was that they be *pure in doctrine;* that they have almost universal acceptance *within the orthodox German Lutheran Church* and have thus received the almost unanimous testimony that they had come forth from the true spirit [of Lutheranism] . . .[51]

Walther's emphasis on purity of doctrine was fully in keeping with the rise of the Confessional Lutheran Revival during this period. Indeed,

---

Kirchen-Agende of 1856. See Norman Nagel, "Holy Baptism and Pastor Walther," in *Light for Our World: Essays Commemorating the 150th Anniversary of Concordia Seminary, St. Louis, Missouri,* ed. John W. Klotz (St. Louis: Concordia Seminary, 1989), 61–82.

50. "Die Gesang-Bücher," *Der Lutheraner* 7 (October 29, 1850): 35, emphasis not original.
51. Walther, "Lutherisches Kirchen-Gesangbuch," 112, as translated in Carl S. Meyer, *Moving Frontiers,* 182. Emphasis not original.

Lutheran, Anglican, and Presbyterian traditions—each in their own way—experienced a renaissance of conservative confessionalism during the mid-nineteenth century, both in America and Europe.[52] Walther and the Missouri Synod would play a significant role on the American side of that equation, and the selection of hymns reflecting this "Old Lutheran" emphasis on purity of doctrine helped to ensure the spread of that commitment among German American Lutherans.[53]

Walther's second consideration—that the hymns be universally accepted by "the orthodox German Lutheran Church"—likewise reflected his commitment to Lutheran orthodoxy, but particularly to Lutheran orthodoxy in its *German* form. As Walther further explained in his *Der Lutheraner* announcement:

> The editors have been fully conscious of the difficulty of their task . . . They can give the assurance that they approached the task with fear and trembling and from the Christian church's *voluminous treasury of German hymnody,* according to the grace which God had given them, selected only those hymns which they recognized as particularly worthy of transmission from children to children's children and of preservation as a treasure, as an *inalienable possession of the German-speaking church.*[54]

That Walther would be focusing his efforts on the production of a German-language hymnal for German-speaking Lutherans is, in itself, unremarkable. Other German Lutheran immigrants were doing much the same.[55] Yet Walther was clearly keen that the hymns selected for his

---

52. See Walter H. Conser, *Church and Confession: Conservative Theologians in Germany, England, and America, 1815–1866* (Macon: Mercer University Press, 1984).
53. In 1855, German Reformed church historian Philip Schaff observed the following taxonomy of American Lutherans: "The *New Lutheran* party is an amalgamation of Lutheranism with American Puritanic and Methodistic elements. . . . The *Old Lutheran* section consists of a portion of the more recent emigrants from Saxony, Prussia, Bavaria, and other countries. . . . Over the experimenting New Lutherans they have the advantage of a fixed principle, a well-formed doctrinal basis, and general logical consistency. . . . The *Moderate Lutheran* tendency strikes a middle course between these two extremes, which are bound together only by the accident of name. . . . Finally, as to worship and Christian life. In the first place, the Old Lutherans have a more or less complete liturgical altar-service, even with the crucifixes and candles burning in day-time; and in all such matters they cleave to historical tradition; while the New Lutherans incline to the Puritanic system of free prayer, the strict observance of Sunday, neglect of the church festivals, and of all symbolical rites and ceremonies; . . ." Philip Schaff, *America: A Sketch of Its Political, Social and Religious Character,* ed. Perry Miller, The John Harvard Library (Cambridge: Belknap, 1961), 150–159. Emphasis not original.
54. Walther, "Lutherisches Kirchen-Gesangbuch," *Der Lutheraner* 3 (June 1, 1847): 112, translated in Meyer, *Moving Frontiers,* 182. Emphasis not original.
55. For example, see J. A. A. Grabau's hymnal, *Evangelisch-Lutherisches Kirchen-Gesang-Buch* (Buffalo: Zahm, 1842).

hymnal would contain only those that were deemed "particularly worthy" among the tens of thousands available, in order to transmit to and preserve for future generations an "inalienable possession of the German-speaking church." What Walther could not foresee was the way in which this "voluminous treasury" would one day transcend its German-language boundaries and be transmitted to a generation of "children's children," who would sing them not in German, but in English.

THE IMPACT OF WALTHER'S HYMNAL

Indeed, Walther's Hymnal has made an impact today *only* because of what was eventually translated from it into English. Of course, becoming fully English-speaking was the Missouri Synod's "manifest destiny," as it had been for every other group of Lutheran immigrants prior. Even as early as 1865, Missouri Synod theologians were acknowledging this inevitability.[56] Nevertheless, it would take more than half a century and World War I before Missourians would finally get serious about transitioning into English.

Hymnologically speaking, there was much that needed to happen in the meantime. For instance, if Walther had for some reason decided in 1847 to also provide an English-language version of his hymnal, or something close to it, he would have had virtually *nothing* to work with in terms of existing translations of German hymns into the English language. At mid-century, there were hardly any existing English translations of German hymns, and the few that did exist were often mechanically stilted and poetically infelicitous, or they were based on faulty German texts that had been corrupted by Rationalism. By the end of the nineteenth century, however, the prolific Catherine Winkworth, along with Jane Borthwick, John Kelly, Frances Elizabeth Cox, Richard Massie, and Missouri's own August Crull had spent their lives producing metrical English translations of German hymns.[57]

All of this, then, made it possible in 1889 for August Crull and the English Evangelical Lutheran Synod of Missouri and Other States (the

---

56. F. W. Föhlinger, "Referat: Bildung evang. luth. Gemeinden under unsern englisch redenden Nachkommen," *Lehre und Wehre* 11 (August 1865): 236, wrote: "Since it is highly probable, judging from previous experience, that our German descendants will fall to the English language, therefore beyond all doubt the Lutheran Church has the sacred duty to see to it that the pure doctrine of the Evangelical Lutheran Church is preserved in the English language for our descendants." Translation from Meyer, *Moving Frontiers*, 357.
57. See "The Translators" in Jon D. Vieker, "The Fathers' Faith, the Children's Song: Missouri Lutheranism Encounters American Evangelicalism in Its Hymnals, Hymn Writers, and Hymns, 1889–1912," Concordia Seminary, St. Louis, Missouri, PhD Dissertation, 2014, 233–240.

smaller, English-speaking sister-synod to the larger German-speaking Missouri Synod) to produce a hymnal of four hundred hymns. Its table of contents even followed the same old-Dresden ordering of hymns that Walther's Hymnal had used. And yet, only half of those hymns were translations from the German. The rest were from non-German, non-Lutheran, English-language hymn writers like Isaac Watts, Charles Wesley, John Newton, James Montgomery, Horatio Bonar, Christopher Wordsworth, and dozens and dozens more. When this hymnal was expanded a generation later, it became the Missouri Synod's first, official, English-language hymnal, the *Evangelical Lutheran Hymn-Book* of 1912.[58] At this point, however, some 60 percent of its hymn texts came not from the German corpus in Walther's Hymnal, but from the wider ecumenical hymnody of nineteenth-century, English-speaking Protestantism.

So, what remained? Do we see a glass half empty or a glass half full? Carl Schalk would suggest a glass half full. In his seminal volume, *God's Song in a New Land*, he magnificently catalogues and tells the story of Lutheran hymnals in America, from the colonial period to the 1990s. But in the often-overlooked "Afterword" to this work, Schalk writes:

> For almost four and one-half centuries Lutheran hymnody has changed and adapted with each successive age, absorbing what it has found useful and edifying in each successive age, rejecting that song which it has found to be contrary to its liturgical, sacramental understanding of worship. . . . This brief overview demonstrates that where Lutherans have been faithful to a Lutheran understanding of the role of music and hymnody in the life and worship of the church, they have sought to embrace that normative core of congregational song birthed by the Reformation.
>
> Where that Reformation song was alive and well in the mouths and hearts of congregations, there was the assurance that the Gospel message of sin and grace, death and rebirth, would continue to resound within the church. Where that normative core was diluted, emasculated, or eliminated from Lutheran hymnbooks, it was a muted message—often a message other than the Gospel—that was to sound out. Through the centuries the church's song has continued to be enriched with the best of the new song of each successive age. But where the church has lost its moorings in the Gospel proclamation so uniquely given expression in the 16th-century chorale, the church's worship has experienced deterioration, decay, and decline.[59]

---

58. Jon D. Vieker, *August Crull and the Story of the Evangelical Lutheran Hymn-Book (1912), Shaping American Lutheran Church Music* (Minneapolis: Lutheran University Press, 2013), 6.
59. Carl F. Schalk, *God's Song in a New Land: Lutheran Hymnals in America* (St. Louis: Concordia, 1995), 183–184.

The charts in "Appendix A" and "Appendix E" of Schalk's volume demonstrate that the hymnals of the Missouri Synod, from Walther's Hymnal onward, were very high on what one could call the "Reformation-choral quotient." Abundantly high, in fact. Walther's Hymnal clearly set the course for Missouri's hymnody going forward. As Dennis W. Marzolf notes:

> Of the texts in Walther's hymnal ... one hundred and seventeen are from the sixteenth century (of which thirty-six are attributed to Luther); two hundred and forty-eight are seventeenth century in origin; thirty-nine have their roots in the eighteenth century, and twenty-one of the texts are anonymous ... The era of classical Lutheranism (1520–1650), as far as Walther was concerned, epitomized the Church when it was basking in the light of pure doctrine.[60]

The giants of German, confessional, Lutheran hymnody are all amply represented in Walther's Hymnal—from the great Reformer, Martin Luther, to the suffering Paul Gerhardt; from the great catechetical hymnist, Nikolaus Herman to the "Silesian Job," Johann Heermann; from the Baroque polymath, Johann Rist to Johann Olearius, Nikolaus Selnecker, and dozens and dozens of others from that great cloud of German Lutheran hymnological witnesses.

In contrast, Schalk's appendices also demonstrate the absence of core Reformation hymnody in several other Lutheran hymnals in his study. For instance, only a sliver of sixteenth-century Lutheran chorales are represented in the *Common Service Book* of the United Lutheran Church in America (seven of 577) or in the *Service Book and Hymnal* (nine of 602). I was told that this contrast in hymnic tradition became an issue on the Inter-Lutheran Commission on Worship (ILCW), which began work in 1966 toward a hymnal that was to serve the Missouri Synod, the American Lutheran Church, and the Lutheran Church in America, the three largest Lutheran church bodies in the United States at the time. When the Missourians came to the ILCW meetings with their sixteenth-century Lutheran chorales and were intent on seeing many of them go into the new hymnal, they sometimes encountered a less-than-enthusiastic response from many of the other Lutherans at the table. Nevertheless, a

---

60. Dennis W. Marzolf, "C. F. W. Walther: The Musician and Liturgiologist," in *C. F. W. Walther: The American Luther*, Arthur H. Drevlow, John M. Drickamer and Glen E. Reichwald, eds. (Mankato: Walther, 1987), 87.

great many Reformation treasures did make their way into the *Lutheran Book of Worship* (LBW) and beyond.[61]

The influence of Walther's Hymnal also reached beyond Missouri into the Wisconsin Evangelical Synod (WELS), the Evangelical Lutheran Synod (ELS), and the Slovak Evangelical Lutheran Church (SELC). Along with Missouri, these confessional Lutheran church bodies were members of the Evangelical Lutheran Synodical Conference of North America.[62] Together they produced *The Lutheran Hymnal* (TLH) in 1941.[63] Regarding the content and lasting influence of TLH, Schalk notes:

> *The Lutheran Hymnal* presented the heritage of Lutheran Reformation hymnody, both in the translations of the texts and the continued adherence to the rhythmic form of the chorale melodies, to a degree not found among the other Lutheran hymnbooks of its time.... As a treasury of that normative core of Reformation hymnody of the 16th century, *The Lutheran Hymnal* was without equal among American Lutheran hymnbooks in the middle of the 20th century.[64]

CONCLUSION

On Sunday, September 9, 1883, a two-day dedication event for a new campus for Concordia Seminary began, drawing an overwhelming crowd of twenty thousand people to St. Louis from around the United States. At an outdoor dedicatory service, an aged C. F. W. Walther ascended the special rostrum that had been constructed for the event and passionately delivered a rousing dedicatory sermon, in which he reflected at length on the blessings of God to the Missouri Synod over the thirty-six years since its birth and the birth of its fraternal twin, Walther's Hymnal:

---

61. Marilyn Kay Stulken, *Hymnal Companion to the Lutheran Book of Worship* (Philadelphia: Fortress, 1981), 614–617 shows that about one hundred German hymn texts from the sixteenth to eighteenth centuries were included in LBW, approximately 18 percent of its hymn corpus. Paul Westermeyer, *Hymnal Companion to Evangelical Lutheran Worship* (Minneapolis: Augsburg Fortress, 2010), 878–879, shows that about seventy-five German hymn texts from the sixteenth to eighteenth centuries were included in ELW, approximately 11 percent of its hymn corpus. *Lutheran Service Book: Companion to the Hymns*, 2:894–95, shows that about 165 German hymn texts from the sixteenth to eighteenth centuries were included in LSB, approximately 26 percent of its hymn corpus.
62. Erwin L. Lueker, Luther Poellot, and Paul Jackson, eds., s.v. "Synodical Conference," *Christian Cyclopedia*, http://cyclopedia.lcms.org. Accessed March 31, 2023.
63. W. G. Polack, *The Handbook to the Lutheran Hymnal* (St. Louis: Concordia, 1942), notes that 248 hymns in TLH were translated from German, approximately 38 percent of its hymn corpus.
64. Schalk, *God's Song,* 168.

The precious books of our church, the confessional writings together with the writings of Luther, rescued from the dust, carried from house to house, came to the forefront and were eagerly read and studied by our people. The genuine Lutheran faith and the Lutheran way of life spread like a prairie fire across the land; God blessed us with a unity of faith and a joy of faith with inner brotherly love, which at times even seemed to turn us back to the days of Luther.... The old pure hymns, filled with the power of faith and the fervor of love, as they were sung by our forefathers, gave music with the old sweet manner. In short, a true Lutheran church, of whom one had sung funeral dirges everywhere, came back to life, rose from the grave, and planted the flag of victory of the pure Gospel over a thousand different places of our great union of states.[65]

The astonishing resurrection of a confessional Lutheranism on American soil was the greatest blessing for which Walther and those gathered gave thanks. The Lutheran Confessions, the writings of Luther, and "the old pure hymns" of the Reformation had inspired hearts to spread the Lutheran message and plant the victory flag of the pure gospel in over a thousand congregations across the fruited plain.

The legacy of Walther's hymnal continues today among those who sing its magnificent treasures in English. The hymns of Luther, Gerhardt, Heermann, and others still sound forth from the mouths of the faithful, and with them, the blessings of joy and peace in the Reformation Gospel:

Nun freut euch, lieben christen g'mein!	Dear Christians, one and all, rejoice,
Und laßt uns fröhlich springen,	With exultation springing,
Dass wir getrost und all' in ein	And with united heart and voice
Mit lust und liebe singen,	And holy rapture singing,
Was Gott an uns gewendet hat,	Proclaim the wonders God has done,
Und seine süße wundertat;	How His right arm the vict'ry won.
Gar theu'r hat er's erworben.[66]	What price our ransom cost Him![67]

Luther, *Achtliederbuch*, 1524

---

65. August R. Suelflow, *Servant of the Word: The Life and Ministry of C. F. W. Walther* (St. Louis: Concordia, 2000), 98–99.
66. C. F. W. Walther, *Kirchengesangbuch für evangelisch-lutherische Gemeinden ungeänderter Augsburgischer Confession* (St. Louis, 1847), no. 243.
67. LSB 556.

8.

A Hymnal for Uniting Lutherans: *Common Service Book with Hymnal,* 1917/18

Paul Westermeyer

The outside cover on the book says *Common Service Book with Hymnal*.[1] The *Common Service Book of the Lutheran Church* is the first half of the book, and *The Hymnal* is the second half. It was published for parish churches in 1917 and in 1918. The 1917 book is "Authorized by The General Synod, The General Council, and The United Synod in the South." After a merger, the 1917/18 book was "Authorized by the United Lutheran Church in America." It appeared again in 1919 in a pocket-size, text-only edition. The Occasional Services were published separately in 1930.

Propers, services, and indices are included. After the contents, the calendar stretches across two pages. There the church year with Feast Days and seasons resembles stained glass windows like the title page shown in Figure 8.1.

Holy Communion is followed by Matins and Vespers. Propers include the Introits, collects, epistles, and gospels. General Prayers include the Litany, Suffrages, and the Bidding Prayer. Two thirds of the psalms, twelve canticles, the passion, occasional services, general rubrics, and prefaces follow. The prefaces are those to the 1888 *Common Service* and to this 1917 book. They give an account of the 1888 and 1917 publications with an overview of Lutheran worship in the nineteenth century in relation to

---

1. *Common Service Book with Hymnal* (Philadelphia and Columbia: 1917, and Philadelphia: 1917 and 1918).

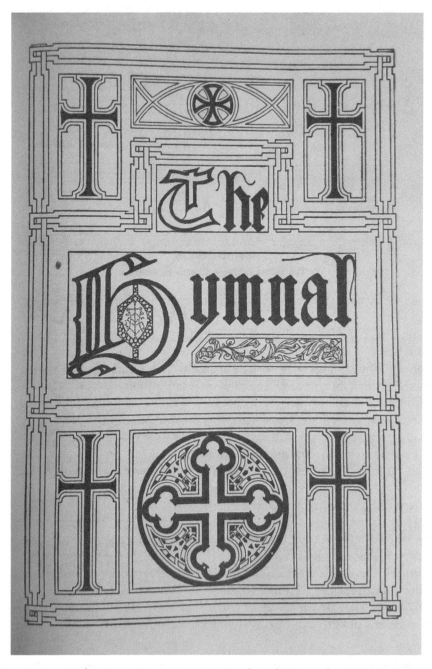

Figure 8.1 Title page, *Common Service Book with Hymnal*, 1917/18.

the sixteenth century and to the church before that in "a Communion of Saints."[2] After the prefaces a paragraph of thanks comes as "The Music of the Book." The services are given four-part Anglican Chant, the hymns four-part harmonizations. They are organized according to the church year, the Word, baptism, confirmation, the Holy Communion, and other topics.

The 1917 book's cover and page margins are slightly larger. Three paragraphs dated "Whitsuntide 1929" were added later, after the original prefaces, with a note that "a revision of the Music Edition of the Common Service [was] authorized by the United Lutheran Church at its convention in . . . 1928." This refers to the simplification of the Order for the Burial of the Dead, the omission of the "Second (Plain Song) Setting of the Services and certain Tables of Lessons." A note says the Plain Song Setting was "still available." Page numbers are changed, the 1917 service book with 320 pages, the 1917/18 one with 310.

A Luther League hymn is added to the first book in an appendix with nineteen alternate tunes for the 577 hymns. The second book omits the appendix, adds the Luther League hymn to the body of the hymns, places alternate tunes with their hymns, and has a new layout. The first hymnal has tunes in four parts followed by the hymns. The second hymnal interlines at least one stanza.

Both books have the same first seven hymn indices: "I. Subjects, II. Originals of Translated Hymns, III. Authors, Translators and Sources of Hymns, IV. Composers and Sources of Tunes, V. Metres, VI. Tunes, and VII. First Lines." The 1917/18 edition added two: "VIII. Topical Index" and "IX. Table of Hymns for Sundays and Festivals of the Church Year."

The hymn numbers and their total (578) are the same in both books, but the different layouts and alternate tunes change the page numbers after hymn number thirty-five. The 1917 book has 656 pages, the 1917/18 edition 631.

The sources of the translated hymns are mostly German and Latin: Greek, nine; Latin, forty-six; German, one hundred and twenty; Swedish, Danish, French, and Italian, two each; and Welsh, one. These proportions reveal a serious problem, the "loss" of the Scandinavian heritage. Scandinavian American Lutherans keenly felt and sharply expressed their

---

2. CSB 1917, p. 315; 1917/18, p. 307.

displeasure.[3] The proportions did not change from a 1912 "Proof Copy"[4] and may not have been intentional but reflect the lengthy struggle of German Americans to get their house in order. The Scandinavian displeasure nonetheless reverberated throughout the next century (see chapter 9).

Most of the 341 translations are by Catherine Winkworth (1829–1885) with fifty-three, and John Mason Neale (1818–1866) with twenty-five. Contributors of the most original hymns are Isaac Watts (1674–1748), twenty-five; Charles Wesley (1708–1788), twenty-one; John Wesley (1703–1791), fourteen; Paul Gerhardt (1607–1676), fifteen; and Reginald Heber (1783–1826), Henry Francis Lyte (1793–1847), and Martin Luther (1483–1546), each with seven. Brief comments accompany some entries in the index. The one for Paul Gerhardt is "Greatest of German and Lutheran hymn writers."

Of the 280 tune sources, twenty-two have more than four tunes, among them Folksong, fifty-one; John Bacchus Dykes (1823–1876), forty-six; William Henry Monk (1823–1889), twenty; Arthur Sullivan (1842–1900), fifteen; John Gauntlett (1805–1876), fourteen; Henry Smart (1813–1901), thirteen; Lowell Mason (1792–1872), ten; and Freylinghausen's *Gesangbuch* (1704), William Henry Havergal, (1793–1870), and John Stainer (1840–1901), each with nine. This reflects a strong English influence. The total of these larger contributors is 277, while the number of German chorale tunes is seventy-four.

The authorizations reflect the merger of the General Synod, General Council, and General Synod South into the United Lutheran Church in America in 1918 and, before that merger, the proposal of the General Council in 1909 that the three groups join in a common hymnal with a common form of the 1888 *Common Service*.

The 1917 *Common Service Book with Hymnal* became the model for Lutheran hymnals published in this country after 1917. "Soon after its adoption by the three original bodies which joined in its preparation, it was in use by the Iowa Synod, the Joint Synod of Ohio, the Norwegian synods, the Missouri Synod, and later by the Augustana and Icelandic Synods."[5] To understand this book one has to examine the study, research, and conflicts of the previous century which culminated in the 1888 *Common*

---

3. For example, see the comments in the *American Lutheran Survey* (October 23, 1918), cited in Carl Schalk, *God's Song in a New Land: Lutheran Hymnals in America* (St. Louis: Concordia, 1995), 162–163.
4. See Schalk, *God's Song*, 160.
5. Schalk, *God's Song*, 219.

Service and which in turn shaped and made the 1917 book possible. That story begins in 1817.

LOST IDENTITIES

In 1817 a hymnal called *Das Gemeinschaftliche Gesangbuch, zum gottesdientslich der Lutherischen und Reformirten Gemeinden in Nord Amerika,*[6] (The Common Songbook for the Public Worship of Lutheran and Reformed Communities in North America), was endorsed and shared by the Pennsylvania Lutherans and the German Reformed. It omitted many classic German chorales, abbreviated others, and did not stimulate congregational singing. It had no services, only prose paragraphs of daily morning and evening prayers and a list of epistles and gospels for the year. The 494 hymns without music were organized by topics. Philip Schaff (1819–1893), the best hymnologist of the time, called it "beneath all criticism."[7]

The groups who shared *Das Gemeinschaftliche Gesangbuch* came to Pennsylvania from the Palatinate in southwest Germany. They shared "union churches," intermarried, and in 1787 founded Franklin College together (later Franklin and Marshall). In 1918 the Lutherans formed the United Lutheran Church in America. In 1934 the German Reformed and the Evangelical Synod of North America joined in the Evangelical and Reformed Church. The Evangelical Synod had Lutheran roots in Prussia where Frederick William III (1770–1840) had tried to unite the Lutherans and the Reformed.

Pietism and Rationalism had diminished distinctions between the Lutherans and German Reformed. Worship for both was a lecture or sermon with prayers, lessons, and hymns, an opening "invocation" and a concluding Benediction. The distinction the people knew was that the Reformed began the Lord's Prayer "Unser Vater" and the Lutherans "Vater Unser." A confession of sins and the Lord's Prayer, if present, were said by the minister alone. Hymn singing had "almost become a 'lost art.'" Revivalism with "American Lutheran New Measures" further reduced the heritages. An awakening led to confessional and Americanizing divisions for both groups. The 1917 book is part of the Lutheran confessional stream.

---

6. *Das Gemeinschaftliche Gesangbuch, Sechste Auflage* (Philadelphia: Mentz und Kovondt, 1847, reprint London: Dalton House, 2018).
7. Philip Schaff, "German Hymnology," trans. T. C. Porter, *Mercersburg Review,* 12/2 (April, 1869): 241.

REFORMED AND LUTHERAN CONFESSIONAL AWAKENINGS

In 1840 John Williamson Nevin (1803–1886) came to the German Reformed Seminary in Mercersburg, Pennsylvania (which in 1871 moved to Lancaster).[8] Two years later the German Reformed congregation there heard a trial sermon by William Ramsey. He "issued an altar call... When the tumult abated, Nevin told the congregation... that while they had got some fairly good exercise they should not assume to have progressed in piety."[9]

"New Measures" included the "anxious bench." In front of an assembly a preacher addressed sinners about their sins. The emotional state was presumed to convert them. This inundated Lutherans and German Reformed. Nevin objected to this practice in his book *The Anxious Bench*.[10] Alluding to the second century ecstatic movement of Montanism in Phrygia, he called New Measures a Montanist "Phrygian dance," "quackery," "solemn tricks for effect," "justification by feeling."[11] Alluding to the British monk Pelagius who came to Rome around 400 CE, Nevin said the anxious bench symbolized a false Pelagian system, conversion the product of the sinner's own will.[12]

Lutherans reacted against Nevin most strongly. In 1833 Lutheran pastor Benjamin Kurtz (1795–1865) became Editor of the *Lutheran Observer*, which supported New Measures. He changed it to a weekly, increased its circulation, gave revivals better coverage than the German Reformed, and said New Measures were the work of the Spirit.[13] An *Observer* correspondent called the anxious bench "the lever of Archimedes, which by the blessing of God can raise our German Churches to the degree of respectability and prosperity in the religious world which they ought to enjoy."[14]

In February 1839, C. F. W. Walther and a group of confessional Saxon Lutherans came to Missouri. A few months later, Johannes Andreas August

---

8. Much of what follows is from Paul Westermeyer, "What Shall We Sing in a Foreign Land? Theology and Cultic ['cultivated'] Song in the German Reformed and Lutheran Churches of Pennsylvania, 1830–1900" (PhD Dissertation, University of Chicago, 1978).
9. Bard Thompson, "The Catechism and the Mercersburg Theology," *Essays on the Heidelberg Catechism* (Philadelphia and Boston: United Church Press, 1963), 60.
10. John W. Nevin, *The Anxious Bench,* 2nd ed., revised and enlarged (Chambersburg: Publication Office of the German Reformed Church, 1844).
11. Nevin, *The Anxious Bench*, 27–29.
12. Nevin, *The Anxious Bench*, 114ff.
13. "Notes on 'The Anxious Bench' by the Rev J. W. Nevin, D. D.'," *The Lutheran Observer*, 12/11 (Nov. 17, 1843).
14. Quoted by Nevin, *The Anxious Bench*, 18, footnote.

Grabau and "Old Prussians," who objected to Frederick William III's Union Church, came to New York. In the South the influential Henkel family of pastors pursued confessional concerns. But the *Lutheran Observer* said that the sixteenth century and Pietism illustrated Lutheranism. It threw away past forms, took up the word of God as its "sword," and used new "exercises" to "kindle the sacred flame."[15]

As time went on, however, Kurtz and the *Lutheran Observer* were challenged. In 1844, the year of Nevin's revised *Anxious Bench*, Philip Schaff joined Nevin at Mercersburg Seminary. He was baptized in Switzerland in the Reformed Church, went to the academy at Kornthal in Württemberg, was confirmed in the Lutheran Church, and lived in Stuttgart in the pietistic Mann household where he began a lifelong friendship with Wilhelm Julius Mann (1819–1892). Mann became the pastor of the large, influential St. Michael and Zion Lutheran Church in Philadelphia. Schaff studied at Tübingen, Halle, and Berlin, lectured in Berlin, and joined Nevin at Mercersburg as Professor of Church History and Biblical Literature. In 1870 he went to Union Seminary in New York, and in 1888 he founded the American Society of Church History.

In 1834 riots in Philadelphia between Irish Catholics and the American Party had caused a fire which burned thirty-nine houses and two Catholic churches. Joseph Berg, Pastor of First German Reformed Church in Philadelphia, preached this anti-Catholic sentiment at the Allentown Synod meeting in 1844. He said German Reformed history was untainted by Rome and could be traced as an unchanging doctrinal monolith via the Waldensians to Polycarp, second century bishop of Smyrna.

Schaff challenged that history in his inaugural address, "The Principle of Protestantism." He said that the Reformation is "the legitimate offspring and greatest act of the Catholic Church" and Protestantism in its true conception is Catholic.[16] The problem was that Protestant concerns for freedom had turned into self-will and private judgment with the subjective diseases of rationalism and sectarianism. He called for an ecumenical confessional recovery with Protestant and Roman Catholic truths fused in an evangelical catholic life stream. Such thoughts also reverberated among Lutherans.

Schaff edited a hymnal as a "selection of spiritual songs from all times of the Christian church for public and church use." His title, *Deutsches*

---

15. G. Scherer, "The New Liturgy," *The Lutheran Observer*, 12/29 (March 14, 1845): 42.
16. Philip Schaff, *The Principle of Protestantism*, trans. John W. Nevin, ed. Bard Thompson and George H. Bricker (Philadelphia: United Church Press, 1964, first published, 1845), 73.

Gesangbuch,[17] (German Songbook), was the same one Lutherans used for their "Wollenweber" hymnal,[18] though theirs was more "Americanizing" than Schaff's. For music both books turned to G. F. Landenberger (1815–1882?), a teacher and organist at the Church in Philadelphia where W. J. Mann was pastor. Landenberger's book used the then current norm of isorhythmic chorale tunes with *Zwischenspielen* between phrases.[19]

LUTHERAN CONFESSIONAL AWAKENING

In 1898, Lutheran pastor H. Frank Scheele (1858–1939) wrote about the 1888 *Common Service*. In this brief 4" × 6" book of 125 pages—not for scholars and theologians, but dedicated "to the young Lutherans of America"—he positively referenced the "Presbyterian" Schaff who "easily stood among the foremost Scholars in this country."[20] Scheele said *The Common Service* was not binding, but had arguments from Scripture, history, and aesthetics. He discussed its parts, practical effects, and benefits, then answered objections. How did Lutherans reach this point?

In 1848 Schaff began the *Kirchenfreund* which his friend the Lutheran pastor W. J. Mann edited later. It attuned Pennsylvania Lutherans to Germanic sources, as did the more confessional groups who had come to America. In 1849 the *Evangelical Quarterly Review* began to oppose the *Observer*. It was first edited by William M. Reynolds (1812–1876), a Lutheran pastor who became an Episcopal priest and was professor of Latin for eighteen years at Gettysburg College (then Pennsylvania College). Charles Philip Krauth (1797–1867) followed Reynolds as Editor. He was a Lutheran pastor who in 1850 marked his retirement as the first President of Gettysburg College with a sermon calling for a renewed acquaintance with the Augsburg Confession. A year earlier *The Missionary*, a weekly paper edited in Pittsburgh by William A. Passavant (1821–1894), entered the fray. Passavant was a Lutheran pastor who brought the Lutheran Deaconess movement to this country and helped to found and administer benevolent institutions.

The Pennsylvania Ministerium requested a new edition of the liturgy in 1850. The New York and Ohio Synods were invited to join the effort. In

---

17. Philipp Schaff, ed., *Deutsches Gesangbuch* (Philadelphia: Lindsay & Blakiston, 1859).
18. *Deutsches Gesangbuch* (Philadelphia: Wollenweber, 1849).
19. G. F. Landenberger, *Choral-Buch für die Orgel mit Zwischenspielen* (Philadelphia: Kohler, 1861).
20. H. Frank Scheele, *The Common Service* (Staunton: Stoneburner & Prufer, 1898), 15.

1855 the result was a *Liturgie und Agende*.[21] In 1860 it received an English translation,[22] recovering some Lutheran elements in a responsive service with congregational participation. The English translation moved closer to the Lutheran form of the Western Mass, and the regular Sunday morning service was the Word Service of the Communion Liturgy.

Beale M. Schmucker (1827–1888) provided much of the scholarship. His father, Samuel S. Schmucker (1799–1873), a graduate of Princeton Seminary, had helped to found Gettysburg Seminary in 1826 and was its first professor for forty years. An advocate of "American Lutheranism," he helped to produce the first General Synod English hymnal, *Hymns Selected and Original*,[23] "used by more than half of all English-speaking Lutherans in America."[24]

Beale M., though an 1847 graduate of Gettysburg Seminary, reacted against the "Puritanic and Pietistic elements of his father."[25] While he was working on the liturgy for the Pennsylvania Ministerium in 1855, his father, Kurtz, and other "American Lutheran" ministers anonymously wrote and then sent the *"Definite Platform"*[26] to General Synod pastors. It argued for removing five "errors" from the Augsburg Confession: the approval of ceremonies of the Mass, private confession and absolution, the divine obligation of the Sabbath, baptismal regeneration, and the real presence of the body and blood of the Savior in the Eucharist.

The anonymity, exclusiveness, and contents of the *Definite Platform* provoked a storm of protest. John N. Hoffman, the pastor of Trinity Lutheran Church in Reading, was the first to object in a hasty, emotional, and practical response.[27] J. W. Mann wrote a more reasoned one. He said

---

21. *Liturgie und Agende: ein Kirchenbuch für die Evangelisch–Lutherische Kirche in den Vereinigten Staaten* (Philadelphia: Kohler, 1855).
22. *A Liturgy for the Use of the Evangelical Lutheran Church By authority of the Ministerium of Pennsylvania and Adjacent States* (Philadelphia: Lindsay & Blakiston, 1860).
23. *Hymns Selected and Original, for Public and Private Worship* (Gettysburg: The General Synod of the Evangelical Lutheran Church, 1828).
24. Joel Lundeen, "Lutheran Hymnbooks in America: A Checklist of Major Titles," 1978 (Vertical File: Hymn books. Archives of the Evangelical Lutheran Church in America, Elk Grove Village, Illinois), 2.
25. Henry E. Horn, ed., *Memoirs of Henry Eyster Jacobs* (written 1906, edited by Horn, 1940, mimeographed, 1974), II, 163.
26. Samuel S. Schmucker, *Definite Platform, Doctrinal and Disciplinarian, for Evangelical Lutheran District Synods; Constructed in Accordance with the Principles of the General Synod* (Philadelphia: Miller & Burlock, 1855).
27. John N. Hoffman, *The Broken Platform: or a Brief Defense of Our Symbolical Books, against Recent Charges of Alleged Errors* (Philadelphia: Lindsay & Blakiston, 1856).

that the Augsburg Confession was misunderstood and misrepresented, that the *Definite Platform* had the errors.[28] He discussed these alleged errors, pointing to the sacramental posture as a Lutheran signature. S. S. Schmucker responded to Mann.[29] Mann then responded to Schmucker by dividing Lutherans into the Missouri and Buffalo Synods on the right,[30] almost everybody else in the center, and American Lutheranism on the left. He called American Lutheranism "something new," Puritanic, and Zwinglian, which removed Lutheran forms of worship so that even singing was not done by the congregation.

Disagreements continued. S. S. Schmucker argued that sacraments—a term he preferred to avoid—had no objective reality. In opposition to Beale's work on the Pennsylvania Ministerium's *Liturgy*, at the General Synod of 1862 the elder Schmucker proposed an "Order of Exercises," avoiding the word "liturgy," though it was called the "Proposed Liturgy."[31] It was a list of anthems, prayers, Scripture, hymns, and sermons. Wary of congregational participation, except maybe hymns, he said that "in the repetition of the Lord's Prayer and Creed the people may unite audibly with the minister if the majority of the congregation decide to do so."[32] This was a preacher's manual, not a Lutheran people's liturgy.

THE CHURCH BOOK

In 1818 the Pennsylvania Ministerium, which had been founded by the Lutheran patriarch Henry Melchior Mühlenberg (1711–1787), initiated The General Synod. This body began in 1820 as an "inclusive federation" of Lutherans in America.[33] Three years later the Ministerium sensed a loss of power within the organization and withdrew. In 1853 the Ministerium rejoined the General Synod, but in 1865 it founded the Lutheran Theological Seminary in Philadelphia as a confessional bulwark. (Gettysburg and Philadelphia seminaries are now United Lutheran Seminary.) The General Synod forced the Ministerium back out a year later, in 1866. The Ministerium then called for a more inclusive body, which led in 1867 to the General Council, "the way of confessional subscription."[34]

---

28. William Julius Mann, *A Plea for the Augsburg Confession, in Answer to the Objections of the Definite Platform* (Philadelphia: Lindsay & Blakiston, 1856).
29. Samuel S. Schmucker, American *Lutheranism Vindicated* (Baltimore: Kurtz, 1856).
30. William Julius Mann, *Lutheranism in America* (Philadelphia: Lindsay & Blakiston, 1857).
31. Samuel S. Schmucker, *Proposed Liturgy of the Evangelical Lutheran General Synod* (s.l., 1864).
32. Schmucker, *Proposed Liturgy*, 6.
33. John Tietjen, *Which Way to Lutheran Unity?* (St. Louis: Concordia, 1966), 13–38.
34. Tietjen, *Which Way to Lutheran Unity?*, 30–47.

As previously noted, in 1850 the Pennsylvania Ministerium had requested a new edition of the liturgy. The one currently in use was from 1847, dependent on the one from 1842 of the Pennsylvania and New York Ministeriums with the Synod of Ohio[35] via the Ministerium's 1818 liturgy.[36] This edition stood in the mold of Frederick Quitman (1760–1832), who had prepared the first influential American English Lutheran liturgy in New York in 1814.[37] Except for hymns, it omitted congregational participation. A preacher's manual, not a liturgy, the church year and Lutheran hymnody were forgotten. It had confessions, prayers, benedictions, lections, ministerial acts like baptism, and rubrics for the Lord's Supper. In place of justification by grace through faith it said, "we praise thee that thou hast graciously revealed to us thy readiness to receive into favor all who cease to do evil and learn to do well."[38]

The Pennsylvania Ministerium's Liturgy Committee included Beale M. Schmucker's historical skills, Charles Porterfield Krauth's (1823–1883) theological ones, and Joseph Augustus Seiss's (1823–1904) editorial ones. Charles Porterfield was the son of Charles Philip Krauth, who in 1838 had prepared *Hymns, Selected and Arranged, for Sunday Schools*.[39] Its cue came from S. S. Schmucker's hymnal of 1828, but it included confessional stirrings. So did a Sunday School hymnal by William Passavant.[40] Charles Porterfield shared his father's confessional awakening, was the first theology professor at Philadelphia Seminary, and wrote the confessional magnum opus, *The Conservative Reformation and its Theology*.[41] Seiss, a Moravian by birth, opposed revivalism with a Lutheran confessional posture and prepared a *Book of Forms* for the people of St. John's in Philadelphia where he was the pastor.[42]

---

35. *Liturgie and Kirchenagende für die Evangelisch-Lutherischen Gemeinden in Pennsylvania, New York, Ohio und den benachbarten Staaten* (Philadelphia: Bötticher, 1842).
36. *Liturgie oder Kirchen-Agende der Evangelisch-Lutherischen Gemeinen in Pennsylvania und den benachbarten Staaten* (Baltimore: Scheffer und Mund, 1818).
37. *A Collection of Hymns and a Liturgy for the Use of Evangelical Lutheran Churches; To Which are Added Prayers for Families and Individuals.* Published by Order of the Evangelical Lutheran Synod of the State of New York (Philadelphia: Billmeyer, 1814), 4.
38. *A Collection of Hymns*, 4.
39. Charles Philip Krauth, *Hymns. Selected and Arranged for Sunday Schools of the Evangelical Lutheran Church, and Adapted to the the Sunday Schools in General* (Philadelphia: Brown, 1838).
40. William A. Passavant, comp. *Hymns Selected and Original, for Sunday Schools* (Baltimore: Kurtz, 1843).
41. Charles Porterfield Krauth, *The Conservative Reformation and Its Theology* (Philadelphia: General Council Publication Board, 1871, reprinted Minneapolis: Augsburg,1963).
42. Joseph A. Seiss, *A Book of Forms for the Use of Christians in the Sanctuary, and the Closet* (Philadelphia: Sherman, 1859).

The Ministerium envisioned what appeared in 1868 as the *Church Book*.[43] Its basis was the 1860 English *Liturgy for the Use of the Evangelical Lutheran Church*. It contained what the people needed for worship in a clearly Lutheran rite, reversing Quitman's pattern. The Word service of Antecommunion was followed by Communion. When the *Church Book* was translated into German in the 1877 *Kirchenbuch*,[44] Vespers took on a more historic shape, and Matins appeared. The *Church Book* and *Kirchenbuch* were widely accepted.

The General Synod, gradually moving away from American Lutheranism, in 1869 published a *Book of Worship* with the "Washington Service" as an alternative to the "Proposed Liturgy" of S. S. Schmucker. Prepared by a Liturgy Committee enlarged to neutralize S. S., it was a compromise between a historic Lutheran service and a list of items.

HYMNODY

Benjamin Kurtz published a *Lutheran Prayer Book* in 1852.[45] Most of its 176 hymns came from S.S. Schmucker's *Hymns Selected and Original*. The forty-six he chose were of the same ilk. Seiss provided an alternative in *The Evangelical Psalmist*.[46] It changed tunes, but it barely touched the texts, which were culled from Schmucker's book with his old numbers, Seiss's new numbers, and an index for both.

Two Sunday School hymnals lived in the wake of *Hymns Selected and Original*. Matthias Sheeligh (1821–1900) enlarged Passavant's work in 1860, and a book for infants also appeared.[47] *Hymns for Sunday Schools* of the General Synod was different,[48] surprising Frederick M. Bird (1838–1908) that such a healthy and cheerful book could have made "so great an advance . . . on what went before."[49]

---

43. *Church Book for the Use of Evangelical Lutheran Congregations by Authority of the General Council of the Evangelical Lutheran Church in America* (Philadelphia: The German Evangelical Ministerium of Pennsylvania, 1868).
44. *Kirchenbuch für Evangelisch-Lutherische Gemeinde. Herausgegeben von der Allgemeinen Versammlung der Evangelische-Lutherische Kirche in Nordamerika* (Philadelphia: File, 1877).
45. Benjamin Kurtz, *Lutheran Prayer Book for the Use of Families and Individuals* (Baltimore: Kurtz, 1852).
46. *The Evangelical Psalmist: A Collection of Tunes and Hymns for Use in Congregational and Social Worship* (Philadelphia: Lindsay & Blakiston, 1860).
47. *Hymns Selected and Original, for Infant Sunday-Schools of the Lutheran Church* (Baltimore: Kurtz, 1860).
48. *Hymns for Sunday Schools* (Philadelphia: Lutheran Board of Publication, 1860).
49. Frederic Mayer Bird, "Lutheran Hymnology," *The Evangelical Quarterly Review*, 63 (July, 1865): 333.

Mann set in motion the first alternative to *Hymns Selected and Original*. He concluded his presidential report to the Pennsylvania Ministerium in 1862 by suggesting that it lead the way for "an improved English Hymn Book."[50] A committee reported no satisfactory available English hymnal and called on Frederick Bird of the New York Ministerium for help.

Frederick Bird's father was a playwright, novelist, editor, and doctor; his grandfather was Philip Mayer, pastor for fifty-two years at St. John's Lutheran Church in Philadelphia. Frederick attended Hartwick Seminary, graduated from Union Seminary, and served as a Lutheran chaplain and pastor in New York and Philadelphia. In 1868, the year the *Church Book* was published, Lutherans lost his expertise. As some other Lutheran and German Reformed pastors were doing, he moved to the Episcopal Church.

Before that, Bird collected "several thousand hymnological works,"[51] knew Charles Wesley's work well,[52] and wrote articles for the *Evangelical Review* about Lutheran English hymnals.[53] He said a hymnal required "*competent knowledge* of Hymnology by the compilers," "severely correct judgment and thoroughly refined taste," and a "broad, liberal, appreciative, catholic spirit."[54] Henry Eyster Jacobs, (1844–1932), who wrote a history of the Lutheran Church in the United States,[55] said Bird's suggestions were "an announcement of the program according to which the hymnal of the Church Book was prepared."[56] The same could be said for the 1917 *Common Service Book with Hymnal*.

Adolph Spaeth (1839–1910) taught New Testament at Philadelphia Seminary and was the pastor at St. Johannis Church. He became the committee's secretary. Not a hymnologist like Bird, he nonetheless knew the terrain well. Bird worked out a list of hymns, consulted with Beale M. Schmucker, and in 1865 a hymnal was in print.[57] After some revisions it was published in 1868 as part of the *Church Book*. Watts and Charles

---

50. *Minutes of the German Evangelical Lutheran Ministerium of Pennsylvania in North America* (Allentown, 1862), 16.
51. Henry E. Jacobs, "The Making of the Church Book," *The Lutheran Church Review*, 31 (October, 1912): 604.
52. Frederic Mayer Bird, *Charles Wesley Seen in His Finer and Less Familiar Poems* (New York: Worthington, 1866).
53. Bird, "Lutheran Hymnology," *The Evangelical Quarterly Review*, 16 (January, 1865): 23–46; (April, 1865): 193–225; and (July, 1865): 328–351.
54. Bird, "Lutheran Hymnology," 337, 339, and 341.
55. Henry Eyster Jacobs, *A History of the Evangelical Lutheran Church in the United States* (New York: Christian Literature Co., 1893).
56. Jacobs, "The Making of the Church Book," 604.
57. *Hymns for the Use of the Evangelical Lutheran Church. By Authority of the Ministerium of Pennsylvania* (Philadelphia: Rodgers, 1865).

Wesley were the foremost contributors, but more than one fourth of it came from foreign sources, especially German.[58] Topics were arranged in approximately the sequence of the Apostles' Creed with the church year blended in. The German *Kirchenbuch* of 1877 also included a hymnal.

The hymnal Spaeth and B. M. Schmucker brought to completion sold well, but there were pockets of resistance in some German-speaking congregations that used the starkly contrasting "Wollenweber" hymnal of 1849. Spaeth said that half of its hymns came from "the period of hymnological decay," that the modern ones were "bombastic, unchurchly, and unscriptural," and that festival seasons of the church year were "poorly supplied."[59] The *Kirchenbuch*, however, included such a large number of sixteenth- and seventeenth-century hymns that even Mann criticized it. He said it seemed to assume that "the Holy Spirit died in the year A.D. 1700."[60]

Sunday school parallels for both the English and German books followed as the General Synod edged toward a more Lutheran posture. In 1866 it decided to revise *Hymns Selected and Original*. With S. S. Schmucker in charge it reduced the number of hymns by half in a new but still topical arrangement. "Revivals" remained, the church year was absent, and subjective elements were emphasized. In 1869 the revised hymnal joined the "Washington Service." Lewis Benson assessed it as "growth in discrimination, but none toward churchliness."[61] The shock for General Synod churches was the presence of service materials. A small number of churches adopted it. S. S. Schmucker suggested that when it was joined to the *Book of Worship* services should be omitted. But a preacher's manual with hymns had seen its day. The General Synod kept morning and evening services. Sales increased.

The English-speaking General Synod felt the impact of immigration. In 1875 George Wenner (1844–1934) reported that ten thousand German communicants were served by one hundred pastors who used German at worship. Wenner, a Yale University and Union Seminary graduate, organized Christ Lutheran Church in New York and served it for sixty-six years. Ecumenical and Lutheran, he helped move the General Synod closer to its Lutheran moorings. Wenner told the General Synod's

---

58. Lewis Benson, *The English Hymn* (Richmond: Knox, 1962, reprint of 1915 edition), 560, counted 167 German translations, forty-two Latin, and eleven Greek. The revision, except for the Latin, added translations.
59. Adolph Spaeth, "Hymnody, Hymn-Books, Luth."*The Lutheran Cyclopedia*, ed. Henry Eyster Jacobs and John A. W. Haas (New York: Scribner, 1905), 238.
60. Horn, *Memoirs of Jacobs*, II, 234.
61. Benson, *The English Hymn*, 561.

German hymn book committee its hymnal should be "small," "objective" and "generally recognized by the church," with texts given "careful and conservative criticism."[62] Wenner saw no reason for a new German collection and suggested the *Deutscher Evangelischer Kirchengesangbuch,* which the Eisenach conference in Germany had prepared in 1853. This was the hymnal Philip Schaff had suggested as a "common ground-work for all new German hymn-books."[63] Though he found it too "archaeological," Schaff praised it for the best texts and melodies. Wenner also applauded it and suggested *Unsere Lieder* for the Sunday School, a Berlin hymnal arranged according to the church year.

MUSIC

Kurtz sought help from unnamed "gentlemen of science as well as refined taste" to select tunes for his 1852 *Lutheran Prayer Book,*[64] but it had novel tunes with short life spans and descants. Seiss provided a musical alternative—not high art divorced from the people, but high quality for practical use with hymn tunes and Anglican chant for the psalms and canticles. He presented to the General Synod his work for the *Evangelical Psalmist* as a companion to *Hymns Selected and Original.* The Synod, though favorably impressed, declined action, so he published it himself.[65] *Psalms and Canticles* was republished seven years later with music for the *Liturgy* of 1860.[66] Charles Porterfield Krauth wrote a ten-page introduction which articulated central Lutheran motifs. The Lutheran church sings, he said, and the "organic structure" of the Lutheran service demands "musical rendering of its responsive parts." He said Popery stole the music from the people by Latin, and sectarianism stole it by incompetent leadership and fashionable choirs which substituted for them.[67]

Others also sensed the need for music. In 1869, a year after the *Church Book* appeared, the General Council appointed a committee to select music for it. Spaeth, an enthusiastic musician who planned extensive musical services, was on the committee. However, it took no action except to suggest that the *Church Book* committee be authorized to review and

---

62. *Proceedings of the General Synod* (27) (Baltimore, 1875), 28.
63. Schaff, "German Hymnology," 245.
64. Kurtz, *Lutheran Prayer Book,* 4.
65. *The Evangelical Psalmist,* 3 and 5. See also the *Proceedings of the General Synod* (Pittsburgh, 1859), 32f.
66. *Psalms and Canticles for the Evangelical Lutheran Churches (from "The Evangelical Psalmist")* (Philadelphia: Book and Tract Society of St. John's Evangelical Lutheran Church, 1867).
67. *Psalms and Canticles,* iii, vi, and vii.

recommend music it might receive. Harriet Krauth (1845–1925) was working on this.

THE CHURCH BOOK WITH MUSIC

Harriet Krauth was Charles Porterfield Krauth's daughter. In 1880 she became Adolph Spaeth's second wife after his first wife died in 1878. She was a singer, organist at St. Stephen's Church in West Philadelphia, hymn translator, music editor, and author. In four years, she furnished music for the entire *Church Book*, grafting high quality English musical branches onto Germanic roots.[68] She improved on Seiss's *Psalms and Canticles* of 1867 by printing the liturgy in full with music distributed throughout at the proper points. This made it easier to use, but it could look forbidding, especially with hymn tunes changed.

Seiss sensed this. His "high-handed individualism"[69] asserted itself. In 1874, part of St. John's Church organized The Church of the Holy Communion. Seiss went with them. He and his organist, Charles Pilling Engelmann (b. 1846), prepared a service book and hymnal.[70] It presumably solved the problems, though it too could look forbidding. Seiss's instincts were tuned to an "elevated" popular taste,[71] however, and his book outsold Harriet Krauth's. Harriet saw it as an unwanted rival.

Rivals or not, Harriet Krauth and Seiss had made English services and hymnals available with music. John Endlich (1819–1892), a musician in Reading, prepared the music for the *Kirchenbuch*. It was published in 1879 with Adolph Spaeth's aid.[72] Endlich chose the rhythmic form of chorale tunes, the musical symbol of the Lutheran confessional revival.

The "Washington Service" did not require service music, nor was the General Synod predisposed to have any. Nevertheless, in 1880 it newly published a service book and hymnal which included Anglican chant for

68. *Church Book for the Use of Evangelical Lutheran Congregations. By Authority of the General Council of the Evangelical Lutheran Church in America. With Music* (Philadelphia: Lutheran Book Store, 1872).
69. Horn, ed., *Memoirs of Jacobs*, II, –71.
70. *Church Song. Part First. Musical Responses, Chants, Etc. Adapted to the Liturgy, Canticles and Psalms of the Evangelical Lutheran Church. Part Second. Metrical Tunes, Adapted to the Church Book of the General Council. The Book of Worship of the General Synod (North). With a Service for the Lord's Supper* (Philadelphia: Lutheran Book Store, 1875).
71. Horn, ed., *Memoirs of Jacobs*, II, –71.
72. J. Endlich, *Choralbuch mit Liturgie und Chorgesängen zum Kirchenbuch der Allgemein Kirchenversammlung* (Philadelphia: Kohler, 1879).

the *Gloria Patri, Kyrie,* and *Gloria in Excelsis*.[73] The General Synod then decided the Lutheran church was a singing one and chose to publish a hymnal with tunes and three principles: prefer the old, inquire into the tune's "churchly" and devotional character, and consider how text and tune relate.[74] "Churchly" was understood with a more pietistic twist than the General Council, but there was common ground. The committee was surprised by the "rapid sale and great popularity of the hymnal." Within two months two printings had been exhausted.[75]

THE COMMON SERVICE OF 1888

Common ground increased. In 1870 John Bachman (1790–1874), a pastor who for fifty-six years had served St. John's Church in Charleston, South Carolina, suggested to his General Synod South—who had separated from the General Synod in 1864—that it appoint delegates to meet and consult with other synods to promote greater uniformity in their books of worship.[76] The General Synod South liked the idea, but it saw no chance that such a proposal would succeed. It therefore took no action. In 1876, however, it put out feelers that asked the committee revising its liturgy to confer with the General Synod and the General Council about one book with the "same hymns" and "the same Order of Services and liturgic forms" for all Lutherans in the United States.[77] In 1878 delegates to the General Synod and General Council were asked to appoint committees "for the purpose of preparing a Service Book."[78] The General Council agreed,

> provided that the Rule which shall decide all questions . . . shall be: The common consent of the pure Lutheran Liturgies of the Sixteenth Century, and when there is not entire agreement among them, the consent of the largest number of those of the greatest weight.[79]

---

73. *Book of Worship with Hymns and Tunes Published by the General Synod of the Evangelical Lutheran Church in the United States* (Philadelphia: Lutheran Publication Society, 1880).
74. *Proceedings of the General Synod* (29) (Wooster, Ohio, 1879), 26–28.
75. *Proceedings of the General Synod* (30) (Altoona, 1881), 19.
76. Luther D. Reed, "Historical Sketch of the Common Service," *Lutheran Church Review*, 36/5 (October, 1917): 501. For additional accounts and documents about the *Common Service* and the *Common Service Book*, see Luther Reed, *The Lutheran Liturgy* (Philadelphia: Muhlenberg Press, 1947), 182–204; Carl F. Schalk, *God's Song*, 157–63, and Carl F. Schalk, *Source Documents in American Lutheran Hymnody* (St. Louis: Concordia, 1996), 120–24.
77. Reed, *Historial Sketch*, 502.
78. Ibid.
79. *Minutes of the General Council* (12) (Zanesville, Ohio, 1879).

The General Synod was not so sure, but in 1883 fifty-five of its ministers petitioned it to settle on "liturgical forms more in harmony with the doctrines and usages of the Evangelical Lutheran Church,"[80] not to prepare a new liturgy, and to begin the study of liturgical matters with the other bodies.[81] The General Council's Rule received tacit approval.

A joint committee included Seiss, Spaeth, and Henry Eyster Jacobs. A subcommittee of B. M. Schmucker, George Wenner, and Edward Traill Horn (1850–1915) did most of the work. Horn succeeded Bachman at St. John's in Charleston and became the committee's secretary, B. M. Schmucker its chair.

Three years later the *Common Service* was prepared. All three bodies adopted it in 1887. The Communion service looked like the one in the 1868 *Church Book* while its Propers, Matins, and Vespers looked like those in the 1877 *Kirchenbuch*. The United Synod South, a union in 1886 of the General Synod South and some independent synods, published it in 1888, as did the General Synod in 1889. The General Council delayed publication to include the Ministerial Acts in an edited *Church Book*. It met in September of 1888, and B. M. Schmucker prepared the copy for a new *Church Book*. A month later he ran with it to catch a train and died on the train from the exertion. The revised edition of the *Church Book* with the *Common Service* was delayed until 1892, at which point the General Council also joined sixty "Additional Hymns" to the hymnal portion of the 1892 *Church Book*. Continuing to move away from American Lutheranism and *Hymns Selected and Original*, in 1899 the General Synod revised its *Book of Worship* in a hymnal with hymn tunes and a musical edition of the *Common Service*.[82]

Jeremiah Franklin Ohl (1850–1941), a Philadelphia Seminary graduate with hymnody, liturgical studies, composing, prison reform, and organ playing among his interests, was a pastor in Philadelphia, director of the Lutheran Deaconess House in Milwaukee, and a city missionary in Philadelphia. He prepared a hymnal for Sunday Schools and the worship of the whole church.[83] Offended by the subjectivity of Sunday School hymnody, he thought that hymns for children ought to have the "great objective realities of the faith"[84] with church hymns best for them. He used the "uncorrupted rhythmic settings of the chorales."[85]

80. *Proceedings of the General Synod* (31) (Springfield, 1883), 47.
81. Ibid., 47.
82. *Book of Worship with Hymns and Tunes* (Philadelphia: The United Lutheran Publication Board, 1899).
83. J. F. Ohl, *School and Parish Hymnal with Tunes* (Philadelphia: Frederick, 1892).
84. Ohl, *School and Parish Hymnal*, 3.
85. Ohl, *School and Parish Hymnal*, 5.

He also prepared a *Service Book* with Matins and Vespers,[86] and in 1913 the General Council put Ohl's *Hymnal* and *Service Book* together under one cover.

Harriet Krauth Spaeth published a new edition of her *Church Book with Music*, altering the service material to conform to the *Common Service*. Harmonized Gregorian Psalm tones and Anglican chant were both given for Antiphons and Psalms. Divided pages with music at the top and psalms at the bottom allowed any psalm to be used with any chant. Tunes for additional hymns were included.

Luther D. Reed (1873–1972) now stood at the center of liturgical, artistic, architectural, and musical work. He taught at Philadelphia Seminary (which moved to suburban Mt. Airy in 1889) and was a primary editor of texts and music for the 1917 *Common Service Book with Hymnal* and for the 1958 *Service Book and Hymnal*.[87] He grew up in Lancaster where his father was the pastor at Christ Church, studied piano and violin, and had undistinguished academic records at Franklin and Marshall College and the Lutheran Seminary at Mt. Airy. At the expense of theology, he studied organ, music theory, Gregorian chant, and became an organist at St. Michael's Church in Germantown where he organized a Glee club, played the violin, and attended concerts.

During his time in seminary Reed began to study the *Common Service* with Henry Eyster Jacobs whose quiet scholarship awakened him to liturgical concerns. He integrated music into the liturgy. In 1895 he was called to Emmanuel Church north of Pittsburgh. There he arranged Gregorian chant and began to study with Harry G. Archer whom he called the best organist in town.[88] They prepared service books of Gregorian chant which led to convocations for organists, choirmasters, and pastors in 1898, 1899, and 1901.[89] Archer and Reed also got Max Reger to compose musical settings.[90]

---

86. J. F. Ohl, *School and Parish Service Book being the Order of Matins and Vespers of the Evangelical Lutheran Church with Music* (Philadelphia: Frederick, 1892).
87. *The Service Book and Hymnal* (Minneapolis: Augsburg, 1958).
88. Luther D. Reed, *At Eventide: Recollections and Reflections* (unpublished typescript, n. d.), 22.
89. Harry G. Archer and Luther D. Reed, eds., *The Psalter and Canticles Pointed for Chanting to the Gregorian Psalm Tones with a Plain Song Setting for Matins and Vespers* (New York: The Christian Literature Company, 1897), Harry G. Archer and Luther D. Reed, eds., *The Choral Service Book containing the Authentic Plain Song Intonations and Responses for the Morning Service, The Order of Matins and Vespers, the Litany and the Suffrages of the Common Service for the Use of Evangelical Lutheran Congregations with Accompanying Harmonies for Organ* (Philadelphia: General Council Publication Board, 1901), *Burial Service; Musical Settings by Harry D. Archer and L. D. Reed* (Philadelphia: General Council Publication Board, 1910).
90. *The Responsories; Musical Settings by Max Reger. A Volume in the Series of Service Books* (Philadelphia: General Council Publication Board, 1914).

THE COMMON SERVICE BOOK AND HYMNAL OF 1917

In addition to convocations like this, as Carl Schalk says, the situation was "ripe" for a common hymnal.[91] In 1897 the General Council suggested that a committee cooperate with other Lutheran bodies to prepare "a Common Book of Worship including, besides the Common Order of Service, Orders for Ministerial Acts, and a Book of Hymns in the English Language." In 1901 a "Proof Copy of a Common Hymnal had been printed" with about 450 hymns, based on an 1899 *Proof Copy of a Proposed new Hymnal* with 541 hymns that Seiss had "prepared" and "published at his own expense." In 1903 a "manuscript of the hymnbook had been completed." In 1907 the Church Book Committee reported that the United Synod South had printed the hymnal with the Common Service, and it already had gone through three editions. This book, though not approved by the General Council and General Synod, apparently had found a place in some of their churches anyway.

In 1909 the General Council met in Minneapolis and invited the General Synod and the United Synod of the South to join it in a final revision of the proposed hymnbook. A subcommittee which included Jacobs, Ohl, and Reed "entered upon a most thorough examination of the arrangement and contents of the Common Hymnal, largely upon the basis of exhaustive studies by Dr. Jacobs." Theodore Emmanuel Schmauk (1860-1920) had suggested this examination which included "not only the entire field of English Hymnody, but translations from the hymns of the Early church, the Latin, German, Swedish, Danish, and Icelandic." Schmauk was born in Lancaster, Pennsylvania, a pastor who had served a church in Lebanon, Pennsylvania, and was editor of the *Lutheran Church Review*. From 1903 until 1920 he was President of the General Council.

The subcommittee's report was complete in 1911, and a printed copy was prepared in 1912. This became the substance of the 1917 hymnal. Schalk saw the "basic strength of the *Common Service Book and Hymnal* ... in its liturgical formulations" and that, "for the first time, a significantly large body of Lutherans were united about a common body of hymnody in their official book of worship." He saw its weakness in not finding sufficient acceptable "literary merit" in translations. The Joint Committee said it "spared no effort or expense in gathering all the books in which English translations of the treasures of Lutheran hymnody in other languages are found," but that "*the great bulk of this material was absolutely unusable.*"

---

91. For further details and sources of quotations about what follows, see Schalk, *God's Song*, 158–63 with the endnotes, and Reed, *The Lutheran Liturgy*, 182–204.

Schalk said this resulted in a "failure to reclaim, to any significant degree, the historic, confessional hymnody of the 16th-century Lutheran formation to which its liturgy paid homage."

This may be termed a weakness, but the Committee may have judged rightly that, aside from the fine translations of German chorales by Catherine Winkworth and the equally fine translations of Latin and other pre-Reformation hymns by John Mason Neale, it could not find English translations that fit the quality hymns required. Schalk's overall analysis was that the 1917 book was a "truly remarkable" *Common Service* "coupled with a hymnbook still quite removed from a distinctly confessional Lutheran collection." That may be hard to maintain unless "confessional Lutheran" means something narrower than the understanding of the book's framers and subtracts their context. One needs to consider the following.

- 15 percent of the book came from the chorale tradition.
- Some chorale tunes were rhythmic, though not all. "Wachet Auf" (No. 5) was rhythmic, but "Ein feste Burg" (No. 195) was isorhythmic.
- This was a hymnal finding its way not in its native land or language, but in the United States in English.
- It represented a Lutheran perspective in which one would expect a strong catholic showing of texts and tunes from the language of the surrounding culture.
- Its framers made discriminating choices which had considerable staying power.

In any case, Luther Reed's assessment was more positive. He found it "quite remarkable that when the new book was organized it had ready for use a complete and carefully prepared service book and hymnal... The organization of the United Lutheran Church and the preparation of the *Common Service Book and Hymnal* were expressions of the American spirit. It spoke in comprehensiveness of plan, catholicity of outlook, compact and practical arrangement, and in the extensive use of the book by the people and clergy throughout the continent."[92]

---

92. Reed, *The Lutheran Liturgy,* 204.

9.

The Scandinavian Hymnal Tradition

Gracia Grindal

The story is told of one Oluf Skriver, who stood outside a Norwegian church in 1529 singing Lutheran hymns loudly in the vernacular and disturbing the priest and worshipers inside the church. When the priest asked him to stop, he announced that he would sit in a tree and keep on singing. For him it was a wonderful thing to sing the gospel in his own language to Norwegian tunes.[1] That encapsulates the beginning of Lutheran hymnody in the North.

To be sure, there were hymns in the North that were sung in the vernacular from the beginning: most well-known would be a day song, Dagvisa, *Den signade Dag* (O day full of grace), one of the earliest Christian hymns in the North.[2] Also, as Gerhoh of Reichsperg (1083–1169) had observed: "All the earth exalts in praise of Christ with vernacular songs, but especially the Germanic people, whose language is especially suited for communal singing."[3] That may have been as important to the development of Lutheran hymnody as anything, making the flowering of hymnody in the Germanic languages almost inevitable.

Sweden's Petri brothers, Olaus (1493–1552) and Laurentius (1499–1572), Denmark's Hans Tausen (1494–1561), and Finland's Mikael Agricola

---

1. H. Blom Svendsen. "Den Nye Kvedskap," *Norsk Salmesang: Arven fra Gammel Tid*, (Oslo: Lunde, 1935), 1: 35. For a similar story see Ulrich S Leupold. "Introduction: The Hymns," LW 53: 191.
2. See Lars Eckerdal. "Den signade dag—den nordiska dagvisan," *Hymnologi Nordisk Tidsskrift*. 39 (October 2010): 93–97.
3. Cited in Anthony Ruff. "Pre-Reformation German Vernacular Hymnody," *Hymns and Hymnody: Historical and Theological Introductions,* ed. Mark A Lampert, et al. (Eugene: Cascade: 2019), 1: 225.

(1510–1577) all returned from their studies in Wittenberg committed advocates of Luther's theology. They quickly translated the Deutsche Messe of Martin Luther and his hymns into their own languages. The Petris returned to Sweden in 1519, well before Luther's first hymnal, but they followed Luther closely. Hans Tausen had studied with Luther in 1523/24 just when the first Lutheran hymnals were published. He had heard the powerful congregational singing in Wittenberg.[4]

The first Swedish hymnal, *Swenska songer eller wijsor* (Swedish songs or folksongs), came out in 1526 by order of King Gustav Vasa. While there is no named editor, the hand of Olaus Petri in the work is almost certain. Several of his hymns are included, among them, *O Herra Gud ditt Helga ord* (Thy sacred word, O Lord of old), two stanzas of which were included in the Augustana *Hymnal 1925* (AH 215). We have no extant copies of the first edition, only some pages from the second, but there is a complete copy of the third from 1536. These editions established a template for later Swedish hymnals. They began with the catechism: the Ten Commandments: *Tesse äre the tiyo buud* (These are the ten commands), the Creed, and Lord's Prayer. Then, translations of old Latin songs such as *A solis ortus cardine* which Luther included in his hymnals. These were followed by hymns on Jesus's parables, such as *Om en rijk man her siunge wij* (About a rich man we are singing). In addition, there are several hymns based on the psalms and canticles like Luther's Psalm 130, *Af diuupsen nödh ropar iach til tich* (Out of the depths I cry to you).[5] Revisions of this hymnal with added hymns continued for more than a century.

The first evangelical Danish service was held in Malmø, still part of the Danish kingdom, on June 1, 1527, led by Claus Mortensen (1499–1575). Mortensen and Hans Olufson (*ca*. 1500–1542) published the first Danish hymnal in 1528, intended for Sundays and daily use. At the same time, they published a Danish version of the Deutsche Messe, *Thet christelighe messze embedhe paa dansche*. It included the hymns for the ordinary, plus hymns for every Sunday. In 1529, they published the two books together.

That same year, Hans Tausen prepared an evangelical vesper service with Danish hymns, antiphons, psalms, and canticles. In 1533, when *Malmø Salme Bogen* (The Malmø Hymnal) appeared, it contained materials from previous hymnals and services, plus new content: new texts, including Tausen's vespers, the hymn mass and fifty-one new Danish

---

4. Anders Malling. "Efterskrift," *Malmø-Salme Bogen 1533*. Facsimile (Malmø: Ljustrycksanstalt, 1967), 289.
5. [*Swenska songer eller wjisor, 1526*], earliest extant edition: *Swenske songer eller wisor nw på nytt prentade*... (Stockholm: Kungl. tryckeriet [Royal printing house], 1536).

hymns. The hymn selections began with evening and morning hymns, translations of Luther's hymns, hymns for the festivals, translated German hymns, three of David's psalms, nineteen hymns based on the catechism and the hymn mass, plus three by Olaus Petri, translated from Swedish. The biblical source for a verse is printed beside it.

In 1567 *Then Swenska Psalmboken förbätret* (The Swedish Hymnbook Improved) was published. The driving force behind this was Laurentius Petri. This hymnal was one in a series reworked and revised since the 1526 hymnal. Much of the original material remained, with additional hymns and psalm paraphrases.

About this time, the Finns produced their first hymnal. The founder of Finnish Lutheranism, Mikael Agricola, had returned from studies with Luther and Melanchthon in 1538. He shared their convictions about the language of worship needing to be in the vernacular.[6] Jacobus Petri Finno (1540–1588) published the first Finnish hymnal in 1583. It contained 101 hymns, the majority translations of Swedish, German, and Latin hymns, with seven by Finno. A later hymnal, *Yxi Wähä Suomenkielinen Wirsikirja* (A Little Finnish Hymnal) (Stockholm: Mouterin, 1614), was edited by Hemming of Masku (1550–1619). He also translated and published a Finnish version of the *Piae Cantiones*, a priceless collection of medieval texts and music. With Sweden's rule over Finland, many Swedish speaking Finns used the early Swedish hymnals and continue to do so as Swedish is an official language in Finland.

A new Danish hymnal, *Den danske Psalmebok* (The Danish Hymnbook) (Copenhagen: Benedicht, 1569) was prepared by Hans Thomissøn (1532–1573). Thomissøn, while not considered a hymn writer, had a sense for the language and worth of the older hymns which made him an ideal editor. He used the materials of the previous hymnals and added over 150 new hymns. The preface included astronomical information such as how to reckon the date for future Easters plus a calendar with saints' days, much reduced from the medieval church, including significant days in the Dano-Norwegian calendar.

In his preface to the hymnal, Thomissøn wrote a charming personal account of the history of Danish hymnody. He included a defense of Lutheran hymnody:

"God's Word is, in itself, lively music that gives comfort and life during our dying needs, and a truly righteous joy in our hearts, but when it

---

6. Toivo Harjunpaa, "An Historical Outline of Hymnody in Finland," *Studia Theologica* 23 (1969): 157.

comes with a lively and sweet melody (which is also God's special gift), it gives the song new power and goes deeper into the heart so that the text, which is the heart of the soul of the song, stirs the heart more and is not easily forgotten."[7]

Thus, he remarked on the importance of finding the right tunes also printed with the texts. There were the usual thirty-seven Latin hymns, corrected or revised, and thirty-five psalms versified, plus a few hymns such as *Den signede dag* (O day full of grace) (LBW 161) from pre-Reformation times. The Danish version of the Deutsche Messe concluded the hymnal. Thomissøn also suggested in his preface that the service end with the singing of the Ten Commandments hymn, and sometimes even the entire catechism so people would learn it.

King Fredrik II (1534–1588) ruled that this hymnal, along with the Danish Bible and the Niels Jespersen's *Gradual* (Copenhagen, 1573), was to be used in "all the schools and no other." All other hymnals were "forbidden." Every church was to have this book, along with the Bible, the book of church ordinances, and the liturgical book "lying on the altar."[8] The hymn section began with the liturgical year, including the singing catechism of Luther; the final section added hymns for the stages of life: marriage, thanksgiving, death and burial, judgment day, and the resurrection. As Denmark's first hymnal commissioned by a king, it continued, with some changes, and with content that has lasted until today. Out of the 268 hymns in it, almost 20 percent remain in the current Danish hymnal.[9]

Although no other Danish hymnal achieved official status until Thomas Hansen Kingo's work in the late seventeenth century, there were many supplements to the Thomissøn hymnal and books by individual writers, none more beloved than the work of Hans Christensøn Sthen (1544–1610), *En liden Vandrebog* (A little Pilgrim Book) (1589), still treasured by Danes.[10] One of Sthen's hymns appeared in translation in America: *Herr Jesus Krist* (Lord Jesus Christ) included in the *Lutheran Hymnary*

---

7. Hans Thomissøn. "Alle gode Gudfryctige Christne i Danmarckis oc Norgis Riger," *Den Danske Psalmebog met mange Christelige Psalmer.* (Copenhagen: Benedicht, 1569; facsimile, 1997), sig. Cviij^r.
8. Jørgen Kjærgaard, *Salme Håndbok: Salmehistorie Med biografier af forfatterne i Den Danske Salmebog 2002.* I (Copenhagen: Vajsenhus, 2003), 68.
9. Kjærgaard, *Salme Håndbok*, 73.
10. See Jens Lyster's reprint of Sthen's collected works, *Hans Christensen Sthens Skrifter* (Copenhagan: Det Danske Sprog- og Litteraturselskab (DSL); Odense: I kommission af Syddansk Universitetsforlag, 1994–2015).

(LH 278), the *Concordia* (CH 218) and (TLH 353) translated by Harriet Reynolds Krauth Spaeth (1845–1925).

Iceland's Marteinn Einarsson (d. 1576), Bishop of Skáholt from 1548–1556, was the first to publish vernacular resources for Iceland. *Ein kristelig Handbog* (A Christian Handbook) (1555) based on the Malmø liturgy of 1535, included an appendix of thirty-five hymns by Martin Luther translated into Icelandic. Several others also produced hymns in Icelandic, but the first official hymnal was not published until 1589 when Bishop Guðbrandur Þhorlaksson (1541–1627) of Hólar compiled *En ný Psalma Bók* (A New Hymnal). It contained 342 hymns.

In his preface Guðbrandur remarked that it was created for two reasons: (1) so people could sing the "true evangelical faith" and (2) it used the conventions of Icelandic poetry going back to Snorri Sturluson (1179–1241).[11] It was intended for home devotions as much as church services.[12] This book remained the Icelandic hymnal until the nineteenth century.

THE SEVENTEENTH CENTURY

The Swede, Finn, and Dano-Norwegian traditions all based their next provisional hymnals on these early hymnals, taking pains to include contemporary authors like Sthen and great hymn writers in Germany. Paul Gerhardt (1607–1676), Johann Heerman (1585–1647) and Johann Rist (1607–1667) were among the more well known in the Nordic countries. Along with these influences, the psalm paraphrases of Calvin's followers came to the North via the work of Ambrosius Lobwasser (1515–1585), whose translations of the French psalm paraphrases into German, *Psalter des Königlichen Propheten David* (Leipzig: Steinmann, 1573), brought a wave of criticism from German Orthodox Lutherans, although his work was admired by both Swedes and Danes.

In the early years of the seventeenth century, during the Baroque era, there was a flowering of individual hymnwriters in the Nordic countries. In Denmark, Thomas Hansen Kingo (1634–1703) was beginning to dominate Dano-Norwegian hymn writing. In Norway two accomplished contemporaries, Petter Dass (1647–1707), and Dorothea Engelbretsdatter (1634–1716) were becoming well known. In Iceland the gifted Hallgrímur

---

11. Kjærgaard, *Salme Håndbok*, 283.
12. On Icelandic hymnal information I am indebted to Karl Sigurbjörnsson, Bishop Emeritus of Iceland, in an email from November 30, 2022.

Pétursson (1614–1674), who had spent his student years in Copenhagen, was making his mark. His *Passíusálmar* (Hymns of the Passion) (1664), fifty hymns still read on Icelandic radio every day of Lent, shaped Icelandic piety for the next generations.

Uppsalapsalmboken (The Uppsala Hymnal) (1645), served as a semiofficial book in Sweden until Bishop Jesper Svedberg's *Then Swenska Psalm-boken* (The Swedish Hymn Book) (1695). It would become the national hymnal that shaped Swedish religious life for the next 124 years. At the king's request, Svedberg began compiling a manuscript that made use of the hymns from the previous hymnals, adding hymns by individual hymn writers such as Laurentius Laurentii Laurinius (1573–1655) who wrote *I Himmelen, i Himmelen* (In heaven above) (ELW 630). Svedberg was also helped by accomplished hymn writers of his day such as Jacob Arrhenius (1642–1725), a professor of history. He was known for his Jesus hymns, one of which, a translation of a German hymn, appeared in Augustana's *Hymnal* 1925 (AH 482) and the *Concordia* (CH 316: *Jesu! Du min fröyd och fromma* (Jesus, Lord, and precious Savior). Another, his own *Jesus är min vän den bäste* (Jesus is my friend most precious), was found in the Augustana *Hymnal* (AH 470). Haquin Spegel (1645–1714), bishop and briefly archbishop of Sweden, was the most productive of the hymn writers at the time, especially in his paraphrases of psalms. Another author, Israel Kolmodin (1643–1709), wrote the hymn *Den blomstertid nu kommer* (The blossomtime is coming), which is still popular in all Nordic countries. ELW 830 uses the Svedberg hymnal's tune from 1697, though with a text called *Hve dýrðlegur er Drottinn* (How marvelous God's greatness), by Iceland's Valdemar Briem (1848–1930).

Svedberg's committee presented its hymnal to the king for publication in 1694. *Den Swenska Psalm-Boken* (The Swedish Hymnal), the *Gamlabok* (The Old Book), became almost a magical totem for Swedes, who would swear by it. Like its predecessors, it included hymns for every Sunday's texts, followed by the gospel and epistle texts with collects and prayers accompanying them, as well as the passion history. In the middle was Luther's *Small Catechism*, the Hustavlan, and then prayers for special occasions concluding with prayers for a "traveling person on land and sea." Svedberg's new hymnal quickly received scorching criticism from other authorities in the Swedish church.

In the end, the king ordered his critics and Svedberg to revise the hymnal and present it again for approval. After much dissent and argument, Svedberg finally presented a new version of the hymnal with many of his works deleted or much changed, ostensibly because of their

Pietism. Many 1694 hymnals were sent to New Sweden for use by the Swedes there.[13]

Thomas Hansen Kingo began establishing himself as a hymn writer as early as the 1670s. He produced a booklet of hymns, *Aandelige Siunge-koors Første Part* (Spiritual Singing Choirs, Part One) (Copenhagen: Eichhorn, 1674) that included three hymns intended for home devotions for morning, noon, and evening, every day of the week, with a morning and evening psalm. The three hymns for the day had the same meter so they could be sung to the same tune, with a rhymed *suk* (prayer) for every day. Vilhelm Loren used some of them in the *Salmebok* of the Norwegian Synod in 1874.

The second booklet, *Aandelige Siunge-koors Anden Part* (Spiritual Singing Choirs, Part Two) (Copenhagen: Eichhorn, 1677), contained hymns written for confession and absolution, some on the passion narrative, and other hymns that fit various topics or occasions such as one on Vanity: *Far, Verden Farvel* (Farewell, world, farewell), and another on Fortune, *Sorrig og Glæden* (Sorrow and gladness), one of Kingo's greatest poems. These hymns were not intended for the Sunday service, but for home devotions. Families now had hymns and prayers to sing or read three times every day.

On March 27, 1683, Christian V commissioned Kingo to prepare a hymnal for all Danish and Norwegian churches. The instructions for the book were precise. He was to prepare a hymnal that would continue the Lutheran emphasis on the centrality of hymns. In addition, it was to fit in with the ritual book of 1685 on which Kingo was working at the time. In 1689, Kingo finished the "Winter Part" for the Sundays from Advent through Easter. After Kingo presented the King his finished work in 1696, his enemies attacked it. Only after significant revisions, including the deletion of fifty-one hymns by Kingo, did it receive royal approval. Once again, like the Svedberg affair, it was a literary loss. Finally, in 1699, Kingo's hymnal, *Dend Forordnede Ny Kirke-Psalme-Bog* (The Official New Church Hymnal) (1699) was approved for publication as the authorized hymnal of the two kingdoms.

PIETISM AND ENLIGHTENMENT HYMNALS

Like the Svedberg hymnal in Sweden, the Kingo hymnal became the unifying text of the Twin kingdoms of Denmark and Norway for the next century, if not longer; it was cherished by many immigrants to America

---

13. For a study of the fate of the 1694 hymnal, see Bengt Wahlstrom, "Exkurs: Den Swedbergska Psalmbokens senare Öden. 1. Översändandet till Amerika," *Studier över Tillkomsten av 1695 Års Psalmbok*. (Uppsala: Almqvists & Wiksells, 1951), 214–239; see also chapter 1, page 22.

and became an important source for Norwegian hymnals in America. In the meantime, Erick Pontoppidan (1696–1764) was commissioned by King Christian VII on September 3, 1736, to compile a hymnal, *Den Nye Psalme-bog* (The New Hymn Book). He charged Pontoppidan to add new hymns for new occasions.[14] It appeared in 1740. The old Lutheran hymns that taught the tenets of the faith no longer spoke to the people so clearly. The title page of the hymnal makes clear its difference from Kingo's: it would provide hymns "for more edifying occasions."[15] This need for *opbyggelse* (edification), a key word in Pietist talk, was strongly felt in the court where Christian VII reigned in a time that was called "state Pietism."

The chief feature of Pontoppidan's hymnal was its organization of the hymns to fit the *ordo salutis* (order of salvation), a practice popular with Pietists. Hans Adolph Brorson had used the *ordo* for his collection of hymns published during the 1730s, culminating in his 1739 collection of hymns, *Troens Rare Klenodie* (Faith's Rare Treasury). Pontoppidan included hymns by Brorson (1694–1764), whose hymns became popular in Norway where they were set to folk tunes by the local cantors (klokkers), thus making them seem like native Norwegian hymns, as is clear from Grieg's setting of *Den store hvide Flok* (Behold, a host) (ELW 425).

Because Pontoppidan's hymnal was not divided up into hymns for every Sunday as had been the tradition through Kingo, pastors now had 259 new hymns that would go with topics on which they preached. This meant the necessity of a hymn board in the church since people could no longer as easily find the hymns for each Sunday as they could in the Kingo hymnal. Pontoppidan also included two hymns by Bergen's poet, Dorothe Engelbretsdatter, *Dagen viger og gaar bort* (Daylight fades and dies away), and *Naar jeg min feil vil skue* (When I behold my errors). While this hymnal had official approval, it was not used as much as Kingo's.

Pietism became a force in Iceland as well. Guðbrandur's hymnal had been reprinted in 1607 with more hymns and republished six times, each time getting bigger as the bishops added the hymns of Hallgrímur Pétursson's *Pássíusálmar* (Hymns of the Passion), and other hymns for the incarnation and resurrection, as well as Kingo's morning and evening hymns. These were to help families with home devotions. By 1772, the hymnal had become so bulky it could not easily be bound. It was then divided into two parts: *Flokkabók* with many new hymns influenced by

---

14. "The King's commission to Pontoppidan, September 3, 1736." Kjærgaard, *Salme Håndbok*, 134.
15. *Den Nye Psalme-Bog* (Copenhagen: Berling, 1740).

Pietism, and the second, *Höfuðgreinarbók*, traditional doctrinal hymns. *Flokkabók* remained popular until the mid-nineteenth century.

In Sweden, Svedberg's hymnal remained almost uncontested in its dominance for a generation. In 1701, Bishop Johannes Gezelius the Younger (1647–1718), made a Finnish version of Svedberg. Like its source, it contained the texts for Sundays and prayers for festivals. It was used until 1886 and still is in some revivalist groups.

In 1717, Georg Lybecker's (*ca.* 1670–1716), hymnal *Moses och Lamsens wisor* (Moses and the songs of the Lamb) was printed. Lybecker, who knew August Hermann Franke (1663–1727) and Johann Anastasius Freylinghausen (1670–1739), advanced the cause of Pietism in Sweden through his preaching and especially his songs. After Lybecker's hymnal the Moravian movement began to influence Swedish religious life. Its songs were first published in Swedish in the book *Sions Sånger* in 1743 and a revised version, *Sions Nya Sånger*, in 1778. Both were published in Copenhagen and smuggled into Sweden because of The Conventicle Act passed in 1726 which banned Moravian gatherings. Nevertheless, it spread widely in the country. The first book of *Sions Sånger/Siionin Virret* (Sion's singer/ Sion's streams) became a standard in Finland and was adopted by the revivals. It continues to be updated and revised in Sweden, Finland, and America even today.

The 1772 *Sions Nye Sånger* became known as the Rutström hymnal. Anders Carl Rutström (1721–1772), a Lutheran pastor, wrote hymns that would influence Lina Sandell and the Rosenius revival. Three Rutström hymns made it to the United States: *Kom, huldaste förbarmare* (Come, Savior dear, with us abide) (AH 298), *Min blodige konung på korsträdets stam* (My Crucified Savior, despised and contemned) (AH 114), and *Lammets folk och Sions fränder* (Chosen seed and Zion's children) (AH 267); as well as appearing in the Augustana *Hymnal*, the first two were included in *Youth's Favorite Songs*, a collection of spiritual songs and American gospel songs edited by Carl L. Manfred (1918–2011) and published sometime in the early 1950s that is still cherished by many.

ENLIGHTENMENT

While the hymnals of the autocratic Baroque era served as the glue that kept the cultures of both traditions solidly unified, by the end of the eighteenth century, new movements changed people's world views. Hymnal committees wanted to find new hymns that recognized those changes.

In Denmark, during the turmoil of the Johann Friedrich Struensee (1737–1772) period, and to some extent because of it, the Enlightenment began to make inroads into the culture. The mentally ill King Christian VII was persuaded by Struensee, the regent of Denmark, to approve several significant reforms in Denmark consistent with Enlightenment thought. This influence also affected the next hymnal in the Dano-Norwegian kingdom. When Struensee was brutally executed for lèse-majesté, a leader of the intrigue against him, Secretary of State Ove Høegh Guldberg (1731–1808), began secretly planning a hymnal with Bishop Ludvig Harboe (1709–1783) that would meet the demands of the day. They wanted hymns that were not so long as those in Kingo's book, and hymns of praise—not the teaching and homiletical hymns in Kingo's and earlier hymnals. The Belletristic Society of Denmark requested that writers send in hymns anonymously, using the new creation centered theology and less of the Baroque themes of repentance and self-abnegation.

To their surprise, they received twenty hymns from Birgitte Boye (1742–1824), a young woman married to a manager of the king's forest in southern Zealand. She won the contest and was invited by the committee to contribute more hymns and work with them on the hymnal. Although the hymnal was approved in 1778 for use in both kingdoms, the hymnal wasn't printed until 1783. When the Guldberg Hymnal, *Psalme-Bog* (Hymn Book) came out, much of it looked like the prior Kingo hymnal with more choices of hymns. The hymnal continued Kingo's arrangement, with hymns for each Sunday of the church year. It included 438 hymns. The committee had kept 132 of Kingo's hymns, and 143 from Pontoppidan's hymnal. Many of those, however, were revised to fit the thought of the day. Most surprising was that it contained 146 hymns by Boye, especially her hymn on the churching of women, *Ved Barsel Koners Kirkegang* (At the new mother's churching), almost surely the first such hymn written by a woman who had given birth. Most of the rest of her contributions had Enlightenment themes.

Although the editors hoped the "simple could find what would strengthen them," in fact it was aimed more at the upper classes. Their protests to the contrary, the stated purpose of their hymnal was the "uplifting of the Spirit for the enlightened."[16]

Boye's star would rapidly fall with the next hymnal of 1798 when most of her hymns would be removed. The Norwegians would keep several of her hymns alive, using three of them as høitids salmer, or festival hymns,

---

16. Guldberg and Harboe, "Aller naadigste Konge!" (To the King) as found in Kjærgaard, *Salme Håndbok*, 148.

that were always sung at the reading of the Gospel at Christmas, Easter, and Pentecost. Two of them, *En frelser er idag oss født; Rejoice* (Rejoice, this happy morn (TLH 79 or LBW 43) and *Han er opstanden* (He is arisen, glorious word) (TLH 189 or LBW 138), endured in America through the *Lutheran Book of Worship*.

The Guldberg hymnal, despite its Enlightenment ambitions, had enough of Kingo and Pontoppidan to satisfy traditionalists. It was brought by many immigrants to America and became a significant source for *Salmebog for Lutherske Kristne i Amerika* (Hymnal for Lutheran Christians) (1874, revised in 1903), the first Norwegian hymnal prepared in America. Ulrik Vilhelm Koren (1826–1910), the editor, kept the Kingo arrangement of hymns for every Sunday which his successors used in the first successful English hymnal of the Norwegians, *The Lutheran Hymnary* (1912). He also included Dorothe Engelbretsdatter's hymn *Dagen viger og gaar bort* (Daylight fades and dies away, SS 482) along with hymns from Birgitte Boye (SS 80, SS 217).

Because tastes changed so quickly during the last decade of the eighteenth century, Denmark decided to produce another hymnal within just a few years of Guldberg. Members of a committee created *Evangelisk-Kristelig Psalmebog* (The Evangelical Christian Hymnal) (1798). They were influenced by the work of Christian Bastholm (1740–1819), who in 1785 put out a proposal to update and shorten the service. He wanted to substitute hymns that were teaching or homiletical with hymns that praised and offered thanksgiving for God's greatness.[17] The music should be tasteful and worthy of the subject. No hymn should be more than eight stanzas. And, finally, everyone should be able to sing with understanding. His proposal, which was tried in the Danish church with disastrous consequences, was also accepted by the editors of the new hymnal.[18]

The *Evangelisk-Kristelig Psalmebog* committee rejected almost all the hymns of Boye. When it appeared, its title was "a hymnal for use in church and home devotions."[19] The table of contents reveals a hymnal divided into three parts: (1) Praise and thanksgiving hymns focused on the being of God and the Trinity; (2) "Hymns of Prayer" that filled out the hymns of the *ordo salutis*; and (3) hymns for the stages of life. While many hymns by previous authors were there, such as those by Kingo or Brorson, they were heavily edited and updated. When it appeared, people

---

17. Christian Bastholm, *Forsøg til en forbedret Plan i den udvortes Gudstjeneste*, 1785, as found in Kjærgaard, *Salme Håndbok*, 154.
18. Bastholm, *Forsøg til en forbedret*.
19. "Evangelisk-kristelig Psalmebog til brug ved Kirke- og Huus-Andagt."

reacted strongly against its revisions, its organization, and especially that the hymns were no longer in the same Sunday order as Kingo's. Worst was that the devil had completely disappeared from the hymnal. All this did was increase the disaffection of the Danish people.

Still, the Icelandic church produced a similar hymnal, *Evangeliskkristileg Messu-saungs og Sálma-Bok* (The Evangelical Christian Hymn Mass and Hymnal) (1801), based on *Den Evangelisk-Kristelig Psalmebog*. Although it received the same criticisms in Iceland as its source in Denmark, the hymnal remained in use for seventy years.

In 1816 Johann Wallin (1779–1839) was asked to prepare a Swedish hymnal to supplant Svedberg. Wallin and his colleagues, Johan Åström (1767–1844), Frans Mikael Franzén (1772–1847), and Samuel Johan Hedborn (1783–1849), had been preparing for such a work for some years, publishing books of *Profsalmer* (Trial Hymns) from 1809 to 1813. By 1815, Wallin and his committee had created a hymnal of 500 hymns to present to the court. The King approved *Den Swenska Psalmboken* (The Swedish Hymnal) on January 29, 1819 for use in the kingdom. Wallin had written 128 hymns, translated 23, and revised 178 of the hymns in the book. Franzén's *Bereden väg for Herren* (Prepare the royal highway, ELW 264) and *O Jesus, än de dina* (Around you, O Lord Jesus, ELW 468), have endured.

Wallin's table of contents shows a different understanding of hymnals from Svedberg. There are no texts for individual Sundays, or prayers, not even the passion of Christ narrative. The book is exclusively hymns, which are arranged theologically, not catechetical. The opening hymn is by Wallin, *Upp, psaltare och harpa* (Strike up, O harp and psaltery) (AH 345). The first part of the hymnal is divided into hymns on the Trinity. The next section, *Christeligt Sinne och Förhållende* (Christian thought and behavior), contains topical hymns from the *ordo salutis* and hymns for special occasions. Some few favorites from Svedberg's hymnal survived. Svedberg's hymn, *Herre, signe du och råde* (Lord, bless us and advise us) (AH 348), revised by Wallin, was the last hymn in the collection as it had been in the 1695 hymnal.

Wallin's hymnal served the Swedish church for more than a century. Swedish immigrants were told to bring with them the revised version of John Henrik Thomander (1798–1865) and Peter Wieselgren (1800–1877). They had edited the original to excise the rationalism of Wallin. Even this revision was not as popular as the songbooks the immigrants knew and loved, especially those by Oscar Ahnfelt and Lina Sandell (1832–1903).

Thirty of Wallin's hymns and translations appeared in Augustana's *Hymnal* and six in the SBH, but only three in the LBW; most famous is his Christmas hymn *Var Hälsad, Sköna Morgenstund* (All hail to you, O blessed morn) (LBW 73), central to Swedish Julotta sevices. Two others appear in the LBW, one a stanza taken from a longer Wallin hymn, *Hör hur tempelsången stiger Kristne, medan vi här vandra* (Christians while on earth abiding) (LBW 440) with the second stanza by Svedberg, his only hymn in the LBW, and *Vi lofve dig, o store Gud* (We worship you, O God of might) (LBW 432). The current Swedish hymnal (1986) contains thirty-one hymns by Wallin and many translations and revisions of older hymns.

NATIONALISM AND ROMANTICISM

As the nineteenth century progressed, nationalism began to affect all of Europe and naturally had an influence on the various hymnals in the Nordic countries. Norwegians, now free of Denmark, began to look for an authentic Norwegian language that was less Danish, while the Finns began searching for their national past and language. This also meant that many of the best hymn writers in each country were often the nation's best poets, and their hymns were as much a part of the cultural heritage of the nation as their other poems.

Archbishop Jakob Tengström (1755–1832) of Finland attempted to adopt the Wallin hymnal for Finnish use, but his attempts were rebuffed. Only after his death did the Finns begin thinking of a new hymnal. Three of Finland's most distinguished poets worked on this hymnal: Johan Ludvig Runeberg (1804–1877), a Finn Swede and Finland's national poet, whose birthday is still celebrated in Finland with a "Runeberg torte"; Elias Lönnrot (1802–1884) the champion of Finnish folklore and compiler of the national epic, *Kalevala*; and Zacharias Topelius (1818–1898), another of Finland's great writers. Together, with other Finnish poets and musicians, they produced both a Swedish and Finnish hymnal in 1886. The Swedish hymnal compiled by Runeberg contained 500 hymns, 261 of which came from the Svedberg hymnal of 1695. The Finnish hymnal contained 75 percent of the hymns from the 1701 hymnal to satisfy the Pietists who loved it. Most of the rest were by Lönnrot.

During this time the Danish church, now separated from Norway, saw the rise of Nicolai Fredrik Severin Grundtvig (1783–1872), who flooded Denmark with his hymns, theological and historical works. His collections of hymns, *Sang-Værk* (Song Work), from 1837, 1839, 1841, until his last in 1870, would, over time, be incorporated into the Danish hymnal.

Several of his hymns, among them, *Kirken den er et gammelt hus* (Built on a rock the Church shall stand) (ELW 652) and *Den Signede Dag* (O Day full of grace), made their way to America.

Bishop Jacob Peter Mynster (1775–1854), who had famously preached in Copenhagen's cathedral to one person, Søren Kierkegaard, was urgent about attracting more people to church by updating worship materials. He essentially agreed with Bastholm and wanted a new hymnal, an idea the King opposed. Nevertheless, Mynster and several others compiled a trial hymnal with only one hymn by Grundtvig, who noted this wryly.

In 1855, a new Danish hymnal, *Psalmebog til Kirke- og Huus-Andagt* (Hymnal for Church and Home Devotions) was approved. It continued the organization of the *Den Evangelisk-Kristelig Psalmebog* with three sections for the Trinity and the last sections for topics in the Christian life. In both the Wallin and Danish hymnals, we can see the influence of Pietism with its concerns for the Christian walk and the Enlightenment's interest in the more theological divisions like the Trinity. Once again, Grundtvig's work was essentially snubbed.

Because Norway was now a twin kingdom with Sweden, the Swedish and Norwegian churches became closer. The long association with Denmark and its hymnic tradition meant that it was difficult to put together a Swedish/Norwegian hymnal. The Norwegian church needed its own hymnal. In 1840, Wilhelm A. Wexels (1797–1866), the popular pastor at Our Savior's in Christiania, tried with *Christelige Psalmer* (Christian Hymns) (1840). One of his many hymns, *O happy day when we shall stand,* has endured in America (ELW 441).

In 1852 the church department in Stockholm asked Magnus Brostrup Landstad (1802–1880) a second time (he had refused the first time) to compile a hymn for Norwegians that used Norwegian, not the Dano-Norwegian of all worship resources until then. Romantic nationalism was rampant in Norway, with its people discovering their Nordic past. Ivar Aasen (1813–1896) was working on Nynorsk, a language based on Norwegian dialects, as Landstad took up his work. Landstad consulted with Aasen about language issues, even though his hymnal does not use Nynorsk.

When Landstad presented his work to the church, *Kirkesalmebog* (Church Hymn Book) (1861), it was sharply criticized, especially by Pastor Johan N. Skaar (1828–1904), a hymnologist who wrote several anonymous articles against Landstad's work in the Oslo paper *Morgenbladet.* Landstad defended his work: he wanted the hymns in the book to be "evangelically Christian and historically of the folk."[20] After a long debilitating conflict, and years of revisions, his *Kirkesalmebog* (Church Hymnal) was officially approved in 1869. However, a few years later in 1873, the hymnal *Psalmebog for Kirke og Hus* (Hymnal for Church and Home) (1873) compiled by Andreas Hauge (1815–1892), son of Hans Nielsen Hauge, appeared and was also approved by the church department. This began a long and difficult period known as the *salmebokstrid* (Hymnal Conflict). While Hauge's book was preferred by the clergy, the people chose Landstad. By the turn of the century over 90 percent of Norwegian congregations used it. A similar debate broke out in America as later immigrants brought Landstad with them, making it the semi-official hymnal of Norwegian American churches in competition with Koren's *Synodens Salmebog* (Synodical Hymnal) (1874). In 1895, a revised version of Landstad, *Salmebog for lutherske Kristne i Amerika* (Hymnal for Lutheran Christians in America) (1895), with a supplement of Norwegian hymns by Norwegian American pastors, was printed by the United Church for use in America. In 1904, the Lutheran Free Church published its version of Landstad's *Salmebog* (1904). Both Dorothe Engelbretsdatter and Birgitte Boye's hymns were well represented here, as was Petter Dass with *Herre Gud, ditt dyre navn og ære* (Lord our God, with praise we come before you) (ELW 730).

Landstad followed the arrangement of hymns for every Sunday. It included, as well, the gospel and epistle texts for each Sunday, the passion narrative and collects for the day. A rather orthodox man, he was not drawn to the Pietism of the Haugeans but could not help but be influenced by them. That influence did not show through in his time, but the compilers of the SBH, when presented with his hymns such as *Naar synderen rett ser sin vaade* (When sinners see their lost condition) (CH 270 and TLH 65) by the Evangelical Lutheran Church (ELC), charged Landstad of being Methodistic.[21]

While the official hymnals of the nineteenth century in all the Nordic countries held sway on Sunday mornings, they were outnumbered by the spiritual songbooks that were now pouring out of the publishing houses. For Swedish Americans, *Hemlandssånger; Songs of the Native Land*, the 1892 Swedish songbook published by the Augustana Lutheran Church, featured over one hundred of Lina Sandell's hymns in a collection of five

---

20. Stig Warnø Holter, "Forfatter," *Nytt Norsk Salmelexicon* (Trondheim: Tapir Akademisk Forlag, 2013), 3: 76.
21. Selmer Berge, "Notes on Hymnal Com." At Pittsburgh PA, June 19–21, 1945 p. I, ii. (Luther Seminary Archives).

hundred. It was far more popular than the version of Wallin they were told to use. The break with the Swedish church led by Paul Petter Waldenström (1838–1917) grew into what became the Missionsförbundet church, and the Covenant in America. They took much of the Swedish song tradition as theirs, so Swedish Lutherans began to shun it as not being Lutheran. Sandell's hymns *Tryggare kan ingen vare* (Children of the heavenly Father, ELW 781), *Blott en dag* (Day by day, ELW 790), *Bred dine vida vingar* (Thy holy wings, ELW 613), and *Jag kan icke räkne dem alla* (The numberless gifts of God's mercies, ELW 683), however, have persisted in American hymnals more than any other Nordic writer but Grundtvig.

In Iceland Bishop Pétur Pétursson (1808–1891) published a new hymnal in 1871. It included 533 hymns but received criticism for being too much like the 1801 hymnal that had been thought too rationalistic. To answer that criticism the bishops of Iceland called the best poets of Iceland together to have them produce a hymnal, *Sálmabók til kirkju og heimasöngs* (Hymnal for Church and Homes) (1886), that was "new and modern." It became known as "The Seven Poets' Hymnal." It contained 650 hymns, 408 of Icelandic origin.

Toward the end of the century, hymnal compilers had to face the liturgical movement coming from the work of Wilhelm Loehe (1808–1872) and the Anglo-Catholics in the Oxford Movement. Gustav Margerthe Jensen (1845–1922) got the church in Norway in 1887 to adopt a prose or chant mass instead of the hymn mass used from 1527, and Uddo Lechard Ullman (1837–1930) in Sweden prepared a revision of the Swedish liturgy adopted in 1894. While hymnals had not really printed liturgies because they were both known and required little from the congregation except Amen, the Apostles' Creed, and Lord's Prayer, hymnals now had to contain scripts for prose worship with responses and readings by the entire congregation.

Another battle was the argument about rhythmic vs. isometric settings of the German chorales. The German scholar Fredrik Layriz (1808–1859) argued that Luther's hymns were rhythmic, not isometric, and urged hymnal compilers to change back to this form. Ullman, the Swedish liturgist, had become a champion of the rhythmic chorale, intriguing President Tufve Nilsson Hasselquist (1816–1891), who wanted to call him to teach at Augustana Seminary, Rock Island.[22] It was his dream that Swedish Augustana would compile a hymnal suitable for Swedes in Sweden and America.[23]

---

22. Gracia Grindal, "The Swedish Tradition in Hymnals and Songbooks," LQ 5 (1991): 443.
23. Grindal, "The Swedish Tradition in Hymnals and Songbooks," 443.

In 1908 Jensen was commissioned to produce a revised version of the Landstad hymnal. He worked on the revision until his death in 1922. A committee finished his work on the hymnal, a revised version of Landstad, in 1926. It remained in use, with another revision in 1953, until 1984 in Norway. In 1924/25, a Nynorsk hymnal, *Nynorsk Salmebok for Kyrkja og Heim og Skule* (New Norwegian Hymnal for Church and Home), was officially approved, featuring the work of Elias Blix (1836–1902), Bernt Støylen (1859–1937), and Anders Hovden (1860–1943).

In Sweden, it was not until 1937 that a new Swedish hymnal, *Den Svenska Psalmboken* (The Swedish Hymnal), was produced. There had been many proposals to prepare such a book through the nineteenth century and into the twentieth. It was mostly a revised version of Wallin's, with many of Wallin's hymns retained. Some suggested it should bear the name of Johan Alfred Eklund (1863–1945) as the editor of this work. It was organized as Wallin's hymnal had been, starting with hymns for the Trinity, the liturgical year, then the sacraments and wedding hymns, followed by hymns from the *ordo salutis*. There is a large section on the times of the year and day, and popular hymns for school opening and closing exercises. A section for the final things is followed by hymns for home devotions especially for children and hymns for worship, including the canticles. It marked the debut of the young pastor Anders Frostenson (1906–2006), who would go on to be considered the most important hymn writer of the century in the Nordic countries. His commitment to writing hymns that were simple and which also used the imagery and language of the day, sparked what became the Hymn Explosion of Scandinavia.

The Finns also approved a modernized and enlarged hymnal in 1938, with a Swedish-language version in 1943, despite the war. Just as World War II was ending, in 1945, the Icelandic church produced a new hymnal, *Sálmabók til Kyrkju og Heimasöngs* (Hymnal for Church and Homes), with 687 hymns.

After the war there were stirrings toward a new kind of hymn that spoke to the now very secular people in their various countries who were not automatically Christians. The Cold War and the threat of nuclear devastation deeply affected many Nordic people, who looked to the west for security while at the same time opposing its massive nuclear arsenal. Later, the Vietnam War, guilt for colonialism, and the needs of the poor in the "Third World" became signature issues for the Nordic nations. Peace became a theme of its emerging hymnody, as did the question of how to proclaim Christ to an increasingly secular age. A commission was established in 1969 to fashion a new Swedish hymnal, the fourth official hymnal of Sweden. It produced an impressive three volume report on its work, *Den Svenska psalmboken: betänkande* (The Swedish Hymnal: Considerations).[24] In the end, the new hymnal would be filled by original texts from Sweden's best writers, Frostenson, Britt G. Hallqvist (1914–1997), Jan Arvid Hellström (1941–1994), and Eva Norberg (1915–2004), who treated current topics. Throughout the 1970s, the hymnal committee worked along with the Finnish church to produce a new hymnal for both churches. Both the Swedish and Finnish hymnals appeared in 1986.

Frostenson, now the dean of hymn writers in Sweden, Norway, and Finland, showed the way with his hymns, closely followed by Britt G. Hallqvist. One of his more popular and controversial hymns was *Guds kärlek är som stranden och gräset* (God's love is like the beach and grasses), which featured new and unbiblical images for God's love like the sands and grass, images which Psalm 90 used to describe the inconstancy of human life. Hallqvist wrote of her doubt: *Lär mig at bedja av hjärtat* (Teach me to pray from my heart). Both Frostenson and Hallqvist also produced charming short hymns telling Bible stories for children. As the Swedish committee worked on its hymnal it began meeting with the Norwegian hymnal committee, also in the throes of making a new hymnal. It would break from the Landstad tradition and meet the same angst of the postmodern age.

Svein Ellingsen (1929–2020) of Norway was writing hymns that also spoke directly to the angst of the modern. He, along with most of the hymn writers of the postwar churches, wrote several hymns to bolster the collection of hymns on the sacraments. His hymn *Fyllt av glede* (Filled with gladness) supplanted the old Kingo baptismal hymn, *Enhver, som tror og bliver døbt* (All who believe and are baptized) (ELW 442). Egil Hovland (1924–2013) wrote the tune as he did for many of Hallqvist's, Ellingsen's, and Eyvind Skeie's new hymns. When the Norwegian hymnal of 1985 came out, it included more than twenty hymns plus many more retranslations and recasting of older, classic hymns by Ellingsen. Two of his hymns are in the current ELW, *Såkorn som dør i Jorden* (Seed that in earth is dying) (ELW 330), and *Vi rekker våre hender frem* (We raise our hands to you, O Lord) (ELW 690). His significant contribution of both hymns and revisions makes it his hymnal, much like Landstad's had been, along with Egil Hovland. Hovland, a Norwegian organist and composer, had grown up in the Bedehus (prayer house) tradition of Norway and

---

24. *Den Svenska psalmboken: betänkande*. 1969 års psalmkommitte, Sweden, (Stockholm: Liber-Förlag, 1981).

knew the spiritual songs of his own tradition as well as the corpus of English and American gospel songs and brought them into the hymnal.

When the Swedish book was printed in 1986 it had the feature of being radically ecumenical. The first 350 hymns were chosen by most of the Christian churches in Sweden and all had participated in the choice of hymns: the Liberal Catholic church (Cecelia), the Salvation Army, Adventists, Freechurch, Methodist, Aliiance, Baptists, Missionkyrkan, and Pentecostals. The second part resembled the Wallin and Svedberg hymnals in its hymn choices. All told there were 700 hymns in the hymnal with many prayers for special occasions.

Global music was just coming into view following the publication of these hymnals. Today no hymnal can be printed without a good mixture of hymns from around the world as well as contemporary settings of old hymns. The Swedish church printed a supplement of new hymns for use in the churches: *Psalmer i 90–talet* (Hymns for the '90s) (1994). In 2018, the church passed a resolution to complete a thoroughgoing revision of the 1986 hymnal, a process that continues.

The Finns also found a new fresh vigor in their hymns from writers such as Anna-Mari Kaskinen (b. 1958), whose hymns dominate the latest Finnish hymnals. She has found composers like Petri Laaksonen (b. 1962), whose music is like much American contemporary worship music, but with a Finnish solemnity. One hymn from this time is the very popular *Armalaulu* (For by grace you have been saved) by Kari Tikka, a composer and conductor in the Finnish Opera. It is now in *Evangelical Lutheran Worship* (ELW 598).

The Danes, sometimes described by Norwegians and Swedes as "anderledes" (otherwise), took a longer time to produce a hymnal using the insights of Frostenson and the work of their Norwegian and Swedish neighbors. After a long period of work the Danes produced an official hymnal in 2002. It, too, was compiled by people who believed in the necessity for new hymns to speak to the time. They did not include many hymns by their most contemporary hymnists such as Lisbeth Smedegaard Andersen (b. 1934), but she is represented in a few hymns and is becoming more and more popular as the decades progress.

The Norwegians published a new hymnal in 2013. Like the Swedes they had produced a hymnal supplement *Salmer 1997* (Hymns 1997) in preparation for a new hymnal planned for 2008, but which did not materialize until 2013. The pressure to include global hymns was strong, and they are present in the collection. Most significant was the pressure to include twenty-three hymns in the language of the Sami, and also

Kvensk, a dialect of Finnish used in Norway. Another question was how many Nynorsk hymns should be included, especially those by Elias Blix, the true master of the language. The committee was enamored with John Bell and the Ionian movement with its Irish tunes for hymns and included many of his in the corpus of hymns. In addition, a charming Christmas song by Norwegian balladeer Alf Prøysen is included, even though its references to Christianity are slight. All told there are 884 hymns; 222 of them were new and had not been in previous hymnals. There are 354 hymns in Nynorsk. Not a few hymns are printed in their original language, Swedish, Latin, and English, such as "Amazing Grace."[25] It also contains Luther's *Small Catechism.*

Some contributors to the 1984 book were still active: Eyvind Skeie, by far the most prolific of Norwegian hymn writers; Ellingsen; Hovland; Trond Kverno; and Sigvald Tveit (1945–2019) were still productive composers at the beginning of the work, but the hymnal took a back seat to the drastic revision of the liturgy from the Jensen liturgy of 1887. Influenced by Vatican II, the Norwegian church embarked on a long process of changing its liturgy, proposing to give congregations the right to design their own versions of a service based on the same liturgy used in the *Evangelical Lutheran Worship* book.

All the Nordic countries are continuing to produce new hymnals or supplements. Iceland has produced a new official hymnal, *Sálmabók íslensku kirkjunnar* (The Hymnal of the Icelandic Church) (2022), which contains 811 hymns with liturgical texts. The Nordic treasuries of hymns, *salmeskatt,* are considered part of their literary heritage. There are popular summer festivals with hymns and gospel songs in these countries, like "Skjærgaards Gospel" in Kragerø, Norway. Organists like Iver Kleive play old folk hymns with the heavy metal guitarist Knut Reiersrud to large audiences, changing how the young hear these old hymn treasures.

Note should be made here of hymnals from the Faroe Islands in 1960 and 1990, *Salmabok Føroya Folks* and *Sálmabók Føroya Kirkju* respectively, and Danish mission fields in the West Indies and Tharangambadi, once Tranquebar, plus Argentina, where a significant number of Danes emigrated; also, various Sami hymnal collections.

Peder Balslev-Clausen wrote that while the mass is constitutive of Roman Catholic worship, for Lutherans it is the singing of hymns.[26] If

---

25. See Vidar Kristensen, "Arbeidet med Norsk salmebok 2013," *Hymnologi: Nordisk tidsskrift.* udgiven af Salmehistorisk Selskab og Nordhymn, 40 (October 2011): 105–114.
26. Peder Clause Balslev, "Salmerne og gudsjeneste," *Hymnologiske Meddelelser,* 18/1(April 1989): 5–29.

one is not able to sing hymns in a Lutheran service, one has not really participated, he argued. If that is true, Lutherans have gotten much of their Lutheran identity through the hymns they have sung in church. Those compiling hymnals know they can weaken traditions by what they leave out from past collections. Not including hymns from those treasuries changes people's identities—in American Lutheranism, for example, there was a conscious change to more Anglo-American hymnody as in the case of the SBH 1958 and German in the case of the LBW 1978.

Every Lutheran tradition passes on a modicum of early hymns from the Reformation and Orthodox period of German hymnody. Joint hymnal committees in America made up of people from all Lutheran traditions in America all voted for the German kernlieder, the English corpus of hymns, and Scandinavian hymns they knew from TLH, but not those with which they were unfamiliar. The ELW, for example, contains no hymns by Landstad or Wallin. The push to be ecumenical has meant that ecumenical offerings are prioritized rather than samplings from smaller unique traditions.

Lutherans in the North continue to write and sing hymns. Unfortunately, many of these rich treasuries (Kernlieder) that used to speak, and might have continued to speak, to American Lutherans with roots in these rich traditions have been ignored by recent American Lutheran hymnal committees. This omission has also kept English speakers of many traditions unaware of the riches from the North that speak the gospel to our contemporary and diverse world.

10.

Chasing Mühlenberg's Dream: From SBH to LBW

Mark A. Granquist

Lutherans are a singing people and have been from the beginning. Insisting that lay people ought to understand and be actively involved in worship, Martin Luther worked to translate medieval hymns into German and to compose new hymns that would preach and teach the new Evangelical faith. Luther was concerned not only that the words be faithful to the gospel, but also that the tunes would be accessible and singable to the average person. From the sixteenth century on, Lutherans developed a rich tradition of hymnody, originally centered in Germany and Scandinavia but expanding as Lutherans moved around the world, first to North America and eventually to the Global South as well. Each movement of Lutherans brought them into contact with new musical traditions that expanded and enriched the base of their own hymnody.

To say that there is a single Lutheran tradition of hymnody might, however, be too simplistic; perhaps it would be better said that there are numerous Lutheran traditions of hymnody, often distinctive by national origins and traditions, or by theological assumptions. The traditions of Lutheran hymnody were centered around the publication of organized and bound hymnals (sometimes referred to as Psalmbooks), which were sometimes produced by official church bodies and sometimes by independent sources. The composition of these hymnals was often contentious, and the selection of hymns to be included (or excluded) was controversial along the lines of theology and taste. Even within national Lutheran traditions there were sometimes sharp controversies over the production of official hymnals. In the eighteenth century the disputes between orthodox and pietist Lutherans often centered around which hymns, and which types of hymns, ought to be included in official hymnals, and Pietists, especially, often created collections of hymns that reflected their own religious determinations. Somewhat later, as religious rationalism crept into various corners of Lutheranism, the fight over appropriate hymns was joined on this level, with hymn writers of a decidedly romantic bent developing new hymns in opposition to the rationalists.

When European Lutherans from Germany and Scandinavia began to migrate to North America during the colonial era, they brought with them their own traditions of hymnody.[1] The ubiquitous "immigrant trunk" filled with their belongings invariably included several religious books, including Lutheran catechisms and devotional writings, collections of Martin Luther's sermons, and of course, psalmbooks and hymnals. Sometimes these psalmbooks were the official Lutheran hymnals, but as often as not they also brought with them unofficial hymnals, generally oriented along pietistic lines. These latter hymnals included many Lutheran hymns of a decidedly subjective variety, matching Pietist theology, and increasingly including Anglo-American evangelical and revival hymns that had been translated into European languages.[2]

When these immigrant Lutherans began to form congregations and denominational structures in North America the questions about which hymnals to use were frequently contentious. The eighteenth-century German American Lutherans came from different regional churches around Germany and brought with them the Lutheran hymns of their local churches, often creating controversy within congregations over which one to use. The great leader of colonial Lutherans, Henry Melchior Mühlenberg, determined that one of his first tasks was to create a common, German-language hymnal for use by Lutheran congregations in North America. But as with the formation of all subsequent American Lutheran hymnals, this was a difficult exercise in construction and compromise. Lay people had definite opinions about their old and cherished hymnals and were often not reticent about voicing their displeasure if the new collections did not include their favorites.

---

1. For a good overview of the hymnody of American Lutherans, see R. Harold Terry, "Lutheran Hymnody in North America," in Mary Kay Stulken, *Hymnal Companion to the Lutheran Book of Worship* (Philadelphia: Fortress Press, 1981), 82–114.
2. On this dynamic, see Mark A. Granquist, "American Hymns and Swedish Immigrants," LQ, 20 (2006): 409–428.

The nineteenth century saw a large migration of German and Scandinavian Lutherans to North America and the subsequent creation of dozens of new Lutheran synods, divided along ethnic and theological lines. Many of the pastors and church leaders of these new Lutheran church bodies were of a decidedly pietistic inclination, although they were what might be termed "churchly" pietists, rather than separatists, and had an appreciation both for the traditions of their national churches and the Pietist renewal movements. They appreciated the old Lutheran chorales and traditional hymns, as well as new, pietistic contributions. Sometimes leaders made the attempt to keep the two traditions separate in different hymnals, to be used in different worship settings. For example, the Swedish-American Lutheran denomination, the Augustana Synod, used a version of the contemporary official hymnal of the Church of Sweden, but also used a separate hymnal called the *Hemlanssånger* (Songs of the Homeland). Some leaders felt that the official hymnal should be used for Sunday morning worship and the *Hemlanssånger* should be reserved for more informal worship services, but this was an artificial construction that was mostly ignored. When the Augustana Synod produced their first English-language hymnals, they included hymns from both traditions in a single volume.[3]

The colonial Lutherans and their descendants made the transition to the use of English in the first decades of the nineteenth century, and soon began to develop English-language Lutheran hymnals. But the second wave, the large nineteenth-century migration of Lutherans to North America, did not crest until right before World War I, and these immigrants largely employed the immigrant languages for worship and hymnody up until then. Their transition to the use of English came in a huge rush during and immediately after the war.[4] Nativist and xenophobic pressures during the war left Lutherans on the defensive; German American Lutherans were special targets of popular pressure, but the loyalty of all groups that worshipped and taught in foreign languages were immediately suspect. Several states passed laws forbidding the use of any language other than English in education and public gatherings, and there were ugly incidents of the persecution of anyone considered "too foreign." American Lutherans had been gearing up for large public celebrations of the four-hundredth anniversary of the Protestant Reformation in 1917,

---

3. See Maria Erling and Mark A. Granquist, *The Augustana Story: Shaping Lutheran Identity in North America* (Minneapolis: Augsburg, 2008), 91–93.
4. On the language transition and Americanization, see E. Clifford Nelson, *Lutheranism in North America, 1914–1970* (Minneapolis: Augsburg, 1972), especially chapter 1.

but these had to be scaled back dramatically, and ended up mainly being Lutheran demonstrations of loyalty to the war effort.

THE TRANSITION TO ENGLISH

The transition to the use of English in worship came extremely quickly. Pressure had already been mounting from younger immigrant Lutherans, already comfortable in English, but their elders who ruled the congregations and denominations did not want linguistic change. War pressures added to these generational tensions, but it was the almost complete cessation of European immigration during and after the war that doomed the immigrant languages. At the beginning of the war, most of these congregations and denominations used the immigrant languages exclusively, but by 1930 the old European languages had almost completely disappeared.

Such a rapid transition was not accomplished gracefully. All elements of denominational life had to be transformed, including worship and hymnody; this was not easy, for many in these immigrant Lutheran denominations were not particularly adept in the use of English. They were forced to assemble new English-language hymnals in a hurry, rushing to translate many of their familiar hymns into the new language. Translation is an art, not a science, and translating the poetic texts of the hymns into a new and different language took linguistic and artistic skills that many within the denominations lacked. Certainly, many of the old sixteenth- and seventeenth-century Lutheran chorales had already been translated into English, though these translations (by Victorian English authors) were closer to paraphrases than strict translations. The new American revival and gospel hymns that they had learned in translation were also not a problem. The issue was those hymns specific to their homelands, especially the pietist and renewal hymns of the eighteenth and nineteen centuries, and the old chorales, especially in the Scandinavian languages. The speed at which these hymns needed to be translated, and the dearth of qualified translators, meant that many of these newly translated hymns were rendered in wooden and imperfect English.

Perfect or not, there was a strong demand for these new hymnals. Among congregations of Norwegian-American Lutherans, most of whom had merged in 1917 from a fractured past, the choice of hymns and hymnals was complicated. The official English-language hymnal of the Norwegian Lutheran Church in America was the *Lutheran Hymnary* of 1912, but it was rivaled by an unofficial hymnal, the *Concordia,* first published in 1916 and expanded in 1932. Uncharacteristically, the two Danish-American denominations pooled their resources in 1927 to produce the *Hymnal for Church and Home*. The Swedish-American Augustana Synod pioneered an early English-language hymnal in 1901, but this temporary expedient was replaced by the *Hymnal* of 1925. The Finnish-American Suomi Synod had their own translations of Finnish hymns, but many congregations used the Augustana Synod *Hymnal*. Various German-American Lutheran groups had similar histories, including the American Lutheran Church's *American Lutheran Hymnal* of 1930 and *The Lutheran Hymnal* (TLH) of the Lutheran Church Missouri Synod published in 1941.

There is one additional element to the development of English-language Lutheran hymnals that is extremely important, but often overlooked: namely, the early development by many of these Lutheran denominations of youth or Sunday School hymnals in English. While their parents and grandparents still worshipped in the immigrant languages, there was a strong demand from the younger generations for hymnals that they could use. Besides drawing from Lutheran sources, these hymnals also often included American gospel and revival hymns, camp meeting songs, and folk songs, all of which became quite popular among the youth. As these younger Lutherans grew into adulthood and achieved leadership in their congregations, they often insisted on including some of these popular hymns in the newly formed English-language American Lutheran hymnals, often to the distress of hymnological specialists who looked down on these traditions and the hymns that they produced.

The transition by all the major Lutheran denominations to the use of English also led to this question: If everyone now spoke English, what reasons were there for the existence of so many different denominations? Their ethnic past was fading, and the expected postwar immigration failed to materialize. There were also positive arguments for greater institutional unity. By the twentieth century, Lutherans had become the third largest Protestant "family" in the United States, but their linguistic isolation and their balkanized structures muted their presence and influence on the national scene, or so the argument went. The mantra for most of the century was unity, and the question was how to overcome separations and achieve this. Unity was, however, much easier to proclaim as an ideal than it was to achieve as a reality.

The first wave of mergers and consolidations came about between 1917 and 1930.[5] As previously noted, the various Norwegian-American

---

5. On the history of Lutherans in North America, see Mark A. Granquist, *Lutherans in North America: A New History* (Minneapolis: Fortress Press, 2015), and E. Clifford Nelson, ed, *Lutherans in North America* (Philadelphia: Fortress Press, 1972).

Lutheran denominations came together in a delicately balanced merger in 1917 to form the Norwegian Lutheran Church in America (NLCA). This was followed in the next year by the union of the three strains of the colonial, Mühlenberg Lutherans into the United Lutheran Church in America (ULCA). And in 1930, three Midwestern German Lutheran denominations (the Iowa, Ohio, and Buffalo synods) formed the American Lutheran Church (1930–1960). This merger did not, of course, include the very large Missouri Synod. Beyond this, in 1918 many American Lutheran denominations formed a cooperative agency, the National Lutheran Council (NLC). This was not a merger, but a national umbrella organization that coordinated Lutheran activities and mission outreach. Eventually, the NLC comprised eight American Lutheran denominations representing nearly two-thirds of Lutherans in the United States. The Missouri Synod, representing most of the other one-third, did not join the NLC.

But progress toward the ideal goal of Lutheran unity was slow. Mergers were often difficult to achieve, and even more difficult to consolidate after the fact; people's institutional loyalties did not automatically follow into the newly merged denominations. Common hymnals were often seen as a crucial aspect of paving the way for merger and consolidation. The Mühlenberg Lutherans had already achieved a common liturgy in the *Common Service Book* of 1888, though a fully common hymnal was not achieved until 1917. In 1921 the Iowa Synod invited the other members of the National Lutheran Council to jointly develop a common hymnal, a task at which they labored for nine years. This project did result in the *American Lutheran Hymnal* in 1930, but it failed to be adopted by most of the NLC members, becoming the English hymnal only of the newly merged ALC. Though they ended up with two hymnals instead of one, the same process of a hymnal preceding a merger also worked for the Norwegian American Lutherans.

This first round of mergers was seen by many as being an initial step to a larger, more comprehensive merger of Lutherans in the United States. This was the era of consolidation in American culture, as institutions in many parts of national life were brought together into ever larger units. The norm for business was the new, large corporations that bundled together businesses of different types and styles. Local school districts and other units of government were similarly consolidated, and on the national level Americans experienced the enormous growth of the federal bureaucracy necessitated by the New Deal of the 1930s and by the defense demands of World War II. The watchword was "efficiency," brought about by ever-larger institutions and economies of scale. Across much of the Protestant community in the United States the watchwords were merger and consolidation.

Lutherans in America very quickly succumbed to this trend, and the mergers of the first round were seen as preliminary to a truly unified Lutheran church in America. But many obstacles blocked the road to this realization. The newly merged churches needed time to develop their own organizations. The Great Depression of the 1930s left the denominations struggling to survive, and World War II (1939–1945) diverted a tremendous amount of time and resources to the war effort. And the question of just who would be invited to the merger negotiations was tricky. The two largest Lutheran denominations, the ULCA and the Missouri Synod, were deeply suspicious of each other. The rest of the Lutheran denominations were in the middle, often leaning one way or the other but never in unison. The NLCA and the ALC were inclined toward Missouri, but Missouri rarely reciprocated their affections, unless on its own terms. "Waiting for Missouri" was sometimes a difficult and exasperating exercise.

THE *SERVICE BOOK AND HYMNAL*

The 1944 annual convention of the ULCA passed a resolution calling for a new, common hymnal for all Lutherans in America. All eight denominations of the National Lutheran Council eventually agreed to this proposal, and in 1945 two commissions, one on liturgy and the other on hymns, began the work of making this new hymnal a reality. Missouri declined to participate, reasoning that it had just introduced its own new hymnal in 1941. The process of developing a new hymnal proceeded apace; the same cannot be said of a parallel process toward a merger of the eight denominations of the NLC, which collapsed in 1952. Out of this collapse came two separate merger processes with four denominations apiece, a pair of groupings that led to the formation of the American Lutheran Church (ALC) in 1960 and the Lutheran Church in America (LCA) in 1962. The Missouri Synod did not join either process. The common hymnal, however, did survive these upheavals, and when produced in 1958 was officially adopted by all eight NLC denominations, and later by the ALC and the LCA. This new *Service Book and Hymnal* (SBH) thus became the common hymnal of two-thirds of Lutherans in North America.

The formation of the ALC and LCA and the introduction of the *Service Book and Hymnal*, however impressive, still did not completely satisfy those who dreamed the big dream of one common Lutheran denomination in the United States with one common hymnal. One of the participants in the formation of the SBH, Dr. Ernest E. Ryden of the LCA, commented in 1965:

> Although the *Service Book and Hymnal* might be rightly regarded as a spiritual and cultural triumph in American Lutheranism, its creators do not look upon it as the final word in a common book of worship. That ideal, they feel, will not be achieved until the other one-third of the Lutherans in the new world cooperate in the creation of such a volume.[6]

Waiting for Missouri, indeed. However, during the 1960s it seemed, for a while, that this dream might actually become a reality. The three major Lutheran denominations were growing closer to each other, and in 1967 all three joined together in a common cooperative body, the Lutheran Council in the USA (LCUSA). A further and meaningful development was the forging of altar and pulpit fellowship between the ALC and the Missouri Synod in 1969, a type of relationship that Missouri had very rarely ever agreed to in the past.

THE *LUTHERAN BOOK OF WORSHIP*

The denominational publishers who print and sell hymnals suggest that the average "pew life" of a bound hymnal is approximately twenty years; after that, congregations need to consider replacing old, worn-out hymnals. As these publishers also enjoy the increased revenue from putting out new hymnals, the "replacement window" is often a good time to consider developing a new worship book. In the mid-1960s the Missouri Synod's 1941 hymnal was almost a quarter of a century old. Instead of a new denominational hymnal, the synod voted in 1965 to propose to the other American Lutheran denominations a cooperative venture to develop a common hymnal for all the Lutheran denominations in North America. The synodical resolution suggested a course of action:

> To pursue a cooperative venture with other Lutheran bodies as soon as possible in working toward, under a single cover: (a) a common liturgical section in rite, rubric, and music; (b) a common core of hymn texts and musical settings; (c) a variant selection of hymns, if necessary.[7]

---

6. Ernest E. Ryden, "Hymnbooks," in Julius Bodensieck, ed., *The Encyclopedia of the Lutheran Church* (Minneapolis: Augsburg, 1965), 2: 1090.
7. Lutheran Church Missouri Synod, "Synodical Resolution" 1965, in Stulken, *Hymnal Companion to the Lutheran Book of Worship*, 111.

Even though the hymnal of the other Lutheran denominations, the SBH, was only seven years old at the time, the ALC and LCA responded favorably to this invitation from the Missouri Synod. In 1966 the three churches established the Inter-Lutheran Commission on Worship (ILCW), soon to be joined by the Evangelical Lutheran Church in Canada (ELCIC).

The ILCW began its work in earnest in 1969 with the publication over several years of a series of booklets entitled *Contemporary Worship*, in which Lutheran congregations were encouraged to explore new hymns and new worship resources ahead of the new hymnal itself. In early 1975 the ILCW published its preliminary listing of hymns for the new resource and received thousands of suggestions from Lutheran congregations around North America, after which the ILCW reexamined and revised the list. Finally, in 1978, the new hymnal, the *Lutheran Book of Worship* (LBW), was published.

But Mühlenberg's 1786 dream of one church and one hymnal for all Lutherans was not to be realized, at least at that time. Internal divisions within the Missouri Synod began to rock the denomination in the late 1960s, and a decidedly conservative president, J.A.O. Preus, was elected in 1969. As conservatives took control of the synod (and as the LCA and ALC moved in more liberal directions), internal dissent within Missouri led to a schism wherein some moderates left the synod to form the Association of Evangelical Lutheran Churches (AELC) in 1976. In 1977 a convention of the LCMS ordered further "doctrinal review" of the proposed LBW, and a special report of a subsequent review committee produced forty-three pages of suggested revisions. As a result, Missouri dropped out of the ILCW at the last minute and proceeded eventually to publish its own new hymnal, *Lutheran Worship*, in 1982. In design and content, the new LCMS hymnal looked very much like the LBW, albeit with the specific changes the review committee had suggested. The LBW did, however, become one vehicle for equipping the other three major Lutheran denominations, the ALC, LCA, and AELC, to begin merger negotiations for a new Lutheran denomination, the Evangelical Lutheran Church in America, formed in 1988.

As has been previously suggested, the centralizing trends within American society in the mid-twentieth century were a strong impetus to both the development of common hymnals and the merger of Lutheran denominations. The ideal was that the experience of Lutheran worship would be uniform across congregations in North America, whether one was attending services in Portland, Maine or Portland, Oregon. In this respect, the local congregation was seen almost as a franchise of the denomination, whose worship life was directed by its national worship staff. However, beginning in the 1960s there were countervailing trends in culture and church away from consolidation and uniformity that created local resistance. New common hymnals, as well as mergers, often created animosity and resistance from local congregations used to their old familiar patterns of worship and hymnody. Lay people mourned the loss of their favorite hymns in the inevitable pruning that resulted in the production of new hymnals, and some congregations resisted the "top-down" imposition of these books in place of their old, tried and true worship resources. The author of this chapter remembers as a youth in the late 1960s that although his father's Augustana congregation in northern Illinois had grudgingly adopted the SBH, the women of the congregation kept all the old "black" 1925 hymnals on shelves in the church library, dusting them regularly because "they might be needed." Other congregations kept the old hymnals in the pew racks alongside the new ones, or bought new, "non-denominational" hymns of a decidedly evangelical cast so that people could sing their own favorite gospel hymns which had been eliminated from the new common Lutheran hymnals. Hymnals can divide as well as unite.

A FIRST ATTEMPT AT UNITY: COMPILING THE SBH

Having surveyed the development of English-language Lutheran hymnals from their beginnings, through the SBH, and to the LBW, it is now time to consider the selection and compilation of the hymns in these latter two hymnals and the dynamics of how these books were produced. Certainly, there was with both hymnals a desire to expand the hymnic horizons of American Lutherans and a search for "excellence" in hymnody, both of which were very good things. But as it was impossible to include every hymn that American Lutherans had known and loved, many hymns from the various immigrant traditions had to be excluded. Beyond this, there were implicit and explicit battles over the definitions of "excellence" and "good taste." Hymnal committees are often small and can be dominated by professional worship scholars or those with definite ideas about what makes for a "good" hymn or hymnal. As Gracia Grindal, a member of the ILCW that produced the LBW, observed, "each hymnal is something of an attack on the previous hymnal."[8]

The work on what would become the SBH began in 1945 with two commissions, one on the liturgy and the other on the hymns. Members

---

8. Gracia Grindal, "Treasured Hymns Unearthed or Buried," *Lutheran Forum*, 49/2 (2015): 25.

of the commissions were representative of the eight church bodies within the NLC, with the number of members somewhat dependent on the relative size of the denominations. The larger denominations—the ULCA, the Augustana Synod, the Evangelical Lutheran Church (the main Norwegian-American group) and the ALC (1930–1960)—had multiple representatives. Smaller traditions, such as the Danish churches, the Lutheran Free Church, and the Finnish Suomi Synod had only one or two representatives, which meant they had much less influence on the process and on the selection of hymns.

The chair of both the liturgy and the hymn commissions and a prime mover in shaping both processes was Luther D. Reed of the Lutheran seminary in Philadelphia. Reed was a prominent scholar in liturgics and hymnody, and his voice was prominent in this process. Other prominent voices on the hymn commission were Paul Z. Strodach and Edward T. Horn III from the ULCA, Ernest E. Ryden of the Augustana Synod, Selmer Berge of the ELC, and Albert Jagnow of the ALC. Because of the size of the ULCA delegation and because of the scholarly influence of its leading representatives, the ULCA had an outsized influence on the formation of the SBH, both on the liturgy and on the selection of hymns.

The overall strategy of the hymnal commission is laid out in detail in several places. Addressing the synodical representatives in 1957, Ernest E. Ryden explained their working guidelines:

> Although no set of rules or principles were ever established by the Commission on a Common Hymnal, the members of the Commission soon arrived at a common understanding relative to the requisites that should be met by every hymn included in the collection. Three of these must be constantly kept in the foreground:
>
> A. It must be Scriptural in language or thought.
> B. It must be devotional in character.
> C. It must be lyrical in quality and exalted in poetic expression.

In its first report to the eight cooperating churches, the Commission stated: "We have no call to preserve mediocracy, triviality, or sentimentality, but should provide our people with hymns that are noble in thought and distinguished in form."[9]

---

9. Ernest E. Ryden, "Review of the Hymns in the New Service Book and Hymnal," in *Program of Introduction for the Service Book and Hymnal of the Lutheran Church, 1957–1958*, 12–13. (unpublished).

In the "Introduction to the Common Hymnal" in the SBH itself, the Commission stated its principles further:

> (it) must be a new work, not simply a conflation of the existing hymnals; it must contain only good hymns providing as a companion for the liturgy, for the full round of the Church Year and the Christian Life; hymns must be devotional rather than didactic or homiletical, and their direction Godward, not manward, the hymnal must be ecumenical in character . . . each hymn must have the highest standard of literary excellence (and) should be exalted in language, noble in thought and reverent in feeling.

Further, this introduction explained some of its difficulties in hymn selection:

> One of the most difficult problems was the application of this final principle, especially to hymns of our own heritage where pressure was great for their inclusion. Inferior translations have been accepted in the past because of the affection felt for the original . . .[10]

These lofty principles, whether established or tacitly agreed upon, guided the selection of the hymns for the new SBH.

The new hymnal contained 602 distinct hymns which were sometimes set to two or even three different tunes. Eighty of the hymn texts were from the Greek or Latin (many translated by English authors in the Oxford Revival tradition), and two-thirds of them were of English or American origin. Most of the tunes were also of Anglican-American origins (English tunes "in abundance"), with eighty German chorales, twelve Swedish, twelve Norwegian, and ten Danish melodies.[11] A detailed analysis of the hymn list of the SBH shows the preponderance of English tunes and texts, with eleven from the English Psalters, nineteen from the Wesleys, twenty-four from the English Evangelical Revival tradition, and dozens (often translations) from the Oxford Revival movement. A primary influence on the hymns in the SBH came from two English hymnals, *Hymns Ancient and Modern* (1861) and *The English Hymnal* (1906).[12]

---

10. "Introduction to the Common Hymnal," *Service Book and Hymnal of the Lutheran Church in America,* Churches Cooperation in the Commission on the Liturgy and the Commission on the Hymnal, 1958, 286.
11. Stulken, *Hymnal Companion,* 109.
12. For a detailed analysis of the hymns in the SBH see William Seaman, *Companion to the Hymnal of the Service Book and Hymnal.* (Commission on the Liturgy and Hymnal, 1976), 1–15.

It seems that there was a definite bias here, not only toward English and American hymnody, but to particular strains of that hymnody coming from the Anglican and Episcopalian traditions which seemed to dominate the hymn selections. As Ralph Quere observed of the formation of the SBH:

> Shaped in many ways by Luther Reed, the *Service Book and Hymnal* of 1958 represented an "ecumenizing" if not an "Anglicizing" of Lutheran worship.[13]

The hymnody of the Victorian era and early twentieth century is strikingly over-represented in the SBH, seemingly suggesting its belief that these hymns represent what its introduction judged "the highest standards of literary excellence." The clear choice in the SBH of the language of the King James Version of the Bible for many of the hymn texts and liturgical elements reinforced this strong tendency toward things Anglican.

A puzzling element of the SBH's hymnological tendencies is in the declaration that "hymns must be devotional rather than didactic or homiletical, and their direction Godward, not manward." It is unclear what the terms "Godward" and "manward" actually mean. What would constitute the difference between the two? As well, the emphasis on "devotional" hymns rather than "didactic or homiletical" seems to run counter to long traditions of Lutheran hymnody.

From Luther on, Lutheran theology insisted that the word of God must be proclaimed clearly in the language of the people, and that this proclamation of the word in preaching and sacrament created faith in the hearers. Hymns in this understanding would seem to be the very definition of a "manward" hymn, the proclamation of God's word to the Christians, creating change in the hearer and the singer. Many of Luther's hymns are strongly homiletical or catechetical (didactic)—these types of hymns are how most Lutherans across time learned their theology and repeated it. The framing of Godward/manward suggests the influence of the mystics or the English metaphysical poets rather than Lutheran theology and tradition.

Also instructive might be the kinds of hymns that were not included in the SBH, most notably hymns of the Anglo-American Evangelical gospel and revival traditions and many of the hymns of the Scandinavian Lutherans, especially those from the nineteenth-century Pietist and

---

13. Ralph W. Quere, *In the Context of Unity: A History of the Development of the Lutheran Book of Worship* (Minneapolis: Lutheran University Press, 2003), 14.

awakening traditions. Given the composition of the hymnal committee, it seems very clear that the representatives of the Scandinavian-American Lutheran denominations could be easily outvoted by the others on the committee, and if the grumblings from that time are to be believed, they probably were. A hint to this comes from the introduction to the hymns in the SBH, where it is observed that

> One of the most difficult problems was the application of this final principle [excellence] especially to hymns of our own heritage where pressure was great for their inclusion. Inferior translations have been accepted in the past because of the affection felt for the original . . .

Certainly, the hurried compilation of English-language Scandinavian-American Lutheran hymnals in the early twentieth century included many clumsy translations of Scandinavian hymnody. But the implicit bias seems to run deeper than this; many of these translations could well have been improved, and it is hard to avoid the conclusion that these hymns were omitted because they did not reach to the majorities' supposed standard of excellence in any translation. The SBH contains no hymns by C.O. Rosenius or Lina Sandell, only two by Hans Brorson, and only a meager selection of Danish and Finnish hymns. The Swedish hymn, "How Great Thou Art," a "Godward" hymn of praise if ever there was one, was omitted, presumedly because of its Pietist origins and association with the Billy Graham revival crusades. This seems a perfect example of Grindal's observation that "each hymnal is something of an attack on the previous hymnal."

There was also an interesting sociological element at work in the formation of the SBH, especially in the Americanization of the immigrant Lutheran populations during the time of its formation. Lutherans in America had already achieved a strong numerical position within American Protestantism, but numbers alone do not make for power or influence, as the Congregationalists, Presbyterians, and Episcopalians can attest. The descendants of the nineteenth-century Lutheran immigrants, now working their way up the socioeconomic ladder in the mid-twentieth century, sought respectability and influence within the dominant and "respectable" world of mainline Protestantism.[14] Many of them jettisoned

---

14. See John E. Groh and Robert H. Smith, eds, *The Lutheran Church in North American Life* (St. Louis: Clayton, 1979), especially the chapters by Leigh D. Jordahl, "American Lutheranism: Ethos, Style, and Polity," 33–55; and Niel M. Johnson, "Lutherans in American Economic Life," 132–164.

their immigrant past and learned the ways and mores of the leading Protestants in their communities. In part, this phenomenon is most assuredly at work in the selection (or rejection) of hymns for the SBH, especially the tendency toward English and American hymns of the Anglican and Episcopal traditions.

The SBH was controversial in some areas of American Lutheranism, especially among Scandinavian-American Lutheran denominations who came to realize that many of the favorite hymns of their particular tradition would not be included in the new hymnal. As the SBH began to take shape, there were rumblings of deep discontent from these quarters. Discontent reached a peak when some in the Norwegian-American Evangelical Lutheran Church suggested that their denomination should publish their own version of the SBH with extra hymns from their own tradition added back in. For a number of reasons this expedient was never adopted, but that such action was contemplated is instructive. The mantra of unity in hymnal and denomination carried the day, although in some areas of American Lutheranism the "Red Hymnal" (SBH) was slow to be adopted.

The SBH was an important development, to be sure, but the fast-changing developments of the 1960s within American Lutheranism seemed to have many longing for further development and modernization of hymnody. Hymn scholar Erik Routley, asked to evaluate the SBH, wrote in 1968:

> In general I think the hymnal presents a very confused notion of what Lutherans in America and other English speaking countries believe, in theology and aesthetics. I think it showed leanings toward the pretentious (which often means the 19th century) and away from the direct (which does not necessarily mean the 20th century). With searching theological criticisms on the part of an editorial board, it could be the basis of a distinguished new collection.[15]

A SECOND ATTEMPT AT UNITY: COMPILING THE LBW

Already in the early 1950s the Missouri Synod began to think about a revision of the TLH, but it was not until the early 1960s that such a movement gained traction. But after discussion within the Missouri

---

15. Erik Routley, "Critique of the Service Book and Hymnal," Preface, p. 1, June 1967, quoted in Quere, *In the Context of Unity*, 21. It is instructive to think that Luther D. Reed was 75 years old in 1958 when the SBH was published, and reflected the aesthetics of an early generation.

Synod, the momentum shifted from a revision to a new common Lutheran hymnal, and the synodical convention of 1965 recommended pursuit of this project. So, in 1966 representatives from Missouri, the ALC, and the LCA formed the Inter-Lutheran Consultation on Worship (ILCW), and in 1967 representatives of the groups met to begin their explorations of what might be possible.

The mid-1960s were a heady time for Lutheran unity in the United States with the formation of the LCUSA and the ILCW. It was soon determined that the work of the latter would produce a completely new hymnal, and not just a revision of the SBH and TLH. The ILCW was organized into four different working groups: two on the liturgy, one on hymn tunes, and one on hymn texts. The liturgical groups made early public impressions beginning in the late 1960s with a series of liturgical publications and contemporary worship supplements to be tried on an experimental basis in Lutheran congregations across the country. The two hymn committees developed their own sets of criteria and began a slow and methodical sifting of hymn texts and tunes, over 2,300 of which were considered by the time they were finished.

The hymn committees were propelled by the revolution in worship music, much of it contemporary, during the 1960s. The language of the texts was to be brought out of the intentionally archaic and often fustian styles of the SBH and TLH. New, more inclusive language was demanded, and hymn texts often were modified along these lines. New tunes and texts often were prized by the committees as a way of modernizing the worship experience. ILCW emphasized that the hymns must be "singable" by the ordinary person in the pews, and for many hymns the emphasis would be on singing in unison, rather than parts. The hymn music had to be "playable" for a wide range of church musicians. In many cases, and to the distress of many, the magnificent old Bach chorale harmonizations were eliminated from the old Lutheran hymns. The old SBL dictum of hymns being "Godward" rather than "manward" was retained, although because of the presence of the LCMS delegates, some of the sixteenth-century Lutheran catechetical or homiletical hymns were retained or re-introduced, including Luther's hymn version of the creed.

Initially, there seemed to be some question as to the nature of the new hymnal itself, and whether it would retain a core of several hundred hymns (to allow for further expansion) or a more fully formed hymnal. There was even a suggestion that it might be loose-leaved to allow for future additions, but this idea was quickly discarded. The ALC and LCA themselves made surveys of their congregation to find out which hymns congregations were actually using, and the results, though predictable, were distressing to some professional hymnologists. By the mid-1970s the preliminary hymn list was coming together, and early in 1975 a list of around five hundred hymns was made public for comments. And comments they received! The ALC offices received over 1,600 responses to the proposed hymn list, and the LCA reported receiving several thousand more. Predictably, the responses centered around those hymns that the ILCW had not included in the hymnal, especially of those that surveys had demonstrated to be congregation favorites. An observer wrote at the time:

> The proposed new Lutheran hymnal has caused the ire of many Lutherans because the committee in charge of the hymnal plans to drop 35 old, familiar hymns. A survey . . . revealed that the two hymns receiving the largest number of votes by Lutheran congregations for inclusion in the new book are "How Great Thou Art" and "Amazing Grace." As one stunned Lutheran comments, "Take that, Johann Sebastian Bach."[16]

Some observers were pleased, however, by the inclusion of newer hymn texts and a few of the Scandinavian hymns that had not made it into the SBH.

By November 1975, the hymn committees met to finalize the hymn list for the new hymnal, which came in at 569 canticles and hymns. A number of the most popular hymns were added back onto the hymn list, including "How Great Thou Art," "Amazing Grace," "Onward Christian Soldiers," and "O Perfect Love," among other older "war-horses." A press release at the time noted that "the denominational review committees feared that elimination of too many of the 'old favorites' would jeopardize the acceptance of the new hymnal." But this release went on to quote the hymn committees as being "deeply concerned about the compromise of standards by the demands for certain sub-standard additions to the body of hymnody."[17] In his 1978 detailed comments to the committee on the hymn list for the new hymnal, Erik Routley acidly commented,

> Presumably you were blackmailed late including "How Great Thou Art." Surely one of the great disasters of our time. (Courage! Courage! You are the people who invented *Ein feste burg* & should have recalled its last stanza when being blackmailed . . .)[18]

---

16. George R. Plagenz, "Let's all rise and sing about Wicked Polly," *The Cleveland Press*, Sunday, November 15, 1975.
17. Erik W. Modean, "Hymns Selected for the New Lutheran Service Book," (New York: News Bureau of the Lutheran Council in the USA, November 18, 1975), 1–3.
18. Erik Routley, "Informal reactions to the Lutheran Hymnal 1978," six-page single-spaced unpublished manuscript, in Leonard R. Flachman, "A Press History of the LBW from the Private Papers of Leonard R. Flachman," Luther Seminary Library, St. Paul, MN.

Certainly, the hymn committees wanted hymns that were singable and that people in the pews wanted to use, but presumably there was sometimes a clash of hymnological aesthetics going on between what the committees wanted and what the Lutheran public desired.

By 1976, then, there had been a great deal of engagement from the ALC and LCA about the hymn list, and modifications made. But the loud silence from Missouri was about to be broken. The LCMS endured a huge set of upheavals in the early 1970s, including the walk-out of most of the faculty and students from Concordia Seminary, St. Louis, and the withdrawal of pastors and congregations to form the breakaway Association of Evangelical Lutheran Churches in 1976; so, it is likely that Missouri's attention was elsewhere. But in 1975, LCMS president J.A.O. Preus appointed nine individuals to consider the new hymnal as it was taking shape. Their reactions were generally predicable: the hymn list as proposed included too many doctrinally questionable hymns, and not enough of the standards from the TLH.[19] In January 1976 the Commission on Worship of the LCMS suggested the appointment of doctrinal reviewers for the proposed hymn list of the LBW, and this review process proceeded through 1976 and into early 1977. In its March 21–25, 1977 meeting the Commission on Theology and Church Relations recommended that the synodical convention that summer take no action on the new hymnal until a "thorough review of its contents had been completed by the CTCR and the seminary faculties."[20] On April 12, 1977, President J.A.O. Preus wrote to Eugene Brand, the director of the LBW project, suggesting a delay in the tentatively-scheduled 1978 publication until the LCMS had time to further review the new hymnal.[21] Brand and others on the ILCW did not agree to this request.

At its convention in the summer of 1977, the LCMS decided to appoint a Special Hymnal Review Committee to examine the new hymnal, and the committee delivered its report to the synod in November 1977. The committee suggested retaining 504 of the 569 proposed hymns, rejecting many hymns as being theologically suspect or inferior, and also suggested adding into the hymnal sixty-six hymns of special interest to the LCMS.[22] This action caused six of the seven LCMS members of the Commission

---

19. Quere, *In the Context of Unity*, 140–142.
20. "CTCR recommends 'State of Protesting Fellowship with ALC deferring action on the new hymnal.'" Press release from the LCMS March 24, 1977, p. 1, in Flachman, "A Press History of the LBW"
21. Letter, J.A.O. Preus to Eugene Brand, April 12, 1977, in Flachman, "A Press History of the LBW."
22. Report and Recommendation of the Special Hymnal Review Committee, in Flachman, "A Press History of the LBW."

on Worship to resign in protest, charging that the proposed changes meant that "there is no longer any real possibility of the Lutheran Book of Worship being accepted by the Lutheran Church-Missouri Synod" regardless of any revisions other cooperating Lutheran churches might make in the book. Further they charged that the real motive for LCMS delaying was not doctrinal, but fear of church fellowship.[23]

The ILCW refused to delay the publication of the new hymnal, now officially to be named the *Lutheran Book of Worship*, which was scheduled for introduction in 1978. The Missouri Synod began to consider the idea of introducing its own version of the hymnal, with the changes in liturgy and hymns that it envisioned. This idea brought a swift retort from the ILCW, which told the LCMS that if it considered such a plan, it could face legal action and copyright restrictions. There were feelings of disappointment and disgust within both the ALC and LCA over these eleventh-hour maneuvers. One ALC observer, composer and music publisher Robert Wetzler, complained:

> Put baldly, this [the LBW] is a Missouri Lutheran hymnal and they don't even plan to use it. They loaded the book with "their" stuff and tampered with just about everything else that is "ours." It is like a repudiation of all non-Missouri musical tastes. And ALC/LCA are buying into this sight unseen. It's as if those of us who don't swallow all this are not "with it" (or are fools or second-rate musicians or not truly Lutheran, somehow). The tastes reflected in this book are not the tastes of most organists, choirmasters, or people-in-the-pews in either the ALC or LCA as I see it.[24]

Yet the new LBW was probably too far along for further changes and the delays such changes would entail. The LBW was introduced in 1978 and was an immediate best seller for the denominational publishers, Augsburg Publishing House (ALC) and Fortress Press (LCA), with over one million copies sold by the end of 1978 and two million sold by 1981.[25] The Missouri Synod proceeded with plans to introduce its own hymnal, named *Lutheran Worship*, which appeared in 1982. In appearances and content, the new LCMS hymnal seemed to be what the 1977 convention had called for; the essential core of the hymnal was based off the LBW,

---

23. "Lutheran group's efforts on hymnal ends in resignations," *Minneapolis Tribune*, Thursday, November 17, 1977, p. 8–B.
24. Robert Wetzler, "Re Lutheran Book of Worship (LBW), August 1978." six-page typescript analysis of the LBW sent to Leonard Flachman, in Flachman, "A Press History of the LBW."
25. Karen Walhof, "The Inter-Lutheran Commission on Worship," fourteen-page manuscript history, May 12. 1981, p. 14, in Flachman, "A Press History of the LBW."

with the deletion of the hymns the CTCR found objectionable and the addition of LCMS-favored hymns that did not make it into the LBW.

Dreams die hard. But by the late 1970s it became clear that despite a flurry of optimism in the 1960s, Mühlenberg's dream of one church and one hymnal was not to be immediately achieved, if ever. The SBH and LBW had two-thirds of American Lutherans using the same hymnal, and those denominations eventually merged into the Evangelical Lutheran Church in America in 1988. But despite decades of work, this was the furthest things would go to date. Certainly, the SBH and LBW included a wide array of new hymns for Lutherans to sing, but in doing so they failed to bring many of the strands of Lutheran hymn traditions, especially from Scandinavia, into fresh new translations for twentieth-century American Lutherans. This was a lost opportunity that later generations must rectify.

11.

An Extraordinary Hymnal Supplement

Daniel Zager

The Lutheran Hymnal 1941 (TLH), "Authorized by the Synods Constituting the Evangelical Lutheran Synodical Conference of North America," enjoyed a long period of use in those Lutheran entities comprising the Synodical Conference. Congregations of the Lutheran Church—Missouri Synod used TLH at least until the 1978 publication of *Lutheran Book of Worship* (LBW) or the LCMS revision—the 1982 *Lutheran Worship* (LW 1982). Indeed, some congregations would use TLH up to the publication of the 2006 *Lutheran Service Book* (LSB). While the Wisconsin Evangelical Lutheran Synod and the Evangelical Lutheran Synod withdrew from the Synodical Conference in 1963 due to doctrinal issues in the LCMS regarding church fellowship practices and historical-critical methods of biblical interpretation, they continued to use TLH until the 1993 publication of *Christian Worship* (WELS) and the 1996 *Evangelical Lutheran Hymnary* (ELS). Thus, for some fifty years TLH established a period of stability for hymn texts and music in this segment of North American Lutheranism. Of course, the corollary of such stability is that newer hymnody was for the most part unavailable to singing congregations, except perhaps for occasional local reproduction and singing of newly written hymns.

During the postwar decades there was a resurgence in hymnic creativity, especially regarding texts. Though it is an awkward phrase, "Hymn Explosion" has been employed frequently to describe this outpouring of new hymn texts, particularly in Great Britain, beginning in the 1960s with

Dunblane Praises 1 and *2* (1965 and 1967).[1] Alan Luff points especially to two supplements published in 1969: "*Hymns and Songs* from the Methodists and *100 Hymns for Today* from the Anglican *Hymns: Ancient and Modern* . . . Here, it is generally acknowledged, we are into the Hymn Explosion itself and not the preparatory matter."[2]

While there was no specific analogue in the United States to the British "Hymn Explosion," that same year of 1969 saw the publication of a particularly important Lutheran hymnal supplement: *Worship Supplement* (WS). The title page specifies its origin: "Authorized by the Commission on Worship, The Lutheran Church—Missouri Synod and Synod of Evangelical Lutheran Churches." Its historical context and intended use are clarified in the foreword, which is worth quoting at length:

> More than a generation has passed since *The Lutheran Hymnal* first appeared in 1941. The intervening years have brought many changes in Christian living that have led to new worship needs. New concerns for social structures, colleges, armed forces, missions, the inner city, and racially and culturally conscious groups have raised a need for updating liturgical and hymnodic materials both as to language and form.
>
> When this need first began to be felt, a thorough revision of *The Lutheran Hymnal* was planned and begun. The project was abandoned several years ago in favor of a program designed to lead to an eventual all-Lutheran hymnal in English. The present *Worship Supplement* was meanwhile chosen to supply the worship needs of the Church until the proposed long-range project could produce a more permanent hymnal. It was adopted as a convenient stage in the development of new types and forms of worship materials which, by meeting demands of changing times and situations, might serve also as a modern experiment in applying timeless truths to timely needs, an attempt to give voice to the cries and joys of today's Christian by means of contemporary creations.[3]

---

1. While Alan Luff registers his preference for the perhaps more elegant phrase "Hymn Renaissance," "Hymn Explosion" remains the most-used historical term for this flowering of new hymns; see Alan Luff, "The Twentieth-Century Hymn Explosion: Where the Fuse Was Lit," *The Hymn: A Journal of Congregational Song* 58/4 (Autumn 2007): 19; see also his earlier article "The Hymn Explosion after 25 Years," *The Hymn: A Journal of Congregational Song* 46/2 (April 1995): 6–15.
2. Luff, "The Twentieth-Century Hymn Explosion," 16.
3. WS, 9. The complete foreword is also available in Carl F. Schalk, *Source Documents in American Lutheran Hymnody* (St. Louis: Concordia, 1996), 142–149. Those pages contain all the prefatory material for both the pew edition (tune-text) of WS as well as the separate Accompaniment Edition.

The "all-Lutheran hymnal" referenced here would appear nine years later—as the LBW of 1978. WS played an important role in setting the stage for LBW and its parallel LCMS version of 1982,[4] simultaneously providing a new and welcome freshness in hymn texts, tunes, and settings that complemented the hymnic content of the by then nearly thirty-year-old TLH.

As Luff discusses the British "Hymn Explosion" he mentions various poets emerging in the 1960s who would become justifiably esteemed for their contributions to Christian hymnody, among them Timothy Dudley-Smith, Fred Pratt Green, Brian Wren, and Christopher Idle. While none of those poets was represented in WS, what is noteworthy is that simultaneous with the British "Hymn Explosion" new poets were also emerging in American Lutheranism, notably via the WS: Jaroslav J. Vajda (1919–2008) and Martin H. Franzmann (1907–1976).

NEWLY WRITTEN TEXTS AND NEWLY COMPOSED TUNES

Jaroslav Vajda was the son of a Slovak Lutheran pastor. After his training at Concordia Seminary, St. Louis (BDiv, 1944) he served as a pastor in bilingual (English/Slovak) Lutheran parishes in Pennsylvania and Indiana (1945–1963) before taking on editorial responsibilities at Concordia Publishing House from 1963 to his retirement in 1986.[5] His hymn text "Now the Silence," coupled with Carl Schalk's (1929–2021) tune NOW, will serve here as an example of a new text and tune in WS.

Martin Franzmann's career illustrates the pliable boundaries between the Lutheran church bodies comprising the Synodical Conference prior to its fracturing in 1963 and its dissolution in 1967. Franzmann was educated in the standard sequence of WELS institutions preparing

---

4. For additional historical background on the movement toward an "all-Lutheran hymnal" see Nancy Raabe, "*Worship Supplement 1969*: The Vatican II of Lutheran Worship?" *Cross Accent: Journal of the Association of Lutheran Church Musicians* 21/2 (July 2013): 22–27. For an assessment of how WS influenced LBW see Randall K. Sensmeier, "The Influence of the *Worship Supplement* on the *Lutheran Book of Worship*: A Legacy of Excellence," *Church Music* 79 (1979): 77–80.
5. LBH–CH 2:717–718. On Jaroslav Vajda's life and work see: Paul Westermeyer, *With Tongues of Fire: Profiles in 20th-Century Hymn Writing* (St. Louis: Concordia, 1995), 138–153; and Jon D. Vieker, "An Interview with Jaroslav J. Vajda," *Hymns in the Life of the Church*, Journal of the Good Shepherd Institute 4 (2003), ed. Daniel Zager (Fort Wayne: Concordia Theological Seminary Press, 2004), 147–159.

pastors: Northwestern Preparatory School and Northwestern College, sharing a single campus in Watertown, Wisconsin (BA, 1928), and Wisconsin Lutheran Seminary (BDiv, 1936). After his college graduation and prior to his seminary studies he taught Greek and English at Northwestern College (1928–1930), returning there, after completing seminary, as professor of classics (1936–1946). In 1946 he was appointed professor of New Testament exegetical theology at Concordia Seminary, St. Louis, serving there until 1969 when he moved to Westfield House, Cambridge, England, the seminary of the Evangelical Lutheran Church of England.[6]

One of Franzmann's hymn translations appeared in the 1941 TLH: "Rise Again, Ye Lion-Hearted" (TLH 470). By contrast, WS included six of his original hymn texts and one translation ("With High Delight"). Of the original hymn texts, "O God, O Lord of Heaven and Earth" will serve here as the primary example of Franzmann's poetry, coupled with Jan Bender's (1909–1994) original tune for this hymn, WITTENBERG NEW.

Vajda "Now the Silence" and Schalk NOW (WS 770)

Exploring *Worship Supplement* for the first time, one could not help but notice this fresh textual and musical expression—designated as "An Entrance Hymn." Unlike most hymns, there is no rhyme scheme, no metrical scheme, indeed no punctuation at all. And the reiteration of the word "Now"—nineteen times! The poet outlines what is about to take place—the Divine Service, where Christ serves us with his gifts of absolution, word, and sacrament. "Kneeling" and "plea" stand for confession, "the Father's arms in welcome" for absolution. "Hearing" and "power" signal the word of God read and preached. The Eucharist is summarized by: "The vessel brimmed for pouring," "body," "blood," and "joyful celebration." "The heart forgiven leaping" may be the most brief and perfect summary of what the Lutheran *Gottesdienst*, the Divine Service, is all about: from the pastor's absolution, through the proclamation of the gospel, to receiving the Lord's body and blood, it is all about forgiveness of sinners by a gracious God. The poetic economy of words is striking and makes this hymn a landmark of twentieth-century Lutheran hymnody. Indeed, Vajda himself stated: "Looking back on the 25th anniversary of

---

6. LSB–CH, 2:335–37. On Martin Franzmann's life and work see: Robin A. Leaver, *Come to the Feast: The Original and Translated Hymns of Martin H. Franzmann* (St. Louis: MorningStar, 1994); Richard N. Brinkley, *Thy Strong Word: The Enduring Legacy of Martin Franzmann* (St. Louis: Concordia, 1993); and Westermeyer, *With Tongues of Fire*, 62–72.

Now the Silence, I see it as the unexpected and unintended watershed for my hymnody, and indirectly for other hymn writing in the last quarter of the 20th-century."[7]

Schalk, who would become a regular collaborator with Vajda, wrote the memorable tune NOW for Vajda's text. Like the text, it is economical in its own way, not only through repetition of phrases (AABBA'C) but, perhaps more importantly, by the melodic interval of the rising perfect fourth, which predominates throughout Schalk's melody, moreover with phrase B being a transposition of phrase A up a perfect fourth. Further, the rhythmic germ of quarter note and eighth note infuses the melody and matches the text perfectly. Characteristic of hymn harmonizations in TLH was a note-against-note sense of verticality, the norm being every melodic note harmonized separately. By contrast, Schalk's harmonization for NOW has a more linear feel, with the harmonic rhythm operating at the rate of each quarter note/eight note unit.

As published for the first time in this 1969 supplement, both Vajda's text and Schalk's tune revealed new hymnic possibilities, quite beyond what singing congregations had experienced in nearly three decades of using TLH. *Worship Supplement* was providing new directions in Lutheran hymnody.[8]

Franzmann "O God, O Lord of Heaven and Earth" and Bender WITTENBERG NEW (WS 758)

When *Worship Supplement* was published in 1969 no other living poet had as many texts included as Martin Franzmann, with six original hymns:[9]

"Thy Strong Word Did Cleave the Darkness"	1954 and 1959
"O Fearful Place, Where He Who Knows Our Heart"	Before 1969
"O Thou, Who Hast of Thy Pure Grace"	Before 1969
"In Adam We Have All Been One"	1961
"O God, O Lord of Heaven and Earth"	1966
"O Kingly Love, That Faithfully"	1966

---

7. Westermeyer, *With Tongues of Fire*, 148.
8. "Now the Silence" was included in LBW but not in LW 1982.
9. The date of writing for each text is drawn from Leaver's "Commentary" section in his *Come to the Feast: The Original and Translated Hymns of Martin H. Franzmann*.

Each of these hymns in its own way reveals Franzmann's brilliant use of the English language, coupled with his theological insights as a New Testament exegete. Here is one brief example from his hymn "O Fearful Place, Where He Who Knows Our Heart" (WS 774, st. 4), designated in WS for "The Church *ANNIVERSARY*":

> O Son of God, who diedst our life to win,
> Here in this house we died thy death to sin,
> And from the dead with thee have raisèd been.

Here in a poetic economy of words Franzmann summarizes Paul's teaching on baptism in Romans 6. "Here in this house"—the church—the sacrament of baptism is administered, and, in Paul's words, "all of us who have been baptized into Christ Jesus were baptized into his death" (Rom 6:3) ("We died thy death"), and "if we have been united with him in a death like his, we shall certainly be united with him in a resurrection like his" (Rom 6:5) ("And from the dead with thee have raisèd been"). This hymn, coupled with a newly composed tune by Richard Hillert (1923–2010), was not, however, included in subsequent Lutheran hymnals.

By contrast, "O God, O Lord of Heaven and Earth" was included in both LBW and LW 1982, though with revisions that did great harm to Franzmann's original text.[10] With distinctive, incisive language Franzmann's hymn declares the story of salvation. God's living finger, which wrote the Ten Commandments on tablets of stone (Exod 31:18 and Deut 9:10), "never wrote that life should be an aimless mote [a small particle or speck], a deathward drift from futile birth." On the contrary, God desired nothing less than his life for man, whom he created "in his own image" (Gen 1:27). Moreover, God gave to humankind the "wondrous gift of liberty," which, however, our first parents misused in their "fatal will to equal [God]," a "rebel will" that brought death instead of the life that God intended for the crown of his creation. But the Savior promised in Genesis 3:15, the "Prince of peace," came to our "house of doom" and "breached all its walls for our release" from the hold of sin and death. When Christ came to "our hall of death" he breathed "our poisoned air"—an apt reference to increasing awareness of air pollution in the 1960s, but even more he would "drink for us the dark despair that strangled man's reluctant breath." Thus, he took on himself the despair of humans who know

---

10. See Leaver, *Come to the Feast*, 50–53, for a detailed critique of the LBW revisions. The 2006 LSB provides a version much closer to Franzmann's original, cf. LSB 834.

that they are unable to live according to God's commands; *for us* Christ walked "the road that leads us back to God." Franzmann's narrative of salvation history is at once similar to Luther's 1524 *Nun freut euch* ("Dear Christians, One and All, Rejoice"), both hymns proclaiming the turn from death and sin to life and salvation. But where Luther's ten stanzas provide him an expansive poetic canvas, Franzmann is more the miniaturist, his exceptionally well-chosen words in only four stanzas being akin to the smallest details in a miniature painting.

"O God, O Lord of Heaven and Earth" is categorized in WS as a hymn for Reformation, and indeed was commissioned by the Lutheran Council in the United States of America (LCUSA) specifically for the 450th anniversary of the Reformation in 1967. In the final stanza Franzmann's text prays that the Holy Spirit "who didst once restore the Church"—the sixteenth-century Reformation movements—might "breathe on thy cloven Church once more . . . in these gray and latter days." With Franzmann's hymn the singing congregation not only proclaims the story of salvation, but also prays that the Spirit will lead the church always to be "the bringer of good news."

Bender's tune WITTENBERG NEW was composed specifically for Franzmann's text, "Wittenberg" in the tune name referring to Wittenberg University in Springfield, Ohio, where Bender was a faculty member at the time that he composed the tune. The tune is unified by the interval of the rising fourth and by repetition of musical phrases, as outlined here:

A	O God, O Lord of heaven and earth,
A'	Thy living finger never wrote
B	That life should be an aimless mote,
	A deathward drift from futile birth.
A	Thy Word meant life triumphant hurled
A'	Through every cranny of thy world.
C	Since light awoke and life began,
D	Thou hast desired thy life for man.

That the tune has sometimes been regarded as difficult for congregational singing is likely due to the combined length of poetic phrases two, three, and four. Sensitive musical leadership will provide for a quick breath after poetic line three. Even acknowledging that one challenge, the tune is perfectly matched to Franzmann's poetry, there are no particular rhythmic difficulties, and the motivic/melodic unity promotes strong congregational singing.

Newly Translated Chorale Texts:
Martin L. Seltz and F. Samuel Janzow

While *Worship Supplement* included strikingly original new texts and tunes, such as those by Vajda/Schalk and Franzmann/Bender, it also played an important role in making accessible older chorales that had not been included in TLH, as well as providing new translations of some chorales already found in the 1941 book. Two translators played significant roles in this aspect of WS: Martin L. Seltz (1909–1967) and F. Samuel Janzow (1913–2001).

Seltz served as a pastor in LCMS parishes in Minnesota, Iowa, and Illinois. As a member of the LCMS Commission on Worship, Liturgics, and Hymnology he was also a participant in the work leading to publication of WS.[11] Particularly noteworthy is his translation of the Advent chorale *O Heiland, reiss die Himmel auf* ("O Savior, Rend the Heavens Wide," WS 706). This text, by Friedrich Spee von Langenfeld (1591–1635), appeared first in seventeenth-century Catholic sources before finding a place in Lutheran hymn collections.[12] Seltz's translation was the first English-language version of this hymn text, which is notable for its strong sense of eschatological yearning.

What makes Seltz's translation so noteworthy is his ability to stay very close to the original German—and its scriptural allusions—while still employing evocative English expressions. Consider, for example, the first stanza:

O Heiland, reiß die Himmel auf,
Herab, herab vom Himmel lauf;
Reiß ab vom Himmel Tor und Tür
Reiß ab, wo Schloß und Riegel für.

O Savior, rend the heavens wide;
Come down, come down with mighty stride.
Unbar the gates, the doors break down;
Unbar the way to heaven's crown.

---

11. LSB–CH, 2:660.
12. LSB–CH, 1:62–63.

The first two lines of the translation capture the sense of Isaiah 64:1: "Oh that you would rend the heavens and come down," the second two lines the sense of Psalm 24:7: "Lift up your heads, O gates! And be lifted up, O ancient doors." Perhaps an even closer connection between original and translation may be seen in stanza six:

> Hier leiden wir die größte Not,
> Vor Augen steht der ewig Tod.
> Ach komm, führ uns mit starker Hand
> Vom Elend zu dem Vaterland.

> Here dreadful doom upon us lies;
> Death looms so grim before our eyes.
> O come, lead us with mighty hand
> From exile to our Fatherland.

Seltz's translation of this Advent chorale was included, in somewhat abbreviated form, in both LBW (38, stanzas 1, 5–7) and LW 1982 (32, stanzas 1–3, 5–7).

Beyond bringing this superb chorale text (and tune) back for American singers, Seltz provided new translations of chorale texts already found in TLH:

701	"Savior of the Nations, Come"	TLH 95	"Savior of the Nations, Come"
714	"In dulci jubilo"	TLH 92	"Now Sing We, Now Rejoice"
741	"The *Victimae Paschali* Celebration"	TLH 187	"Christ Is Arisen"

For "Savior of the Nations, Come" Seltz provided a new translation for lines 3 and 4 of stanza 3, and all of stanzas 4–6. LBW would use his translation of stanzas 3 and 4, while LW 1982 would use a new translation by F. Samuel Janzow.

Seltz's translation of "In dulci jubilo" freely mixes lines of Latin and English, with sometimes awkward results, as, for example, in the first four lines of stanza 1:

> In dulci jubilo
> Sing "Alleluia," lo!
> See our Joy reclining
> Here in praesepio!

LBW would turn to a three-stanza translation by John Mason Neale (1818–1866), while LW 1982 would use a new translation by Janzow.

In WS Seltz's translation of the Easter hymn "Christ Is Arisen" was joined with the Easter sequence *Victimae paschali laudes,* the former inserted as congregational song between sections of the Easter sequence. With minor alterations his translation was taken into LBW as a separate hymn, there preceding "Christians to the Paschal Victim." LW 1982 again drew on Janzow for a new translation. Both the 2006 hymnals—ELW and LSB—use Seltz's translation of *Christ ist erstanden,* attesting to the enduring quality of his work as a translator of chorales.

F. Samuel Janzow was an ordained LCMS pastor (Concordia Seminary, St. Louis, 1936) who served as pastor at Luther-Tyndale Church in London, England (1936–1947), and at Trinity Lutheran in Trimont, Minnesota (1948–1954). He was also a scholar of English literature, serving as professor of English at Concordia Teachers College, River Forest (now Concordia University Chicago) from 1954 to his retirement in 1981, along the way earning a PhD in English from the University of Chicago in 1968.[13] Janzow's two translations in WS (708, "We Praise, O Christ, Your Holy Name," and 712, "Let All Together Praise Our God") are dwarfed in quantity by his twenty-eight translations in LW 1982, together with his larger project for Concordia Publishing House that resulted in "translations of all 37 of Martin Luther's hymns."[14]

Why would WS include Janzow's new translation of *Gelobet seist du, Jesu Christ* (WS 708), which was already to be found in TLH (TLH 80, unknown translator, 1858)? Like Seltz's translation of *O Heiland, reiss die Himmel auf,* Janzow prizes a translation closer to the German original. Consider, for example, the first stanza:

Gelobet seist du, Jesu Christ,
Daß du Mensch geboren bist
Von einer Jungfrau, das ist wahr;
Des freuet sich der Engel Schar.
Kyrieleis.

---

13. On Janzow's life and work as a hymn writer and translator see David W. Rogner, *Dawnlight Breaks: The Hymn Texts and Translations of F. Samuel Janzow,* Shaping American Lutheran Church Music (Minneapolis: Lutheran University Press, 2014). See pages 18–19 for a tabular list of Janzow's original texts and translations in WS, LBW, LW 1982, and LSB.
14. Rogner, *Dawnlight Breaks,* 6.

We Praise, O Christ, your holy name.
Truly human child you came,
From virgin born; this word is true.
Your angels are rejoicing too.
Kyrieleis! [WS 708]

All praise to Thee, eternal God,
Who, clothed in garb of flesh and blood,
Dost take a manger for Thy throne,
While worlds on worlds are Thine alone.
Hallelujah! [TLH 80]

The TLH translation omits reference to the virgin ("Jungfrau") in line three, and to the angels rejoicing in line four ("Des freuet sich der Engel Schar"), both key elements in the Christmas narrative. Janzow's translation is appropriately closer to the German original. Consider also stanza four:

Das ewig Licht geht da herein,
Gibt der Welt ein' neuen Schein;
Es leucht' wohl mitten in der Nacht
Und uns des Lichtes Kinder macht.
Kyrieleis.

The Light Eternal, breaking through,
Made the world to gleam anew;
His beams have pierced the core of night,
He makes us children of the light.
Kyrieleis! [WS 708]

Thou camest in the darksome night
To make us children of the light,
To make us in the realms divine,
Like Thine own angels round Thee shine.
Hallelujah! [TLH 80]

The first two lines of the TLH translation pick up the imagery of the third and fourth lines of stanza *four* of the German original: "night" ("Nacht") and "children of the light" ("Lichtes Kinder"), while lines three and four of the TLH translation pick up on lines three and four of stanza *six* of the German:

> Und in dem Himmel mache reich
> Und seinen lieben Engeln gleich.

Thus, the unknown translator in TLH conflated two lines each from stanzas four and six of the original into what is TLH stanza four.

So, again, why include Janzow's translation of a chorale already available in TLH (and likely not sung nearly as often at Christmas as the familiar carols)? Janzow's translation is often more faithful to the original, depriving the singer of neither details nor nuances in the German text. On the other hand, his translation of the concluding stanza seven is not literal but still poetically rich:[15]

> Das hat er alles uns getan
> Sein groß Lieb zu zeigen an.
> Des freu sich alle Christenheit
> Und dank ihm des in Ewigkeit.
> Kyrieleis.

> Such grace toward us now fills with light
> Length and breadth and depth and height!
> O endless ages, raise your voice;
> O Christendom, rejoice, rejoice!
> Kyrieleis! [WS 708]

As the first in what would be a longer line of hymnal supplements published for use by Lutherans in North America, *Worship Supplement* presented some entirely new poetic and musical expressions not found in existing Lutheran hymnals (1941 TLH, 1958 SBH). New hymn texts and tunes, such as those by Vajda/Schalk and Franzmann/Bender, or a first English translation of a chorale coupled with its historic tune (*O Heiland, reiss die Himmel auf*) are examples. But this supplement was also a vehicle

---

15. By contrast LSB 382 provides a more literal translation of stanza 7:
All this for us our God has done
Granting love through His own Son.
Therefore, all Christendom, rejoice
And sing His praise with endless voice.
Alleluia!

for experimentation, providing new translations of hymns already available. Would congregational singers, pastors, and musicians make use of a new translation such as Janzow's "We Praise, O Christ, Your Holy Name"? Was there value in translations that were more faithful to the original than were some of the older, existing translations? Both Seltz and Janzow provided new translations that would not only enrich the hymnic repertory but would also provoke these important questions as Lutherans in North America worked toward compilation of that anticipated new hymnal, the 1978 LBW.

EXPANDING THE REPERTORY OF HYMNS

Thus far the focus has been on select individuals who created new texts (Vajda and Franzmann), tunes and settings (Schalk and Bender), and translations (Seltz and Janzow) for *Worship Supplement*. As important as these newly created vehicles were for Gospel proclamation and worship, so too were texts, tunes, and translations of existing materials that were not brand new, but, rather, new to North American Lutherans who had been using TLH exclusively for nearly thirty years. With no intention of being comprehensive, what follows here is a consideration by topic of some of the riches that came into American Lutheranism by way of WS, many of those materials subsequently being included in LBW and LW 1982—often, of course, marked by variants, which will not be traced here.[16]

Sixteenth-Century German Hymns

Among sixteenth-century German hymns included in WS are:

722   *Herr Christ, der einig Gotts Sohn* (The Only Son from Heaven)

This text is by Elisabeth Cruciger (*ca.* 1500–1535), one of the poets who worked with Luther to provide new hymns "in the vernacular which the people could sing during mass."[17] Significantly, this hymn was included in two of the very first Lutheran hymnals published in 1524 by two rival printers in Erfurt.[18] The hymn was included in LBW and LW 1982, as in WS designated for Epiphany.

---

16. Remembering here a conversation with Carl Schalk, who put it succinctly: "Hymnal committees love to tinker." An invaluable source for detailed tracing of textual variants is LSB–CH, vol. 1.
17. LW 53: 36 (from the *Formula missae*, 1523).
18. On the 1524 Erfurt hymnals see especially Chapter 2, pp. 51–53.

768 *In dir ist Freude* (*In Thee Is Gladness*)

This hymn comes from a 1598 collection of Latin and German songs for Christmas and New Year's compiled by Johann Lindemann (1549–1631) and joined to Italian dance music published in 1591 by Giovanni Gastoldi (*ca.* 1554–1609). Included in neither TLH nor SBH, this hymn has been widely accepted in North American Lutheran books since its appearance in WS. It is an ideal example of how WS added to our congregational repertories hymns that—in retrospect—we may wonder how we ever lived without.

Nineteenth-Century American Hymn Tunes

Nineteenth-century American hymn tunes from southern folk traditions are not part of TLH. From *Southern Harmony* (1835) WS took the tune JEFFERSON for use with the Advent text "Come, Thou Long-Expected Jesus" (705) and THE SAINTS DELIGHT for Franzmann's text "In Adam We Have All Been One" (759). The tune CONSOLATION for another Advent hymn, "The King Shall Come When Morning Dawns" (707) is drawn from *Kentucky Harmony* (1816). All three of these texts and tunes were included in LBW and LW 1982. The same cannot be said of WS 752, where the text Son of God, Eternal Savior is coupled with an early American tune LORD, REVIVE US. While that text was included in both LBW and LW 1982 it was joined to the seventeenth-century Dutch tune IN BABILONE.

Hymns from Britain and Ireland

WS truly supplemented TLH by providing American Lutheran singers a taste of the riches of British and Irish hymnody. KING'S LYNN (WS 756, "From All Thy Saints in Warfare" and WS 784 "O God of Earth and Altar") is an English folk tune transcribed by Ralph Vaughan Williams (1872–1958), who, in addition to being a preeminent twentieth-century English composer, was a collector of English folksongs. WS 756 also provided a textual possibility unknown in TLH, but carried forward in subsequent Lutheran hymnals, namely, a three-stanza hymn where the second stanza is inserted as needed to observe a particular saint's day, the possibilities including sixteen separate stanzas for various saints and apostles. The hymn was taken into both LBW (177–178) and LW 1982 (193–194), both under the title "By All Your Saints in Warfare."

As a composer of hymn tunes, Vaughan Williams was represented in TLH by only a single tune SINE NOMINE (TLH 463, "For All the Saints Who from Their Labors Rest"). WS added two more of his hymn tunes: KING'S WESTON (WS 743, "At the Name of Jesus") and DOWN AMPNEY (WS 755, "Come Down, O Love Divine"), both subsequently taken into LBW and LW 1982. WS 725, "My Song Is Love Unknown," joins a remarkable seventeenth-century English text to a beautiful melody composed specifically for that text by a contemporary of Vaughan Williams, the English composer John Ireland (1879–1962). Here again WS provides a text and tune that we wonder how we previously lived without, that hymn being taken into LBW and LW 1982, as well as most subsequent Lutheran hymnals.

Among Vaughan Williams's extensive body of compositions is "Three Preludes Founded on Welsh Hymn Tunes" (1920), settings for organ of BRYN CALFARIA, RHOSYMEDRE, and HYFRYDOL. Of these three tunes only HYFRYDOL was found in TLH. WS made those other two Welsh tunes available to LCMS Lutherans, SBH having already included BRYN CALFARIA and RHOSYMEDRE, the latter coupled in SBH with the text "My Song Is Love Unknown," rather than Ireland's tune LOVE UNKNOWN. Both BRYN CALFARIA and RHOSYMEDRE were subsequently included in LBW and LW 1982. Finally, in this category of hymns from Britain and Ireland, WS made available the wonderful nineteenth-century Irish folk song that is joined to the text "I Bind unto Myself Today the Strong Name of the Trinity," the tune named ST. PATRICK'S BREASTPLATE,[19] also included in LBW and LW 1982.

Christmas, Holy Week, and Easter

Commonly heard at Christmas, but not included in TLH for congregational singing, were hymns such as: "Angels We Have Heard on High" (WS 711), "Gentle Mary Laid Her Child" (WS 716), and "What Child Is This" (WS 719), the latter with its remarkable second stanza that so strongly links Christ's incarnation and passion. Here WS added Christmas melodies and texts already widely known, heard, and sung, thus expanding the repertory in immediately useful ways. These Christmas hymns were taken into LBW (except for "Gentle Mary Laid Her Child") and LW 1982.

In addition to "My Song Is Love Unknown," WS included for Holy Week John Mason Neale's translation of the Latin hymn "Pange lingua

---

19. For extensive background on both text and tune, see Joseph Herl's essay in LSB-CH, 1:692–700.

gloriosi" by Venantius Fortunatus (530–609). In WS (728) the text was joined to a new tune FORTUNATUS NEW, composed by Carl Schalk just three years before WS was published. Schalk's tune is a model of musical economy, not only in its overall form AA'B but also in its opening melodic and rhythmic gesture (first measure), which infuses the hymn melody, making it at once memorable and easy for a singing congregation to assimilate.

WS included the following Easter hymns new to TLH singers, all of which have found wide acceptance in subsequent Lutheran hymnals in North America, including LBW and LW 1982:

733 "At the Lamb's High Feast We Sing"
734 "With High Delight Let Us Unite" [Martin Franzmann trans.]
738 "Come, Ye Faithful, Raise the Strain"
742 "This Joyful Eastertide"

While the categories and hymns cited here to demonstrate how WS expanded the repertory of hymns for congregational singers steeped in nearly thirty years of exclusive use of TLH is necessarily selective, it does demonstrate the impact of WS, particularly on its two successor books: LBW and LW 1982. WS did what a supplement is designed to do, namely, to introduce texts, tunes, and translations new to a particular group of congregational singers, knowing that some expressions will last while others may not. A supplement, then, is, by definition, necessarily provisional and somewhat experimental, but WS was clearly a significant step toward the full new Lutheran hymnals that would be published in 1978 and 1982, both serving well until their successors, ELW and LSB, were published in 2006.

NEW POSSIBILITIES IN HYMN SETTINGS

Worship Supplement was published in two physical volumes: a text and tune pew edition for use by congregants, and an accompaniment edition for use by organists or pianists.[20] Because TLH provided a four-part harmonization for every hymn, a single volume served congregational singers as well as organists. Thus, a new and distinguishing feature of WS—and one not to be taken for granted—was the elevation of organ accompaniment of hymns as a distinctive musical phenomenon requiring its own published

---

20. *Worship Supplement: Accompaniment Edition* (St. Louis: Concordia Publishing House, 1969).

resource. Moreover, the accompaniment edition normally provided *two* settings for each hymn:

> In most instances, two harmonizations are provided for each hymn, the first in a simple style for piano or organ without pedal or with optional pedal, the second in an idiomatic polyphonic texture for organ with obligatory pedal. . . . The harmonizations have been freshly and carefully prepared. . . . The second settings are written in the distinctive idiom and technique of the organ. Because of their somewhat polyphonic fabric, they presuppose skillful players and require meticulous performance.[21]

The composers of these organ settings were Theodore Beck, Jan Bender, Paul Bunjes, Richard Hillert, and Carl Schalk.

By promoting a more linear-oriented musical language in hymn accompaniment, as opposed to the consistently vertically-oriented, note-against-note harmonizations in TLH, it is fair to say that the WS Accompaniment Edition opened up an alternative musical language in hymn accompaniment. A ready case in point would be the treatment in WS of chant melodies. The Christmas hymn "Of the Father's Love Begotten" is found in TLH (98) and in WS (721), the main textual difference being that WS omits TLH stanza four. One suspects that the reason WS included this hymn was to rectify the musical harm done to the beautiful melody DIVINUM MYSTERIUM in TLH, which straitjacketed this thirteenth-century chant melody into a 4/4 rhythm, making the hymn vertically rather than horizontally oriented. In this instance WS provided a single accompaniment, by Bunjes, that allows the melody to predominate, the lower voices providing slower-moving harmonic support.

The accompaniments for two other chant melodies in WS show similar sensibilities. The Advent hymn "Creator of the Stars of Night" (703), CONDITOR ALME SIDERUM, receives two settings by Hillert, the first in three voices, the second in four voices, both linear-oriented and highlighting the chant melody. Similarly, Schalk's two settings of JAM LUCIS, "Before the Ending of the Day," show a three-voice and four-voice texture, respectively, with the chant melody moving in eighth notes and the supporting voices in quarter notes. In all three of these examples WS demonstrated how to harmonize a linear chant melody in ways unknown in TLH, thus opening a new musical potential for the accompaniment—and singing—of this category of congregational song.

---

21. From the Preface to the *Worship Supplement: Accompaniment Edition*, 6.

During the 1960s Lutheran church music publishers such as Augsburg Publishing House and Concordia Publishing House began to supply organists with collections of alternative hymn accompaniments (or reharmonizations). Among such publications that predate WS and its accompaniment edition were three collections composed by Bender, which presage the kind of accompaniments found in WS, aptly characterized, in the preface to the Accompaniment Edition, as having a "somewhat polyphonic fabric."[22] Bender's collections from the 1960s, all published by Concordia Publishing House, include:

The Hymn of the Week: Organ Settings (1961)
New Organ Settings for Hymns and Chorales, Set I, Set II (1963)

His 1961 collection, for example, included spare, linear-oriented settings of two chant-based hymn melodies: VENI EMMANUEL and DIVINUM MYSTERIUM, thus providing alternative accompaniments to TLH 62 and 98, respectively. The 1963 collections included, for example, magnificent settings of JESAIA, DEM PROPHETEN (Set I) and CHRIST IST ERSTANDEN (Set II), both of which show Bender's imaginative use of a variety of textures, including unison passages and pedal point.

Bender's accompaniment settings in WS (and those of his fellow WS composers) thus grew out of a context rooted in the previous three decades of composed chorale accompaniments in Germany, which, from the 1960s, were then taken up by American Lutheran composers in a variety of ways. In WS Bender's accompaniments for NUN KOMM, DER HEIDEN HEILAND (WS 701) and NUN BITTEN WIR (WS 753), for example, follow the pattern described in the Accompaniment Edition's preface, with the first setting being in three parts, the second—utilizing for the most part the same bass voice—being in four parts. The three-part settings are more than an accommodation to musicians of less training; they allow the organist to provide musical and registrational variety over the course of a multi-stanza hymn. Among Bender's best accompaniments in WS are those for IN DIR IST FREUDE (WS 768). While there are two settings, they do not differ greatly from one another, both being in four parts.

22. Of course, Bender was not inventing something brand new; rather, he was adding to (and building on) similar repertory by contemporaneous twentieth-century German composers, such as Hans Friedrich Micheelsen (1902–1973) and many others, who composed chorale accompaniments for organists. Bender, teaching in the United States from 1960, was applying such musical procedures not only to the chorale repertory but to a broader spectrum of hymns as well, see, for example, his settings of SINE NOMINE or TALLIS' CANON in Set II of his *New Organ Settings for Hymns and Chorales*.

The "somewhat polyphonic fabric" noted in the preface may be seen here in various ways. For example, the first four melodic pitches are imitated by the tenor voice at a distance of three quarter-notes, and, because that opening melodic gesture is immediately repeated, the continuing interplay between soprano and tenor voices enlivens the accompaniment. Bender also uses to good effect an occasional quarter note rest in the bass voice on a strong beat, the bass line resuming on the subsequent weaker beat and providing a rhythmic "kick" to the overall harmonization (see, for example, the second full measure and the textual phrase "Jesus, Sunshine of my heart," with the expected bass note on the first syllable "Je–" delayed by a beat). While one hesitates to call such small procedures "compositional strategies," they are nonetheless the kinds of things that a skilled composer can do (in a confined space) to inject energy into the musical texture and avoid a vertical note-against-note harmonization in favor of a more polyphonic approach.

★ ★ ★

Worship Supplement provided new texts, tunes, translations, and new musical possibilities in hymn accompaniments. It expanded the hymn repertory of American Lutherans who had used TLH exclusively for nearly thirty years. Apart from brand new items, WS brought old items that were, in fact, new to this segment of American Lutheranism, including chorales then unknown to American Lutherans, Latin hymns and their chant melodies, nineteenth-century American hymn tunes, hymns from Britain and Ireland, and previously unknown hymns to enrich festival seasons of the church year. There was a real richness in WS—some of which carried over to the next two generations of Lutheran hymnals (1978/1982 and 2006), and some of which went no further than WS. But that is the nature of a *supplement*. The next generation of Lutheran hymnals would draw ever more deeply on, for example, the riches of British hymnody, while the 2006 hymnals would provide something that was lacking in WS: namely, ethnic hymnody. In fact, WS was the first of what would be many more Lutheran hymnal supplements, each of them experimenting with new possibilities.[23]

---

23. Chapter 12 in this volume traces, albeit briefly, subsequent supplemental and ethnic hymnals.

12.

Hymnals 2024

Daniel Zager and Robin A. Leaver

The study of influential American Lutheran hymnals does not, of course, end with the 1978 *Lutheran Book of Worship*. The production of hymnals has continued apace—particularly in this time of a continuing "hymn explosion" in the United States, and the concomitant richness of new hymns, both poetically and musically. Moreover, during the last quarter of the twentieth century and the early decades of the new millennium there has been an increasing awareness of the global nature of the church.[1] That recognition has led to new possibilities in ethnic hymnody from various regions of the world—translated into English to enrich American hymnals. One also notes a heightened awareness of the need for Lutheran hymnals in Spanish and French for the use of Lutherans in the Americas beyond predominantly English-speaking regions. What follows in this chapter is a necessarily brief consideration of three categories of Lutheran hymnals produced from 1991 to the present: (1) five hymnal supplements, (2) six full hymnals for English-speaking Lutherans, and (3) four full hymnals for Spanish- and French-speaking Lutherans in the Americas.

Hymnal supplements have provided an important means for Lutheran church bodies to evaluate hymnic expressions that are new—not only in the sense of recent origin, but also "new to Lutherans," based on hymns absent from predecessor hymnals. For the historian, hymnal supplements have a particular benefit, providing a series of snapshots from specific

---

1. See, for example, the 1996 "Nairobi Statement on Worship and Culture: Contemporary Challenges and Opportunities," in *Christian Worship: Unity in Cultural Diversity*, ed. S. Anita Stauffer, LWF Studies (Geneva: Lutheran World Federation, 1996), 23–28.

times and places, showing church bodies wrestling with questions of the function and purpose of hymns and hymnals, and ultimately with larger theological and liturgical considerations concerning the role of sung proclamation and praise in the church's worship life.

The full hymnals produced by Lutheran church bodies from 1993 on, all of which remain in use, are difficult to consider historically without some distance of time. Nevertheless, those hymnals are cited here, with excerpts from their prefatory statements, and brief mention of a few characteristics—especially relating to new hymn texts—in each of those full hymnals. In due course, such hymnals will receive historical appraisal, particularly in light of the hymnals that will eventually succeed them. Note, this chapter considers only hymns—not orders of service—providing brief descriptions of hymnals and supplements published for use by Lutherans in North America from 1991 to 2022, thus aligning with the first hymnals of 1524, which contained hymns but not orders of service.

HYMNAL SUPPLEMENTS

Beginning in the 1990s and extending into the new millennium, Lutheran church bodies in the United States have been active in planning, compiling, and publishing hymnal supplements—books that fill two important functions. First, they provide a way to make newer hymns available to congregational singers, especially *between* the publication of full hymnals or worship books, which appear (at best) every twenty-five to thirty years. Second, they provide these church bodies an important means of evaluating potential new hymns for such a projected full hymnal. In that second sense hymnal supplements are somewhat experimental in nature and provide a kind of sifting process, the expectation being that not all the hymns included in a supplement will eventually find their way into a full hymnal. All three major Lutheran church bodies in the United States (ELCA, LCMS, WELS) published hymnal supplements during the last three decades, such supplemental volumes revealing not only the various strands of hymnody being considered for a forthcoming full hymnal, but also showing the ever-evolving nature of hymnic creativity, poetically and musically, denominationally and internationally. Five supplements, published between 1991 and 2020, are cited and briefly described here in chronological order to show how these church bodies (and publishers) build successively on one another's work by tapping into some of the same emerging streams of hymnody.

1991. *Hymnal Supplement 1991.* Chicago: GIA Publications.

Of the five hymnal supplements considered here this one alone was compiled and published without a connection to an American Lutheran church body. Rather, it was conceived by one of the most prominent publishers of hymnals for Roman Catholics in the United States: GIA Publications (originally: Gregorian *I*nstitute of *A*merica). But it emerged as a response to, and an update of, the *Lutheran Book of Worship*, as editors Robert J. Batastini and John Ferguson note in their preface:

> Since the appearance of the Lutheran Book of Worship in 1978, several trends have occurred which evidence the need for new worship materials for the 1990's: (1) a virtual explosion of new hymnody; (2) an ever-increasing awareness that the language of worship should be sensitive to all people; (3) the continuing need and desire of diverse worshipping communities for a wider range of musical styles and expressions. *Hymnal Supplement 1991* is GIA's response to the above. (iv)

Thus, while not specifically a Lutheran supplement, *Hymnal Supplement 1991* (HS 1991) was prompted by the fact that LBW was then thirteen years old and already—in the estimation of some—showing some deficiencies in an age when the "hymn explosion" continued apace, in the United States as well as in Great Britain. (In publication terms, while the British phenomenon was a "hymn explosion," here in the United States it was as much a "*hymnal* explosion" as a "hymn explosion.") The preface also identifies Lutheran contributors and consultants to this volume, among them Richard Hillert, Carl Schalk, Randall Sensmeier, Marilyn K. Stulken, Mons Teig, Ralph Van Loon, and Paul Westermeyer.

The preface states that the volume contains "much that is old . . . and much that is new" (iv). For example, the group of thirteen psalm settings includes two psalms (in English translations by Daniel G. Reuning) taken from the "Becker Psalter" (1628, 1640, 1661) of Heinrich Schütz (1585–1672), as well as six psalm settings by Joseph Gelineau (1920–2008). Similarly, among the hymns for Christmas is a seventeenth-century chorale by Christian Keimann (1607–1662): *Freuet euch, ihr Christen alle* ("O Rejoice, All Christians, Loudly"—with an updated translation, based on TLH 96, by Sensmeier), coupled with Andreas Hammerschmidt's (1611/12–1675) sturdy tune FREUET EUCH, IHR CHRISTEN, a hymn from TLH that was not taken into LBW. Among the newer hymns for Christmas is Jaroslav Vajda's "Before the Marvel of This Night," with Schalk's beautiful tune MARVEL. Among the other new texts in HS 1991 are hymns by Timothy

Dudley-Smith, Fred Pratt Green, Vajda, and Brian Wren; new tunes include those by Calvin Hampton, Hillert, David Hurd, Richard Proulx, and Schalk. Perhaps most notable, however, is the presence of texts and music by David Haas, Marty Haugen, and Michael Joncas, names absent from LBW but prominent in more recent Roman Catholic hymnals published by GIA. Their hymns would continue to appear in Lutheran supplements and hymnals following HS 1991.

1995. *With One Voice: A Lutheran Resource for Worship.* Minneapolis: Augsburg Fortress.

This hymnal supplement was "developed by the Publishing House and the Division for Congregational Ministries of the Evangelical Lutheran Church in America" (5) "as an additional volume of resources for Lutherans at worship" (4). The "Introduction" goes on to articulate a rationale for *With One Voice* (WOV):

> A quick glance at this resource will reveal that to sing "with one voice" [Rom 15:6] does not imply uniformity of expression. The "one voice" of the Church represents an amazingly diverse fabric, many songs of many cultures in many styles, woven together by the one Spirit. The size of *With One Voice* allows only a sampling of these many songs, but the breadth represented here is a witness to the Church's unity in diversity and an encouragement to communities to cultivate a variety of expressions when they gather, rather than dividing themselves by style of worship or music. (4)

Published only four years after HS 1991, WOV builds on and extends the kind of diverse musical expressions found in that earlier supplement. Among the various musical strands in WOV, the African American spiritual is well represented. Hymns from Africa include examples from South Africa, Tanzania, Nigeria, and Ghana. Spanish-language hymnody is included as well, facilitated by knowledgeable translators Madeleine Forell Marshall and Gerhard Cartford. These various strands of ethnic hymnody are among the most notable contributions brought forward in WOV. Women hymn writers in WOV include Susan Palo Cherwien, Ruth Duck, and Delores Dufner, OSB. Among American hymn writers represented are Carl P. Daw, Herman G. Stuempfle Jr., and Jaroslav Vajda, along with British poets Timothy Dudley-Smith, Fred Pratt Green, Christopher Idle, and Brian Wren (with five hymns). HS 1991 brought the texts and music of Marty Haugen to the attention of Lutherans, and his hymnody is well represented in WOV, along with that of Daniel Schutte ("I, the Lord of

Sea and Sky"), David Haas ("Blest Are They"), and Michael Joncas ("On Eagle's Wings"). Finally, the music of Jacques Berthier for the community of Taizé in France is also found in WOV, as it was in HS 1991. Thus, WOV built on the 1991 GIA supplement but added a richer component of various ethnic hymn repertories.[2]

1998. *Hymnal Supplement 98.* St. Louis: Concordia Publishing House.

"Prepared by the Commission on Worship of The Lutheran Church—Missouri Synod." The Introduction to this book states:

> *Hymnal Supplement 98* is intended to serve the Church with additional resources for worship. Intentionally a supplement, it is not a replacement for the hymnal. . . . Gathering hymns from a wide range of time, place, and Christian community, this supplement is a catholic collection. It recovers the use of some Bach chorales while expanding the repertoire to hymnody of Africa, China, and Latin America. It includes some of the earliest texts of the Church while adding the voices of 20th-century authors and composers. (5)

The chorales alluded to are Bach's harmonizations of (1) the tune ERMUNTRE DICH (from his "Christmas Oratorio") for the hymn "Break Forth, O Beauteous Heavenly Light" and (2) the tune O JESULEIN SÜSS, for the hymn "O Jesus So Sweet, O Jesus So Mild." Among the ethnic hymns are two not found in the earlier supplements cited above: one from Ethiopia, "When I Behold Jesus Christ" and one from China, "Greet the Rising Sun." Among the hymns common to WOV and HS98 are: "Sing with All the Saints in Glory," "Thine the Amen, Thine the Praise," "Go, My Children, With My Blessing," and "Christ, Mighty Savior" with Richard W. Dirksen's marvelous tune INNISFREE FARM. Those few examples illustrate the pattern of one supplement borrowing hymns brought forward by an earlier supplement. But at the same time each supplement introduces newly identified or newly written hymns. To cite only a few from HS98: Thomas Troeger's insightful Easter text "These Things Did Thomas Count As Real"; an exceptional text on Baptism, "God's Own Child, I Gladly Say It," by Erdmann Neumeister (1671–1756), translated by Robert E. Voelker; a catechetical hymn on the Lord's Supper, "What Is This Bread?" with text by Frederic W. Baue, derived from Luther's Small Catechism, with a tune by Jean Neuhauser Baue; and Joy F. Patterson's text

---

2. There is a hymnal companion for WOV: Marilyn Kay Stulken, *With One Voice: Reference Companion* (Minneapolis: Augsburg Fortress, 2000).

of comfort so applicable to our day, "When Aimless Violence Takes Those We Love." Moreover, there are texts from British hymn writers Timothy Dudley-Smith and Fred Pratt Green not found in earlier Lutheran hymnals cited here: Dudley-Smith's Passion Week text, "No Tramp of Soldier's Marching Feet" and Green's wonderful hymn on vocation, "How Clear Is Our Vocation, Lord," coupled with C. Hubert H. Parry's tune REPTON. HS98, like the two earlier supplements cited here, includes a selection of Berthier's Taizé settings. Finally, HS98 introduces the hymns of Stephen P. Starke and provides more of Herman G. Stuempfle Jr.'s hymns than do the earlier supplements. Starke is a prolific and gifted hymn writer whose texts would find further inclusion, particularly in LSB 2006.[3]

2008. *Christian Worship: Supplement.* Milwaukee: Northwestern Publishing House.

"Authorized by the Commission on Worship of the Wisconsin Evangelical Lutheran Synod." The foreword to this book states:

> *The Lutheran Hymnal* (TLH) served congregations of the Wisconsin Evangelical Lutheran Synod from 1941 to 1993. In 1993 *Christian Worship: A Lutheran Hymnal* (CW) took its place as the primary hymnal in the church body. It was the consensus of those who worked on the "new" hymnal that it should not serve for as many years as TLH. It was the vision of those committee members and the WELS Commission on Worship that a hymnal should serve 25 to 30 years. Over the course of that many years, worship resources change and worship practice in the church body might change as well.
>
> *Christian Worship: Supplement* (CWS) is making its appearance in 2008, 15 years after the production of CW, or "midway" between hymnals. Already there have been significant changes in the worship resources available. Producing a supplement is a way to take advantage of such changes and to assist worshipers, worship planners, and worship leaders in making use of these new resources. (6)

Compared to HS98, CWS included even more hymns by Stephen P. Starke and Herman G. Stuempfle, Jr.—eight original texts from each poet. (Both poets had figured prominently in the 2006 LSB, Stuempfle as well in the 2006 ELW.) The work of WELS's own poets and musicians also found a place in CWS. Laurie Gauger (text) and Grace Hennig (music) provided

---

3. There is a hymnal companion for HS98: *Hymnal Supplement 98 Handbook*, ed. Paul J. Grime and Joseph Herl (St. Louis: Commission on Worship, LCMS, 1998).

a striking hymn for Lent: "What Grace Is This!" Peter Prange wrote a particularly fine hymn for the feast of St. Michael and All Angels: "Christ, the Lord of Hosts, Unshaken." Kermit Moldenhauer provided a new tune for Luther's Easter hymn "Christ Jesus Lay in Death's Strong Bands." While one might well be reluctant to give up Luther's own tune CHRIST LAG IN TODESBANDEN, there can be no doubt that this new alternative is quite a strong, singable tune. CWS was the first of the Lutheran supplements or hymnals to include texts and music of the Irish songwriters Keith and Kristyn Getty, "There Is a Higher Throne," as well as the collaboration of Keith Getty (music) and Stuart Townend (text). CWS provides three hymns from the latter, including the very popular "In Christ Alone." The Foreword to CWS notes that "Some hymns are more suited to organ accompaniment while others are more suited to piano accompaniment. Still others work with either or with guitar accompaniment" (7). Like the supplements preceding this one chronologically, the availability of piano as well as organ for hymn accompaniment is presupposed.

2020 *All Creation Sings: Evangelical Lutheran Worship Supplement.* Minneapolis: Augsburg Fortress.

The subtitle of *All Creation Sings* (ACS) makes clear that it is related to the 2006 ELCA hymnal *Evangelical Lutheran Worship* (ELW). The introduction to ACS explains the relationship of these two books:

> The introduction to *Evangelical Lutheran Worship* noted: "The Christian assembly . . . worships in the midst of an ever-changing world." Beginning in 2017 just after the tenth year since the release of *Evangelical Lutheran Worship*, structured conversation and consultation took place in the ELCA to consider how support for the ongoing renewal of worship might respond to this reality of fast-paced change in church and society. In 2018 research was conducted to assess the interest in a liturgy and song supplement that would serve the broad spectrum of worshiping communities, and it helped identify the content that would best address the needs and concerns that have emerged over the previous decade and more. The results provided valuable information and affirmed a plan for timely development of a supplemental volume that would accompany *Evangelical Lutheran Worship.* (4)

With respect to the hymns included in ACS, the introduction states further: "a body of assembly song, including many newer expressions since 2006, has been selected to address some of those same needs and themes but also to support worship through the liturgical year"

(5). Some of those "needs and themes" are articulated further in the introduction:

> The song of all creation, and thus our song too, includes words and melodies of lament, of indignation, of pleading, and ultimately of hope in God's presence and mercy. These prayers and songs concern not only the health of our planetary home but also the health of human beings and human community in a time when socioeconomic imbalance, tensions around ethnic and gender identity, and global pandemic (to name a few) threaten our common life—and in a time when people face new challenges to the wholeness of their own bodies and minds. (6)

The hymnic content of ACS is organized first by liturgical year and then by topic, the topics in ACS being almost exactly the same as in ELW in terms of both order and wording. "Healing" (ELW) becomes "Healing, Wholeness" in ACS, and "Stewardship" in ELW is combined with "Creation" in ACS. Ruth Duck's prayer for healing, "When We Must Bear Persistent Pain," is included in the section "Healing, Wholeness." In the section "Justice, Peace" David Bjorlin's text "Build a Longer Table" offers that idea as a counter to "not a higher wall," and "Build a broader doorway, not a longer fence." In the "Creation, Stewardship" category Mary Louise Bringle's text "Can You Feel the Seasons Turning" addresses our very current reality of climate change and asks at the end:

> Called by God to serve as stewards
> Till earth's garden greens and thrives,
> Can we learn in time to listen?
> Can we turn and change our lives? (ACS 1065)

Bringle is represented in ACS with twelve hymns, Susan Palo Cherwien with seven original hymns and a new translation of Luther's *Mitten wir im Leben sind*.[4]

FULL ENGLISH-LANGUAGE HYMNALS FROM LUTHERAN CHURCH BODIES IN AMERICA

The goal here is to identify the full hymnals published during the last three decades for use by American Lutherans. The commentary includes: (1) excerpts from prefatory statements in the hymnals, especially statements

---

4. There is a hymnal companion for ACS: Paul Westermeyer, *Assembly Song Companion to All Creation Sings* (Minneapolis: Augsburg Fortress, 2023).

that indicate intent and speak to the balance of old and new hymns, and (2) just the briefest mention of a few of the newer poets included in these books. Obviously, any kind of comprehensive evaluation of a denominational hymnal is beyond the scope of this volume; moreover, a certain chronological distance is essential for a dispassionate evaluation of any hymnal. These volumes are all currently in use by the various Lutheran church bodies in North America.

1993. *Christian Worship: A Lutheran Hymnal.* Milwaukee: Northwestern Publishing House. Authorized by the Wisconsin Evangelical Lutheran Synod.

When *Christian Worship: A Lutheran Hymnal* (CW 1993) was published in 1993 it provided the Wisconsin Evangelical Lutheran Synod (WELS) their first alternative to *The Lutheran Hymnal* (TLH) since the publication of that book in 1941. Fifty-two years with the same hymnal was clearly a lot, and it was perhaps no surprise that CW 1993 "achieved over 90% coverage [among WELS congregations] in its first year."[5] The introduction to CW 1993 states:

> The phrase "new/revised" in the synodical resolution was interpreted to mean a hymnal which **preserved** the Christian and Lutheran heritage of liturgy and hymns from *The Lutheran Hymnal* and at the same time **improved** and **expanded** it. Much of the familiar content of *The Lutheran Hymnal* has been preserved. (8)

> The overall intent of those who prepared *Christian Worship: A Lutheran Hymnal* was to produce a Lutheran hymnal that was at once forward-looking and also enriched by the faith and worship experience of the whole Christian church of the past. Specifically the goal was to deliver to the church a strongly Christ-centered book, bringing together liturgies and a large number of hymns celebrating the life and atoning work of Jesus. (9)

The goal of retaining the best of the past (preserving) while adding new expressions as well (expanding) is the common challenge faced by many hymnal committees. With respect to the hymns in CW 1993 the Introduction notes:

> The hymn section of the new hymnal has a familiar look. Over 400 hymns have been retained from *The Lutheran Hymnal*, though many have undergone a slight updating of language.... The hymn section also has a

---

5. Michael Schultz, "The Future of Worship in WELS from the perspective of a new hymnal project," (2013), 27. www.worshipandoutreach.org/writings/blog/the-future-of-worship-in-wels

new look and sound. The last three decades have seen a strong resurgence of creativity and interest in the writing of hymns. Therefore, congregations will enjoy a greater variety of hymns than formerly. In addition to Lutheran chorales and traditional English hymnody, a wide selection of plainsong hymns, spirituals, folk hymns from Appalachia, Wales, Ireland, and elsewhere, gospel hymns, and contemporary hymns in different styles are included. In addition to new texts and new melodies, a somewhat freer and fresher type of harmonization has been furnished for some of the hymns; descants and guitar chords are supplied for a few others. (9)

Among hymns "from the last three decades" now brought to WELS congregations for the first time were texts by Timothy Dudley-Smith, Martin H. Franzmann, Fred Pratt Green, Michael Joncas ("On Eagles' Wings"), and Jaroslav Vajda, as well as WELS hymn writers Kurt Eggert, Werner H. Franzmann, and James P. Tiefel.[6]

2021. *Christian Worship: Hymnal.* Milwaukee: Northwestern Publishing House.

Christian Worship: Hymnal is authorized by the Wisconsin Evangelical Lutheran Synod.

As stated in the 2008 *Christian Worship: Supplement*, WELS determined to provide a new full hymnal within a generation (twenty-five to thirty years) after CW 1993, rather than allowing for another 50-year-plus monopoly of the kind exerted by TLH from 1941 to the appearance of CW in 1993. Thus, precisely fifteen years after CW 1993 the Supplement appeared in 2008, with the next new full hymnal—CW 2021—appearing twenty-eight years after its predecessor full hymnal. The introduction to CW 2021 states:

> Like its predecessors, this hymnal celebrates our worship heritage with an eye to the future. Gifted poets, artists, and musicians don't stand by idly while the church marches on. The majority of hymns and rites you'll find here are time–tested and approved, but there are also worthy texts and musical settings that are fresh and new. (iv)

By including 657 hymns, CW 2021 has the capacity to offer both the "time-tested and approved" as well as the "fresh and new." In that latter

---

6. There is a hymnal companion for CW 1993: C. T. Aufdemberge, *Christian Worship: Handbook* (Milwaukee: Northwestern Publishing House, 1997). Particularly helpful is the provision of the original German text for Lutheran chorales.

category, and continuing the pattern begun in the 2008 CWS, CW 2021 offers thirteen hymns by the Irish songwriter/composer team of Stuart Townend and Keith (and Kristen) Getty, uniquely among recent Lutheran hymnals in America. Lutheran hymn writers Herman G. Stuempfle Jr. and Stephen P. Starke are each represented by ten original texts.

1996. *Evangelical Lutheran Hymnary.* St. Louis: MorningStar Music Publishers.

Prepared by the Worship Committee of The Evangelical Lutheran Synod, Mankato, Minnesota.

The Evangelical Lutheran Synod (ELS) is one of the smaller Lutheran church bodies in the United States, with roots in the Norwegian Evangelical Lutheran Church in America organized in 1853. The *Evangelical Lutheran Hymnary* (ELH) has no introductory comments stating intent or reflecting on the balance of older and newer hymns. It contains 602 hymns organized topically and by church year. Though the roots of the ELS are Norwegian, a separate index of "Translated Hymns" reveals sixty-nine hymns translated from "Norwegian/Scandinavian" languages, but 256 from German, many of those being chorales. Indeed, ELH is the only current American Lutheran hymnal where one can find, for example, English-language versions of chorales such as *Ich ruf zu dir, Herr Jesu Christ* or *O Mensch, bewein dein Sünde groß*. Hymns by late twentieth-century poets are more limited in ELH, with, for example, one hymn each by Timothy Dudley-Smith, Fred Pratt Green, Christopher M. Idle, Stephen Starke, and Jaroslav J. Vajda, and three hymns by Martin H. Franzmann.

1999. *This Far by Faith: An African American Resource for Worship.* Minneapolis: Augsburg Fortress.

Since this hymnal refers to itself as a supplement, it might be thought to be in the wrong section of this chapter. However, the world "supplement" occurs neither in its title nor subtitle, and the hymnal appears to have been conceived as a stand-alone, full liturgical and hymnic resource, in contrast to usual supplements that are trial collections of new hymns in a kind of interim step toward a new full hymnal at some point in the future.

This resource has been developed by a cooperative inter-church process involving the Evangelical Lutheran Church in America and the Lutheran

Church—Missouri Synod. Each church body has been responsible for its own review process.

This resource is recommended for use in the Evangelical Lutheran Church in America.

The prefatory matter in TFBF includes a five-page essay "Worship and Culture: An African American Lutheran Perspective," followed by a second five-page essay "Leading African American Song." From the first essay on "Worship and Culture":

> Yet the challenge of transmitting the gospel to people of African descent in the Americas has been exacerbated by the "peculiar institution" of slavery and the seemingly intractable legacy of racism. In succeeding decades, as they continued to be baptized and catechized under Lutheran auspices, African Americans frequently found that their vernacular expressions of worship and song were not recognized by the wider Lutheran community. (9)
>
> As the first African American worship supplement prepared for use among Lutherans, *This Far by Faith* joyfully joins this conversation in progress. It is a proposal for addressing issues of worship from a perspective of particular culture and at the same time being faithful to the worship patterns of the church through the ages. To that end, this volume provides an important contribution to the global discussion on worship and culture by making available to African American Lutherans and to the wider church some of the riches of African American liturgy and song. (11)

TFBF, organized by church year and then by topic, includes 264 "Hymns and Songs," not all of them of African American origin. The Easter section, for example, includes Herbert Brokering's hymn "Alleluia! Jesus Is Risen," set to David Johnson's wonderful tune EARTH AND ALL STARS. In the section "The Word" we find Luther's "A Mighty Fortress Is Our God" in the isometric version from LBW, and in the "Witness" section Daniel Schutte's "I, the Lord of Sea and Sky." Such additions to TFBF neither overwhelm nor detract from the riches of African American song brought forward in this resource.

In 2006 the two largest Lutheran church bodies in America—the ELCA and the LCMS—each published new hymnals; these two books continue to serve many of the Lutheran congregations in the United States.

2006. *Evangelical Lutheran Worship*. Minneapolis: Augsburg Fortress.

Evangelical Lutheran Worship is approved for use in the Evangelical Lutheran Church in America.

Evangelical Lutheran Worship is approved for use in the Evangelical Lutheran Church in Canada and is commended to this church as its primary worship resource.

From the Introduction to *Evangelical Lutheran Worship* (ELW):

At the beginning of the twenty-first century, *Evangelical Lutheran Worship* continues the renewal of worship that has taken place over the three centuries Lutherans have been on the North American continent and in the Caribbean region. During this time, renewal efforts have been marked by a movement from a variety of Lutheran immigrant traditions toward a greater similarity of liturgical forms and a more common repertoire of song. . . . In the twentieth century, the consolidation of various immigrant Lutheran church bodies and those more established on this continent was reflected in the primary worship books used by mid-century, namely *Service Book and Hymnal* and *The Lutheran Hymnal*. In 1978 *Lutheran Book of Worship* was published, the fruit of an ambitious inter-Lutheran project that sought to unite most North American Lutherans in the use of a single worship book with shared liturgical forms and a common repertoire of hymnody.

The years since the publication of *Lutheran Book of Worship* have seen many changes within the church and the world. . . . A growing awareness of the interrelatedness of the world, coupled with new understandings of the world's diverse cultures, has had implications also for the church as the one body of Christ throughout the world. The use of language continues to develop in response to context and societal change, as does the use of more than one language in worship. Forms of musical expression have blossomed, and churches have embraced many of these forms for use in worship.

Evangelical Lutheran Worship is a core rather than a comprehensive resource. The collection of materials is more expansive than its predecessor; it reflects a body of prayer and song that our churches consider worthy to hold in common; and, in many contexts, it will provide most or all of what is needed for the assembly's worship. Still, it is not possible or necessary for a single worship book to contain all the expressions of worship desired in every context by an increasingly diverse church. The book contains notable representatives of a wide variety of liturgical texts and musical forms that point to repertoires outside this volume.

Evangelical Lutheran Worship represents the gifts of the breadth of the church of Christ, and prizes the words and songs we hold in common with other Christians. At the same time, it treasures and extends the particular accents of our Lutheran inheritance as gifts to the whole church. (7–8)

As in WOV, the 1995 supplement, the African American spiritual is well represented in ELW. ELW also excels in the amount and variety of hymns drawn from the large body of Spanish–language hymnody. From twenty-first-century writers, the hymns of Marty Haugen, Delores Dufner, OSB, Susan Palo Cherwien, and Herman G. Stuempfle Jr. are particularly well represented.[7]

2006. *Lutheran Service Book*. St. Louis: Concordia Publishing House.

Prepared by The Commission on Worship of The Lutheran Church—Missouri Synod.

From the Introduction to *Lutheran Service Book* (LSB):

Within the Lutheran tradition, the wedding of the Word of God to melody was modeled by the reformer himself. Martin Luther had a high regard for music and urged the Church to use it wisely as a vehicle for proclaiming the Gospel. "Next to theology," he wrote, "I accord to music the highest place and the greatest honor." Retaining the best of pre-Reformation hymnody, as well as adding a great number of new hymns to the Church's song, Luther and succeeding generations of hymnwriters continue to inspire the faithful to lift their voices in praise and thanksgiving to the triune God. (viii)

Lutheran Service Book now continues the Church's song into the twenty-first century. Officially accepted at the Synod's 2004 Convention, *Lutheran Service Book* is a careful blending of the best of *The Lutheran Hymnal* and *Lutheran Worship*. It offers treasured melodies and texts that have nourished God's people for generations. (ix)

In every age God also blesses His people by raising up hymnwriters who have honed their craft to create rich and fresh expressions of praise. Produced during the most prolific period of English-language hymn writing in the history of Christendom, *Lutheran Service Book* delivers a rich feast of Gospel-centered hymns from every age and from many lands. (ix)

One such hymnwriter providing "fresh expressions" is Stephen P. Starke, LSB including twenty-seven of his original texts and thus providing the church yet new means for sung proclamation and praise. LSB also drew generously from the treasure of new hymn texts by Timothy Dudley-Smith and Herman G. Stuempfle Jr., while not ignoring the rich heritage

---

7. There is a hymnal companion for ELW: Paul Westermeyer, *Hymnal Companion to Evangelical Lutheran Worship* (Minneapolis: Augsburg Fortress, 2010).

of Lutheran hymnody, including twenty-seven texts by Luther and seventeen by Paul Gerhardt.[8]

SPANISH- AND FRENCH-LANGUAGE HYMNALS FOR LUTHERANS IN THE AMERICAS

1991. *Cantad al Señor.* St. Louis: Concordia Publishing House.

Cantad al Señor includes 111 hymns, organized around the church year (hymns 1–24) and then by topic. Committee members for this hymnal project came from Argentina, Guatemala, Mexico, Panama, the United States, and Venezuela.

1998. *Libro de Liturgia y Cántico.* Minneapolis: Augsburg Fortress.

Developed by and recommended for use in the Evangelical Lutheran Church in America.

After a selection of Psalms and a section entitled "Canticas Liturgicas," the section of "Himnos y canticos" is organized by church year (275–378) and then by topic (379–624).

2009. *Liturgies et cantiques Luthériens.* Winnipeg: Éditions de l'Église Luthérienne du Canada.

Préparé par le Comité liturgique francophone de l'Église luthérienne du Canada.

Members of the committee were David Saar and David Somers, pastors in the Lutheran Church—Canada.

Hymn section: 307–740. The hymns are categorized according to the same headings used in LSB, this hymnal being a French-language counterpart to LSB.

2022. *Himnario Luterano.* Macomb, MI: Lutheran Heritage Foundation.[9]

---

8. There is a hymnal companion for LSB: *Lutheran Service Book: Companion to the Hymns*, ed. Joseph Herl, Peter C. Reske, and Jon D. Vieker, 2 vols. (St. Louis: Concordia, 2019).

9. A review of *Himnario Luterano* by Geoffrey R. Boyle, in *Concordia Theological Quarterly* 87 (April 2023): 185–187, very helpfully compares this hymnal to its two predecessors: *Culto Cristiano* (1964) and *Cantad al Señor* (1991).

On July 20, 2022 the Lutheran Heritage Foundation (www.lhfmissions.org) announced that "The new Spanish Lutheran Hymnal (*Himnario Luterano*) has been released in the Dominican Republic. 19,000 copies have been printed and are now on their way to Lutheran churches throughout North, Central and South America. . . . At almost 1,100 pages in length, *Himnario Luterano* contains nearly 670 hymns, 90 Psalms, 5 orders of Divine Service, 2 Matins services, 2 Vespers services, Luther's *Small Catechism* and more."

INTERNATIONAL AND GLOBAL HYMNALS

Toward the end of 1523, a handful of hymns in the vernacular were gathered together in Wittenberg to form the first Lutheran hymnal in the *Achtliederbuch* of 1524. Now, five hundred years later, there are few countries or languages that are without Lutheran hymnals.

In the second half of the twentieth century, as the world recovered from the disruption and disunity of a world war, different worldwide movements for unity and cooperation came into being. One of them was the Lutheran World Federation (LWF), founded in 1947: "a global communion of churches in the Lutheran tradition, living and working together for a just, peaceful, and reconciled world." The inaugural LWF Assembly was held in Lund, Sweden, in 1947, the first of what has become a LWF tradition: an Assembly of delegates from all the member churches that meets every six or seven years to consider issues of common concern. Each day begins with worship, which of necessity must be multilingual. For the second Assembly held in Hanover in 1952, a multilingual hymnal was prepared with the single-word title *Laudamus* ("We praise" from *Te Deum laudamus*). Appropriately, it was given a bilingual subtitle: *Hymnal for the Lutheran World Federation. Gesangbuch für den lutherischen Weltbund*. For each of the next five Assemblies a new edition of *Laudamus* was prepared: second edition, Minneapolis, 1957; third edition, Helsinki, 1963; fourth edition, Evian, 1970[10]; and fifth edition, Budapest, 1984.

Although in the first instance *Laudamus* was designed for the daily worship of the respective Assembly, it was not restricted to this use, as explained in the foreword to the fifth edition:

---

10. This edition was edited by Ulrich S. Leupold, the editor of LW 53, *Liturgy and Hymns* (1965).

Over the years, *Laudamus* has become widely known, and its use has broadened accordingly. No longer is it intended for assemblies only. It is used increasingly in ministries to tourists and itinerants where its multilingual aspect is especially important. It finds use in many meetings of Lutherans around the world, and even in other international ecumenical gatherings.[11]

Nevertheless, the hymnal was shaped by its function as the songbook for daily worship of the international Assemblies:

> For reasons that are mostly pragmatic, the hymn collection [*Laudamus*] remains rather conservative. When people meet together for only a few days of worship and work, there is little time or inclination to learn new things in order to worship.[12]

Therefore, although the collection of 154 hymns does contain a few hymns from Asia, Africa, and Latin America, "the hymnal is still characterized by a core of classic Lutheran hymns of Northern European origin."[13] For its time *Laudamus* provided what was needed when Lutherans who sing in different languages came together to worship. There was a growing realization that more was required than a simple collection of hymns in different languages. Thus, the last edition of *Laudamus* was for the Budapest Assembly of 1984, and the worship of later Assemblies became increasingly global in scope and content, a trend that is observable in the hymnals reviewed in the earlier part of this chapter.

In 2019, in preparation for the five-hundredth anniversary of the publication of the *Achtliederbuch* in 1524, the Lutheran World Federation, in collaboration with the Liturgical Institute of Leipzig University under the leadership of Dr. Uwe Steinmetz, initiated a five-year study project for its 148 member churches in ninety-nine countries. The goal was for each area to explore their Lutheran heritage and identity in an international context. With an overall title for the project of *Pilgrimage, Freedom, Belonging: Lutheran Hymns and Rites 2024*, the aim was:

> to experience the diverse ways of spirituality and mission in which our member churches embody the Lutheran tradition in diverse cultural contexts. Within new horizons of economic, political, scientific,

---

11. Carl H. Mau, Jr., "Foreword," *Laudamus*, 5th ed. (Budapest: Lutheran World Federation, 1984), v.
12. Mau, "Foreword," *Laudamus*, v–vi.
13. Mau, "Foreword," *Laudamus*, v.

technological and psycho-social developments, we want to discern ways in which we creatively express law and gospel, faith and works, nature and grace, justification and sanctification, freedom and vocation—marks of our common Lutheran heritage.[14]

The eight hymns of the *Achtliederbuch* provided the framework for the project:

> The *Achtliederbuch* of 1524 documented the reformation movement for the first time through a collection of eight songs previously printed on pamphlets. The eight songs form a snapshot of the heartfelt concerns by the young movement, the first attempt of situating the reformation ideas in the relationship with the world and God in song forms.
>
> Following the inspiration of the *Achtliederbuch*, the *Global Achtliederbuch 2024* documents a collection of music and liturgical elements (rites) that sketch out hopes and visions of being Christian in a Lutheran tradition from a global perspective in our age and presents a mosaic of Christian expressivity in contemporary language and sound in the cultures of the seven world regions of Lutheranism. As the vertical eighth region, the liturgical heritage of Luther is reflected in its historical development, its transformational processes, and in relation to its situatedness in socio-cultural contexts in the Lutheran world regions today. [15]

The LWF member churches encompass the world in seven horizontal regions: (1) Africa; (2) Asia; (3) Central Eastern Europe; (4) Central Western Europe; (5) Latin America and the Caribbean; (6) Nordic Countries; and (7) North America. The eighth is the vertical region of history: Luther's hymnic and liturgical heritage. Between Reformation Day, October 31, 2022, and the end of February 2023 Lutherans in each of the seven world regions were encouraged to submit new hymns and liturgies in the musical idioms and styles that express the culture and ethnicity of their particular region, including new arrangements of Lutheran chorales. During the first half of 2023 an editorial team chose what was to be included, and later the same year the new truly global hymnal was typeset and printed; it now carries the simpler title *The Global Songbook 2024*, though some still think of it as *The Global Achtliederbuch*

---

14. For the background see Uwe Steinmetz, "Rites and Hymns of the Anthropocene. Formierungsprozesse christlicher Identität in Liturgien und Musik des weltweiten luthertums," *Kerygma und Dogma* 67/4 (2021): 306; and https://www.hymnsandrites2024.org/ accessed 4/30/2023.
15. https://www.hymnsandrites2024.org/book-2024/ 5/1/2023.

2024. The hymnal is made up of around two hundred songs, mostly written and composed within the last few decades, together with others that originated in more recent times as part of the world-wide project. The hymnal had a fairly limited print-run. This is because it is available on-line, where readers can find additional arrangements for voices and instruments and explore hymnological and liturgical developments. As the first hymnals originated from Wittenberg and from thence to the world, so the presentation of *The Global Songbook 2024* to the world was from Wittenberg on June 29, 2024, followed by similar beginnings in other world regions thereafter.

In the same way that the first five hundred years of Lutheran hymnals began with the *Achtliederbuch*, so the second five hundred years has begun with the *Global Achtliederbuch*.

"A New Song We Now Begin."

Select Bibliography

Ameln, Konrad. "Das Achtliederbuch vom Jahre 1523/24." JbLH 2 (1956): 89–91.

———. *The Roots of German Hymnody of the Reformation Era*. St. Louis: Concordia, 1964.

———. "Das Klugsche Gesangbuch, Wittenburg 1529: Versuche einer Rekonstruktion." JbLH, 16 (1971): 159–162.

———. "Luthers Kirchenlied und Gesangbuch: Offene Fragen." JbLH 32 (1989): 19–28.

Bachmann, Johann Friedrich. *Zur Geschichte der Berliner Gesangbücher*. Berlin: Schultze, 1856.

Bialek, Roland. "Das Gesangbuch und sein Einband." JbLH 39 (2000): 191–211.

Blankenburg, Walter. "Das Gothaer Cantionale Sacrum," JbLH 15 (1970): 145–153.

———. "Johann Walters Chorgesangbuch von 1524 in hymnologischer Sicht: Zum Beginn der Geschichte des evangelischen Kirchenliedes vor 450 Jahren." JbLH 18 (1973/74): 65–96.

———. "Der Einfluß des Kirchenliedes des 17. Jahrhunderts auf die Geschichte des evangelischen Gesangbuches und der Kirchenmusik." In *Das protestantische Kirchenlied im 16. und 17. Jahrhundert: Text-, musik- und theologiegeschichtliche Probleme*, edited by Alfred Dürr and Walther Killy, 73–85. Wiesbaden: Harrassowitz, 1986.

Blume, Friedrich. *Protestant Church Music: A History*. New York: Norton, 1974.

Böhme, Franz M. *Altdeutsches Liederbuch: Volkslied der Deutschen nach Wort und Weise aus dem 12. bis zum 17. Jahrhundert*, 3rd ed. Leipzig: Breitkopf & Härtel, 1925.

Böker-Heil, N., and H. Heckmann, and I. Kindermann, eds. *Das Tenorlied. Mehrstimmige Lieder in deutschen Quellen 1450–1580*, 3 vols., Kassel: Bärenreiter, 1979–1986.

Bosinski, Gerhard. "Joachim Slüter und Luthers Gesangbuch von 1529," *Theologische Literaturezeitung*, 108 (1983): 705–722.

Brecht, Martin. *Martin Luther*, 3 vols. Stuttgart: Calwer, 1981–1987; *Martin Luther*, translated by James L. Schaaf. Philadelphia: Fortress Press, 1985–1993.

Brown, Christopher Boyd. "Devotional Life in Hymns, Liturgy, Music, and Prayer." In *Lutheran Ecclesiastical Culture, 1550–1675*, edited by Robert Kolb, 205–258. Leiden: Brill, 2008.

Bunners, Christian. *Johann Crüger (1598–1662): Berliner Musiker und Kantor, lutherischer Lied– und Gesangbuchschöpfer*. Berlin: Frank & Timme, 2012.

———. *Paul Gerhardt: Weg, Werk, Wirkung*, rev. ed. Berlin: Buchverlag Union, 1993.

Clarke, Martin V. "'Come, All You People' Lutheran Influences on the Spread of Global Hymnody." CLM 337–350.

Classen, Albrecht, ed. *Deutsche Liederbücher des 15. und 16. Jahrhunderts*. Münster: Waxmann, 2001.

Cyprian, Ernst Salomon. *Die Hauskirche, oder erbauliche Schrifften, welche zu häuslicher Übung der Gottseligkeit mit sonderbarem Nutzen gebrauchet werden können*. Gotha: Reyher, 1739.

Czaika, Otfried. "A Vast and Unfamiliar Field: Swedish Hymnals and Hymn-Printing in the Sixteenth Century." In *Celebrating Lutheran Music: Scholarly Perspectives at the Quincentenary*, edited by Maria Schildt, Mattias Lundberg, and Jonas Lundblad, 125–138. Uppsala: Universitet, 2019.

de Laix, Esther Criscuola. "'Before Our Time': Latin and Lay Latinity in Early Lutheran Hymnals." *Celebrating Lutheran Music: Scholarly Perspectives at the Quincentenary*, eds. Maria Schildt, Mattias Lundberg and Jonas Lundblad. Uppsala: Universitet, 2019, 17–32.

Dürr, Alfred, and Walther Killy, eds. *Das protestantische Kirchenlied im 16. und 17. Jahrhundert: Text-, musik- und theologiegeschichtliche Probleme*. Wiesbaden: Harrassowitz, 1986.

Fischer, Albert F. W. *Das deutsche evangelische Kirchenlied des 17. Jahrhunderts*, ed. Wilhelm Tümpel, 6 vols. Gütersloh: Bertelsmann, 1904–1916.

Fischer–Krückeberg, Elisabeth. "Johann Crüger's Praxis pietatis melica," *Jahrbuch für Brandenburgische Kirchengeschichte* 26 (1931): 27–52.

Georgius, Theophilus. *Allgemeines Bücher- Lexicon, In welchem nach Ordnung des Dictionarii die allermeisten Autores oder Gattungen von Büchern zu finden* . . . Leipzig: Georgius, 1742.
Glover, Raymond F., ed. *The Hymnal 1982 Companion*. New York: Church Hymnal Corporation, 1990–1994.
Gottschaldts, Johann Jacob. *Sammlung von allerhand auserlesenen Lieder-Remarqüien In Sechs Teilen*. Leipzig: Martini, 1748.
Graff, Paul. *Geschichte der Auflösung der alten gottesdienstlichen Formen in der evangelischen Kirche Deutschlands*. Göttingen: Vandenhoeck & Ruprecht, 1937–1939.
Grimm, Jürgen. *Das Neu Leipziger Gesangbuch des Gottfried Vopelius (Leipzig 1682): Untersuchungen zur Klärung seiner geschichtlichen Stellung*. Berlin: Merseburger, 1969.
Grindal, Gracia. "Hymnals." In *Dictionary of Luther and the Lutheran Traditions*, edited by Timothy J. Wengert, et al., 350–352. Grand Rapids: Baker, 2017.
———. *Preaching from Home: The Stories of Seven Lutheran Women Hymn Writers*. Minneapolis: Fortress Press, 2017.
———. "The Swedish Tradition in Hymnals and Songbooks," LQ 5 (1991): 435–468.
Hase, Martin von. "Ein Enchiridionfund (Erfurt, Johannes Loersfelt 1525)." *Archiv für Reformationsgeschichte* 39 (1942): 254–255.
———. "Die Drucker der Erfurter Enchiridien." JbLH 2 (1956): 91–93.
Herl, Joseph. *Worship Wars in Early Lutheranism: Choir, Congregation, and Three Centuries of Conflict*. New York: Oxford University Press, 2004.
———, Peter C. Reske, and Jon D. Vieker. *Lutheran Service Book: Companion to the Hymns*. St. Louis: Concordia, 2019.
Hillerbrand, Hans J. *The Oxford Encyclopedia of the Reformation*, 4 vols. New York: Oxford University Press, 1996.
Jenny, Markus. "Luthers Gesangbuch." *Leben und Werk Martin Luthers von 1526 bis 1546: Festgabe zu seinem 500. Geburtstag*. Edited by Helmar Junghans, 1: 301–321 and 2: 825–832. Berlin: Evangelische Verlagsanstalt, 1983.
———, ed. *Luther's Geistliche Lieder und Kirchen gesänge: Vollständige Neuedition in Ergänzung zu Band der Weimarer Ausgabe* [= AWA 4]. Cologne: Böhlau, 1985.
Junghans, Helmar, ed. *Leben und Werk Martin Luthers von 1526 bis 1546: Festgabe zu seinem 500. Geburtstag*. Berlin: Evangelische Verlagsanstalt, 1983.

———. *Martin Luther und Wittenberg.* Munich: Koehler & Amelang, 1996.
Kadelbach, Ada. "Das 'Achtliederbuch' vom Jahre '1523/1524': Zu unserer Faksimile-Bielage." JbLH 50 (2011): 30–34.
Koch, Eduard Emil, and Richard Lauxmann. *Geschichte des Kirchenlieds und Kirchengesangs der christlichen, insbesondere der deutschen evangelischen Kirche,* 3rd ed. Stuttgart: Belser, 1866–1877; reprint, Hildesheim: Olms, 1973.
Korth, Hans-Otto and Wolfgang Miersemann, eds. *Praxis Pietatis Melica: Edition und Dokumentation der Werkgeschichte,* 2 vols. in 5. Halle: Franckesche Stiftungen, 2014–2024.
Kouba, Jan. "Die ältest Gesangbuchdruck von 1501 aus Böhmen." JbLH 13 (1968): 78–112.
Kümmerle, Salomon. *Encyklopedie der evangelischen Kirchenmusik.* Gütersloh: Bertelsmann, 1888–1895; reprint Hildesheim: Olms, 1974.
Leaver, Robin A. *"Goostly Psalmes and Spirituall Songes": English and Dutch Metrical Psalms from Coverdale to Utenhove 1535–1566.* Oxford: Clarendon, 1991.
———. "Hymnals." *The Oxford Encyclopedia of the Reformation.* Edited by Hans J. Hillerbrand, 2: 286–89. New York: Oxford University Press, 1996.
———. "Hymnals." *The Encyclopedia of Protestantism.* Edited by Hans J. Hillerbrand, 2: 908–920. New York: Routledge, 2004.
———. *Luther's Liturgical Music: Principles and Implications.* Minneapolis: Fortress Press, 2017.
———. *The Whole Church Sings: Congregational Singing in Luther's Wittenberg.* Grand Rapids, MI: Eerdmans, 2017.
Lundberg, Mattias, Maria Schildt, and Jonas Lundblad, eds. *Lutheran Music Culture: Ideals and Practices.* Berlin: de Gruyter, 2021.
———, ———, ———, eds. *Celebrating Lutheran Music: Scholarly Perspectives at the Quincentenary.* [CLM] Uppsala: Uppsala University, 2019.
Lundeen, Joel. "Lutheran Hymnbooks in America: A Checklist of Major Titles," 1978. Vertical File: Hymn books. Archives of the Evangelical Lutheran Church in America, Elk Grove Village, Illinois.
Messmer, Franzpeter. *Altdeutsche Liedkomposition. Der Kantionalsatz und die Tradition der Einheit von Singen und Dichten.* Tutzing: Schneider, 1984.
Oettinger, Rebecca Wagner. *Music as Propaganda in the German Reformation.* Aldershot: Ashgate, 2001.
Olearius, Johann Christoph. *Evangelischer Lieder-Schatz darinn allerhand Auserlesene Gesänge.* Jena: Bielke, 1705–1707.

———. *Jubilirende Lieder-Freude: Bestehend in erster Aufflage derer allerersten A. C. 1524. und 1525. in Druck gegangenen Lutherischen Gesängen zur Vermehrung schuldigster Devotion und Danckbarkeit, bey dem Andern von Gott verliehenen Lutherischen Reformations-Jubilaeo*. Arnstadt: Meurer, 1717.

Paasch, Kathrin, ed. *"Mit Lust und Liebe singen": die Reformation und ihre Lieder. Begleitband zur Ausstellung der Universitäts- und Forschungsbibliothek Erfurt/Gotha in Zusammenarbeit mit der Stiftung Schloss Friedenstein Gotha, 5. May bis 12 August, 2012*. Gotha: [Universitäts- und Forschungsbibliothek], 2012.

Polack, William Gustave. *The Handbook to the Lutheran Hymnal*. 3rd ed. St. Louis: Concordia, 1958.

Rathgeber, Christina. "The Reception of Brandenburg-Prussia's New Lutheran Hymnal of 1781," *The Historical Journal* 36 (1993): 115–136.

Reckziegel, Walter. *Das Cantional von Johann Hermann Schein: Seine geschichtlichen Grundlagen*. Berlin: Merseberger, 1963.

Riederer, Johann Bartholomäus. *Abhandlung von Einführung des teutschen Gesangs in die evangelischlutherische Kirche überhaupts und in die nürnbergische besonders: wobey auch von den ältesten Gesangbüchern und Liedern so bis zum Tode Lutheri herausgegeben und verfertigt worden gehandelt wird*. Nuremberg: Endter, 1759; facsimile, Leipzig: Zentralantiquariat, 1975.

Röbbelen, Ingeborg. *Theologie und Frömmigkeit im deutschen evangelischlutherischen Gesangbuch des 17. und frühen 18. Jahrhunderts*. Göttingen: Vandenhoeck & Ruprecht, 1957.

Rößler, Martin. "Die Frühzeit hymnologischer Forschung." JbLH 19 (1975): 123–86.

———. *Geistliches Lied und kirchliches Gesangbuch*. Berlin: Strube, 2006.

Ryden, Ernest E. "Hymnals." In *The Encyclopedia of the Lutheran Church*. Edited by Julius Bodensieck. Minneapolis: Augsburg, 1965, 2: 1072–1090.

Schalk, Carl F. *The Roots of Hymnody in The Lutheran Church—Missouri Synod*. St. Louis: Concordia, 1965.

———. *God's Song in a New Land: Lutheran Hymnals in America*. St. Louis: Concordia, 1995.

———. *Source Documents in American Hymnody*. St. Louis: Concordia, 1996.

Schlüter, Marie. *Musikgeschichte Wittenbergs im 16. Jahrhundert: Quellenkundliche und sozialgeschichtliche Untersuchungen*. Göttingen: V&R unipress, 2010.

Schulz, Frieder. *Martin Luther. Ein Betbüchlein mit Kalender und Passional Wittenberg 1529.* Kassel: Stauda, 1982.
Scribner, Robert W. *For the Sake of Simple Folk: Popular Propaganda for the German Reformation.* Oxford: Clarendon, 1994.
Seaman, William R. *Companion to the Service Book and Hymnal.* Minneapolis: Commission on the Liturgy and Hymnal, 1976.
Seibt, Ilsabe. *Friedrich Schleiermacher und das Berliner Gesangbuch von 1829.* Göttingen: Vandenhoeck & Ruprecht, 1998.
Sommer, Ernst. "Das Gesangbuch von Valentin Bapst, Leipzig 1545: Eine kritische Betrachtung der Melodien." JbLH 11 (1966): 146–161.
Stapel, Wilhelm, ed. *Luthers Lieder und Gedichte: Mit Einleitung und Erläuterungen.* Stuttgart: Evangelisches Verlagswerk, 1950.
Stauffer, S. Anita., ed. *Christian Worship: Unity in Cultural Diversity.* LWF Studies. Geneva: Lutheran World Federation, 1996.
Steinmetz, Uwe. "Rites and Hymns of the Anthropocene. Formierungsprozesse christlicher Identität in Liturgien und Musik des weltweiten luthertums," *Kerygma und Dogma* 67/4 (2021): 306–325.
Stulken, Maralyn Kay. *Hymnal Companion to the Lutheran Book of Worship.* Philadelphia: Fortress Press, 1981.
———. *With One Voice: Reference Companion.* Minneapolis: Augsburg Fortress, 2000.
Veit, Patrice. *Das Kirchenlied in der Reformation Martin Luthers: Eine thematische und semantische Untersuchung.* Stuttgart: Steiner, 1986.
Vieker, Jon D. "C. F. W. Walther: Editor of Missouri's First and Only German Hymnal," *Concordia Historical Institute Quarterly* 65/2 (1992): 62–64.
———. *August Crull and the Story of the Evangelical Lutheran Hymn-Book (1912).* Minneapolis: Lutheran University Press, 2013.
Voigt, Louis. *Hymnbooks at Wittenberg: A classified catalog to the collection of Hamma School of Theology, Wittenberg School of Music Thomas Library.* Springfield: Chantry, 1975; a major heading was unfortunately omitted—*General Synod of the Evangelical Lutheran Church in the U.S.A.*—which should have been inserted before no. 283.
Volz, Hans. "Die Wittenberger Gesangbuchdrucker Joseph Klug und Hans Lufft." JbLH 4 (1958/59): 129–133.
Wackernagel, Philipp. *Bibliographie zur Geschichte des deutschen Kirchenliedes im XVI. Jahrhundert.* Frankfurt: Heyder & Zimmer, 1855; reprint, Hildesheim: Olms, 1961.

———. *Das deutsche Kirchenlied von der ältesten Zeit bis zu Anfang des XVII. Jahrhunderts.* Leipzig: Teubner, 1864–1877; reprint, Hildesheim: Olms, 1964. The major part of Vol. 1 (pages 365–817) is a substantial supplement to Wackernagel's 1855 *Bibliographie zur Geschichte des deutschen Kirchenliedes.*

Walther, Carl Ferdinand Wilhelm Walther. *Kirchen-Gesangbuch für evangelisch-lutherische Gemeinden ungeä̈nderter Augsburgischer Confession, darin des sel[igen] Dr. Martin Luthers und anderer geistreichen Lehrer gebräuchlichste Kirchen-Lieder enthalten sind*, ed. C. F. W. Walther. St. Louis: Verlag der deutschen evang. luth. Gemeinde u. A. C. 1847. English version: *Walther's Hymnal: Church Hymnbook for Evangelical Lutheran Congregations of the Unaltered Augsburg Confession.* Translated and edited by Matthew Carver. St. Louis: Concordia, 2012.

Watson, Richard and Emma Hornby, eds. *The Canterbury Dictionary of Hymnology.* <http://www.hymnology.co.uk>

Weber, Édith. "'Nota contra Notam' et ses incidences sur le Choral Luthérien et sur le Psautier Huguenot," JbLH 32 (1989): 73–93.

Wegener, Johann. "Das erste Wittenberger Gemeindegesangbuch." *Monatsschrift für Gottesdienst und Kirchliche Kunst* 4 (1899): 7–11.

Wennemuth, Heike. "Bibliographie deutschsprachiger Gesangbücher: Ein Forschungsprojekt an der Universität Mainz." JbLH 42 (2003): 216–220. Description of the research project of the University of Mainz, a database of German language hymnals, accessible from: https://gesangbuchbibliographie.uni-mainz.de/index.php

Westermeyer, Paul. *Assembly Song Companion to All Creation Sings.* Minneapolis: Augsburg Fortress, 2023.

Wissemann-Garbe, Daniela. "Neue Weisen zu alten Lieder: Die Ersatzmelodien im Klugschen Gesangbuch," JbLH 37 (1998): 118–138.

Zahn, Johannes. *Die Melodien der deutschen evangelischen Kirchenlieder*, 6 vols. Gütersloh: Bertelsmann, 1889–1893; reprint Hildesheim: Olms, 1963. Vol. 6 is a detailed bibliography of hymnals that include music.

Zedler, Johann Heinrich. *Grosses vollständiges Universal Lexicon Aller Wissenschafften und Künste* (Leipzig: Zedler, 1731–1754).

Contributors

Mark A. Granquist is the Lloyd and Annelotte Svendsbye professor of the history of christianity at Luther Seminary, St. Paul, Minnesota. Before this he taught at St. Olaf College and Gustavus Adolphus College. A historian of the Lutheran experience in North America, his publications include *Lutherans in America: A New History* (Fortress Press, 2015) and *A History of Luther Seminary, 1869–2019* (Fortress Press, 2019), among other books. He served as an editor of the *Dictionary of Luther and the Lutheran Traditions* (Baker, 2017) and serves as the editor of the journals *Word & World* and the *Journal of the Lutheran Historical Conference*.

Paul J. Grime serves as professor, dean of the chapel, and vice president of spiritual formation at Concordia Theological Seminary, Fort Wayne, Indiana. From 1996 to 2007 he was executive director for the Commission on Worship of The Lutheran Church–Missouri Synod. During that time, he was project director for the development of that church's hymnal, *Lutheran Service Book* (Concordia, 2006). His degrees are from Valparaiso University, the College-Conservatory of Music at the University of Cincinnati, Concordia Theological Seminary, and Marquette University. He is the composer of numerous hymn preludes and editor of *Lutheran Service Book: Companion to the Services* (Concordia, 2022).

Gracia Grindal graduated from Augsburg College in 1965 and earned an MFA in poetry at the University of Arkansas (1969). She then taught creative writing at Luther College. While there, she worked on the Hymn Text Committee of the *Lutheran Book of Worship* (1978). In 1984 she began teaching at Luther Seminary. Her *Preaching from Home*, a book about six Scandinavian hymn writers, was published in 2011 by Fortress Press. She has written over eight hundred hymn texts for the Revised Common Lectionary and other occasions, plus many translations of Scandinavian hymns, biographies of several Norwegian American women, and several books of poetry, including *Jesus the Harmony: Gospel Sonnets for 366 Days* (Fortress Press, 2021).

Joseph Herl is professor of music at Concordia University, Nebraska, and research professor at the University of Illinois at Urbana-Champaign, where he directs the Hymn Tune Index (hymntune.library.illinois.edu). His books include *Worship Wars in Early Lutheranism*, which received the 2005 Roland Bainton Prize of the Sixteenth Century Society and Conference. He was editor, with Peter C. Reske and Jon D. Vieker, of *Lutheran Service Book: Companion to the Hymns* (Concordia, 2019), and in 2018 he received Concordia University's annual teaching award.

Robin A. Leaver is emeritus professor of sacred music at Westminster Choir College, Princeton, New Jersey. He has also taught at the Juilliard School, Yale University, and Queen's University, Belfast, Northern Ireland. Dr. Leaver has served on the executive committee of the Hymn Society of Great Britain and Ireland, is a past president of the Internationale Arbeitsgemeinschaft für Hymnologie, and was a member of the editorial committee that produced the Episcopal *Hymnal 1982 Companion* (1991–1996). He has served as a consulting editor for the *Jahrbuch für Liturgik und Hymnologie* since 1976 and is a past president of the American Bach Society. In addition to various Luther and Bach studies, he is also the author of numerous books, articles, and entries in reference works in the cross-disciplinary areas of liturgy, church music, theology, and hymnology.

Dianne M. McMullen is John Howard Payne professor of music and college organist at Union College in Schenectady, New York. Previously she taught at Adelphi University, UCLA, and the University of Michigan-Dearborn. She is coeditor, with Wolfgang Miersemann, of *Johann Anastasius Freylinghausen. Geistreiches Gesangbuch. Edition und Kommentar* (six volumes, 2004–2020). She has received grants from Fulbright, DAAD, and others. In addition to her work on Freylinghausen, she currently studies Renaissance dance music and nineteenth-century Swiss Reformed music. She holds degrees from Smith College (A.B. music) and the University of Michigan-Ann Arbor (M.M. organ performance, Ph.D. musicology). She has served as a church organist in Michigan, New York, and Massachusetts.

Markus Rathey is the Robert S. Tangeman professor at Yale University, where he teaches music history at the Institute of Sacred Music and the Divinity School. Before his tenure at Yale, he was post-doc at the hymnological graduate center "Geistliches Lied und Kirchenlied" at Mainz

University. His publications include a book on the German hymn writer and composer Johann Rudolph Ahle (Wagner, 1999) and a monograph on Bach's *Christmas Oratorio* (Oxford, 2016), as well as an introduction to *Bach's Major Vocal Works* (Yale, 2016). He has authored hymn commentaries for the *Handbuch zum Evangelischen Gesangbuch* (Vandenhoeck & Ruprecht, 2000–) and the Swiss *Ökumenischer Liederkommentar* (Theologischer Verlag Zurich TVZ, 2000–); he is also the author of numerous articles on hymn writers for the encyclopedia *Die Musik in Geschichte und Gegenwart*, 2nd edition (Bärenreiter,1994–).

Jon D. Vieker is associate professor of Practical Theology and Dean of Chapel at Concordia Seminary, St. Louis. Vieker received a BA in music from California Lutheran University, Thousand Oaks, California, and M.Div., STM, and PhD degrees from Concordia Seminary, St. Louis, Missouri. His areas of academic interest include the study of hymns, hymn writers, and hymnals, especially as viewed through the history of American Lutheranism and the wider American ecclesial context. Vieker served as assistant director for the LCMS Commission on Worship during the research, development, editing and production of *Lutheran Service Book* and its core companion volumes. He later served as senior assistant to the president of the LCMS.

Paul Westermeyer is emeritus professor of church music at Luther Seminary, where he also served as cantor and directed the Master of Sacred Music degree program with St. Olaf College. Before that he taught at Elmhurst College. A past president of the Hymn Society and editor of *The Hymn*, he wrote the hymnal Companions for *Evangelical Lutheran Worship* (Fortress Press, 2006) and *All Creation Sings* (Augsburg Fortress, 2020). His degrees are from Elmhurst College, Lancaster Seminary, Union Seminary's School of Sacred Music, and the University of Chicago. His life's work has been devoted to studying the church's music and hymnody.

Daniel Zager is retired from the Eastman School of Music (University of Rochester) where he served for twenty-one years as associate dean and head of Sibley Music Library and associate professor of music, teaching sacred music courses in both the musicology and organ departments. He holds the BMus degree in organ performance from the University of Wisconsin-Madison and a PhD in musicology from the University of Minnesota. He was a member of the Hymnody Committee for the *Lutheran Service Book* (Concordia, 2006), and is the author of *Lutheran Music and Meaning* (Concordia, 2023).

Index

Achtliederbuch (Gutknecht, Nuremberg, 1524), 27–28, 45–52, 57, 179, 280–283
   Luther's hymns, 46–49
   Speratus's hymns, 13, 78–79
   reprint of 1717, 14, 16
Agricola, Johann, 42, 44, 78
Agricola, Mikael, 203, 205
American Lutheranism, 25, 154, 160, 189–223, 232–244
   quest for a united hymnal, 25, 28–30, 229–30, 233, 239–40, 268, 280
Arnstadt, 2, 6–7, 16
Augsburg, 15–16, 44–46, 55

Bach, Johann Sebastian, 3, 10n36, 107, 133, 240–41, 269
   as organist, 3, 19n52
   as possible hymnal collector, 10n36
   cantatas, 17–19, 107
Becker, Cornelius, 76, 86, 103, 267
Berlin, 26–27, 109, 115, 128, 130, 142, 187, 195
Bird, Frederick M., 192–93
book auctions, 4–11
book dealers, 11–12
Bourgeois, Loys, 86

British hymn writers and composers, 175, 184, 201, 220
broadsides, 1, 34–39, 44–45, 48, 51, 61
Brorson, Hans Adolph, 155, 210, 213, 238
Brussels, 37–38
Bugenhagen, Johannes, 59–61
Busch, Peter, 8–10, 15–16, 19
Buxtehude, Dietrich, 3

Calvisius, Seth, 92–94, 97–98, 106, 118
Cantional (Schein, Leipzig, 1627/45), 98–101, 121
Cantionale Sacrum (Gotha, 1646), 102–104
Carpzov [II], Johann Benedict, 17
Chorgesangbuch (Walter, Wittenberg, 1524), 6, 16, 54–58, 60–62, 71, 75, 77, 81
Church Book (Philadelphia, 1875), 190, 192–93, 195–199
Common Service Book with Hymnal (Philadelphia, 1917/18), 28, 177, 197, 200–201
confessional awakenings, 186–88
Cruciger, Caspar, 43, 53, 63, 79
Crucuger, Elisabeth, 18, 43, 53, 79, 257

Crüger, Johann, 20, 106–07, 109–10, 120, 122–29, 131, 133, 137

Den danske Psalmebok (Thomissøn, Copenhagen, 1569), 205–207
Den Nye Psalme-bog (Pontoppidan, Copenhagen, 1740), 210
Den svenska psalmboken [I] (Svedberg, Stockholm, 1694), 22, 208–209
Dend Forordnede Ny Kirke–Psalme–Bog (Kingo, Copenhagen, 1699), 209–210, 212
Deutsche Messe (Luther, Wittenberg, 1526), 65–66, 70, 76, 204
Deutsches Gesangbuch (Schaff, Philadelphia, 1859), 188
Dresdnisches Gesangbuch (Tittmann, Dresden, 1796), 166–167, 172

Enchiridia (Erfurt, 1524), 14, 16, 51–53, 57, 78
Enchyridion (Wittenberg, 1524–26), 55–58, 60–62, 78, 80
English, transition to, 227–31
Enlightenment. *See* Rationalism/Enlightenment
Erfurt, 36, 51–53, 103, 134, 142, 257

Formula missae (Luther, Wittenberg, 1523), 39, 43–45, 60, 72
Franck, Johann, 115–116, 131
Franck, Melchior, 101–102, 106
Francke, August Hermann, 114, 134–135, 141–142, 211
Freylinghausen, Johann Anastasius, 20, 133–136. *See also Geist-reiches Gesang-Buch* (Freylinghausen, Halle, 1704–14)
Fünfzig Geistliche Lieder (Osiander, Nuremberg, 1586), 86–88, 90

Gaine, Hugh, 23–24
Georgius, Theophilus, 7, 11–12
Geistliche lieder (Klug, Wittenberg, 1529 and later editions), 67–80
Geistliche Psalmen und Lieder (Widmann, Nuremberg, 1604), 94
Geist-reiches Gesang-Buch (Freylinghausen, Halle, 1704–14, and reprints), 110, 128, 140–149, 153
controversial reception, 139–142
textual and musical criticism, 142–154
Gerhardt, Paul, 25, 115–116, 118, 128–131, 138–139, 165, 177, 179
Germantown, PA, 23, 199
Geystliche lieder (Bapst, Leipzig, 1545), 73, 80–82, 110
global perspectives, 1, 2, 30, 221, 225, 265, 268–269, 272, 276, 280–283
Gotha, 102–104
Gottschaldt, Johann Jacob, 6
Götze, Georg Heinrich, 3, 8–9
Grundtvug, N. F. S., 215–216, 218
Guldberg, Ove Høegh, 212–213
Gutknecht, Jobst, 45–46

Haberkorn, John, 23–24
Hamburg, 3, 13–14, 16, 109, 141
Hannover, 8–10, 18–19, 23, 129, 134
Hassler, Hans Leo, 94, 102
Hegenwalt, Erhart, 41–42, 45
"hymn explosion," 29, 219, 245–247, 265, 267
hymnal collectors and collections, 3–10, 10n37, 12, 193
hymnal supplements, 256, 263, 265–267
hymnals brought by immigrants to America from Germany, 23–24, 27, 154, 159, 174–175, 227

from Scandinavia, 209, 213–214, 217–218, 227
Hymns Selected and Original (S. S. Schmucker, Gettysburg, 1828), 189, 192–194, 198
Hymns, Selected and Arranged (C. Philip Krauth, Philadelphia, 1838), 191

Jacobi, Johann Christian, 23–24
Jacobs, Henry Eyster, 193, 198–200
Jespersen, Niels, 206
Jonas, Justus, 42, 55, 59, 61, 76

Kingo, Thomas Hansen, 206–207, 209–210, 212–14
Kirchengesäng (Hassler, Nuremberg, 1608), 94, 102n32
Kirchengesangbuch (Eisenach, 1853), 195
Kirchengesangbuch (Walther, St. Louis, 1947), 169–173, 175–179
Kirchengesange (Calvisius, Leipzig, 1597), 92–93, 98, 118–119
Kirchen Geseng (Vulpius, Erfurt, 1604), 94–95, 97–98, 103, 105
Klug, Joseph, 6, 19, 43, 54, 57, 69
Krauth, Harriet, 196, 199, 207
Kurtz, Benjamin,186–187, 189, 192, 195

Landstad, Magnus Brostrup, 216–217, 219–220, 223
Laudamus (LWF), 280–281
Leipzig, 92, 98, 105–107, 111, 161, 281. *See also* Vopelius, Gottfried
book dealers; 11–12
churches, 17–18, 76
Lübeck, 3, 5, 109
Luther, Martin

affinity with folk-song and news ballad, 33–39, 52
beginnings of his hymn-writing, 1, 40, 74
catechetical connections, 63–69, 73, 75
encouragement of others to write hymns, 40–41, 43, 75–76, 82
early hymnals, 14–15, 19, 45
from broadside to hymnal, 43–45
hymns and liturgical reform, 59–62
later hymnals during his lifetime, 80–82
revisions of older folk hymns, 40, 78
revisions of his own hymns, 58
See also Deutsche Messe; Formula missae; Geistliche lieder
Lutheran Book of Worship (Minneapolis, 1978), 178, 213, 232–244
Lutheran Worship (St. Louis, 1982), 233, 243, 245, 278

Malmø, 204, 207
Marburger Gesang-Buch (Nuremberg, 1699, and later editions), 22–23
Mayer, Johann Friedrich, 3, 5, 7–8, 12–14, 16
Michael, Rogier, 86, 92, 96–98
Mortensen, Claus, 28, 204
Mühlenberg, Henry Melchior, 24–25, 28, 154, 190, 226, 230, 233

Neale, John Mason, 184, 201, 254, 259
Neu Leipziger Gesangbuch (Vopelius, Leipzig, 1682), 105–106
Nevin, John Williamson, 186–87
Nuremberg, 22, 43, 45–46, 48–49, 60, 79, 89, 111

Olearius, Johann Christoph, 3–6, 8–9, 14–16, 19
Osiander, Lukas, 20, 86–92, 95, 97–98, 107–108

Petri, Olaus and Laurentius, 28, 203–205
Pétursson, Hallgrímur, 208, 210, 218
pietism, 26, 128–129, 134, 160–162, 185, 187, 209–211, 216–17, 226–227
Pontoppidan, Erick, 210, 213
Pott, Johann Ernst, 17
Praetorius, Michael, 96–98, 120
Praxis Pietatis Melica (Crüger, Berlin, 1640 and later editions), 20, 127–129, 133, 137
Prussian Union Church, 26, 159
Psalme-Bog (Guldberg, Copenhagen, 1783), 212–213
Psalmodia Germanica (Jacobi, London, 1722, and later editions), 23–24. *See also* Gaine, Hugh

Ramminger, Melchior, 45–46
Raselius, Andreas, 89, 91–92, 96–97
Rationalism/Enlightenment, 160, 162–164, 166–167, 172, 175, 185, 187, 211–215, 226
Reed, Luther D., 199–200, 235, 237, 239n15
Regensburg, 89–92
Rist, Johann, 5, 17, 126, 138, 177, 207
Routley, Erik, 239, 241

Sachs, Hans, 78–79
Salzburg immigrants, 22
Sauer, Christoph, 23
Scandinavian/Nordic hymnals, 1–2, 29–30, 183–184, 207, 215, 219–223, 237–239, 275

Danish, 28, 203, 206–207, 209, 212, 214, 216
Finnish, 205, 211, 215, 219–221
Icelandic, 207, 210, 214, 218–219, 222
Norwegian, 207, 210, 215–216, 219–220, 222
Swedish, 22, 204, 208–209, 211, 216, 218–221, 227
Schaff, Philip, 174n53, 187–188, 195
Schalk, Carl, 21, 24, 176, 178, 200, 248–249, 260–261, 267–268
Schein, Johann Hermann, 20, 92, 96–107, 111, 118, 121–122, 125, 255
Schelle, Johann, 17, 106
Schamelius, Johann Martin, 148–149
Schmucker, Beale M., 189, 193–194, 198
Schmucker, Samuel S., 189–190, 192, 194
Schütz, Heinrich, 76, 86, 106, 125, 137, 267
Seiss, Joseph A., 192, 196, 198, 200
Serpilius, Georg, 7–8
Service Book and Hymnal (Augsburg, Minneapolis, 1958), 177, 199, 231–232, 234–237
Spaeth, Adolph, 193–195, 198–199
Spalatin, Georg, 40–42, 44, 75–76
Spalding, Johann Joachim, 26
Spener, 128–130, 134
Spengler, Lazarus, 43, 58, 79
Speratus, Paul, 13–14, 26, 43–48, 51–52, 77–79
Steiner, Heinrich, 44, 46
Stifel, Michael, 42, 58, 78
Sunday school influence, 191–192, 194–195, 198, 229
Svedberg, Jesper, 208–209, 211, 214–215, 221

[*Swenska songer eller wjisor*, O. Petri, Stockholm, 1526], 204

Tausen, Hans, 28, 203–205
Telemann, Georg Philipp, 3
Tenorlied, 54, 85–86, 88
The Lutheran Hymnal (St. Louis, 1941), 178, 229, 246, 270, 273, 278
Then Swenska Psalm-boken [II] (Svedberg, Stockholm,1695), 208–209
Then Swenska Psalmboken förbätret (L. Petri, Stockholm, 1567), 205
Tittmann, Karl Christian, 166–167

Ulhart, Philipp, 45–46

Voigt, Louis, 21
Vopelius, Gottfried, 20, 103, 105–107
Vulpius, Melchior, 94–95, 97–98, 103, 105

Wallin, Johann, 214–216, 223
Walter, Johann, 54, 56, 58, 71, 96. See also *Chorgesangbuch*

Walther, Carl Ferdinand Wilhelm, 159–165, 168–170, 172–175, 177–179, 186
Wartburg, 50, 65
Watts, Isaac, 176, 184, 193
Wesley, John and Charles, 154, 176, 184
Winkworth, Catherine, 112n9, 175, 184, 201
Wittenberg, Allerheiligenstift, 42, 54–55, 59–61
  broadsides, 1, 43–45, 47–48, 56–57
  churches, All Saints (castle), St. Mary (parish), 40, 55–56
  early hymnals, 6, 14–15, 19–20, 54–58, 64, 82
  liturgical reform, 59–62
  Scandinavian students, 28, 203–204
  theological faculty's censure of Freylinghausen's hymnal, 140, 143–147, 150–153
  winter of 1523–24, 39–43
  See also Enchyridion (Wittenberg); *Geistliche lieder* (Klug)

Lutheran Quarterly Books

Living by Faith: Justification and Sanctification, by Oswald Bayer (2003).

Harvesting Martin Luther's Reflections on Theology, Ethics and the Church, essays from *Lutheran Quarterly*, edited by Timothy J. Wengert, with foreword by David C. Steinmetz (2004).

A More Radical Gospel: Essays on Eschatology, Authority, Atonement, and Ecumenism, by Gerhard O. Forde, edited by Mark Mattes and Steven Paulson (2004).

The Role of Justification in Contemporary Theology, by Mark C. Mattes (2004).

The Captivation of the Will: Luther vs. Erasmus on Freedom and Bondage, by Gerhard O. Forde (2005).

Bound Choice, Election, and Wittenberg Theological Method: From Martin Luther to the Formula of Concord, by Roberg Kolb (2005).

A Formula for Parish Practice: Using the Formula of Concord in Congregations, by Timothy J. Wengert (2006).

Luther's Theological Music: Principles and Implications, by Robin A Leaver (2006).

The Preached God: Proclamation in Word and Sacrament, by Gerhard O. Forde, edited by Mark C. Mattes and Steven D. Paulson (2007).

Theology the Lutheran Way, by Oswald Bayer (2007).

A Time for Confessing, by Robert W. Bertram (2008).

The Pastoral Luther: Essays on Martin Luther's Pastoral Theology, edited by Timothy J. Wengert (2009).

Preaching from Home: The Stories of Seven Lutheran Women Hymn Writers, by Gracia Grindal (2011).

The Early Luther: Stages in a Reformation Reorientation, by Berndt Hamm (2013).

The Life, Works, and Witness of Tsehay Tolessa and Gudina Tumsa, the Ethiopian Bonhoeffer, edited by Samuel Yonas Deressa and Sarah Hinlicky (2017).

The Wittenberg Concord: Creating Space for Dialogue, by Gordon A. Jensen (2018).

Lutheran Quarterly Books

Luther's Outlaw God: Volume 1: Hiddenness, Evil, and Predestination, by Steven D. Paulson (2018).

The Essential Forde: Distinguishing Law and Gospel, by Gerhard O. Forde, edited by Nickolas Hopman, Mark C. Mattes, and Steven D. Paulson (2019).

Luther's Outlaw God: Volume 2: Hidden in the Cross, by Steven D. Paulson (2019).

Minister's Prayer Book: An Order of Prayers and Readings, Revised Edition, edited by Timothy J. Wengert, Mary Jane Haemig, Chris Halverson, and Robert Harrell (2020)

The Augsburg Confession: Renewing Lutheran Faith and Practice, by Timothy J. Wengert (2020).

Luther's Outlaw God: Volume 3: Sacraments and God's Attack on the Promise, by Steven D. Paulson (2020).

Stories from Global Lutheranism: A Historical Timeline, by Martin J. Lohrmann (2021).

Teaching Reformation: Essays in Honor of Timothy J. Wengert, edited by Luka Ilić and Martin J. Lohrmann (2021).

Experiencing Gospel: The History and Creativity of Martin Luther's 1534 Bible Project, by Gordon A. Jensen (2023).

Face to Face: Martin Luther's View of Reality, by Robert Kolb (2024).

A New Song We Now Begin: Celebrating the Half Millennium of Lutheran Hymnals 1524–2024, edited by Robin A. Leaver (2024).

Sola: Christ, Grace, Faith, and Scripture Alone in Martin Luther's Theology, by Volker Leppin (2024).